Praise for *Evil Geniuses*

"Essential, absorbing, infuriating, full-of-facts-you-didn't-know, saxophonely written . . . [Kurt Andersen] is a graceful, authoritative guide, and he has a Writer-with-a-capital-W's ability to defamiliarize the known."

—ANAND GIRIDHARADAS, *The New York Times Book Review*

"[A] lively, engaging chronicle . . . Andersen brings his distinctive brilliance [to] this revisionist history of contemporary inequality, imbuing it with freewheeling cultural savvy and political sensibility."

—*The National Book Review*

"Andersen always writes with curiosity and intelligence, and in *Evil Geniuses*, [he] chronicles the switchback of the American Dream, from the more fair and democratic promise of the New Deal to the 'deliberate reengineering' of our society by the rich and the political right."

—*Literary Hub*

"A history book written like a police procedural that [tracks] the murder of a country, an economic and moral decline that began just when the U.S. was becoming more fair and equal . . . So good, it should be assigned reading . . . Kurt Andersen [has] a rare talent."

—*Toronto Star*

"*Evil Geniuses* is Kurt Andersen at his riveting best—a genuinely original exploration of the forces that have shaped today's economy and society, and what can be done to repair the damage."

—MATTHEW D'ANCONA, former columnist for *The Sunday Telegraph* and *The Guardian,* former editor of *The Spectator*

"The book is . . . terrifically entertaining and engaging. . . . The elements he is able to pull together and weave into a narrative that so convincingly pinpoints how we arrived at this moment are consistently novel and interesting."

—*Chicago Tribune*

"[A] great, really important, exceptionally well-done, extraordinarily timely book . . . It's brilliant and the best summation of how we got here that I've ever read."

—DAVID ROTHKOPF, *Daily Beast* columnist

"This is the one book everyone must read as we figure out how to rebuild our country. With lucid writing and head-snapping insights, Kurt Andersen explores how a confederacy of the right and big business, with unabashed greed, deliberately reengineered our economy. To fix that will require understanding the roots of the problem. . . . A triumph."

—WALTER ISAACSON, author of *The Code Breaker*

"Nostalgia is the antithesis of history. Andersen brilliantly exposes how nostalgia—the strategic oversimplification of our past—has erased complexity and friction from our country's narrative to serve a single goal: to preserve the status quo for the benefit of those in power. *Evil Geniuses* documents how history and nostalgia are engaged in hand-to-hand combat that may determine our future."

—KEN BURNS, director of *The Civil War* and *The Roosevelts: An Intimate History*

"How did the United States turn from its long-standing egalitarian ideals to its present course of socially and morally catastrophic inequality? Kurt Andersen interrogates the past half century with characteristic intellectual ambition and literary bravado to find out. At once cultural history, memoir, and riff, *Evil Geniuses* explains how our country found its way into this predicament, and how we might yet get out of it."

—Jacob Weisberg, author of *The Bush Tragedy* and *Ronald Reagan*

"*Evil Geniuses* is a vivid catalog of American sociopolitical history—a dedicated deep dive into this country's paradoxical legacy of innovation and ego, with Andersen as its clear-eyed, masterful archivist."

—Rebecca Carroll, author of *Surviving the White Gaze*

"Back when the idea of *President Reagan* still seemed a stretch and *President Trump* was barely a joke, some serious, smart, committed people with vast appetites and little shame—right-wing intellectuals and billionaires, CEOs and Washington hustlers—launched a long war to create a paradigm shift and rewrite our social contract to their benefit. Andersen's dazzling, mind-bending, must-read chronicle of that fifty-year crusade explains how it happened, why it succeeded, and, unsettlingly, what that victory means: America is now *theirs*."

—John Heilemann, host of Showtime's *The Circus,* co-author of *Game Change* and *Double Down*

"Wow. *Evil Geniuses* is engaging, enraging, enthralling, appalling; a true tour de force. And most of all, it's the truth—about how these rapacious bastards have picked this country's bones for the last fifty years, and what the rest of us need to do to turn the tables. . . . Exactly the book we need right now."

—Michael Tomasky, editor of *The New Republic*

"In this sweeping jeremiad, journalist Andersen traces the origins of today's economic inequality and political dysfunction. . . . A cohesive argument backed by hard data and stinging prose. Readers will get a clearer picture of how the U.S. got to where it is today."

—*Publishers Weekly*

By Kurt Andersen

Evil Geniuses

You Can't Spell America Without Me (co-author)

Fantasyland

True Believers

Reset

Heyday

Turn of the Century

The Real Thing

EVIL GENIUSES

EVIL GENIUSES

The Unmaking of America: A Recent History

KURT ANDERSEN

RANDOM HOUSE
NEW YORK

2021 Random House Trade Paperback Edition

Published in the United States by Random House, an imprint and division of Penguin Random House LLC, New York.

Random House and the House colophon are registered trademarks of Penguin Random House LLC.

Some passages in *Evil Geniuses* were originally published in a different form in *Vanity Fair*.

Originally published in hardcover in the United States by Random House, an imprint and division of Penguin Random House LLC, in 2020.

LIBRARY OF CONGRESS CATALOGING-IN-PUBLICATION DATA
Names: Andersen, Kurt, author.
Title: Evil geniuses : the unmaking of America : a recent history / by Kurt Andersen.
Description: New York : Random House, [2020] |
Includes bibliographical references and index.
Identifiers: LCCN 2020017081 (print) | LCCN 2020017082 (ebook) | ISBN 9781984801357 (trade paperback) | ISBN 9781984801364 (ebook)
Subjects: LCSH: Wealth—Political aspects—United States—History. | Big business—United States—History. | Corporate power—United States—History. | Democracy—United States—History. | United States—Economic conditions. | United States—Social conditions. | United States—Politics and government.
Classification: LCC HC110.W4 A53 2020 (print) | LCC HC110.W4 (ebook) | DDC 330.973—dc23
LC record available at https://lccn.loc.gov/2020017081
LC ebook record available at https://lccn.loc.gov/2020017082

Printed in the United States of America on acid-free paper

randomhousebooks.com

2nd Printing

Book design by Susan Turner

For Anne and Kate and Lucy

"We must make our choice. We may have democracy, or we may have wealth concentrated in the hands of a few, but we can't have both."

—Louis Brandeis

"The crisis consists precisely in the fact that the old is dying and the new cannot be born; in this interregnum a great variety of morbid symptoms appear."

—Antonio Gramsci

"Strategic inflection points . . . can mean an opportunity to rise to new heights. But it may just as likely signal the beginning of the end."

—Andy Grove

CONTENTS

INTRODUCTION

When you reach your fifties, it gets easier to notice the big ways in which the world has or hasn't changed since you were young, both the look and feel of things and people's understandings of how society works. A half-century of life is enough to provide some panoramic perspective, letting you see and sense arcs of history firsthand, like when an airplane reaches the altitude where the curvature of the Earth becomes visible.

Some of the arcs of historical change are obvious, their paths as well as their causes. The equality and empowerment of women is one of those big *duh* ones. But other important historical arcs, more complicated or obscure, have to be figured out.

That's how I came to write my last nonfiction book, a not-so-obvious American history called *Fantasyland: How America Went Haywire*. I'd noticed that in so many ways, as Stephen Colbert joked on the first episode of his old nightly show, America had become increasingly "divided between those who think with their head and those who *know* with their *heart*." From the 1960s and '70s on, I realized, America had really changed in this regard. Belief in every sort of make-believe had spun out of control—in religion, science, politics, and lifestyle, all of them merging with entertainment in what I called the fantasy-industrial complex. In that book I explained the deep, centuries-long history of this American knack for creating and believing the excitingly untrue. As soon as I finished writing *Fantasyland*, we elected a president who was its single most florid and consequential expression ever, a poster boy embodying all its themes.

But that long-standing, chronic American condition that turned into an acute crisis is just half the story of how and why we've come to grief these last few decades. This other part concerns the transformation of our social system that started in the 1970s and '80s, helped along by a simultaneous plunge into compulsive nostalgia and wariness of the new and unfamiliar. Whereas *Fantasyland* concerned Americans' centuries-old weakness for the untrue and irrational, and its spontaneous and dangerous flowering since the 1960s, *Evil Geniuses* chronicles the quite deliberate reengineering of our economy and society since the 1960s by a highly rational confederacy of the rich, the right, and big business.

From my parents' young adulthood in the 1930s and '40s through my young adulthood in the 1970s, American economic life became a lot more fair and democratic and secure than it had been when my parents were children in the 1920s and early '30s. But then all of a sudden around 1980, that progress slowed, stopped, and in many ways reversed.

I didn't start fully appreciating and understanding the nature and enormity of that change until the turn of this century, after the country had been transformed. In 2002, when several spectacular corporate financial frauds were exposed and their CEO perpetrators prosecuted, I published a long screed in *The New York Times* blaming Wall Street. "If infectious greed is the virus, New York is the center of the outbreak," I wrote, because it

> is also, inarguably, the money center of America and the world, the capital of capitalism. . . . It was New York investment bankers who drove the mergers-and-acquisitions deal culture of the 80's and 90's and who most aggressively oversold the myth of synergy that justified it. . . . It was they . . . who invented the novel financial architectures of Enron and WorldCom. It was the example of New York investment bankers, earning gigantic salaries for doing essentially nothing—knowing the right people, talking smoothly, showing up at closings—that encouraged businesspeople out in the rest of America to feel entitled to smoke-and-mirrors cash bonanzas of their own.

A few years later, one very cold morning just after Thanksgiving, I had another slow-road-to-Damascus moment from whatever I had been (complacent neoliberal?) to whatever I was becoming (appalled social democrat?). I was actually on the road to Eppley Airfield in Omaha after my first visit to my hometown since both my parents had died, sharing a minivan jitney from a hotel with a couple of Central Casting airline pilots—tall, fit white men around my age, one wearing a leather jacket. We chatted. To my surprise, even shock, both of them spent the entire trip sputtering and whining—about being baited and switched when their employee ownership shares of United Airlines had been evaporated by its recent bankruptcy, about the default of their pension plan, about their CEO's recent 40 percent pay raise, about the company to which they'd devoted their entire careers but no longer trusted at all. In effect, about changing overnight from successful all-American middle-class professionals who'd worked hard and played by the rules into disrespected, cheated, sputtering, whining chumps.

When we got to the airport, I said goodbye and good luck and, at the little bookstore there that contains a kind of shrine to the local god Warren Buffett and his company Berkshire Hathaway, bought a newspaper. In it I read an article about that year's record-setting bonuses on Wall Street. The annual revenues of Goldman Sachs were greater than the annual economic output of two-thirds of the countries on Earth—a treasure chest from which the firm was disbursing the equivalent of $69 million to its CEO and an average of $800,000 apiece to *everybody else* at the place.*

This was 2006, before Wall Street started teetering, before the financial crash, before the Great Recession. The amazing real estate bubble had not yet popped, and the economy was still apparently rocking.

I was writing a regular column for *New York* magazine, so after reading and thinking some more, I summarized my understanding of how an egregiously revised American social contract had been put in place, take it or leave it, without much real debate.

"This is not the America in which we grew up," I wrote.

By which I meant America of the several very prosperous decades

*Historical sums of money are pretty meaningless because of inflation—$1,000 in 2020 is the same as $850 in 2010, $500 in 1990, $150 in 1970, and so on. So throughout this book, unless I specify otherwise, all dollar amounts are inflation-adjusted, even when I don't mention that I've rendered a historical sum in "today's dollars" or that it was "equivalent to" the larger present-day amount.

after World War II, when "the income share of the superrich was reasonably cut back, by more than half. The rich were still plenty rich, and American capitalism worked fine." I wrote about how, since the 1980s, "the piece of the income pie taken each year by the rich has become as hugely disproportionate as it was in the 1920s," how "an average CEO now gets paid several hundred times the salary of his average worker, a gap that's an order of magnitude larger than it was in the 1970s," and how most Americans' wages had barely budged. I wrote that "during the past two decades we've not only let economic uncertainty and unfairness grow to grotesque extremes, we've also inured ourselves to the spectacle." By *we* I meant the mostly liberal, mostly affluent New Yorkers and other cosmopolites who read *New York*.

After this twenty-five-year "run of pedal-to-the-metal hypercapitalism," I wrote, it was "now time to ease up and share the wealth some. Because the future that frightens me isn't so much a too-Hispanic U.S. caused by unchecked Mexican immigration, but a Latin Americanized society with a . . . callous oligarchy gated off from a growing mass of screwed-over peons." We needed to take seriously the rising anger and disgust about an American economic system that seems more and more rigged in favor of the extremely fortunate.

> Populism has gotten a bad odor, and not just among plutocrats—for most of the political chattering class, it is at least faintly pejorative. But I think that's about to change: When economic hope shrivels and the rich become cartoons of swinish privilege, why shouldn't the middle class become populists?

I remember thinking, *This* was why my professors in college had used the terms *political economics* and *the political economy* as distinct from simply *economics* and *the economy*. For one thing, *economics* has the connotation of pure science, suggesting that organizing production and pay and investment and taxes and all the rest is just . . . math. Whereas *political economics* contains the crucial reminder that real-life societies and economies are the result of all kinds of fights and negotiations and feelings and choices about the rules of the game, what's fair, what's not, what to maximize, how to optimize for the majority instead of maximizing only for some powerful minority. It's fine to call it *the economy* when we're discussing what's happening month to month or year to year—the ups and downs in the stock market and rates of employment and inflation and growth. Whereas if we're talking about the whole megillah, the way we've structured our capitalism versus the versions in Canada or Denmark or Russia or China, I think *political economy* is much better. The economy is weather, the political economy is climate.

I also thought: *Mea culpa*. For those last two decades, I'd prospered and thrived in the new political economy. And unhurt by automation or globalization or the new social contract, I'd effectively ignored the fact that the majority of my fellow Americans weren't prospering or thriving.

I seldom have epiphanies, but a few months later, in 2007, I happened to have another, this one concerning the culture, and it would eventually cross-fertilize with my new sense of the hijacked, screwed-up political economy. This second aha moment started with an observation I had one morning concerning personal style. Looking at a photo in the newspaper taken twenty years earlier of a large group of very stylish people on a U.S. city street, I closely examined the way each of them looked, their clothes and hair and makeup. They were virtually indistinguishable from people of the present day. I thought about that, conducted some research, and realized it was a broad phenomenon, true throughout the culture—music, design, cars, more. Apart from cellphones and computers, almost nothing anymore that was new or just a bit old looked or sounded either distinctly new or distinctly old.

This was not only not the America in which I'd grown up, when the look and feel of things changed a lot every decade or so, *it wasn't the way things had worked in the modern age, for a century or two*. In the past, certainly in my lifetime and that of my parents and grandparents, over any given twenty-year period, whenever you glanced back, you'd notice how culture and what was deemed current changed unmistakably from top to bottom. Since the dawn of the modern, ordinary people could date cultural artifacts and ephemera of the recent past and previous eras. During the twentieth century, each *decade* had its own signature look and feel. By the late 1960s, the 1950s looked *so '50s,* and by the early 1980s, the 1960s looked *so '60s*. But then, starting in the 1990s, that unstoppable flow of modernity—the distinctly *new* continuously appearing and making styles seem old—somehow slowed and nearly stopped. The dramatic new change in the culture seemed to be that things were no longer dramatically changing.

How strange.

And *why*? The shortest and simplest answer is that a massive counterreaction to multiple overwhelming waves of newness on multiple fronts, one after another, sent all sorts of Americans, for all sorts of different reasons, to seek the reassurance of familiarity and continuity wherever they could manage to find or fake it.

The first wave was in the 1960s, a decade in which *everything* seemed relentlessly new new *new.* Which for several years felt exciting and *good* to most Americans, and the novelty glut seemed under control by the forces of reason and order. But then came the upheavals of the second half of the 1960s, when society and culture changed startlingly in just a few dozen months. In the early 1970s, exhausted by that flux, still processing the discombobulating changes concerning gender and race and sex and other norms, people all at once started looking fondly back in time at the real and imaginary good old days. Enough with the constant shocks of the new! Hollywood revived and celebrated the recent past in a big way, right away, with nostalgia-fests like *American Graffiti, Happy Days,* and *Grease.* Soon nostalgia for *all* periods kicked in throughout all media and all cultural forms with a breadth and depth that were unprecedented in America.

As people gave themselves over to finding and fondling quaint things that had been stored away in the national attic during the century of novelty and progress, we inevitably amended our view of the entire American past, romanticizing and idealizing it, tending to ignore the bad parts. As it turned out, curating and then *reproducing* pieces of the past extended beyond pop culture and style into politics and the economy. I'm not saying the freshly nostalgia-swamped culture of the 1970s and '80s *caused* people to become more politically conservative. But it wasn't a coincidence that the two phenomena emerged simultaneously. They operated in tandem. The political right rode in on that floodtide of nostalgia, and then, ironically, the old-time every-man-for-himself political economy they reinstalled, less fair and less secure, drove people deeper into their various nostalgic havens for solace. This new fixation of the culture on the old and the familiar didn't subside. It became a fixed backward gaze. Then almost without a pause came another wave of disruption and uncertainty, caused by the digital technologies that revolutionized the ways people earned livings and lived, and which made economic life for most people even more insecure. And the culture in turn focused even more compulsively on recycling and rebooting familiar styles and fashions and music and movies and shows.

Then we moved onto the weird next stage, the latest stage that I first noticed in the 2000s, after my double-take at that old photo—the *stasis:* in addition to letting the past charm us, in the 1990s we also stopped creating the fundamentally, strikingly new, perfecting a comfortable *Matrix* illusion that in some sense the world wasn't really changing all that much.

As I was working on *Fantasyland,* reading and thinking about American history, I noticed more connections between the two phenomena—between our simultaneous switch in the 1970s and '80s to a grisly old-fashioned political economy *and* to a strenuously, continuously familiar culture. Which led me to spend a couple of years reading and thinking more deeply about both.

A *lot* more deeply about the economics and politics. That's what I'd mainly studied in college, but since then I'd mostly just read the news, skimmed along day to day and month to month like anybody whose job never required knowing a lot about deregulation, antitrust, tax codes, pensions, the healthcare industry, the legal fraternity, constitutional law, organized labor, executive compensation, lobbying, billionaires' networks, the right wing, the dynamics of economic growth, stock buybacks, the financial industry and all its innovations—so many subjects of which I was mostly ignorant.

My immersion was revelatory. Reading hundreds of books and scholarly papers and articles and having conversations with experts made me more or less fluent in those subjects and, more, taught me many small things and one important big thing: what happened around 1980 and afterward was larger and uglier and more multifaceted than I'd known. *Inequality* is the buzzword, mainly because that's so simple and quantifiable: in forty years, the share of wealth owned by our richest 1 percent has doubled, the collective net worth of the bottom half has dropped almost to zero, the median weekly pay for a full-time worker has increased by just 0.1 percent a year, *only* the incomes of the top 10 percent have grown in sync with the economy, and so on. Americans' boats stopped rising together; most of the boats stopped rising at all. But along with economic *inequality* reverting to the levels of a century ago and earlier, so has economic *insecurity,* as well as the corrupting political power of big business and the rich, *oligarchy,* while economic *immobility* is almost certainly worse than it's ever been.

Before I started my research, I'd understood the changes in the 1970s and '80s hadn't all just . . . *happened,* spontaneously. But I didn't know how long and concerted and strategic the project by the political right and the rich and big business had been. One of my subjects in *Fantasyland* is how conspiracy-theorizing became an American bad habit, a way our chronic mixing of fiction and reality got the best of us. Of course there are secretive cabals of powerful people who work to make big bad things happen, actual conspiracies, but the proliferation of conspiracy *theories* since the 1960s, so many so preposterous, had the unfortunate effect of making reasonable people ignore real plots in plain sight. Likewise, the good reflex to search for and focus on the complexities and nuances of any story, on grays rather than simple whites and blacks, can tend to blind us to some plain dark truths.

I still insist on a preponderance of evidence before I draw conclusions. I still resist reducing messy political and economic reality to catchphrases like "vast right-wing conspiracy" and "the system is rigged," but I discovered that in this case the blunt shorthand is essentially correct. It looks more like arson than a purely accidental fire, more like poisoning than a completely natural illness, more like a cheating of the many by the few. After all, as the god of the economic right himself, Adam Smith, wrote in capitalism's 1776 bible, *The Wealth of Nations:* "People of the same trade seldom meet together, even for merriment and diversion, but the conversation ends in a conspiracy against the public, or in some contrivance to raise prices."

Evil Geniuses is the book I wish had existed a dozen years ago to help clarify and organize and deepen and focus my thinking and understanding and anger and blame. Like most people over the past decade, I'd noticed this fact here or that infographic there about inequality or insecurity or malign corporate power, but quickly moved on, flittered off to the next headline. But then I decided to go deep into the weeds in order to understand, then come out of the weeds to explain what I'd learned as clearly as I could. I wanted to distill and gather and connect the important facts and explanations in one compact package, to make a coherent picture out of all the puzzle pieces. There are lots of facts and figures in here, but not much jargon at all. By chronicling CEOs and billionaires and intellectuals and zealots and operators planning and strategizing for years, together and apart, networking and plotting, even memorializing some plots in memos—so many jaw-dropping *memos*—I've tried to tell a compelling story as well as make a persuasive argument about what's become of us.

So how did big business and the very rich and their political allies and enablers manage to convince enough Americans in the 1970s and '80s that the comfortable economic rules and expectations we'd had in place for half of the twentieth century were obsolete and should be replaced by an older set of assumptions and protocols?

Most people at the time didn't realize just how immense and pervasive the changes were and certainly not where they'd lead. Reagan's election and landslide reelection were plainly big deals, *some* sort of national mandate, but at the time the 1980s seemed more like a post-1960s reversion to the historically typical, not really its own moment of wrenching transformation. Whereas during the 1960s, everyone was aware we were experiencing a great turning point in culture and politics, with almost everything changing in obvious ways—like how in the '30s people were aware in real time that the Depression and New Deal were transformative, the beginning of a new America. The specific policy changes in the 1980s were profound in the aggregate, but beyond the nostalgic Reaganite Morning in America and freer-free-markets messaging, most of the changes were complicated and esoteric and seemed small, so they had a stealth quality. It didn't feel quite like a paradigm shift because it was mainly carried out by means of a thousand wonky adjustments to government rules and laws, and obscure financial inventions, and big companies one by one changing how they operated and getting away with it—all of it with impacts that emerged gradually, over decades. Social Security and Medicare benefits were not cut, the EPA wasn't abolished, labor unions weren't banned. As it turned out, the 1980s were the '30s but in reverse: instead of a fast-acting New Deal, a time-release Raw Deal.

But the reengineering was helped along because the masterminds of the economic right brilliantly used the madly proliferating nostalgia. By dressing up their mean new rich-get-richer system in old-time patriotic drag. By portraying low taxes on the rich and unregulated business and weak unions and a weak federal government as the only ways back to some kind of rugged, frontiersy, stronger, *better* America. And by choosing as their front man a winsome 1950s actor in a cowboy hat, the very embodiment of a certain flavor of American nostalgia.

Of course, Ronald Reagan didn't cheerfully *announce* in 1980 that if Americans elected him, private profit and market values would override all other American values; that as the economy grew nobody but the well-to-do would share in the additional bounty; that many millions of middle-class jobs and careers would vanish, along with fixed private pensions and reliable healthcare; that a college degree would simultaneously become unaffordable and almost essential to earning a good income; that enforcement of antimonopoly laws would end; that meaningful control of political contributions by big business and the rich would be declared unconstitutional; that Washington lobbying would increase by 1,000 percent; that our revived and practically religious deference to business would enable a bizarre American denial of climate science and absolute refusal to treat the climate crisis as a crisis; that after doubling the share of the nation's income that it took for itself, a deregulated Wall Street would nearly bring down the financial system, ravage the economy, and pay no price for its recklessness; and that the federal government he'd committed to discrediting and undermining would thus be especially ill-equipped to deal with a pandemic and its consequences.

Rather, when we were promised in 1980 the wonderful old-fashioned life of Bedford Falls, we didn't pay close enough attention to the fine print and possible downsides, and forty years later here we are in Pottersville instead, living in the world actually realized by Reaganism, our political economy remade by big business and the wealthy to maximize the wealth and power of big business and the well-to-do at the expense of everyone else. We were hoodwinked, *and* we hoodwinked ourselves.

Our wholesale national plunge into nostalgia in the 1970s and afterward was an important part of how we got on the road toward extreme insecurity and inequality, to American economic life more like the era of plutocrats and robber barons of the 1870s. All our clocks got turned back—the political and economic ones by design, the cultural ones more or less spontaneously. Economic progress ended, and cultural innovation stagnated except in information technology, where unchecked new industrial giants arose—resembling those of that first Gilded Age. The morphing of the nostalgia addiction into cultural paralysis in the 1990s helped to keep us shackled in an unpleasant perpetual present ever since. That cultural stasis, almost everyone and everything looking and sounding more or less the way they did a generation ago, provided daily reinforcement of the sense that the status quo is permanent and unchangeable across the board—in other words, a kind of fatalistic hopelessness of the kind that was standard before democracy existed, before revolutions, before the Enlightenment. We've thus been discouraged by the culture as well as by much of politics from imagining that the economy might be radically redesigned and remade once *again,* encouraged to think that fundamental change is either no longer possible or no longer desirable or both. If the present is more or less indistinguishable from the recent past, why won't the future be pretty much the same as the present but with more robots? There are the gadgets and bits of fresh software, but otherwise we have become unaccustomed to the new, many of us skeptical and afraid of the new, confused about how to think of the past or cope with the future.

Unlike longing for a fairer economy of the kind we used to have, which would require a *collective* decision to bring back, the itch of cultural and social nostalgia is easy for *individuals* to scratch and keep scratching. So for many Americans, who spent several decades losing their taste for the culturally new and/or getting screwed by a new political economy based on new technology, fantasies about restoring the past have turned pathological. Thus the angriest organized resistance to the new, the nostalgias driving the upsurge of racism and sexism and nativism—which gave us a president who seemed excitingly new because he asserted an impossible dream of restoring the nastily, brutishly old. The recent wave of politicized nostalgia is global, of course, taking over governments from Britain to Russia to India. But those countries at least have the excuse of being ancient.

"We respect the past," President Obama said of Americans when I was just beginning work on this book, right before he was replaced by President Trump, "but we don't *pine* for it. We don't fear the future; we grab for it. We are boisterous and diverse and full of energy, perpetually young in spirit." As was his wont, he was being aspirational, wishful, reminding us of our better angels. It was his gentle, upbeat way of saying hey, you know, folks, we really *have* been obsessively pining for the past and excessively fearing the future.

But he was correct about our history and founding national character: *openness to the* new *was a defining American trait*. From the start, four centuries ago, we were eager to try the untried and explore the uncharted, even or especially when it looked risky or terrifying. Americans' innovative, novelty-seeking, risk-taking attitudes were key to most of the country's exceptional successes. The United States was a self-consciously new species of nation, the first one invented from scratch and based on new conceptions of freedom and fairness and self-government and national identity. Our story at its best was a process of collectively, successfully imagining, embracing, and exemplifying the new—then gloating whenever the rest of the world followed our lead.

Of course, that process of perpetual reinvention and refreshment always involved tension between people pushing for the new and people resisting it, sometimes with existential ferocity: irreconcilable differences over status quos resulted first in the American Revolution and then in the Civil War and then the politics of the Depression. In our history so far, at the critical junctures, the forces of the new have eventually triumphed over the anciens régimes.

Almost a half-century ago, the country began a strange hiatus from its founding mission of inventing and reinventing itself in pursuit of the new and improved. Since then Americans have gotten variously confused and contentious and paralyzed concerning the old days, about which parts of the American past can or can't and should or shouldn't be restored. So the essential new national project I'm proposing here is paradoxical: a majority of us have got to rediscover and revive the old defining American predisposition to reject old certainties and familiar ways, plunge forward, experiment, imagine, and then try the untried.

It's important to revisit and dissect and understand what happened when this rigging began and the swamp was filled, and not just to know who to blame for our present predicament. Rather, as we attempt to fix the terrible mess that an unbalanced, unhinged, decadent capitalism has made of America, the revamping of our political economy that started fifty years ago is also an essential case study for envisioning the next fifty. Because if you need proof that ideas have power and that radical change is possible, it's there in the rearview mirror. Evil genius is genius nonetheless. In the early 1970s, at the zenith of liberal-left influence, an improbable, quixotic, out-of-power economic right—intellectuals, capitalists, politicians—launched their crusade and then kept at it tenaciously. The unthinkable became the inevitable in a single decade. They envisioned a new American trajectory, then popularized and arranged it with remarkable success. How was that fundamentally different American future—that is, our present—designed and enacted? And how might it happen again in the other direction? There are lessons to be learned: having big ideas and strong convictions, keeping your eye on the ball, playing a long game. There are also some relevant cautionary tales from the last few decades—it'd be nice if in success the left could avoid some of the viciousness, lying, cynicism, nihilism, and insanity that overtook the right after victory.

Earlier I called the rich right and big business and libertarian ideologues highly rational. Selfishness *is* rational up to a point, even extreme and cruel selfishness, and this elite confederacy won its war by means of cold-blooded rationality. On the other hand, their increasingly essential political allies in this project are among the most irrational, emotional, unreasonable, and confused Americans of all—religious nuts, gun nuts, conspiracy nuts, science-denying nuts, lying-blond-madman-worshiping nuts. The response to the pandemic showed vividly how this unholy alliance operates: for months early in 2020, right-wing media and the president pursued a two-track propaganda effort that made a catastrophe worse. Fantasyland's magical thinking and conspiracism and mistrust of science fueled the widespread denial of and indifference to the crisis, and fused with the evil geniuses' immediate, cold-blooded certainty that a rapid restoration of business-as-usual must take precedence over saving economically useless Americans' lives.

What I said at the end of *Fantasyland* I'll restate (and I first drafted this paragraph, it's important to note, a year before COVID-19 existed): societies do come to existential crossroads and make important choices.

Here we are. The current political and economic situation wasn't *inevitable,* because history and evolution never are. Nor is any particular future. Where we wind up, good or bad, is the result of choices we make over time—choices made deliberatively and more or less democratically, choices made by whoever cares more or wields more power at the time, choices made accidentally, choices ignored or otherwise left unmade. Even before the pandemic and its economic consequences, and before the protests and chaos following the murder of George Floyd, we were facing a do-or-die national test comparable to the big ones we passed in each of the three previous centuries—in the 1930s, the 1850s and '60s, and the 1770s and '80s. Forgive the *Hero's Journey* talk, but this is America's Fourth Testing.

We can continue down our recent paths. We can leave in place, as is, the 1980 paradigm shift in the political economy and its suicidal excesses that have made most Americans worse off. We can maintain a superficially unchanging culture to fool and comfort ourselves. We can rage against the irreversible social and demographic changes. We can treat the imminent tsunami of technological transformations of work and life the same way we've dealt with the tech revolution so far—by letting it *just happen* according to the preferences of big business, letting it overwhelm us and reshape the economy and society without any collective vetting or negotiation or consensus.

We can, in other words, fail to change what needs changing—and thereby guarantee America's continued decline and fall. Or we can try to make fairer, smarter choices about which new to accept and which old to recover and how to shape them. We can rediscover the power of collective action and the government to make progress. We can actually aim for a new, *improved* America. This present inflection point really isn't just a matter of changing the ways we think and operate in order to escape national doom. After we pass through the latest recession (or depression), the technological *possibilities* for a flourishing of abundance and leisure might actually allow us to design and build a twenty-first century that's closer to utopia than to dystopia.

How do we aim for that future, one more like *Star Trek* than *Mad Max*?

One way is by emulating the social premises and promises and policies that are in place elsewhere in the rich, developed world. In the 1980s some of the smartest of these societies redoubled their commitment not only to markets but also, unlike us, to making their market economies work for the majority and for the long run, by buffering economic insecurity and inequality and other downsides of new technologies and the newly globalized economy.

I'm inclined to believe the theories that American history tends to run in cycles, sociopolitical and economic eras that last for decades before the pendulum swings in a different direction. My hunch and hope is that we're at the end of the long era that began forty-odd years ago, and that America may now be on the verge of positive change and a bracing cascade of the wildly new and insanely great. But it won't happen by itself. Pendulums must be pushed.

PART ONE

A Brief History of America

1

Land of the New: America from 1600 to 1865

I've referred to America as Fantasyland, but it was always also Tomorrowland. Four hundred years ago, back in the time that we think of as totally rustic and primitive Frontierland, *new* was in the name—the New World. That was the brand from the start, exciting and attractive because it was an entirely unfamiliar blank slate. People by the thousands left Europe, abandoning the *Old* World, sailing to the New World to improvise new lives and new ways of life, to invent new identities. The new inhabitants created new communities they called New England, New Netherland, New Amsterdam, New Hampshire, New Salem, New York, New Orleans, New Haven, New London, New Jersey, new everything.

The religion of the newcomers was itself new—Protestantism had existed for less than a century when the English Protestant settlers arrived. The particular sects of the early settlers were all so feverishly new—Puritans (here to build the New Jerusalem), Quakers, Shakers, Mennonites, Amish, Methodists, Baptists—that they required a new place, empty of too many disapproving white people, in which to practice and propagate their peculiar faiths. And then, uniquely in Christendom, Americans proceeded to create and spin off *new* new religions, massively successful ones, from Mormonism to Christian Science to Pentecostalism to Scientology—as they continue to do.

Here in America we embraced and encouraged, as no other country had before us, a new and different approach to making and selling things—entrepreneurialism, whereby almost anybody was unusually free to give any business (or religion) a go. "The discovery of America offered a thousand new paths to fortune," Alexis de Tocqueville wrote after spending most of 1831 crisscrossing the United States, "and placed riches and power within the reach of the adventurous and the obscure. . . . The passions which agitate the Americans most deeply are not their political but their commercial passions. . . . Americans affect a sort of heroism in their manner of trading [that] the European merchant will always find . . . very difficult to imitate."

The young Tocqueville had been dispatched by the French government to the young United States to study its new approaches to incarceration, but he chronicled and marveled at *every* variety of non-European novelty he came across. "A new science of politics is indispensable to a new world," he wrote in *Democracy in America,* and Americans' "love of novelty" was being restrained only by lawyers and "their superstitious attachment to what is antique."

He realized that the American character derived from a self-conception of being new and always embracing the new.

> The inhabitants of the United States are never fettered by the axioms of their profession; they escape from all the prejudices of their present station; they are not more attached to one line of operation than to another; they are not more prone to employ an old method than a new one; they have no rooted habits, and they easily shake off the influence which the habits of other nations might exercise upon their minds from a conviction that their country is unlike any other, and that its situation is without a precedent in the world. America is a land of wonders, in which everything is in constant motion, and every movement seems an improvement. The idea of novelty is there indissolubly connected with the idea of amelioration. No natural boundary seems to be set to the efforts of man; and what is not yet done is only what he has not yet attempted to do.

In America, *the idea of novelty is indissolubly connected with the idea of amelioration,* new equals improved, progress apparently built in.

The creation of America and then the United States coincided exactly with the Age of Enlightenment, the early 1600s to late 1700s. Ours was a nation built from scratch meant to embody the best Enlightenment principles and habits of mind. Freedom of thought and speech. Embrace of reason and science. And most importantly for this discussion, a foundational belief in the idea of human progress. The United States was a self-conscious incarnation of the modern idea of purposeful, rapid progress—that is, of seeking and expecting one's life and society to be perpetually new and improved.

So our expectation of constant social and cultural change has its roots in the new Enlightenment thinking in which America's founders and many of its people were steeped. But the country's birth also occurred simultaneously with an explosion of the materially new as well. You probably imagine, as I did, that the average European's standard of living gradually improved as the Middle Ages ended in the 1400s. In fact, in the economies of America and Britain, measured by the average person's share of total production, as the economist Robert Gordon says, "there was virtually no economic growth before 1750." And that changed only because in the 1760s and '70s practical large-scale steam engines were perfected, just as manufacturing was being otherwise mechanized. Suddenly life was transformed: the industrial revolution began at the same moment as our Revolution. In fact, one reason Americans fought the war was because the English back home weren't eager for the colonies to industrialize and had even banned some kinds of manufacturing in America. When victory came, it seemed all of a piece, like providence or destiny: an amazing new nation, amazing new technology, amazing new systems of manufacture and transportation—land of the free, home of the new.

It wasn't just a one-time change, this sudden proliferation of intertwined new technology and new economics starting around 1800, the change from muscle-powered labor and zero-sum economic stasis to steam-powered growth, boom and done. The enthusiastic embrace of *new* new technologies and new businesses and new ways of living became a permanent American condition, the beginning of perpetual flux, an ongoing flood of newness. Once the economy was growing at a rate beyond that of the population, each citizen's share of the economy increasing by 1 or 2 percent a year, and thus doubling in size every couple of generations, constant change in all parts of American life was essentially guaranteed. It meant there were new sorts of businesses and jobs, new relationships between workers and bosses, new kinds of buildings and bridges, new and more and bigger newspapers, new varieties of hope and dreams for oneself and one's children and grandchildren, and some new kinds of unpleasantness and misfortune as well.

Tocqueville wasn't the only young European to understand how this commitment to the endlessly new was the defining feature of the zeitgeist from which the United States emerged. Karl Marx never visited America, and as a young man at a moment of political fervor in quasi-feudal Europe, he could not foresee the resilience of new, industrializing political economies like ours to adapt and thrive for another century or two. But in 1848 he absolutely nailed the new condition of perpetual, contagious reinvention that America most purely exemplified. "Constant revolutionizing of production, uninterrupted disturbance of all social conditions, everlasting uncertainty and agitation distinguish [this] epoch from all earlier ones," twenty-nine-year-old Marx and his twenty-seven-year-old co-author Friedrich Engels wrote in their *Manifesto*.

> All fixed, fast-frozen relations, with their train of ancient and venerable prejudices and opinions, are swept away, all new-formed ones become antiquated before they can ossify. All that is solid melts into air, all that is holy is profaned, and man is at last compelled to face with sober senses his real conditions of life.

One way the new political economy could sustain itself in the United States was the exceptional western expanses that were available for settlement. Before America existed, the word *frontier* had exclusively meant the boundary between two countries, but then we gave it its new and enduring American meaning—the frontier was thenceforth the endpoint of the settled and familiar and the exciting start of new and barely known lands. The technologies that were built out so giddily and fast, steam-powered railroads and electric telegraphy, kept our frontier line moving west, allowed more millions of people, new immigrants and descendants of former immigrants, to fashion new lives in new towns and cities closer to the frontier. In less than twenty years, from the early 1840s to 1860, America's railroads grew from about 3,000 miles to 30,000, and its telegraph lines from 38 miles to 50,000.

If an American disliked being a factory worker or any other kind of wage slave, he could light out for the territory ahead of the rest, or at least sustain himself with the fantasy of doing so, to homestead or build the railroad or hunt for gold or silver or for suckers to grift. He or even she could leave an overfamiliar old hometown for some new place to become someone new, with a reworked or fictitious identity. In the early 1900s, for instance, one of my grandfathers escaped his strict Mennonite community in Pennsylvania, where his family had lived for a century after arriving from Germany; moved by himself twelve hundred miles west to Nebraska, where he'd never been and knew nobody; became a lawyer, an occupation for which he hadn't been educated, and a Unitarian, a religion previously unknown to him; and met a socialist and suffragist, probably his first ever, whom he married just as women won the right to vote.

In the Old World, it had taken half a millennium for a few ancient cities to grow from populations of thousands to hundreds of thousands. In the United States, new cities were conjured into existence and managed to grow that much in a few decades. Chicago went from five thousand people to more than half a million in thirty years. New York, doubling in size every decade or two, reached a half-million population in 1848. In my novel *Heyday,* set in New York that year, a practitioner of the new medium of photography considers the astonishing new high-tech *brightness* of his suddenly enormous city.

> To be modern, he thought, is to be artificially aglow . . . gaslight spreading into every parlor and respectable street . . . the laughably large new panes of plate glass that amounted to architectural magician's tricks . . . the unearthly rays of light beaming from burning lime that transformed any actor on a stage into a shining angelic or demonic figure; the new, exceptionally *yellow* yellow paints and new bright red printers inks, all mixed up by chemists in laboratories; the telegraph wires that sparked and blushed against the night skies. . . . Modern America glows.

Newness generated on such a scale at such speed was probably unprecedented in human history—and then with the addition of telephones and *electric* lights and skyscrapers and cars, and airplanes overhead, those huge new cities became new all over again.

Back in 1850, before railroads extended even to the Mississippi River, San Francisco grew in two years from a town of five hundred to a city of 25,000, the largest west of Chicago. That was thanks to the Gold Rush, which instantly added a dreamier new piece to the modern American dream—that anybody could get rich overnight. The Gold Rush was the beginning of California's evolution into the most American part of America, a place where every kind of new is created and thrives and then gets adopted by the rest of the country and the world—new religions, new forms of entertainment (movies, television, theme parks), new technologies (aerospace, digital), new lifestyles based on driving, on dressing down, on being outdoors, on lifestyle perfectionism.

California would become internationally synonymous with the casual as well as the new. But from America's earliest days, foreign visitors like Tocqueville noted this new culture's characteristic informality, in dress, in speech, in the lack of deference by common people for the elites. So did astute natives like Walt Whitman, who in a single sentence of his preface to *Leaves of Grass* pointed to both of these defining habits of Americans—"the picturesque looseness of their carriage" and "the President's taking off his hat to them, not they to him," as well as their extreme "welcome of novelty." The counterculturalism of the 1960s, an extremely picturesque extreme ultra-looseness, was just one of a series of self-consciously *new* modes that have serially defined the American zeitgeist before and since—the Transcendentalist and Bowery B'hoy subcultures of the 1830s and '40s, the Jazz Age of the 1920s, the TV-besotted 1950s, the 1970s Me Decade, the yuppie 1980s, the hip-hop 1990s—each of which made daily life look and feel new all over again for new generations of Americans.

During the nineteenth and twentieth centuries, new technologies applied to making and growing and mining and moving and communicating things drove economic growth. "If there is one thing that economists agree on (and there are not many)," the economist and innovation expert Mariana Mazzucato writes, it "is that technological and organizational changes are the principal source of long-term economic growth and wealth creation," perhaps as much as 80 percent of it. It's a cycle in which "inventions are overwhelmingly the fruits of long-term investments that build on each other over years." Those two centuries of growth continued to make the country seem perpetually fresh and to enable Americans' characteristic optimism and taste for the new.

Along the way, a people who defined themselves as seekers and personifications of novelty, rushing toward a blindingly bright future, also sought occasional respite from the accelerating shocks of the new. Almost as soon as the new United States was established, Americans developed an occasional cultural tic, indulging in nostalgic entertainments of a whole new kind, most notably for American times and places they themselves hadn't experienced. Our forefathers created a nostalgia industry that fictionalized our recent past, turning Daniel Boone and Buffalo Bill Cody into living celebrity-hero artifacts and reenactors of the frontier days, in the nineteenth century devouring James Fenimore Cooper's romantic stories of the untamed eighteenth century. *Walden* was driven by Henry David Thoreau's nostalgia for the era of his childhood in the 1820s and '30s, before railroads and the telegraph, and his dreamy wish "not to live in this restless, nervous, bustling, trivial Nineteenth Century." As that century turned into the even more restless, nervous, bustling twentieth, the United States relentlessly modernized and urbanized. Then came our biggest act of national nostalgia, creating and moving en masse to suburbs, brand-new green and peaceful simulations of old-time American towns and villages and homesteads.

But the suburbs of the twentieth century also embodied an ugly nostalgia, of course, because they were places to which native-born white Americans could escape the city to live almost exclusively among their own kind. America's tragic flaw is our systemic racism, and it's a residue of a terrible decision our founders made to resist the new and perpetuate the old: the enslavement of black people. Slavery had ended in most of Europe by the 1500s, but not in its colonies in the New World and elsewhere. France and Spain and Britain outlawed their slave trades and slavery itself decades before the United States did, and they found it unnecessary to fight civil wars over the issue. Tsarist Russia emancipated its serfs before democratic America emancipated its slaves. On abolition we were not early adopters.

The most important foundations for slavery, of course, were racism and economics. In the antebellum South, enslaved blacks constituted half of all wealth and generated a quarter of white people's income. But white Southerners also clung to slavery due to nostalgia for the time when slavery wasn't under serious challenge by their fellow citizens, and anticipatory nostalgia for the idealized present they feared losing—as a governor of Tennessee wrote after the Civil War, for "the cotton fields, alive with the toiling slaves, who, without a single care to burden their hearts, sang as they toiled from early morn till close of day." White Southern nostalgia was also for the fictional feudal pasts depicted in the novels of Walter Scott, set in ye olde England and Scotland, published in the 1820s and '30s, and particularly, phenomenally popular in the American South because the fictions served to romanticize their own slave-based neofeudalism. Mark Twain blamed secession and the Civil War on such Southern "love [of] sham chivalries of a brainless and worthless long-vanished society."

The brand-new party of the North was the most progressive party—Republicans were not just antislavery but in favor of building railroads and public universities and giving free land to homesteaders. Lincoln and his party of the new won the war that killed 4 percent of American men in four years, the equivalent of 7 million today. The country at large looked to be more or less back on an Enlightenment path and catching up with the rest of the civilized world—letting go of the hopelessly obsolete and irrational, changing dramatically when necessary. Despite powerful backlashes along the way (the South's replacement of Reconstruction with Jim Crow, the fundamentalist Christian upsurge of the early 1900s, the resistance to civil rights a half-century later, the insidious and ongoing systemic racism), over the long run the country was more open to the new than fixated on the past. Progress fitfully prevailed. For most of the twentieth century, most Americans seemed to have permanently learned lessons about the mortal dangers of pathological nostalgia and resistance to change, so that a large governing majority remained committed to making America perpetually new.

2

Land of the New: An Economic History from the 1770s to the 1970s

To recap:

1. While not everything new is good or desirable, an exceptional *openness* to the new was America's factory setting.
2. We call the desirable new *progress*.
3. From the late 1700s to the late 1900s, economic growth helped make the United States perpetually new, thus enabling social progress.
4. Economic growth comes overwhelmingly from incorporating new technologies into the way work is done.

I want to return to that last point, and to what I said earlier about how, just as the United States was giving birth to itself 250 years ago, the steam-powered industrial revolution began turning a society of farmers and artisans into one of workers tending machines in factories and elsewhere, thereby permitting the U.S. economy to grow and grow.

That's all true, but it's not the whole truth. Because as I've said, and as I'll now explain in more detail, every economy, including ours, is a political economy. So here's a crucial fifth point:

5. One way or another, we *chose* and *choose* as a society how to make economic use of new technologies *and* of the new wealth that results from economic growth.

Of course, when I say "as a society," I mean the people who exercise effective power over the choices a society makes. For instance, even before the game-changing steam-powered contraptions of the industrial age came along after 1800 and transformed the nature of more and more jobs, bosses for a century or two had been redesigning work to suit themselves. During this so-called *industrious* revolution, manufacturers began gathering their artisanal workers each day into buildings that they began calling factories. Thus gathered, a Cornell University historian of work explains, "the labor could be divided and supervised. For the first time on a large scale, home life and work life were separated. People no longer controlled how they worked, and they received a wage instead of sharing directly in the profits."

The industrial revolution's great American celebrity promoter Eli Whitney became famous in the 1790s, just out of Yale, for inventing a machine that was at the center of America's industrial revolution—a new, improved cotton gin that mechanized the process of removing the dozens of seeds from each cotton boll. At the time, growing cotton was a new and very small part of American agriculture. One worker using just his or her hands spent a whole day to produce one pound of clean cotton. But using Whitney's gin, that output suddenly leaped to twenty or twenty-five pounds per day. In the early 1800s, cotton replaced tobacco as the biggest U.S. export, and production increased 3,000 percent over the next half-century.

The cotton gin is a perfect illustration of the economic fact to which I keep returning: a new technology makes workers more efficient, increased productivity results in more profits, and the economy grows. But as I've also said, every economy is a political economy, and the story of the cotton gin is also an extreme illustration of that fundamental truth. Cotton growing happened in the South, of course, and the people whose productivity dramatically improved were enslaved African Americans, at least two-thirds of whom worked producing cotton. And the profits that dramatically improved as a result, of course, all went to the plantation owners. So this remarkable piece of new technology, in addition to driving overall U.S. economic growth, was responsible as well for making slavery a foundation of the U.S. economy.

Eli Whitney also happens to be a fabulous case study of the overenthusiasm and overpromising that surround technological progress—especially at moments of revolutionary economic change, such as the early nineteenth and early twenty-first centuries. We learn in school that Whitney came up with another, more foundational piece of the industrial revolution: manufacturing things out of standardized bits and pieces, *interchangeable parts,* from gears and levers then to Ethernet plugs and semiconductor chips now.

Coming off the success of the cotton gin, young Whitney convinced the new U.S. government that he was their man to mass-produce ten thousand muskets, even though he knew nothing about making guns. Two years later, after failing to meet his contractual deadline, he went to Washington to keep his remorseful buyers on the hook. His state-of-the-art musket was taking a *bit* longer than expected to get right, he told President Adams and President-elect Jefferson and the secretary of war, because it would consist entirely of fantastic new interchangeable parts, meaning that manufacture would be cheaper and faster, and repair easier. He spread a hundred metal pieces on a tabletop. *Sirs, here before you are all the ordinary parts from ten of my new gunlocks,* he explained. *Hand me one of each, any you wish, at random, and from those, using only a screwdriver, I shall assemble a working apparatus!* Which he proceeded to do, wowing everyone, getting his deadline extended, more money, and a contract for still *more* muskets.

Whitney's demonstration in Washington, however, had been almost all show. According to the MIT technology historian who wrote the definitive account of that episode, "Whitney must have staged his famous 1801 demonstration with specimens specially prepared for the occasion. It appears that Whitney purposely duped government authorities" into believing "that he had successfully developed a system for producing uniform parts." (*Vaporware* would be the word coined two centuries later.)

The inventor and nail manufacturer Jefferson, who'd been excited for years about the prospect of interchangeable parts, was wildly enthusiastic. Not long after the faked demo, he wrote a letter of introduction on Whitney's behalf to the governor of Virginia, his protégé James Monroe. Whitney "has invented moulds & machines for making all the pieces of his locks so exactly equal," the president wrote, and thus "furnishes the US. with muskets, undoubtedly the best they receive." None of that was true. In fact, Whitney wouldn't deliver any muskets to the government until 1809, nine years later, and interchangeable parts weren't perfected until after his death.*

Whitney was absolutely honest when he admitted in 1812 that the whole point of using identical, interchangeable parts to make things in factories would be to render old-fashioned craftspeople obsolete—that is, "to substitute correct and effective operations of machinery for the skill of the artist." This new way of organizing production, and using technology to replace skilled workers with cheap unskilled workers, was known at the time as the American System.

I also told not-the-whole-truth in the last chapter when I wrote that the industrial revolution made the average citizen's share of the economy start growing. That's true, but is also misleading, as are many statements involving mathematical averages.† For the first half of the 1800s, workers in the industrializing economy didn't actually get a fair share of the new bounty. In fact, their overall incomes probably stagnated or shrank, while the capitalists' share doubled, dramatically increasing inequality. Which led many people starting in the 1840s in America and Europe to imagine that these booming new capitalist systems were unsustainably unfair and might presently bust.

In Britain, a twenty-four-year-old executive at a cotton mill near Manchester, the son of one of the company's founders, wrote in an 1845 book that "the most important social issue in England [is] the condition of the working classes, who form the vast majority of the English people. What is to become of these propertyless millions who own nothing and consume today what they earned yesterday?" The "industrialists," this young industrialist wrote, "grow rich on the misery of the mass of wage earners," but "prefer to ignore the distress of the workers."

The writer was Friedrich Engels, about to become Karl Marx's lifelong friend, collaborator, and patron. Instead of collapsing, the new capi-

*Jefferson did include this boilerplate disclaimer near the end of his letter to Monroe about Whitney: "I know nothing of his moral character."

†A note on averages: a few times I've been in rooms with a hundred ordinary people and my acquaintance Warren Buffett, which meant the average person's net worth in those rooms was nearly $1 billion.

talist system adapted. America's has always been a free-market economy, but as a *political* economy, the society constantly redesigns and tweaks the system and enforces its operating rules and norms. And so from the mid-1800s onward, as new technologies kept making workers more productive—by 1840 the productivity of U.S. factory workers exceeded Britain's—and as the economy kept growing, workers started getting a proportionately larger share of the enlarging pie, and then they kept doing so. To use the other standard metaphor again, for the next century and a half, all boats rose together.

That principle of economic fairness was at the heart of our American social contract as we evolved from rough-and-ready start-up nation to successful global superpower. It didn't happen because the new capitalists of the 1840s suddenly became kind and began sharing their wealth, like Dickens's Ebenezer Scrooge.* Encouraging virtue among the well-off—that is, creating good, strong social norms and shaming violators—does have a place in this story. But the big shift toward economic fairness that began in the later 1800s was the result of a new system of controls that we democratically built into our political economy.

"Private economic power is held in check by the countervailing power of those who are subject to it," the supremely lucid economist John Kenneth Galbraith wrote in *American Capitalism* in 1952. "The first begets the second." *Countervailing power* is a political economic concept that Galbraith nailed down. From the late 1800s through the 1900s, that power was organized and built throughout U.S. society by citizens and workers and customers to check and balance the new and rapidly growing power of big business. We almost only talk about "checks and balances" concerning Washington politics, presidents versus Congress versus the federal courts. But economies—especially modern free-market economies, loosely supervised day to day, operating mostly without government commanders-and-controllers—also need systems of checks and balances.

It can be useful to think of an economy as a game, the highest-stakes game there is. As in D&D or backgammon or Chutes and Ladders, some

*Charles Dickens's fantasy of a capitalist's redemption and Engels's chronicle of real-life Scrooges indifferent to their employees' misery are a matched pair: Engels was writing *The Condition of the Working Class in England* in Manchester at the end of 1843, just as Dickens wrote and published *A Christmas Carol* in London.

players are extremely avid and others have better things to do, some players are very skilled and others just . . . keep tossing the dice. But unlike other games, in the economy *everyone* is a player. And we all need one another to keep playing forever. Because the whole point is never-ending play, without overwhelmingly decisive, permanent winners or so many losers the game doesn't work as well as it can and should. All games have rules, but unlike other games, the rules by which an economy operates only *seem* like they're handed down by a godlike game designer—whereas in fact, they're amended and sometimes dramatically rewritten by the players over time.

Meanwhile, back in real-life American economic history, starting in the 1800s the industrial revolution changed the game, modern corporations formed, and one player, big business, began acquiring unparalleled new economic and political power. A major inherent advantage that business has over other players in the economic game is its centralized, undemocratic nature: no matter how sprawling companies and financial institutions may be, they have headquarters, strategies, and bosses who give orders that are obeyed—whereas individual workers and customers and small businesses and citizens in this vast country are . . . individuals, spread out, disparate, disorganized, relatively powerless.

So individual Americans got together and organized new checks and balances in the new economy. Workers formed unions. "The operation of countervailing power is to be seen with the greatest clarity in the labor market where it is also most fully developed," Galbraith wrote in *American Capitalism.* Just thirty years earlier, in the 1920s, "the steel industry worked a twelve-hour day and seventy-two-hour week with an incredible twenty-four-hour stint every fortnight when the shift changed. No such power is exercised today," by bosses in the 1950s, only because the overworked workers had risen up and "brought it to an end." That is, during the 1930s, in addition to enacting a minimum wage and child labor laws, citizens through their government created a system that let workers' unions organize and negotiate fairly, and instantly union membership more than tripled. By the 1950s, a third of all jobs at private companies had been unionized.

But the new countervailing power wasn't just about employees forcing businesses to share more of their profits. Citizens elected legislators and governors and presidents to enact new rules concerning how big business could and couldn't conduct itself in other ways, and created new regulatory agencies to enforce those rules. Some of the agencies and missions were very specifically purpose-built to discourage businesses from harming and killing people. In 1906 we created the Food and Drug Administration to prevent the sale of dangerous food and phony medicines, just as in 1970 we created the Environmental Protection Agency to prevent businesses from putting too many toxins into the air and water and land.

Before and after the turn of the twentieth century, America decided that even if businesses weren't physically harming people, a few companies had simply become too large and too powerful for the good of our economy and our democracy—the so-called corporate trusts. In 1910 President Theodore Roosevelt, a rich Republican, said that "corporate funds" used "for political purposes" were "one of the principal sources of corruption" and had "tended to create a small class of enormously wealthy and economically powerful men whose chief object is to hold and increase their power." Antitrust laws were passed to prevent corporations from using their economic power to keep prices unfairly high or wages unfairly low. For a century, those laws saw to it that if one or a few big companies controlled the supply of basic products or services in a region or the whole country—railroads, gasoline and steel, electrical and telephone service, banking, TV and radio—those companies had to be more closely regulated. Or broken up into smaller, less powerful enterprises that would compete with one another—the way we did in the early 1900s to the new companies that controlled 90 percent of the suddenly humongous markets for petroleum (Standard Oil) and cigarettes (American Tobacco). The government's enforcement of these laws kicked into even higher gear under the New Deal in the 1930s; in a decade, the Justice Department's antitrust division grew from 15 lawyers to 583.

America also decided in the early 1900s that it would be fairer and more sensible to fund the federal government mainly by a new direct tax on the incomes of the affluent, with progressively higher taxation percentages on higher incomes. Which meant that a quarter-century later, in the 1930s, we could afford to decide that in this country becoming old should no longer mean becoming poor. In 1940, the year Social Security benefits started, *three-quarters* of Americans sixty-five and older lived in poverty; by 1980 the average retiree was getting the equivalent of $14,000 a year from the federal government, a universal basic income for the old.

The countervailing powers that we built into our free-market political economy from 1880 until 1980 did not amount to an *anti*capitalist conversion. Rather, it was really the opposite, essential to the system's evolution and renewal, making our version of capitalism more fair, less harsh, and politically sustainable, a robust foundation for a growing middle class whose spending fueled more economic growth and a society that made most of its citizens reasonably content and proud. "The economic philosophy of American liberals had been rooted in the idea of growth," the influential sociologist Daniel Bell wrote in the 1970s, around the time he taught a seminar I took in college. "One forgets that in the late 1940s and 1950s," it was labor leaders "and other liberals [who] had attacked the steel companies and much of American industry for being unwilling to expand capacity. The idea of growth has become so fully absorbed as an economic ideology that one realizes no longer how much of a liberal innovation it was." Even as Democratic president Harry Truman was launching the Cold War in 1950 to protect capitalist America from foreign Communists, he emphasized in his State of the Union speech that the country needed an even tougher antitrust law to protect our system from falling "under the control of a few dominant economic groups whose powers will be so great that they will be a challenge to democratic institutions." Restraining excessive business power was a bipartisan consensus. A decade later President Dwight Eisenhower, a moderate Republican, boasted in his final State of the Union address about his eight years of "vigorous enforcement of antitrust laws."

Citizens also created hundreds of other important nodes of countervailing power outside government and the labor movement. In many places—such as Nebraska, where I grew up—citizens chose to own and operate their own local electric and gas systems, and farmers formed cooperatives that gave them leverage in the marketplace. Blue Cross (1929) and Blue Shield (1939) were founded as national nonprofit associations to provide inexpensive medical insurance at one rate for anybody who wanted to sign up, regardless of their age or health or how they earned a living.* Later on, philanthropic foundations created out of the spare prof-

*The year I was born, my parents had a Blue Cross insurance policy for which they paid, to cover themselves and my three siblings and me—in today's dollars, adjusted for inflation—the equivalent of $700 a year.

its of old industrial fortunes became countervailing forces: with karmic perfection, for instance, the foundation created by the son of the founder of the Ford Motor Company began funding environmental organizations in the late 1960s.

All the new laws and formal codes and institutionalized arrangements we enacted to increase fairness and security and to look out for the common good also had the effect of reinforcing the norms from which they emerged, the American attitudes and informal codes concerning fairness and mutual social obligation. It was a virtuous cycle. In 1965 the CEOs of the largest U.S. corporations were paid twenty times as much as their average employees not because it would've been *illegal* to pay them one hundred times as much, but because to do so would've struck everyone as unacceptably unfair. Yes, government started providing Social Security and then, in the 1960s, Medicare and Medicaid, but during the same period more and more companies *voluntarily* provided more and more generous health insurance plans and pensions. In 1939 barely 5 percent of Americans were covered by insurance for hospitalization, but by the mid-1950s it was 60 percent. Over the same brief period, the fraction of American workers set to get fixed pensions from their companies went from just 7 percent to one-fourth of them, on its way to a majority by the 1970s.

In short, the main players in the political economy, business and employees and customers and citizens, worked out a rough power equilibrium that felt more or less fair, which helped keep the economy prospering and growing. This balancing act, and all the new social safety nets and cushions and backups we created, allowed the American economy to evolve quickly and momentously during the 1900s as technology kept improving productivity and putting people in new kinds of jobs—by and large better jobs until the 1980s. In 1900 four in ten working Americans were farmers, but in the 1950s fewer than one in ten had anything to do with agriculture, and by 1970 it was 3 percent. Similarly, between the end of World War II and 1970, the fraction of workers in manufacturing shrank from almost half to a quarter—because by 1970 half the workforce, all those tens of millions of would've-been farmers and factory workers, were earning their livings in offices and stores. In other words, before the twentieth century was over, agriculture and manufacturing between them had gone from employing 76 percent of all workers to just 10 percent.

For most Americans, it didn't play out too badly, especially during the excellent third economic quarter of the century. If you were lucky enough to be a thirty-year-old in 1970, you were 92 percent certain of having a higher standard of living than your parents had had when they were your age. From the 1940s through the '70s—when our richest citizens were paying rates of 70 and 80 and 90 percent on the millionth dollars they earned each year—U.S. productivity and GDP per person *and* median household income after inflation all *doubled*.

"Productivity isn't everything," the Nobel Prize–winning economist Paul Krugman has written, "but in the long run it is almost everything. A country's ability to raise its standard of living depends almost entirely on its ability to raise its output per worker." A country's willingness to raise the majority of its people's standard of living in sync with increasing productivity and growth—to *share* the good fortune fairly—depends, of course, on politics.

3

Approaching Peak New: *The 1960s*

It's true, there was no Internet yet.* But nobody young or even youngish today has lived in an America where almost *everything* seemed constantly, excitingly new, where celebrating newness in every realm was a kind of giddy, overriding national passion. In the early 1960s the United States was still taking its post–World War II victory laps, which seemed to be spiraling upward toward an ever better, shinier future. Vaccines for crippling and deadly childhood diseases were new. Suburbs were still new, television was still pretty new, color television and live transatlantic television (beamed by the Telstar satellite) were *totally* new.

Rock music was new, and couples dancing without touching was newer. Driving our Mustangs and Vista Cruisers on interstate highways (and wearing seatbelts) was new. Steel-and-glass high-rises were new. Shopping malls were new, as were credit cards and plastic everything else, along with Dacron, Spandex, fast food, frozen food, instant food,

*Although the Internet was invented in the 1960s—its fundamental technologies were developed starting in 1963, and the prototype system ARPANET transmitted its first computer-to-computer message in 1969.

and ubiquitous artificially colored food. We even had two new states, the first since olden times.

Air travel was new, and only a lucky minority of Americans had ever flown. The space program was an apotheosis of newness, as well as a genuine national obsession. We had a new president, the youngest ever, who'd prebranded his administration as the New Frontier, and in a famous speech about "the new frontier of science and space" right after the first U.S. astronaut had orbited the Earth, he promised we'd "go to the moon in this decade."* A week later a TV series set one hundred years in the future, *The Jetsons,* premiered in prime time, and three months after that the president spoke at the groundbreaking ceremony for the U.S. pavilion at the New York World's Fair, which he said would show the world "what America is going to be in the future." And so it did. My most vivid memory of my tenth year was a trip to Chicago, my first to a big city, and the afternoon we spent at the Museum of Science and Industry, where I had a long-distance Picturephone conversation with a stranger at the Bell System's World's Fair pavilion in New York City. General Motors' fair pavilion was called Futurama. General Electric's, called Progressland, had been designed by the Disney Company, and Walt was at that moment dreaming up his masterwork in Florida, the Experimental Prototype City of Tomorrow, EPCOT.

A majority of American women making themselves *appear* new by coloring their hair (and a small minority by surgically enhancing their faces and bodies) was a new phenomenon. This midcentury mania for the new had its downsides, particularly when combined with Establishment hubris. Among the unfortunate effects was the national consensus that the way to deal with urban neighborhoods full of old buildings (and black people) in older cities was wholesale demolition and replacing them with massive new buildings and highways. In 1963 New York City began demolishing one of its two grand railway terminals, Pennsylvania Station, just fifty-three years old—mainly because it was not new. Federally funded "urban renewal," as its promoters had just rebranded it, wrecked and maimed many more neighborhoods than it renewed or revived. Just

*"We set sail on this new sea," Kennedy said in that famous speech, "because there is new knowledge to be gained, and new rights to be won," because we'd "be enriched by new knowledge of our universe and environment, by new techniques of learning and mapping and observation, by new tools and computers."

before the policies of the best and brightest in Washington started destroying villages in Vietnam in order to save them, a kind of nonlethal dress rehearsal had taken place in American cities.

When we talk about The Sixties, we usually mean the full-on Vietnam War era, not the first few years of the decade. The differences between 1963 and 1969 were dramatic—the clothes, the hair, the sound, the language, the *feelings*—and the changes happened insanely fast, in a couple of thousand days from shiny earnest Apollonian Progressland to crazed and furry Dionysian hordes. However, once you start thinking of America over its whole history as *the land of the new,* that abrupt segue from the square 1960s to the wild 1960s makes a lot more sense.*

Having successfully survived the Depression (by means of the New Deal) and won World War II (in the end by means of a wholly new weapon), America shifted into high gear and for two decades cruised along, blithely speeding into the future. Transformative federal laws—Medicare and Medicaid, the Civil Rights and Voting Rights acts, the Immigration and Nationality Act, all enacted in a single year's time, the year of the New York World's Fair—seemed strikingly new but also the inevitable next phase of modern American progress, the planned, sensible, well-managed new. Then all of a sudden, in 1965, a warp drive kicked in and blasted the country into an uncharted galaxy of psychedelic anti-Establishment angry and ecstatic anything-goes *super*-new.

But nearly all the big 1960s changes, the various different varieties of new, had a common source, in addition to the deep-seated national predisposition: after twenty-plus years of exceptional prosperity and increasing economic equality that were both still going strong, a critical mass of Americans felt affluent and secure, which made their native self-confidence and high expectations for the next new thing still more intense. That run of shared affluence allowed the grown-ups in charge to decide we could afford Medicare and Medicaid and the various War on Poverty experiments, and it eased the way for more people to obey the better angels of their nature concerning equality for African Americans and women.

After a generation of Depression and world war, the thriving new

*After all, Apollo (rational, reasonable, orderly) and Dionysus (instinctual, emotional, sensual) were brothers, both arrogant sons of Zeus.

political economy also inclined people to have lots more children. Those children were raised almost as if they were a special new subspecies who required more tenderness and understanding than previous humans, the new approach famously codified by Dr. Benjamin Spock's mega-bestseller *Baby and Child Care,* published in the first year of the baby boom. Distinctly new, faintly futuristic, immensely popular toys were invented and manufactured *just for these new modern children*—when I was between three and eleven, Frisbees, Hula Hoops, Slip 'N Slides, and Super Balls all appeared. Most of that stupendous mob became teenagers during the 1960s. There were half again as many young people in America during the 1960s as there'd been just fifteen years earlier.

Adolescents by their nature can be attention seekers who feel they have a unique understanding of truth and virtue, but until the American 1960s, probably no generation anywhere ever had been the center of so much attention or had their specialness so extravagantly validated by their elders. In the 1960s *any* sort of distinct national teenage sensibility and culture were still new phenomena, having emerged only in the 1950s along with rock and roll. What's more, the booming political economy also meant that more of them than ever before were gathered together on college campuses. This new concentration was ideal for maximizing the contagious spread of new cultural values and turning ecstatic-righteous-angry adolescence itself into a kind of ideology. When the parents of baby boomers had been young, 1 or 2 million attended college at any given time; in the fall of 1969, 8 *million* students were in college, four out of ten of them women.

Women of no earlier generation had been able to prevent pregnancy reliably, but in 1960 the Food and Drug Administration approved the Pill, and by 1965 it was the contraceptive of choice. Among the new technologies of the last hundred years, only penicillin, television, and computers reshaped life as much. A single new pharmaceutical freed unmarried young people to have more sex more casually than had ever been possible—in other words, to create entirely new social norms almost overnight. The Pill embodies and straddles the earlier and later parts of the decade—an artifact of corporate science and the technology of convenience that enabled free-for-all grassroots social transformations, from the World's Fair to Woodstock in a single astounding leap.

The baby boomers' lurch into anti-Establishment sex-drugs-and-rock-

and-rollism was also a result of their coming of age with a whole new underlying existential angst: the USSR acquired intercontinental nuclear missiles only in the late 1950s, and the new possibility of instant global apocalypse surely helped predispose a critical mass of American kids to become hedonists, renegades, utopians, and/or nihilists, at least temporarily. But that was only a hypothetical war. When the actual war came in 1964 and 1965, just as the oldest boomers turned eighteen and nineteen, it triggered the full-scale countercultural reaction—then kept fueling it as the U.S. deployment in Vietnam increased from a few thousand advisers to 445,000 troops in less than two years, and as the rate at which young Americans were killed increased eventually to five hundred per week.

One of the ideas underlying this book is that until recently the look and feel of American life dramatically changed every couple of decades, making the world seem continuously new. During the 1960s, the decade of maximum American new, everything dramatically changed every couple of *years.* The whole society was suddenly geared to run on the time frame of youth, when two years is a large fraction of one's life.

In the summer of 1963 Martin Luther King, Jr., the avatar of nonviolent civil rights protest, led the marvelously peaceful March on Washington. Just two years later, in the summer of 1965, the Watts riot was the first of the mega-uprisings by African Americans, and in 1966 the Black Panthers and the rest of the non-nonviolent black power movement emerged.

At the end of 1963, the *Times* ran a long front-page article with the headline GROWTH OF OVERT HOMOSEXUALITY IN CITY PROVOKES WIDE CONCERN. But after the 1969 riot during a police bust of the LGBTQ patrons of the Stonewall Inn in Greenwich Village, a long front-page *Times* article was headlined HOMOSEXUALS IN REVOLT.

In 1963 the journalist (and suburban housewife) Betty Friedan published *The Feminine Mystique,* shocking America with her declaration that this was "a country and . . . a time when women can be free, finally, to move on to something more" than housewifery. Even though her book was a *Times* bestseller for weeks, the first article referring to Friedan at length apparently wasn't published in the paper of record until 1965—about a female ad executive ridiculing Friedan in a speech at an advertising convention. But then in the spring of 1968, the *Times Magazine* ran a long, approving article by a woman referring to Friedan's new

National Organization for Women (NOW) and reporting that "feminism, which one might have supposed as dead as the Polish Question, is again an issue." Not many weeks later, after a feminist anarchist shot Andy Warhol (and a journalist), the president of the New York NOW chapter appeared in court on her behalf.

"We must back Lyndon Johnson in 1964," instructed Students for a Democratic Society (SDS), *the* 1960s organization for young leftists, "not only for what he could be, but because he is at least a responsive politician with a certain amount of freedom to move in a positive direction." Five years later, after the assassinations of Martin Luther King and Bobby Kennedy and the teargassing and beating by Chicago police of antiwar protesters at the Democratic National Convention, SDS declared "the need for armed struggle as the only road to revolution" in the United States.

In 1965 fewer than a million Americans had ever smoked marijuana, not even one-half of 1 percent. By the end of the decade, a majority of college students had smoked, and more than 24 million Americans in all, one in six citizens of smoking age.

In early 1965 the big hit singles were "King of the Road" by Roger Miller, "Mrs. Brown, You've Got a Lovely Daughter" by Herman's Hermits, "It's Not Unusual" by Tom Jones, and the Beatles' "Eight Days a Week." In the fall of 1966 the Beatles recorded the psychedelic "Strawberry Fields Forever," and three months after its release came the simultaneous holy-moly newness of *Sgt. Pepper's Lonely Hearts Club Band* and Jimi Hendrix's *Are You Experienced.*

In 1964 long hair on men meant just over their ears and foreheads; by 1966 it meant down to their shoulders and beyond. In 1964 the shortest hemlines were just above the knee. In 1966, according to a female writer for *The New York Times,* "the Today girl, the With-it, the In girl . . . the new girl in fashion" wore skirts "at least 4 inches above the knee," which was "a flag of protest, an emblem of morals and mores in transition." In 1964 an adult wearing blue jeans in a city was eccentric, but in 1968 a *Times* story reported that "on five continents," blue jeans had become "the lingua franca of young male fashion."

A new fashion for longer hair, shorter skirts, and jeans? Those seem trivial in retrospect, but at the time they struck serious middle-aged adults as deeply, meaningfully new. Short skirts, the photographer Irving Penn said in a 1966 newspaper story, are "spitting in the eye, protesting against bourgeois values and generations past, against the Establishment. It's real protest. Much of the news isn't fit to print. Things are happening, and that's what the young are lifting their skirts about." Four years later, in his huge bestseller *The Greening of America*—"There is a revolution coming . . . the revolution of the new generation"—the Yale professor Charles Reich devoted thousands of words to such revolutionary signifiers. The "choice of a life-style is not peripheral, it is the heart of the new awakening," because wearing "wrinkled jeans and jackets made of coarse material" was "a deliberate rejection of the . . . look of the affluent society." And "the violence with which some older people have reacted to long hair [on young men] shows that they feel a threat to the whole reality that they have constructed and lived by." And "marijuana is a maker of revolution, a truth-serum."

From the end of World War II through the New York World's Fair, as I've described, the future looked pretty fabulous to most Americans, but then during the roiling late 1960s people got confused and scared of the new. Specifically concerning what computers implied for the future of work and jobs, however, the consensus suddenly did the reverse: for two decades, experts had worried about where automation was leading our economy, but starting in the late 1960s the smart set couldn't wait to get to superautomated Tomorrowland.

A significant early worrier had been the mathematician Norbert Wiener—college graduate at fourteen, Harvard professor at nineteen, at MIT the godfather of artificial intelligence—who back in 1948 published *Cybernetics,* a groundbreaking book that gave a new technological field a name. It was remarkably popular, and talking about it to a reporter back then, Wiener succinctly and accurately foresaw the future of work—that is, our present. Just as "the first industrial revolution devalued human labor" such that "no pick-and-shovel ditch-digger can sell his services at any price in competition with a steamshovel," before too long the second industrial revolution would completely automate a factory

> without a human operator . . . Such machines will make it very difficult for the human being to sell a service that consists of making routine, stereotyped decisions. The electronic brain will make

these logical decisions more cheaply, more reliably, and, of course, more quickly.

In an article he wrote right afterward in 1949 for the *Times* (that wasn't published because the editor demanded too many rewrites), Wiener elaborated. "These new machines have a great capacity for . . . reducing the economic value of the routine factory employee to a point at which he is not worth hiring at any price." So unless we change "our present factory system . . . we are in for an industrial revolution of unmitigated cruelty. . . . We can be humble and live a good life with the aid of the machines, or we can be arrogant and die."

Reading Wiener then, young Kurt Vonnegut was inspired to write his first novel, *Player Piano,* which depicted that cruel, arrogant, dystopian American future. In the early 1960s plenty of Washington studies and reports appeared warning of the existential challenges of automation. In 1964 the Oxford mathematician and AI expert who was about to advise Stanley Kubrick on creating HAL for *2001: A Space Odyssey* wrote that although "this point is made . . . seldom outside of science fiction," in fact "the first ultraintelligent machine is the last invention that man need ever make," raising the "possibility that the human race will become redundant."

But then in 1967 Herman Kahn, an inspiration for the title character in Kubrick's previous movie, *Dr. Strangelove,* said not to worry, keep loving the new—automation would lead in no time to four-day workweeks and three months of vacation for everybody. And to the utopian youth of the late 1960s, computer-generated ultra-prosperity looked sweet: if work would soon become unnecessary, conventional ambition could be abandoned. The New Left's favorite living Marxist, Herbert Marcuse, wrote that automation was "the first prerequisite for freedom" to give every individual "his time, his consciousness, his dreams." In fact, Marx himself, a century earlier in notebooks first unearthed and published in the 1960s, foresaw a pleasant future with "an automatic system of machinery . . . itself the virtuoso, with a soul of its own," to which "the human being comes to relate more as watchman and regulator to the production process itself." And in the bestselling 1969 book that coined the term *counterculture,* the author, a young Bay Area professor, wrote that "economic security" was "something [young Americans] can take for granted" now because "we have an economy of cybernated abundance that does not need their labor." In general the utopians at that giddy moment didn't very carefully address how capitalism in the United States and other countries would have to change to avoid Wiener's economic future of unmitigated cruelty.

As the 1970s began, the cultural and political Sixties were still going full tilt, accelerating. Single-sex colleges were all rushing to go co-ed—Princeton, Yale, Bennington, and Kenyon in 1969, Johns Hopkins, Colgate, the University of Virginia, and Williams in 1970. A year earlier a half-million young people had assembled for Woodstock, a new species of American event, and another, record-breaking half-million had assembled in Washington, D.C., to protest the Vietnam War. The New Left spun off a terrorist faction that was setting off an average of ten bombs a week in government buildings and banks around America. A constitutional amendment to lower the voting age from twenty-one to eighteen was about to be passed by Congress (unanimously in the Senate, 401–19 in the House), then ratified by the states in a hundred days, faster than any amendment before or since. Congress promptly passed another constitutional amendment, one to guarantee equal rights for women, by margins almost as large.

Given how much had changed during just the last few years, if that tidal wave of new continued through the 1970s—and why wouldn't it?—what additional shocking changes might lie just ahead?

In fact, in the early 1970s, we had reached Peak New.

PART TWO

Turning Point

4

The 1970s: An Equal and Opposite Reaction

"Everything happened during the sixties," the dystopian fiction writer J. G. Ballard said after they ended. He'd turned thirty in 1961, the optimal age to be a trustworthy real-time chronicler of that decade.* "Thanks to TV, you got strange overlaps between the assassinations and Vietnam and the space race and the youth pop explosion and psychedelia and the drug culture. It was like a huge amusement park going out of control."

I was only fifteen at the end of the 1960s, but it really was like that, even though not the *entire* park was haywire, and some astoundingly great new attractions (civil rights, expanded social welfare, feminism, and environmentalism) were being built at the same time. *Future Shock,* published in the summer of 1970, became one of the bestselling books of the decade. "This is a book about what happens to people when they are overwhelmed by change," wrote the authors, whose lecture in Omaha I excitedly attended at fifteen, "the shattering stress and disorientation that we induce in individuals by submitting them to too much change in too

*Norman Mailer was a bit older, thirty-six as the decade began, but Tom Wolfe turned thirty in 1960, Joan Didion in 1964, and Hunter Thompson in 1967.

short a time," the "roaring current of change . . . so powerful today that it overturns institutions [and] shifts our values."

At that same moment, as the besotted forty-two-year-old Professor Reich at Yale published *The Greening of America,* the more typical reaction to the tumult was that of Harvard's fifty-one-year-old professor Daniel Bell, definitely not feeling groovy. "No one in our post-modern culture is on the side of order or tradition," he wrote in a famous essay called "The Cultural Contradictions of Capitalism." He despaired that the "traditional bourgeois organization of life—its rationalism and sobriety—no longer has any defenders in the culture."

As with all zeitgeists, not everybody and probably not even most people were entirely on board with the spirit of the time. Frightened and angry reactions to the culturally and politically new had germinated instantly. For many people during the 1960s, the perpetual novelty that had been at the heart of modern American capitalism and modern American culture changed from amazing and grand to disconcerting and traumatic. What Marx and Engels had written 120 years earlier about capitalism's collateral impacts was coming true, too true—*all fixed relations swept away, all new-formed ones antiquated before they can ossify, all that is holy profaned, all that is solid melts into air.* In culture, Bell wrote in that 1970 essay, there was now an overriding

> impulse towards the new and the original, a self-conscious search for future forms and sensations. . . . Society now . . . has provided a market which eagerly gobbles up the new, because it believes it to be superior in value to all older forms. Thus, our culture has an unprecedented mission: it is an official, ceaseless searching for a new sensibility. . . . A society given over entirely to innovation, in the joyful acceptance of change, has in fact institutionalized an *avant-garde* and charged it—perhaps to its own eventual dismay—with constantly turning up something new. . . . There exists only a desire for the new.

As people get older, they do tend to lose interest in the new. And what I call Peak New has a statistical demographic underpinning: Americans' median age had been in the teens and twenties for our whole history, and it was dropping again in the 1950s and '60s—but then after 1970 it began increasing, quickly, the average American getting two or three years older each decade. By 1990 it reached thirty-three, higher than it had ever been, and it has continued going up toward middle age.

During the 1970s, just coming off the ’60s and their relentless avant-gardism, people really did feel exhausted, ready to relax and be reassured. Even lots of people who were delighted by the 1960s, by the new laws intended to increase equality and fairness and by the loosey-goosier new laissez-faire cultural sensibilities and norms, were in a kind of bewildered morning-after slough. In response, more and more Americans began looking back fondly to times before the late 1960s, times that seemed by comparison so reassuringly familiar and calm and coherent. In other words, that curious old American nostalgia tic expressed itself as it hadn’t for decades—in fact, it took over with an intensity and longevity it never had before. The multiple shocks of the new triggered a wide-ranging reversion to the old. It turned out Isaac Newton’s third law of motion operates in the social universe as well as physics: the 1960s actions had been sudden and powerful, and the reactions starting in the 1970s were equal and opposite, with follow-on effects that lasted much, much longer.

Some of the origins of this 1970s plunge into nostalgia, in fact, had showed themselves a bit earlier. Paradoxically, as America was approaching Peak New during the 1950s and ’60s, some members of the cultural avant-garde led the way in making the past seem stylish, embracing certain bits and pieces of the old days in order to be unorthodox, *counter*cultural, cooler. It was selective stylistic nostalgia as a way of going against the grain, rejecting earnest upbeat spic-and-span corporate suburban midcentury America. Back in the 1950s, when *vintage* applied only to wine and automobiles, the Beats and beatniks had bought and proudly worn used clothes from the 1920s and ’30s. Jack Kerouac’s *On the Road,* the classic cutting-edge Beat novel, is actually an exercise in nostalgia, as the critic Louis Menand says, published and set in 1957 but actually “a book about the nineteen-forties,” the “dying . . . world of hoboes and migrant workers and cowboys and crazy joyriders.” His cool 1950s characters, Kerouac wrote, all shared “a sentimental streak about the old days in America, . . . when the country was wild and brawling and free, with abundance and any kind of freedom for everyone,” and the character Old Bull Lee’s “chief hate was Washington bureaucracy; second to that, liberals; then cops." The simultaneous folk-music revival, from which Bob Dylan emerged, also consisted of cool kids scratching the same nostalgic American itch ahead of everyone else. College students and hepcats in the early 1960s also rediscovered and worshiped 1940s movies like *Casablanca* and *The Maltese Falcon* at smoky revival movie theaters.

In 1964 Kerouac's road-trip buddy Neal Cassady joined young Ken Kesey and his band of protohippies, driving them across America from the Santa Cruz Mountains to New York City to visit, yes, the World's Fair. They were pioneering inventors of the counterculture—which presently became a mass phenomenon and inherited some of the Beats' sentimental streaks concerning the American old days. Even as youth circa 1970 thought of themselves as shock troops of a new age, part of their shocking newness was nostalgic cosplay. Dressed in reproduction nineteenth-century artifacts—blue jeans, fringed leather jackets, boots, bandanas, hats, men mustachioed and bearded—they fancied themselves hoboes and cowboys and joyriders and agrarian anarchists as they got high and listened to "Maggie's Farm" (Bob Dylan), "Up on Cripple Creek" (the Band), and "Uncle John's Band" (the Grateful Dead). Overnight they made the uncool old Victorian houses in San Francisco cool. The vision of the future sold starting in 1968 by the *Whole Earth Catalog,* the counterculture's obligatory omnibus almanac, was agrarian and handmade as well as—*so* ahead of the curve—computerized and video-recorded.

In 1969, at the Woodstock Festival, the music of the final performer, Jimi Hendrix, was absolute late '60s, disconcertingly and deliciously freaky and vain. Playing right before him, however, had been a group almost nobody knew. Sha Na Na, led by a Columbia University graduate student, sang cover versions of a dozen rock and doo-wop songs from 1956 to 1963, wearing 1950s-style costumes and doing 1950s-style choreography. To the crowd and to the *Woodstock* movie audiences in 1970, this was spectacularly surprising and amusing. It was intense *instant* nostalgia, a measure of just how much and how quickly everything had changed. Songs only six or twelve years old, the music of their childhoods and earlier adolescence—"Jailhouse Rock," "The Book of Love," "At the Hop," "Teen Angel," "Duke of Earl"—already seemed *so ridiculously dated.* Even at the event that remains a defining peak moment of a revolutionary new age that had only just gotten started—the phrase *Woodstock Generation* actually preceded *baby boomers*—Americans began turning backward for the reassuring, unchallenging gaze back at a past that wouldn't change or surprise or shock.

Nostalgia was the charming sanctuary to which people retreated to feel better during their post-1960s hangover—and then never really left. They were encouraged by a culture industry that immediately created a wide-ranging nostalgia division of a kind that hadn't existed before.

The Last Picture Show, set in 1951, came out in 1971, made tons of money, and won Oscars. The musical *Grease,* set in 1959, appeared in 1971, became the most popular movie of 1978 (featuring Sha Na Na, who by then had their own popular TV variety show), and ran on Broadway for the whole decade. *The Way We Were,* the fifth most popular movie of 1973, was set mainly in the 1950s. George Lucas's *American Graffiti,* set in 1962, was the third most popular movie of 1973 and softened the ground for the premiere a few months later of its TV doppelgänger *Happy Days,* which in 1976 spun off *Laverne & Shirley,* set in the late 1950s and early '60s. *Animal House,* also set in 1962, came out in the late 1970s and was one of the most successful movies of the decade.

"I saw rock and roll future and its name is Bruce Springsteen," an influential young rock critic wrote in a review of a live performance in 1974, then helped make it so by becoming his producer for two decades. Hearing the seventy-year-old Springsteen singing his songs today, rhapsodizing about characters and tales of his youth, the nostalgia seems earned and real. But back in the early 1970s, as a twenty-four-year-old, he came across as a superior nostalgia act, an earnest higher-IQ Fonzie. He "seems somewhat anachronistic to many—black leather jacket, street-poet, kids-on-the-run, guitar as switchblade," another influential young rock critic wrote in his positive review of *Born to Run* in 1975. "Springsteen is not an innovator—his outlook is rooted in the Fifties; his music comes out of early rock 'n' roll, his lyrics from 1950s teenage rebellion movies and beat poetry."

It wasn't just the American 1950s on which American pop culture suddenly, lovingly gorged in the 1970s. *Every era* became a nostalgic fetish object. During the 1970s, fans of the Grateful Dead began bathing in nostalgia for the late 1960s, "obsessively stockpiling audio documentation of the live Dead," as the cultural historian Simon Reynolds explains, indulging their "deepest impulse: to freeze-frame History and artificially keep alive an entire era." And that has continued into the twenty-first century—"the gentle frenzy of Deadheads is a ghost dance: an endangered, out-of-time people willing a lost world back into existence."

"Everything Old Is New Again" became a pop hit in 1974 for a reason. *The Godfather* (1972) fetishized the look and feel of the 1940s, *The Great Gatsby* (1974) of the 1920s—and at the heart of both were notions central to the emerging American economic zeitgeist: "It's not personal, it's strictly business," as Michael Corleone said, and greed and ostentatious wealth and gangsterism were all hereby cool. Most of the earnest bits in Woody Allen's work consist of nostalgia, starting in 1972 with *Play It Again Sam. Most* of the most popular movies released in 1973 trafficked in twentieth-century nostalgia, including the gorgeous Depression of *The Sting* and *Paper Moon. The Waltons,* a sentimental TV drama set during the Depression and World War II in a small Virginia town, premiered in 1972 and ran until 1981. Even the one enduring *new* Hollywood genre that arose in the mid-1970s and early '80s, what Lucas and Steven Spielberg created with *Star Wars* and *Raiders of the Lost Ark,* was actually just a big-budget revival of an old genre, forgettable action-adventure B movies and serials from the 1930s and '40s and '50s.

In the 1970s I was too young to perceive this sudden total national immersion in nostalgia as unprecedented and meaningful, so I've wondered since if it only looks like that in retrospect. I was therefore delighted, as I was almost finished with this book, to discover a somewhat shocked contemporaneous account of the phenomenon. It's a remarkable Rosetta Stone.

Robert Brustein, the dean of the Yale School of Drama at the time, published a magazine essay in 1975 called "Retread Culture." Back then, by today's standards, revivals and remakes and multiple sequels were still extremely rare. The first modern superhero movie (*Superman,* 1978) hadn't yet been made. But Brustein was struck by the strangeness of "the current nostalgia boom," the "revivals of old stage hits," "retrospectives of films from the thirties and forties by auteur directors, authentic looking reconstructions of period styles in new films," "revived musical forms," and so on. "Much of contemporary American entertainment," he wrote, "is not so much being created as re-created," each "recycled commodity" presented in the place of something actually new.

And he connected this change in popular culture to changes in political and social sentiment, as some kind of reaction to "a deep American discontent with the present time." This was still five years before Reagan was elected president.

> The culture is partially reflecting America's current conservative mood. A nation which always looked forward is now in the process of looking backward, with considerable longing for the real or imagined comforts of the past. Where audiences once were eager for what was novel and innovative, they now seem more comfortable with the familiar, as if they wished to escape from contemporary difficulties into the more reassuring territory of the habitual and the known.

He saw too that what made the nostalgia different than earlier blips of cultural revivalism was "its multiplicity and universality," turning out reproduction antiques in every part of the culture.

> Why, it is even becoming difficult to identify a distinctive look for our age which is not a compound of past fashions. The cut of our trousers, the shape of our dresses, the style of our furs, coiffures, cosmetics and jewelry, our very advertising techniques and printing models, are all derived from earlier periods—a mishmash of the frontier West, Art Deco, and the flapper era.

Brustein mentioned E. L. Doctorow's fine novel *Ragtime,* a big best-seller at the time that was also esteemed by the elite, about to win the very first National Book Critics Circle Award for fiction. Historical fiction hadn't been considered *literary* fiction for quite a while, but suddenly it was respectable again.

Seeming to be strikingly modern wasn't exactly the same as looking like something from the future, but the two had frequently overlapped during the twentieth century, especially in design and art—in the 1930s, for instance, the concrete slabs of Frank Lloyd Wright's Fallingwater and Raymond Loewy's streamlined locomotives were both. That overlap of the new and the futuristic maxed out in 1964 and 1965, the World's Fair years, the years the newly coined phrases *Jet Age* and *Space Age* achieved their peak usage. The hot women's fashion line of 1964 consisted of short Lycra-and-plastic dresses printed with giant bright stripes and dots. In fashion, Simon Reynolds suggests that 1965 was "the absolute pinnacle of Newness and Nowness." In the later 1960s, "almost overnight, everything stopped looking futuristic" in fashion and instead became riffs on the exotically foreign or—because in the '60s the past was an especially foreign country—the bygone "Victoriana, Edwardiana, twenties and thirties influences." All at once, the past started to seem charming to many more people, while purely excited, hopeful visions of the future came to seem naïve or absurd.*

Earlier I mentioned midcentury urban renewal as an example of America's love for the new turning single-minded and reckless. It was like an autoimmune disease, when misguided antibodies destroy healthy human tissue. But even as that demolition of old buildings and neighborhoods was going full speed, local activists (in New York City most of all) and a few enlightened owners (in Omaha, for instance) started to beat it back—another example of how American citizens have placed essential checks and balances on excessive and misguided power. *The Death and Life of Great American Cities,* by the Manhattan journalist-turned-activist Jane Jacobs, became the manifesto of a successful and powerful new movement in 1961; by the end of the decade, historic preservation was fully institutionalized, and in the 1970s saving and renovating nice old buildings and neighborhoods was becoming the default.†

At the same moment, architecture and urban planning rediscovered the amusements and lessons of history. Architects were designing *new* buildings with columns and pitched roofs and pediments and colorful finishes—a so-called postmodern reaction by elite architects, who used the old-fashioned design moves and materials that the modernist elite had declared taboo for half a century. What began in the late 1960s and '70s as fond, bemused takes on old architectural styles morphed during

*Which is why starting in the 1970s, for instance, the humorist and illustrator Bruce McCall could have a career painting panoramas of fantastical flying machines and infrastructure for the *National Lampoon* and then *The New Yorker,* grand futures as if depicted by overoptimists of the past, what he called "retro-futurism."

†Between 1964 and 1969, university architecture schools began teaching preservation; the first old American factory was turned into a warren of upscale shops (in Ghirardelli Square in San Francisco); the Manhattan neighborhood where artists had started moving into old industrial lofts was named SoHo, and New York City created a commission that could prevent developers from demolishing historic buildings and neighborhoods; Congress passed the National Historic Preservation Act; and Seattle created the Pioneer Square Historic District.

the '80s into no-kidding reproductions of buildings from the good old days. Serious architects and planners calling themselves New Urbanists convinced developers to build entirely new towns (first and most notably Seaside, Florida), urban neighborhoods (such as Carlyle in Alexandria, Virginia), and suburban extensions (The Crossings in Mountain View, California) that looked and felt like they had been built fifty or one hundred years earlier, with narrow streets and back alleys and front porches. A convincingly faux-old baseball park, Camden Yards in Baltimore, established a new default design for American stadiums.

That two-step rediscovery of the past—at first amused and a bit ironic, but soon wholeheartedly sincere, making the old and uncool cool and then *normal*—was a sensibility shift made by tens of millions of lifestylizing Americans not yet known as the creative class. During the 1970s, *retro* became a trendy word.

The Official Preppy Handbook became a crypto-nostalgic bestseller in 1980 by good-naturedly satirizing a certain archaic strain of rich white American privilege as if the 1960s cultural upheavals hadn't happened. Everyone started using the new term *comfort food,* only a bit ironically, to destigmatize old-fashioned American dishes that were familiar, unchallenging, unvirtuous—biscuits, cupcakes, meatloaf, grits, mashed potatoes, macaroni and cheese. The meaning was soon extended to celebrate any and all of our newly unshackled and unapologetic tastes for the old and familiar. J. G. Ballard wrote that right after World War II, which ended when he was fifteen, "people simply became uninterested in the past"—*until* the 1970s, he noticed in the 1990s, when suddenly "nobody was interested in the future. Now they are only interested in the past in a sort of theme-park-like way. They ransack the past for the latest design statement."

But as it turned out, not just for design statements and lifestyle inspirations. Thirty years ago my friend Paul Rudnick and I wrote a cover story for *Spy* about how the recent spate of "Hollywood nostalgia productions [had] portrayed the fifties and early sixties as something to be pined for, something cute and pastel colored and fun rather than racist and oppressive." And how in the 1980s, when we were writing, the new omnipresent nostalgia meant that "you can become Dan Quayle," the forty-two-year-old conservative Republican vice president, "or you can become part of the irony epidemic. Or if you're of a mind to organize an absolutely nutty

George Hamilton memorial limbo competition at the country club, *both*." In other words, post-1960s irony turned out to be "a way for all kinds of taboo styles to sneak past the taste authorities—*don't mind us, we're just kidding*—and then, once inside, turn serious." America in the 1970s and '80s gave itself permission not only to celebrate the old days but also to reproduce and *restore* them. Picking and choosing and exploiting elements of the past extended to politics and the political economy.

To understand how that worked, how the opening of the nostalgia floodgates throughout culture helped the political tide to turn as well, it's useful to look back barely a generation—when it spectacularly *failed* to work in the *early* 1960s. The national political right had tried demonizing liberal modernity before enough Americans were fatigued or appalled by accelerating newness for politicians to exploit that reaction successfully.

Barry Goldwater—a conservative Republican when that wasn't redundant, a not-very-religious right-winger when that wasn't an oxymoron, a libertarian before they were called that—halfheartedly tried to use the incipient cultural backlash when he ran for president in 1964. He'd gotten into politics fighting the New Deal when it was still new, and ever since had advocated for the U.S. economy taking a sharp right turn or full U-turn back to the days before the 1930s. Milton Friedman, an avatar of that ultra-conservative economic strain the same age as Goldwater, was one of his advisers when he was the Republican nominee, the most right-wing nominee ever. He proposed cutting personal and corporate income taxes by 25 percent for starters, scrapping new and imminent socialist programs like Medicare and food stamps, keeping Social Security from getting any more generous, and ending "this cancerous growth of the federal government."

The political economy (including maximum anti-Communism) was his overriding focus. But none of that appeared in the half-hour campaign ad that a team of Goldwater operatives produced and bought time to run on 150 NBC stations just before the 1964 election. The film is an extraordinary artifact, remarkably ahead of the curve for its hysterical depiction of the scary new—teenagers, black people, protests, unbelievers, cosmopolitanism run amok. It was a propaganda ur-text for today's ongoing American culture war, which at the time almost nobody considered a war. It tied together and sensationally stoked all of the embryonic backlashes.

The film starts without narration for ninety seconds, just an exciting quick-cut montage of young people doing the Twist, a crowd of black people singing on a city street, cops arresting people, a pair of apparently gay men, topless go-go dancers, all intercut with shots of a recklessly speeding car and with a soundtrack of frenzied rock guitar riffs. As the narrator begins his voice-over, cut to the Statue of Liberty, a small town and its church, white children obediently pledging allegiance to the flag—then cut back to another frenzied montage of black people protesting and being arrested and some white people having too much fun, in particular dancing women shot from behind or without tops. That's the structure of the entire thirty-minute film, three parts decadence interposed with one part good-old-fashioned America, back and forth. "Now there are *two* Americas," the narrator begins,

> the other America—the other America is no longer a dream, but a *nightmare*. . . . Our streets are not safe, immorality begins to flourish—we don't want this. . . . The new America—ask not what you can give but what you can *take*. . . . Illegitimate births swell the relief rolls. . . . Teenagers read the headlines, see the TV news, anything goes now. . . . They see the cancer of pornography festering.

Cut to an extremely long sequence of porn film posters, strip club marquees, and paperback covers including *Call Me Nympho, Jazz Me Baby,* and *Male for Sale*. All of which were, in fact, public rarities.

> But the new America says, "This is free speech." In the new America the ancient moral law is mocked. "Nation under God—who's He?" . . . No longer is a uniform a symbol of authority. The rules of the game have been changed now. . . . Up through the courts of law, justice becomes a sick joke, new loopholes allegedly protecting freedom now turn more and more criminals free on the nation's streets. . . . By new laws it's not the *lawbreaker* who is handcuffed, it is the *police*. . . . Vigilante committees, good citizens, grope for a solution.

Cut to shots of the U.S.-Mexican border—from more than half a century ago.

> Over the borders—*dope*. Narcotics traffic setting a new depraved record. And the victims so often are the defenseless—the kids. . . . How did this happen? Is there a reason we seemed to have changed so much in so short a time?

A *really* short time—according to this film, the moral decay got bad only during the previous eleven months, since the assassination of the "young, inspiring" President Kennedy. After NBC asked for deletions of "60 of the most risqué seconds," Goldwater at the last moment decided not to air the film, even though his campaign sent two hundred prints to conservative groups to show all over the country.

He lost by a landslide to President Lyndon Johnson, of course, whose share of the vote remains the largest ever. At the time one takeaway was that right-wing economic ideas were a total political nonstarter, anachronisms that would remain so. But in fact the Goldwater campaign was just the first rollout of a new American political template, an unsuccessful beta test. It tried to exploit popular unease with the culturally new as a way to get a green light for the rollback that Goldwater and the serious right *really* cared about—a restoration of old-style economic and tax and regulatory policies tilted toward business and the well-to-do.

That lashing of cultural fear to political economics was just ahead of its time. Because 1964 was before the proliferation of hippies and marijuana and psychedelics, before a large feminist movement emerged and workplaces started filling with unprecedented numbers of women. It was before U.S. combat forces went to Vietnam, before the antiwar movement blossomed. It was before violent crime really shot up—murders in the United States increased by half during the five years from 1964 to 1969, and in New York City by that much in just two years, from 1966 to 1968.

Goldwater's landslide defeat was before the epic black uprisings that came later in the 1960s (Watts, Newark, Detroit) along with the black power movement. But it was just after a couple of years of spectacular civil rights demonstrations and confrontations and *immediately* after the Civil Rights Act became law—which is why the Goldwater film had so many shots of unruly black people and why five of the six states Goldwater won were in the Deep South.

It was also before a critical mass of white people outside the South started feeling the way most white Southerners felt—besieged by blacks, their whiteness no longer quite such a guaranteed all-access VIP pass. It was before wallowing in nostalgia for a lost Golden Age ruined by meddling liberal outsiders from Washington and New York, previously a white Southern habit, became such a common white *American* habit. It was before respectable opinion, having spent a century trying to make ethnic tribalism seem anachronistic and wrong, began accepting and embracing a lot of it. "One of the central themes in the culture of the 1970s was the rehabilitation of ethnic memory and history as a vital part of personal identity," the leftist professor Marshall Berman wrote in his wonderful 1982 book *All That Is Solid Melts into Air: The Experience of Modernity*. "This has been a striking development in the history of modernity. Modernists today no longer insist, as the modernists of yesterday so often did, that we must cease to be Jewish, or black, or Italian, or anything, in order to be modern."

Goldwater was trounced before fantasies about the old days became a craze and then a national cultural default. As he prepared to announce his presidential candidacy, the Arizona department store heir appeared on the cover of *Life* magazine—circulation 8 million, 1960s America's single most respectably glamorous mass media pedestal—wearing a cowboy hat, work shirt, and blue jeans, cuddling his horse. But like his OMG-decadence-black-people-chaos film, that too was ahead of its time in 1963—more than a decade before the post-1960s nostalgic counter-reaction made a majority of Americans ready to fall hard for a prospective Old West president in a Marlboro Man getup.

By 1971, however, nostalgia was seriously cross-fertilizing with grassroots political attitudes. That's when the comedy *All in the Family* went on the air and became for six years the most popular American television show. The premise was Archie Bunker's perpetual politicized anger at post-1960s America, but the show's theme song, sung by the Bunker character and his wife, was a piece of cutting-edge nostalgia combining resentment *and* fondness about politics *and* culture.

Didn't need no welfare state . . .
Girls were girls and men were men

Mister, we could use a man like Herbert Hoover again . . .
I don't know just what went wrong
Those were the days

Richard Nixon won the presidency twice, in 1968 and 1972, but both times mainly due to Archie Bunkerism, to reaction against the 1960s' cultural tumult and new civil rights policies, *not* out of any popular cry for freer markets. In 1968, Nixon and his Democratic opponent, Hubert Humphrey, received essentially identical fractions of the vote, but sociologically it wasn't close: the combined vote of Nixon and George Wallace, the white-supremacist third-party candidate, was 57 percent, an anti-hippie-anti-Negro-anti-crime landslide. In 1972 Nixon won in an actual landslide over his Democratic opponent, Senator George McGovern—61 percent of the vote, forty-nine states, still the third-biggest margin in U.S. presidential election history—because hippies were still proliferating and antiwar protests and bombings by New Left fugitives were still happening.*

The nightmare of the new that had been depicted in 1964 in that Goldwater film had been more than realized in just eight years—LSD! free love! Woodstock! blasphemy! women's lib! gay rights! anti-Americanism! riots! bombings!—and was now at the center of the conservative political pitch. Some of those visceral negative reflexes in the late 1960s—confusion, disgust, anger—had started to congeal, become fixed. Many of the people who'd had strong spontaneous reactions in 1967 had by 1972 turned into full-on cultural reactionaries, actively encouraged by the organized political right.

The sloganeering had improved. "A spirit of national masochism prevails," Nixon's vice president famously said, "encouraged by an effete corps of impudent snobs who characterize themselves as intellectuals." In the spring of 1972, during the primaries, a liberal Democratic senator was anonymously quoted in an article warning that "the people don't know McGovern is for amnesty, abortion, and legalization of pot."

*And the anti-civil-rights backlash was still erupting: George Wallace ran in 1972 in the *Democratic* primaries and won six states, including Michigan and Maryland, and got almost as many votes in all as McGovern.

The Nixonians condensed that into an effective alliterative caricature of McGovernism—Acid, Amnesty, and Abortion.*

Paradoxically, the other big reason President Nixon got reelected by such an enormous margin in 1972 was because on policy he did not swim against the lingering, dominant leftward ideological tide. Unlike Goldwater, he wasn't committed to a superaggressive global anti-Communist crusade but instead oversaw the slow-motion U.S. surrender in Vietnam ("peace with honor") and the remarkable U.S. diplomatic opening to Communist China and détente with the Soviet Union. Unlike the Goldwater right (as I'll discuss in the next chapter), he definitely did not try to roll back Johnson's Great Society social welfare programs, let alone FDR's New Deal. His administration actually built upon them. He wasn't a liberal, just a canny, stone-cold cynic going with the liberal flow.

Economic equality, as a result of all those countervailing forces I talked about, was at its peak in the mid-1970s. It was the same in the United States then as it is in Scandinavian countries today, the share of the nation's wealth owned by nonwealthy Americans larger than it had been since measurements began. The system was working pretty well, and the national consensus about fairness endured. People took for granted all the progress we'd achieved. It really seemed irreversible.

*In fact, McGovern supported marijuana decriminalization, not legalization; blanket amnesty for draft resisters but not military deserters; and each state continuing to decide its own abortion laws. And the Democratic senator who so effectively slagged him behind his back, Thomas Eagleton, became his vice-presidential nominee.

5

The 1970s: Liberalism Peaks and the Counterrevolution Begins

More Americans more intensely loathed President Nixon the whole time he was in office than they loathed any Republican president before Donald Trump. That was partly because Nixon was simply so unlikable. It was partly because of his policies, in particular continuing and widening the war in Southeast Asia. But they also hated him as a result of *when* he happened to be president. Liberals at that time couldn't appreciate that Nixon wasn't really governing much to the right of the three previous *Democratic* presidents. He was a moderate conservative adapting to a very liberal era, so the liberals of that era gave him no special credit.*

In addition to the diplomatic openings to the Communist powers, military budgets under Nixon decreased, despite the ongoing war in Vietnam. And he ended the military draft. But even more, his domestic and economic policies were not particularly friendly to business and the rich,

*Likewise, conservatives in a conservative era twenty years later would give Bill Clinton no credit for his moderately conservative policies—balancing the federal budget, continued deregulation of business, tightening welfare eligibility, signing tough anticrime legislation, and so on. Clinton gets credit and blame for inventing political "triangulation" in the 1990s, but Nixon did it first.

or approved of by his party's right wing. In 1969 he supported and signed a bill that abolished investment tax credits for business and, for the rich, he increased capital gains taxes and cut off loopholes by introducing a minimum tax. His administration created several whole new regulatory bureaucracies targeting business, between 1970 and 1972 alone establishing the Consumer Product Safety Commission, the Occupational Safety and Health Administration, and the Environmental Protection Agency—the last empowered by two expansive new laws that set strict standards on air and water pollution. After he signed the Equal Employment Opportunity Act to root out racial and gender discrimination, his administration quadrupled its staff and increased its enforcement power, almost tripled the budget for civil rights enforcement, and instituted the first affirmative action policies throughout government to hire more nonwhite workers.

"I am now a Keynesian in economics," the president said in 1971, officially surrendering to the New Deal consensus, certifying his rejection of the Goldwater right. He proved it beyond doubt that summer by undertaking a radical intervention in the free market, ordering a three-month freeze of all U.S. prices and wages in order to slow inflation—a year after Milton Friedman himself had warned there was "nothing that could do more in a brief period to destroy a market system" than imposing "governmental control of wages and prices." Afterward, even though our market system wasn't destroyed, Friedman called Nixon's action "deeply and inherently immoral."

Nixon also significantly enlarged the U.S. welfare state, making cost-of-living increases in Social Security automatic, creating an entirely new benefit for disabled workers, and expanding the food stamp program. He often *rhetorically* and sincerely attacked federal programs for the poor—they engaged in "paternalism, social exploitation and waste" of a "seemingly inexhaustible flood" of money—but it was just lip service. During his five and a half years in office, federal spending on social services doubled. He would have gone even further if Congress had cooperated. Democrats controlled the House and Senate, but with smaller majorities than during the Kennedy and Johnson administrations. Nixon proposed a universal health insurance plan not unlike Obama's Affordable Care Act, which Republicans forty years later would call socialism. Still more remarkably, his administration pushed a grand welfare reform plan that would have provided a guaranteed basic family income equal to around $16,000, thereby tripling the number of Americans receiving public assistance and quadrupling federal social welfare spending altogether.*

I've catalogued this despised Republican president's leftish policies in the early 1970s to suggest how accustomed Americans had become over the previous forty years to their national government cushioning them from some of the sharpest insecurities and injustices of raw capitalism. During the more conservative 1950s, President Eisenhower, who fashioned himself a "modern Republican," had said that "only a handful of reactionaries harbor the ugly thought of breaking unions and depriving working men and women of the right to join the union of their choice" and "hold some vain and foolish dream of spinning the clock back to days when organized labor was huddled, almost as a hapless mass." During the 1960s the political historian Richard Hofstadter noted the inevitable complacency that liberal success had created. Earlier in the century, he wrote, "the United States had an antitrust movement without antitrust prosecutions," whereas now it had "antitrust prosecutions without an antitrust movement."

Problems like companies busting unions and having excessive market power seemed to have been more or less solved, or at least were properly policed. In the 1960s, IBM's president and CEO until 1971, the son of the founder, published a book all about his earnest vision of virtuous capitalist stewardship. The company's official "basic beliefs" were to treat individual employees respectfully, provide great customer service, and achieve "excellence"—plus to act in society's general interest, all balanced with trying to make a reasonable profit. It wasn't just PR. Americans took for granted their modern, softened, fairer free-market political economy. It had been moving in the direction of progress for most of a century—faster at the beginning of the 1900s, slower in the 1920s, very fast in response to the crash and Depression in the 1930s, a bit slower in

*Nixon also supported the constitutional amendment guaranteeing equal rights for women and signed the Title IX law that required full-fledged school athletic programs for girls. In addition, his administration was the first to enable Native American tribal autonomy, and it increased the National Endowment for the Arts' budget by 500 percent. A 1971 bill passed by both houses of Congress, getting the votes of most Senate Republicans, would have created federally funded childcare centers nationwide, available to every family and free for poor and lower-middle-class ones—but the president finally vetoed it at the urging of his young right-wing aide Pat Buchanan.

the 1950s, fast again in the 1960s through the early 1970s. It seemed that while the forward progressive momentum occasionally slowed, it would never permanently stop or move *backward*.

Over on the economic right, meanwhile, especially among people who owned or ran or advised big businesses, the flip side of that liberal triumphalism around 1970 was the opposite of complacency—it was alarm, dread, panic. The national consensus remained in favor of government acting on behalf of the public good, requiring business to operate fairly and cleanly and affluent people to pay high taxes, giving a hand to the poor. In 1964 and 1965 the Democrats had actually reduced the top personal income tax rates on the richest Americans from 91 to 70 percent—but after that everything was moving in the wrong direction. In the late 1960s antibusiness attitudes among the U.S. public spiraled out of control along with the general distrust of the Establishment. That default antipathy was now mainstream and not diminishing.

Respectable opinion seemed to have turned against big business so *quickly* and so *hard*. An exposé of the dangers of synthetic pesticides, Rachel Carson's *Silent Spring,* had become a number-one bestseller for months and introduced the idea of "the environment" to millions of Americans, which led directly to the creation of the EPA. There was young Ralph Nader, the tenacious lawyer-investigator-activist out of Harvard Law School, whose own damning exposé of corporate irresponsibility, *Unsafe at Any Speed: The Designed-In Dangers of the American Automobile,* became a bestseller in 1966 and by the end of the year inspired a new federal regulatory bureaucracy to improve car safety. As the 1970s began, Nader was an immensely effective antibusiness celebrity expanding his purview and appeared on the cover of *Time* for a story about "The Consumer Revolt." *Time* marveled that Ford's CEO and chairman, Henry Ford II, was now "acknowledging the industry's responsibility for polluting the air and asked—indeed, prodded—the Government to help correct the situation. The auto companies must develop, said Ford, 'a virtually emission-free' car, and soon." By then Nader had assembled a team of even younger lawyer-investigator-activists who were making trouble for other big businesses. Only in private, meeting with auto executives, was the Republican president willing to vent, saying that these liberal activists "aren't really one damn bit interested in safety or clean air, what they're interested in is destroying the system, they're enemies of the system."

The survey firm Yankelovich, Skelly & White had started asking Americans every year whether they agreed with the statement that "business tries to strike a fair balance between profits and the interests of the public." In 1968, 70 percent still agreed; in 1970, only 33 percent did. Capitalists were freaking out. So were true-believing free-market intellectuals, who were never very numerous and had lately felt pushed even further to the fringe. All those various "countervailing powers" that had been built up for a century on behalf of citizens and workers seemed to have become crazily supercharged.

The early 1970s still felt like the very late '60s. *Maybe* the revolutionary madness was peaking, but so far the grassroots reactionaries were reacting only against the rapidly changing *culture*—against the new policy of busing of black students to white schools, against acid, amnesty, and abortion, against empowered women. The national flip-flop concerning the Equal Rights Amendment tracks that cultural moment perfectly.

In the spring of 1972, the 535 members of Congress passed the ERA with only thirty-two nay votes. Just a week later the legislature of Republican Nebraska, where I still lived, became the second state to ratify that amendment to the Constitution—unanimously, 38–0—and by summer it had been ratified by another nineteen, including Idaho, Texas, Kansas, West Virginia, Kentucky, and Tennessee. Hard-core cultural conservatives, who hadn't been much of an organized national political force, were suddenly galvanized to stop this new abomination. And so less than a year after rushing to approve the explicit guarantee that "equality of rights shall not be denied on account of sex," Nebraska was a bellwether again, becoming the first state to *rescind* its ratification. At that very moment, at the beginning of 1973, the U.S. Supreme Court happened to decide by a vote of 7–2 that abortion was an implicit constitutional right. So with ERA ratification stopped in its tracks, the freshly mobilized cultural right now turned its attention to trying to recriminalize abortion.

But those kinds of backlash by the religious and the provincials weren't directly doing besieged corporate America and the *serious* right, the economic right, any good at all. *Silent Spring*, *Unsafe at Any Speed*—and then in the fall of 1970, denouncing big business more existentially, Reich's *Greening of America*. It appeared with every possible mainstream blue-chip imprimatur: Yale law professor, prestigious major publisher,

Times bestseller list for nine months—and a third of the book filled almost an entire issue of *The New Yorker,* so that tens of thousands of members of the business classes could have a savage countercultural attack on their oppressive and doomed capitalist system delivered directly to their doorsteps.

Reich told *New Yorker* subscribers that they and/or their well-compensated friends and neighbors were all prisoners of "an inhuman consciousness dominated by the machine-rationality of the Corporate State" that "literally cares about nothing else than profits" and that had added "to the injustices and exploitation of the nineteenth century" by the robber barons a new "de-personalization, meaninglessness and repression" that threatens "to destroy all meaning and all life."

He specifically ridiculed the die-hard economic right-wingers,

> the businessmen who were the most vocal in their opposition, [who] had a pathological hatred of the New Deal, a hatred so intense and personal as to defy analysis. Why this hatred, when the New Deal, in retrospect, seems to have saved the capitalist system? Perhaps because the New Deal intruded irrevocably upon their make-believe, problem-free world in which the pursuit of business gain and self-interest was imagined to be automatically beneficial to all of mankind, requiring of them no additional responsibility whatever. In any event, there was a large and politically powerful number of Americans who never accepted the New Deal even when it benefited them, and used their power whenever they could to cut it back.

It was a sign of those triumphalist liberal times that Reich referred to haters of the New Deal in the past tense, as if such weird old coots were extinct.

In fact, exactly two weeks before America's most elite weekly published Reich's astounding hurrah for revolution, and exactly two blocks west on Forty-third Street in Manhattan, America's most elite daily published its antithesis, a manifesto telling businesspeople that they should literally care about nothing other than profits and that they had no additional responsibility to society whatever. The essay was as intemperate and self-righteous as *The Greening of America,* and in the end it had more consequence. According to the economist Mariana Mazzucato, it became the modern "founding text . . . in many ways, of corporate management."

It was written by Milton Friedman, the University of Chicago libertarian economist, and published across five pages of *The New York Times Magazine* under the headline A FRIEDMAN DOCTRINE—THE SOCIAL RESPONSIBILITY OF BUSINESS IS TO INCREASE ITS PROFITS. Friedman had become famous during the 1960s, as the decade of free speech and anything-goes outlandishness made his outlandish ideas seem worthier of consideration in respectable circles. The opening spread of the splashy *Times* article is decorated with headshots of a few of the new breed of meddling crypto-socialists—an EPA official, a federal consumer protection bureaucrat, members of Nader's legal team that was prodding GM to reduce car emissions and hire more black people.

The essay is a cri de coeur for cold-heartedness. Friedman had made the same basic case in his 1962 book *Capitalism and Freedom,* but like Barry Goldwater, it was a bit ahead of its time. By 1970 Friedman had concentrated and supercharged his arguments, moved to high dudgeon by what had happened in the late 1960s—"the present climate of opinion, with its widespread aversion to 'capitalism,' 'profits,' the 'soulless corporation' and so on." He viciously derided the squishy-minded business executives and owners and shareholders who'd come to believe—that is, *pretended* to believe—that they had any duty to decency or virtue or anything but making money and (grudgingly) obeying the law.

He used the phrase "social responsibilities" in scare quotes a dozen times and did the same with "social conscience" and even "social." Any hypothetical "major employer in a small community" who spent money "providing amenities to that community" was simply indulging in "hypocritical window-dressing," tactics "approaching fraud"—and indeed, Friedman had "admiration" for miserly owners and managers "who disdain such tactics." The "influential and prestigious businessmen," bleeding hearts "who talk this way" about corporate responsibility—responsibility "for providing employment, eliminating discrimination, avoiding pollution and whatever else may be the catchwords of the contemporary crop of reformers"—were indulging "a suicidal impulse" by "preaching pure and unadulterated socialism." They were "unwitting puppets of the intellectual forces that have been undermining the basis of a free society."

In 1970 it was stunning for such a figure—leader of the so-called Chicago School of economics, *Newsweek* columnist, respected if not yet quite mainstream—to deliver such a ferocious polemic at length, particularly in the *Times*. In *A Christmas Carol,* the businessman Scrooge is redeemed only when he abandons his narrowly profit-mad view of life—and for a century his name had been a synonym for nasty, callous miserliness. In *It's a Wonderful Life,* the businessman Mr. Potter is the evil, irredeemable, un-American villain. Here was Milton Friedman telling businesspeople they'd been misled by the liberal elite, that Scrooge and Potter were heroes they ought to emulate proudly.

Although Friedman was reacting *against* the 1960s surge in support for social and economic fairness, and wanted the political economy to go back in time, he did so *in the new spirit of the 1960s*. With ultra-individualism freshly flowing in all directions, *everyone* wanted to feel free to do their own thing, including selfish businessmen angry about the intensified suspicion of business. For those readers, seeing the righteous candor and militancy of the Friedman Doctrine in *The New York* fucking *Times* a year after Woodstock was thrilling, liberating. *Capitalists of the world, unite! You have nothing to lose but your chains—chains of "social conscience," chains of self-loathing guilt!* I don't mean this as a joke, or poetically. Two ascendant countercultures, the hippies and the economic libertarians, shared a brazen prime directive: *If it feels good do it, follow your bliss, find your own truth.*

Of course, profits are a prime goal for any business enterprise, as well as the goal most easily measured. When push really comes to shove, business owners' need to make profit will inevitably count for more than any duty they feel to employees, customers, or society. But in the real world, where humans operate businesses somewhere in the large range between break-even and maximum profitability, they always have leeway to be unnecessarily and uneconomically fair, trustworthy, decent, and responsible—that is, to take slightly smaller profit margins for the sake of good values and virtuous norms. Friedman, and fellow free-market purists ever since, constantly refer to Adam Smith, who came up with the "invisible hand" idea in the 1700s. But they distort him. Smith also argued in favor of sensible government intervention to improve and optimize free markets.

Within a few years of the Friedman Doctrine, elite executives-in-training internalized and felt free to espouse it. Asked in a class in the late 1970s at Harvard Business School about a hypothetical CEO who discovers his product could kill customers, young Jeff Skilling said he "would keep making and selling the product. My job as a businessman is to be a profit center and to maximize return to the shareholders. It's the government's job to step in if a product is dangerous." (Two decades later as CEO of the big energy company Enron, Skilling was the main organizer of the vast financial fraud that destroyed the company and for which he served twelve years in prison.)

As for the government protecting the public from profit-mad companies, Friedman's doctrine included a heads-I-win-tails-you-lose catch-22. Any virtuous act by businesses beyond what the government legally requires is simpering folly, yet according to him and the economic right, almost any government regulation of business for the public good is oppressive "statism," the beginning of the end of freedom and democracy. Friedman's was an extreme capitalism, unhindered by any human feeling or moral compunction—or by the public interventions and guardrails with which we'd improved it since the nineteenth century. His vision of a free-market system was a *reductio ad absurdum* purification of our well-tempered and actually successful one, a fundamentalist capitalism.

Just as Friedman was preparing to throw down his gauntlet in that summer of 1970, an Establishment éminence grise not prone to hysteria also began raising alarms about rampant anticapitalist sentiment. Lewis Powell was a top lawyer in Virginia, a former president of the American Bar Association who served on many corporate boards. Among his clients were Philip Morris, the largest cigarette company, as well as the main tobacco industry trade group—whose products the federal government had recently declared carcinogenic and for good measure, in the spring of 1970, had banned from being advertised any longer on television. At a big annual Southern business conference that summer, Powell delivered a keynote speech in which he warned that "revolution could engulf this country" because the U.S. political economy was "under broad and virulent attack" by "white and black radicals" whose "heroes are Fidel Castro, Che Guevara, Ho Chi-minh and Mao Tse-tung" and who behave like "Hitler and his storm troopers."

In his speech, Powell said that because "the media and intellectual communities of our society [have] built up these extremists into national figures of prominence, power and even adulation," made them "lionized on the campus, in the theater and arts, in the national magazines and on television," more and more young Americans, "often from our finest homes, [are] vulnerable to radical 'mind-blowing'" and now believed "the destructive criticism . . . that our free enterprise system is 'rotten' and that somehow we have become a wholly selfish, materialistic, racist and repressive society." And concerning "this incongruous support of revolution," he quoted none other than Milton Friedman and his warnings about the media and intellectual establishments exposing "the foundations of our free society" to "wide-ranging and powerful attack . . . by misguided individuals parroting one another and unwittingly serving ends they would never intentionally promote."

But that was just to be a first draft. A year later Powell was still alarmed, still fuming, and wrote a longer, more elaborate manifesto that eventually became widely known. One of his neighbors in Richmond, a retail-chain president and local politician, was a national officer of the U.S. Chamber of Commerce, the country's main organization of businesspeople. Powell's friend pushed him to take the next step—to draft a national counterrevolutionary strategy and plan of action, like he'd done as a colonel in Air Force intelligence planning D-Day. For the thirty-four-page memorandum he submitted to the chamber's leadership and staff, marked CONFIDENTIAL and entitled "Attack on American Free Enterprise System," Powell borrowed heavily from his speech the year before, which he'd called "The Attack on American Institutions."

He reused the "system is under broad attack" meme as well as the Milton Friedman quote and added his own version of the Friedman Doctrine's class-suicide trope. "One of the bewildering paradoxes of our time is the extent to which the enterprise system tolerates, if not participates in, its own destruction." That is, why were millionaire-funded universities and rich publishers and owners of TV network news divisions (that aired "the most insidious type of criticism of the enterprise system" providing the venues for attacks on business? The enemies he'd warned about before, Che and Mao, were replaced in this memo by celebrity traitors within the American elite. Nader, "a legend in his own time and an idol of millions of Americans," was "the single most effective antagonist of American business," and "Yale Professor Charles Reich in his widely publicized book 'The Greening of America'" had made a "frontal assault on the free enterprise system." Throughout academia and the news media were "those who propagandize against the system, seeking insidiously and constantly to sabotage it," along with their fellow travelers in government who have "large authority over the business system they do not believe in." He went further than he had the year before in his speech, now suggesting that leftist government bureaucrats were intentionally pursuing anticapitalist ends.

It was the red scare of the 1940s and '50s all over again—except this time the right's problem was that the general public *wasn't* scared at all of crypto-socialism, now galloping instead of merely creeping. Powell encouraged his readers to feel like victims—"the American business executive is truly the 'forgotten man.'" But he also told them they were pathetic: "The painfully sad truth is that . . . the boards of directors and the top executives of corporations great and small and business organizations . . . have responded—if at all—by appeasement, ineptitude and ignoring the problem."

It was an *existential* problem, with the "survival of what we call the free enterprise system" in doubt. Polite American "businessmen have not been trained or equipped to conduct guerrilla warfare" against such subversion, but now they needed to mobilize for a massive counterinsurgency, a project requiring "long-range planning and implementation . . . over an indefinite period of years, in the scale of financing available only through joint effort, and in the political power available only through united action and national organizations. . . . This is a long road and not one for the fainthearted."

Powell proposed waging this war on four fronts—in academia, the media, politics, and the legal system—and doing so with unheard-of budgets and ferocity. For the first two fronts, they would need to find and fund scholars and other intellectuals "who do believe in the system . . . who will do the thinking, the analysis, the writing and the speaking" to effect "gradual change in public opinion." Political power needed to "be assiduously cultivated . . . [and] used aggressively . . . without embarrassment and without the reluctance which has been so characteristic of American business." In order to tilt the game decisively in the direction of capital, capitalists needed to copy the ACLU, "labor unions, civil rights groups and now the public interest law firms"—that is, create judicial activism in reverse. "The judiciary may be the most important instrument for social, economic and political change," Powell advised. "This is a vast area of opportunity" if "business is willing to provide the funds"—and indeed the whole war would "require far more generous financial support from American corporations than" any such effort "ever received in the past."

Finally, the courtly and decorous Powell advised: No more Mr. Nice Guy. From now on, no businessmen should be "tolerant . . . of those who attack his corporation and the system." Rather, they should "respond in kind," engage in "confrontation politics. . . . There should be no hesitation to attack the Naders . . . and others who openly seek destruction of the system" nor "to penalize politically" any and all opponents.

Three months after Powell submitted his master plan to the U.S. Chamber of Commerce, he was nominated by Nixon and quickly confirmed as a U.S. Supreme Court justice. A year later, that made his secret memo newsworthy enough to be leaked to a reporter. But it didn't become a big story. Justice Powell had been privately intemperate before he was on the Court . . . so? The economic mainstream was still flowing toward the left, and libertarians were still powerless cranks. Nobody was alarmed by old man Powell's alarmist call to arms.

But one of the effects of that leak was that the Chamber of Commerce in 1972 released the entire confidential Powell Memo to its entire membership. Which meant that people in business and on the wealthy right, who'd regarded Friedman's *Times* essay as a kind of motivational St. Crispin's Day speech delivered by their Henry V, now had an actual battle plan from an experienced and distinguished general, their Duke of Richmond. According to the *New Yorker* journalist Jane Mayer in her important 2016 book *Dark Money*, the Powell Memo "electrified the Right, prompting a new breed of wealthy ultraconservatives to weaponize their philanthropic giving in order to fight a multifront war of influence over American political thought." Among the electrified were the youngish industrial heir Richard Mellon Scaife, who during the 1960s had included Powell in a conservative discussion group—okay, *cabal*—plotting to keep America from moving too far left economically. The rich young right-winger Charles Koch, who'd recently taken over his family oil company in Kansas, was also a close reader of the memo.

As I've said, I'm disinclined to explain history or current events in terms of conspiracies, neat just-so stories that impute too much genius and power to conspirators. If Lewis Powell had never written his memo or if it had never been widely distributed, the right's campaign to reconstruct our political economy might have proceeded more or less as it did. Around the same time, right-wingers in Washington had started talking about the need to create more militant and effective institutions.

But beyond the particular galvanizing effects of the Powell Memo, it and the earlier, virtually unknown Powell speech clearly show the state of mind of the rich right and a lot of the capitalist Establishment at the time—frightened, angry, and motivated to resist before it was too late. Ignored for decades, the memo is now an uncanny and invaluable forensic artifact of the early 1970s for making sense of the remaking of our system that began at that moment.

Conspiracy theories, because they tend to emulate fiction, often imagine Dan Brownian plots with great secrets at their centers. But from 1972 on, Justice Powell's playbook wasn't secret at all. For instance, in a 1974 speech Charles Koch gave to business executives in Dallas, he quoted its final line—"*As* the Powell Memorandum points out," he said, without further explanation, "'business and the enterprise system are in trouble, and the hour is late.'" He assumed that everyone in his audience was familiar with it.

Almost nobody else was paying much attention to the new movement and generational project for which Powell's memo was a piece of founding scripture. Center-left hegemony and (thus) complacency were real. According to that annual national Yankelovich survey asking people if "business tries to strike a fair balance between profits and the interests of the public," Americans were continuing to fall out of love with even the nicer, fairer U.S. capitalism of the time—from 33 percent who'd agreed in 1970 about that "fair balance" down to just 19 percent in 1974 and 15 percent in 1976. A campaign by business and the far right to push conventional wisdom and our political economy itself back to the 1920s, or further? A very long shot, faintly ridiculous, arguably impossible.

But big business and the extremely rich got the memo. They'd been trolled and attacked during the late 1960s, felt besieged, and started imagining or pretending to imagine that some kind of socialist revolution might actually happen. They were becoming, pardon the expression, *class conscious* and began organizing and mobilizing for a long-term struggle.

6

The 1970s: Building the Counter-Establishment

The newly militant capitalists, superrich industrial heirs, and leaders of the largest corporations promptly began executing a version of Powell's plan—a version, in fact, much more ambitious than he'd urged on the Chamber of Commerce. The mission was twofold: turn elite discourse and general public sentiment more in their favor, and wheedle and finagle the federal government—the discredited federal government—to change laws and rules in their favor. The goal was to create a powerful counter-Establishment. What they accomplished in a decade was astonishing. It astonished even them.

Changing the skeptical consensus in academia would be a gradual project, but the rich right realized it could instantly create a few faux mini-universities to crank out business-friendly public policy research and arguments. Until then, think tanks, as they'd come to be called in the 1960s, conceived of themselves as nonpartisan and objective, not really in the business of aligning with particular politicians or pushing particular programs. In 1970 the conservative think tank in Washington, the American Enterprise Institute (AEI), had a tenth the funding of the big established liberal one, the Brookings Institution, a staff of ten, and only two resident scholars. By the end of the decade AEI's budget was equal to Brookings's, and its staff had grown to 125.

The Hoover Institution at Stanford had been around for years, as a foreign policy library founded by Archie Bunker's man Herbert Hoover before he became president. In the 1960s, shortly before Hoover died, he gave the place an aggressive new mission, "to demonstrate the evils of the doctrines of Karl Marx—whether Communism, Socialism . . . or atheism." He installed a new director, a right-wing economist who'd worked for the U.S. Chamber of Commerce and run AEI. The strictly international focus remained—until 1972, when the Hoover Institution announced that it would now be "devoting the same amount of attention to 'the social and political changes taking place in this country.'" By the end of the 1970s, the annual budget had quintupled and the endowment increased from $20 million to $300 million, and former governor Reagan and Milton Friedman were Hoover Institution fellows.

Instead of merely *leaning* right on economics, as in the past, these new and reborn think tanks would be explicitly, unapologetically political and right-wing. The most important 1970s benefactors of the think tanks and the rest of the new counter-Establishment were, in addition to Scaife and Charles and his brother David Koch, the beer heir Joseph Coors and the industrial heir John Olin. All five have curiously similar backgrounds. They grew up in the middle of the country, between the Alleghenies and the Rockies, and all five were heirs to industrial fortunes that their fathers or grandfathers started amassing in the old days, before the New Deal. All but Scaife ran their eponymous family companies, and all but Olin were young, members of the so-called Silent Generation.*

In the early 1970s they all felt besieged by the federal government and demonized by the business-skeptical spirit of the age. As an operator of oil refineries, Koch Industries was now under permanent scrutiny by the new EPA. Coors faced suits and boycotts for racial discrimination and a sudden gigantic federal estate tax liability. The Olin Corporation was one of the largest manufacturers of the pesticide DDT—which the EPA had just banned. "My greatest ambition now," John Olin said in the

*Curiously, four of the five trained as chemical engineers at MIT or Cornell—and had fathers who'd also studied chemical engineering at MIT or Cornell.

1970s, "is to see free enterprise re-established in this country. Business and the public must be awakened to the creeping stranglehold that socialism has gained here since World War II."

Scaife's boast to Jane Mayer, decades later, that he'd funded "133 of the conservative movement's 300 most important institutions," suggests the ambition and ultimate scale of the network of start-ups they began building in the 1970s—those three hundred are just the *"most important"* think tanks and foundations and programs and law firms and advocacy and lobbying groups. David Koch was explicit about this long-game strategy of donating large sums over many years to a large number of new right-wing nonprofits. His goal was

> to minimize the role of government and to maximize the role of the private economy. . . . By supporting all of these different organizations, I am trying to support different approaches to achieve those objectives. It's almost like an investor investing in a whole variety of companies. He achieves diversity in balance. And he hedges his bets.

In fact, not just almost *like* what an investor does: the absolutely direct effect of the Kochs' political donations was to maximize their income and wealth, and to minimize the taxes they paid.

The most important of the think tanks, as it turned out, was an entirely new one dreamed up by a pair of young right-wingers born a year apart, both German-American Catholic midwesterners who worked for middle-of-America right-wing members of Congress. In 1973 Coors gave the two the equivalent of $1.5 million to start the Heritage Foundation. Soon Olin was contributing as well, and Scaife donated millions a year for decades.* Heritage started publishing papers and making arguments to the right of the conservative mainstream—turning Social Security into an optional system, for instance, and denying food stamps to striking workers. "We are different from previous generations of conservatives," one of the cofounders, Paul Weyrich, explained later. "We are radicals,

*Another funder of Heritage and other right-wing start-ups was Richard DeVos, a cofounder of Amway, the unorthodox, somewhat cultish Michigan-based merchandising company that was the subject of a Federal Trade Commission investigation in the 1970s. He was the father-in-law of Trump's secretary of education, Betsy DeVos.

working to overturn the present power structure of the country." What's more, within Washington's ideological ecology, the existence of Heritage had the effect of making AEI seem comparatively reasonable and centrist.

Because it meant to maximize its political influence and impact, Heritage's ultra-conservatism encompassed the two big strange-bedfellow constituencies within the Republican right, the libertarians and the uncomfortable-with-liberty fundamentalist Christians. The second most influential right-wing think tank born in the 1970s, Charles Koch's creation, was the strictly libertarian Cato Institute. He poured in the equivalent of $10 million to $20 million to get it going and tens of millions more afterward.

Libertarianism was definitely outside the mainstream. In the early 1970s, at a conference in Washington of what its organizer Milton Friedman called "free enterprise radicals," he said that it was "important for people of our political persuasion to come together and realize that they're not such kooks as they are sometimes made to appear in their communities." Among his fellow kooks at that meeting was the not-yet-widely-known economic consultant and Ayn Rand associate Alan Greenspan. The new Libertarian Party's 1972 presidential candidate, an entirely unknown philosophy professor then and now, won a total of 3,674 votes nationally.

For a few years during the 1970s, Charles Koch published a stylish-looking San Francisco–based magazine called *Libertarian Review*. In it he wrote an essay that reiterated the gists of the Friedman Doctrine and the Powell Memo but went further, arguing that their "movement . . . for radical social change" must seek to take over American conservatism, radicalize it. Businesspeople and mainstream conservatives ought to support the extreme libertarian demands of "'the (radical) agitator,'" Koch wrote, because "'the more extreme demand of the agitator makes the politician's demand seem acceptable and perhaps desirable.'" But who read the *Libertarian Review*? And who'd ever heard of this Charles Koch guy?

Slowly but surely, the little movement made progress against progress. In 1974, for instance, a few weeks after Nixon resigned, President Ford named Greenspan chairman of his Council of Economic Advisers. His surrogate spouse at the swearing-in was sixty-nine-year-old Ayn Rand herself.

• • •

The right-wing mediascape was still tiny, a few small magazines with circulations in the tens of thousands, the most important of them William F. Buckley's *National Review,* and hardly any radio; cable news and the Internet didn't exist. The only influential right-wing venue of any scale was the daily opinion pages of *The Wall Street Journal,* whose circulation had recently passed 1 million on its way to more than 2 million. In 1972 the young editor Robert Bartley took over the section and enforced a more rigorously hard-edged screw-the-liberals libertarian economic line in the new post-1960s spirit, more unapologetically antitax, antigovernment, pro-wealthy. He hired Irving Kristol, a prominent former leftist who had been so undone by the countercultural 1960s that he'd turned into the original neoconservative—a teacher and intellectual who began savaging in America's capitalist-class daily paper, "the New Class," "our scholars, our teachers, our intellectuals, our publicists," liberals now "engaged in a class struggle with the business community for status and power."

Starting in the 1970s, too, plain old-fashioned Republican tax hatred acquired a new set of academic rationales, thanks to a new generation of economists—and Bartley's *Wall Street Journal* editorial page was their absolutely indispensable corner of the public square. "Our page was the forum," Bartley said a decade later. "These people had to find each other. And they had to have publicity to get other economists thinking about it. It wouldn't have happened without someone playing the role of broker."

Bartley hired a right-hand man at the *Journal,* Jude Wanniski, a former columnist at the *Las Vegas Review-Journal.* One of his duties was cultivating and handling a young economist at the University of Chicago business school—ambitious, eccentric, second-tier—named Arthur Laffer. Laffer's particular brand of old wine in a new bottle was the idea that by dramatically slashing tax *rates* on big business and the rich, you'd make people work and earn and invest more, producing such fountains of prosperity that tax *revenues* would grow enough to prevent excessive federal deficits or draconian budget cuts. Do the math! A 35 percent tax on $2 million in income generates the same amount as a 70 percent tax on $1 million. Everybody wins! Theoretically. Because only the rich would definitely and immediately win. Wanniski made up a legitimate-sounding name—supply-side economics. For anyone else to benefit, what Democrats since the Depression had called trickle-down economics also had to operate—that is, the supply-side tax cuts (and deregulation) would have to make businesses boom and rich people profit so gloriously that some of that money trickled down to produce jobs and better paychecks for the little people.

During the 1970s Bartley, Wanniski, and Laffer had regular dinners, often weekly, sometimes with Kristol, near the *Journal*'s offices in Manhattan's financial district. In 1974 Kristol commissioned Wanniski to write a ten-thousand-word article about Laffer and his notions for the policy journal he ran, *The Public Interest,* thus introducing them to the intellectual world. The premise of the essay was that the last few years of high inflation and slow economic growth proved that conventional economists had no clue, and that the young genius renegade Laffer could bring about a "'Copernican revolution' in economic policy."

At the same time, according to Wanniski, he went to Washington to drum up interest there in the radical-tax-cut revolution. He met with the new White House chief of staff, Donald Rumsfeld, who in turn ordered his deputy to meet with Wanniski and Laffer. And so over drinks at a restaurant three blocks from the White House, Laffer explained himself to the deputy White House chief of staff, Dick Cheney, by sketching on a cocktail napkin what later became known as the Laffer Curve, as if it were some well-established principle of economics.

In 1976 Wanniski introduced supply-side talking points to the *Journal*'s readers. By then Laffer was teaching at the USC business school in Los Angeles, which made it easy for him to throw a dinner party for Governor Reagan—and teach him the supply-side catechism—just before he announced he'd be running for president in 1980. "Supply side economics," the political journalist Sidney Blumenthal wrote in his remarkably good 1986 book *The Rise of the Counter-Establishment: The Conservative Ascent to Political Power,* "was a theology spawned almost overnight" but "presented as radically innovative" as well as "ancient wisdom." It was "so old"—from the arguments fifty and eighty years earlier against income taxes and the New Deal—"that it seemed incredibly new." Theologically dogmatic, both old *and* new—and as Wanniski wrote in his Copernican revolution article, a magical cure for our problems that "would not involve a period of suffering" or "politically impossible prescriptions." It was a work of evil genius.

• • •

As the 1970s proceeded, the gates of all sorts of mainstream bastions opened up to intellectuals and ideas from the economic right, giving conservatism and libertarianism shiny new imprimaturs, and thereby made the liberal gatekeepers feel more exquisitely, magnanimously liberal. The Ford Foundation awarded a grant worth the equivalent of $1.8 million to AEI, the conservative think tank.* *The New York Times* hired William Safire, a speechwriter for Nixon (and his nasty criminal vice president, Spiro Agnew), as one of its main political columnists—and the Pulitzer authorities soon gave Safire a prize, as they did a year later to the *Journal*'s Bartley. Nobel Prizes for economics went both to Friedman and to his Austrian émigré mentor, Friedrich Hayek, in the 1970s. Harvard had two young superstars of the libertarian right on its faculty, the philosopher Robert Nozick and the economist Martin Feldstein.† Nozick's 1974 book *Anarchy, State, and Utopia* argued that anything beyond minimal governmental activity, such as redistributing any money from rich people to poor people, is immoral—and won the National Book Award. Feldstein was skeptical of Social Security and government unemployment benefits and even generous health insurance provided by employers. A decade after the *Times Magazine* delivered the Friedman Doctrine and eight months before Reagan was elected president, it published a long, gushing profile of Feldstein for its 3 million Sunday readers, headlined SUPERSTAR OF THE NEW ECONOMISTS. The opening scene depicted him as an exciting celebrity at a conference of Wall Street executives—and seemed to love "the fact that so titillates his audience—he is a conservative," "the most influential among a cluster of young conservative economists" who say the economy had been "overregulated and overtaxed into deep trouble."

Making old right-wing economic ideas seem fresh and respectable

*That wasn't enough to prevent Henry Ford II, so environmentally woke in 1970, from resigning in a huff in 1977 from the board of the Ford Foundation because it was too "anticapitalist."

†One data point refuting the notion that elite universities are strictly leftist indoctrination camps: from 1984 through 2019, Harvard's introductory undergraduate economics course was taught only by conservative professors—first Feldstein, who served as Reagan's chief economic adviser, then his student Greg Mankiw, who was George W. Bush's chief economic adviser.

was essential, but so was making them *operational*. As the Powell Memo had instructed, Scaife two years later provided the funds to some members of Governor Reagan's staff in California to create the Pacific Legal Foundation, a new kind of pro bono right-wing law firm devoted to litigating against government regulations, especially environmental ones. A few years later Coors put up the money for another, the Mountain States Legal Foundation.

But the main location for weaponizing right-wing ideas, this grand project to undermine and roll back twentieth-century reforms of the political economy, was naturally Washington, D.C. The correct senators and House members had to be helped or hurt, elected or beaten; Congress and the executive branch had to be aggressively lobbied and effectively bribed; laws had to be defeated and passed; the tax code had to be made easier on the rich and big business; and regulations on business had to be blunted or repealed.

The Chamber of Commerce and the other main business organization, the National Association of Manufacturers, had arisen at the turn of the twentieth century during the Progressive Era, to oppose unionization, and they later fought the New Deal. Because they were so large, representing Ford and General Electric as well as thousands of local widget companies, they tended to be cumbersome and ineffectual. In other words, for decades corporate executives and the rich simply hadn't been exercising maximum political leverage—not even to cadge government treats for particular corporations but definitely not, as Powell complained in his memo, to serve the interests of the capitalist side.

You'll notice I didn't say capitalist *class*. I've never had any hesitation using the terms *working class* or *middle class,* of course, but as an educated American liberal coming of age in the 1970s, I learned it was simple-minded and vulgar-Marxist to speak of the economic overlords and the very rich as a class or even as capitalists. And while I still resist defaulting to conspiracist explanations, pieces of this story do look and swim and walk and quack an awful lot like ducks—that is, resemble a well-executed conspiracy, not especially secret, by the leaders of the capitalist class, at the expense of everyone else.

In late 1971, as the Powell Memo was still fresh and essentially secret but rippling through America's C-suites, the chairmen and CEOs of General Electric and Alcoa started dreaming up a powerful new alliance of exclusively *big* businesses, like theirs, that would exercise serious power in Washington in a way that hadn't been done since the old days, before the Crash of 1929 and the New Deal and the deaths of the last of the original industrial oligarchs.

The heads of GE and Alcoa met in early 1972 in Washington with Nixon's Democrat-turned-Republican treasury secretary, John Connally, and Federal Reserve chairman Arthur Burns—who emphatically told them, according to a participant, that business had "to shape up in sophistication and techniques in Washington or go down the political tube."* Weeks later, the GE and Alcoa organizers convened other CEOs from among America's largest corporations at a private men's club on Manhattan's Upper East Side called the Links, and made it official. A year later, at the same club, they merged their group with some similar new antiunion, antiregulation, antitax cabals created by other suddenly militant CEOs, and the Business Roundtable was born. Unlike their weaker, wankerish predecessor groups, the Business Roundtable would consist *only* of the CEOs of the *biggest* businesses, and they were all expected to attend important strategy and decision-making meetings themselves and lobby elected officials personally.† Organized labor had had its run, and now it was time for organized capital to give it a serious go.

Not for a few more years, after Washington had dispensed with Watergate and Nixon, did the press barely begin noticing these new pieces of the emerging counter-Establishment. In 1975 the *Times* published a front-page story about the spectacular success of "a carefully organized lobbying effort, chiefly directed by a little-known organization whose members are all giant corporations"—the Business Roundtable. In the Democrat-majority House, by means of CEOs personally lobbying, the Roundtable managed to kill a bill to expand the enforcement of laws against excessive corporate power.

The same year *The Washington Post* ran a story announcing its discovery that Joseph Coors had been "funneling millions of dollars to new right-wing groups, mainly based in Washington." The world was still

*At the beginning of the Great Depression, when the young Burns taught economics at Rutgers University, one of his most devoted students was Milton Friedman.

†Not-so-fun fact: In 2019, nearly half a century after the Business Roundtable formed, no less than 83 percent of its 182 CEO members—among them its chairman Jamie Dimon, Jeff Bezos, Tim Cook, Michael Dell, and Stephen Schwarzman—were still white men.

largely unaware of the Kochs and their funneling. The *Times* passingly mentioned each of them, apparently for the first time, in 1979—"David Koch, a New York lawyer," because he was going to be the Libertarian Party's 1980 vice-presidential nominee, and his brother in a separate story simply for being so extremely rich yet so little-known. But staying in the shadows was a strategic choice back then. For one of the annual libertarian conferences that Charles Koch sponsored during the 1970s, he wrote a paper recommending that because their "radically different social philosophy" could attract "undesirable criticism," exactly "how the organization is controlled and directed should not be widely advertised." Even when he finally stepped out from behind the curtain two decades later, he told a reporter, "I don't want to dedicate my life to getting publicity."* During the 1970s his Cato Institute apparently wasn't mentioned at all in the *Times,* and the Heritage Foundation only very occasionally.

"History doesn't repeat itself but it *rhymes,*" Mark Twain is alleged to have said. As I discussed earlier, the Civil War had been a struggle between plunging forward and clinging to the past, between new and old Americas. As soon as the war ended, the country underwent an explosion of nostalgia and mass-market corniness and self-celebratory Americana—Currier & Ives pictures, John Philip Sousa marches, the new Christmas and popular music industries, the six-month-long U.S. Centennial Exhibition in Philadelphia with a reproduction seventeenth-century "New England Farmer's Home" and colonial windmill.

And then a century later, history rhymed. In the 1960s our struggles were between old and new, once again involving race and a war, this time a foreign war, that terribly divided Americans. And in the 1970s as in the 1870s, we got a nostalgia explosion: the pop cultural nostalgia, the social nostalgia among Archie Bunkers for more subservient blacks and women—and a de facto economic nostalgia among the wealthy for the unregulated businesses and untaxed fortunes of the 1920s and earlier, the economic foundation of what Twain in 1873 named the Gilded Age.

*Not until 1994 did the *Times* run an article all about the Kochs, and then almost entirely about their business—it included just two paragraphs (of sixty) about their two decades of world-changing political work.

The political reality of that first Gilded Age was that wealthier and more powerful businessmen than ever before bribed and otherwise improperly influenced U.S. officials and legislators on a much bigger scale than ever before. Then during the 1900s laws and norms restigmatized and criminalized the most brazen corruption and indifference to the public good. Organized Washington lobbying by big business and the rich was relatively small-scale, even when Senate majority leader Lyndon Johnson was distributing Texas oil money to senators to persuade them to vote his way in the 1950s—until history started rhyming in the 1970s. Along with capitalists' post-1960s-specific ideological grievances—the loss of public and political respect and support, the second-guessing and meddling by citizens and their government—they were also eager to enrich themselves directly the ways their capitalist forebears had done in the old days.

In 1971 about 175 big companies had full-time lobbyists—that is, "public affairs offices"—in Washington. By 1978 five hundred did, and just four years later, in the second Reagan year, nearly 2,500 corporations employed Washington lobbyists. While today a *majority* of senators and congresspeople become lobbyists when they leave Congress, in 1975, as a definitive *Washington Post* history of modern lobbying explains, "the rare hiring of a former member of Congress as a lobbyist made eyebrows rise." In other words, as the 1970s played out, behind and beneath all the fervent and wonky ideological arguments for unfettered capitalism lay a particular type of animal spirit—piggishness.

And 1975, remember, was in the very wake of Watergate. Much of the Watergate criminality had been funded by the Nixon reelection campaign, to which corporations and rich individuals had secretly donated large sums of cash, actual bags of paper currency. So even as suddenly jacked-up, lobbying-mad corporations began systematically ravishing the federal government, the Watergate scandal prompted Congress to pass campaign finance rules to limit donations' size and disclose who was giving. The newly politicized corporations promptly subverted those new rules in order to increase their power in Washington. A report by AEI, the conservative think tank, smirkingly explained at the time how those reforms had unintentionally "legitimized the role of corporations and business-related groups in federal elections, greatly improving their position vis-à-vis labor and other social interests."

By the fall of 1975, three hundred corporations and business groups had set up one of these new species of donation pipelines—political action committees. The new Federal Election Commission ruled that it was entirely up to a company's executives, without their shareholders' approval, to decide which campaigns and candidates to fund. Two months later, in a case brought by both conservatives and liberal civil libertarians, the Supreme Court ruled that donors not formally connected to candidates—such as corporate PACs—could contribute to political causes as much as they wanted. And in another important case, the Court ruled that corporations were free to finance state and local referenda unrelated to their business.* Corporations, they decided, just like citizens, have free speech rights that may not be limited.

Thus began a "quiet revolution," the head lawyer of the National Association of Manufacturers marveled at the time, by "corporations in the political arena, which would not have been possible only four years ago." And right after the decision removing limits from PAC donations, the number of business PACs increased from three hundred to twelve hundred, generating gushers of money that helped triple the cost of campaigns for a House seat by the mid-1980s, which in turn gave PACs more power, and so on it has gone ever since, a vicious cycle corrupting democracy.

Once again the economic right and big business keenly channeled and twisted the democratic anti-Establishment 1960s spirit. The first spectacular 1960s protests had happened in 1964 in Berkeley, where pissed-off, idealistic students refused en masse to submit to the university's rules restricting public political activity—the Free Speech Movement. The free speech movement launched just a decade later by pissed-off rich adults with a long-term strategy to pursue their economic interests was at least as transformative and consequential.

*The majority opinion in this second case, *First National Bank of Boston v. Bellotti,* was written by . . . Justice Lewis Powell. That decision formed the foundation for the Court's definitive *Citizens United v. Federal Election Commission* decision in 2010 that invalidated limits on campaign spending by groups that candidates don't officially, directly control.

7

The 1970s: From a Bicentennial Pageant to a Presidency

I mentioned how Milton Friedman's confrontational bluntness and zealotry—*telling it like it is,* in 1960s-speak—gave his 1970 manifesto oomph and traction. In fact, ironically, it was a particular set of quintessentially late-1960s attitudes that endured and made America ripe for the project undertaken by the economic right starting in the 1970s. It wasn't so much that people were suddenly primed to respect and glorify business and businesspeople as they had sometimes done in the past. Rather, the reflexive fear and loathing of the government that had become a left-countercultural *and* right-wing reactionary habit during the 1960s grew and spread during the 1970s and found new expressions.

The murderousness (and incompetence) of the Vietnam War, together with the misconduct of the FBI and intelligence agencies in spying on antiwar groups, and the war on drugs, were one set of reasons to hate the federal government in the 1960s and '70s. For some white people, passage and enforcement of laws to help black Americans were another. Violent crime continued to increase in the 1970s, especially in cities, on its way to more than doubling again—which meant that government was failing, and although Washington had next to no involvement with local law enforcement, it was Washington that had passed civil rights laws and expanded antipoverty programs, so it was easy for racist and racist-ish whites to conflate all that and blame Washington for the new criminal mayhem. The increase in violent crime also prompted modest gun control—which in turn provided people who liked guns excessively with a new, self-righteous, 1960s-style individualist reason to despise and fear the government.

Every two or four years, a gold-standard academic survey asks Americans if they "trust the government in Washington to do what is right just about always, most of the time, or only some of the time?" In 1964, 77 percent of them said always or most of the time. By 1970 that majority had shrunk to 54 percent, where it remained for a couple of surveys. But the Vietnam War continued, and we continued losing it. The one universally approved recent U.S. government achievement, the manned space program, was abruptly kaput. Starting in the 1970s, the phrase *good enough for government work* became a piece of viral snark. And of course, there were the Watergate crimes committed by Nixon and his lieutenants. Between the surveys of 1972 and 1974, the Washington-trusting cohort of Americans shriveled to 36 percent. In the next presidential election, the incumbent Republican president said in a debate that the "considerable anti-Washington feeling throughout the country . . . is misplaced," but his Democratic anti-Washington opponent won after saying, in the same debate, that he would undertake "a great reduction in agencies and programs" and end the "gross waste of money."

Once a large majority of Americans came to believe that the federal government was uninspiring or incompetent or corrupt or evil, as they rapidly had over the previous decade, it was going to be a lot easier for the economic right to persuade people that regulating big business and taxing the rich were just plain *wrong*. Those people wouldn't necessarily become crusaders for free enterprise, but if they started focusing more of their resentment and anger on the federal government, the smart right-wingers knew, it could have the same effect.

On the first Sunday of 1976, Washington journalism's elder statesman at the time, James Reston, the former editor of *The New York Times* and then its main political opinion writer, wrote a column called "Presidential Job Description." He said that "a new majority in America, . . . increasingly self-concerned and even cynical, is not impressed by . . . the smooth theatrical conservative nostalgia of Ronald Reagan." Yet over the next month Reagan ran an extremely close second to President Ford in the Iowa and New Hampshire primaries and very nearly won the nomination. As that presidential election got going, another leading political journalist noted that "layered over everything" in the political landscape "are apathy, nostalgia and cynicism."

Reston's idol Walter Lippmann, the great American political commentator and author who'd recently died, had derided politicized nostalgia sixty years earlier, at the beginning of his career and the modern age. "Men generally find in the past what they miss in the present," he wrote.

> For most of us insist that somewhere in the past there was a golden age. But people who are forever dreaming of a mythical past are merely saying that they are afraid of the future. The past which men create for themselves is a place where thought is unnecessary and happiness is inevitable. The American temperament leans generally to a kind of mystical anarchism.

In 1976 the Republicans were not yet the party of unhinged mystical anarchism they became over the next four decades. Rather, after the unhappiness, unfriendliness, cynicism, paranoia, and finally the high crimes of Richard Nixon, Americans were eager to install Mr. Rogers in the White House—that is, sincere, low-key, straightforward Jimmy Carter, a devoutly Protestant goody-goody complete with toothy smile and cardigan sweater whom Reston hadn't even mentioned as a contender in his New Year's election preview.

The choice was between two basically boring, moderate nice guys whom nobody'd heard of a couple of years earlier—a governor running against Washington, Carter, and a lifelong Washington congressional hack who stepped in to replace Nixon's criminal vice president and then pardoned Nixon for his crimes, Gerald Ford. Not only did Carter appear to be Nixon's opposite, he also seemed to fit the zeitgeist's nostalgia requirement: a farmer from a small town called Plains, a Sunday school teacher, and on race a latter-day Atticus Finch.

Electing Jimmy Carter in the fall of 1976 was a natural follow-up to the U.S. bicentennial summer. The bicentennial commemorations were a surprisingly big-deal reboot of national solidarity—a Fourth of July nostalgiapalooza that came along at a ripe moment. In addition to the two hundredth national birthday party, they served as a de facto celebration of the end of the Sixties hangover that had included the finales of Vietnam (1975) and Watergate (1974). I'd just graduated college and arrived in New York City, where people—jaded, sophisticated *New Yorkers*—were fully, enthusiastically engaged in this Americana spectacle. The Grand Parade of Sailing Ships, sixteen old square-riggers each a hundred yards long, gliding into the harbor as if from out of the nineteenth century and past the Statue of Liberty! Plus dozens of military ships disgorging thousands of excited sailors all over the city, *On the Town* come to life!

But after hopeful visions of old-fashioned American virtue helped elect him, Jimmy Carter couldn't manage to play the nostalgia card worth a damn, and *President* Carter never came across as a leading man. Americans don't require presidents (or leading men) to be cheerful or manly all the time, but in the modern era they really can't abide mopes and wimps and scolds.

The previous paradigm shift in the U.S. political economy, embodied and enacted by the New Deal in the 1930s, had been triggered by economic catastrophe—a quarter of all workers suddenly unemployed, the pay of the ones still working significantly cut, savings wiped out by the failures of almost half the banks, stock prices down 89 percent in three years. Nothing remotely as horrible as the Great Depression happened in the 1970s to persuade Americans to make a sharp right turn or reverse course from the country the New Deal had built. Our successful free-market system, as rebuilt in the 1930s and tweaked since, had not teetered or collapsed. In fact, despite a recession, the 1970s were a great decade for business: from 1970 to 1979, corporate profits overall nearly doubled, getting higher than they'd been since 1951. Inequality was as moderate as it had been in the twentieth century. But two very unpleasant and unfamiliar new economic conditions—high inflation year after year and much higher-priced oil and gasoline—made citizens more willing to accept big changes in the economy.

For the three decades since the Truman administration, inflation had been practically imperceptible, mostly running between 1 and 3 percent, as it is in the twenty-first century and has been for three decades. But from 1973 to 1975, the annual rate of inflation rose from less than 4 percent to more than 12 percent, and in 1980 it nearly reached 15 percent. The prices of everything were increasing by half or more every few years. Inflation made for a sense of out-of-control flux that almost nobody enjoyed, as if the 1960s' dismaying rate of change were continuing but without any of the good or fun parts. In a decade, prices more than doubled, meaning that the value of cash savings shrank by more than half. Interest rates on loans naturally doubled as well. Many Americans were disconcerted, angry, and a little panicky. If your middle-class salary doubled between 1973 and 1980, for instance, your purchasing power didn't actually increase *at all,* and yet because of inflation, your marginal federal tax rate could have gone from 24 to 30 percent. Which might well incline you in the next election to vote for the candidates of a Republican Party that was starting to make lower taxes its central promise.

When inflation had begun creeping higher at the end of the 1960s, the economy was still growing fast. But in the mid-1970s there was a double whammy—crazily inflating prices were accompanied by a long economic recession, a combination so unusual the new word *stagflation* was coined. In fact, it was a triple whammy: during the 1970s in America (as in the whole developed world), a *post*–post–World War II slowdown in growth and productivity was becoming apparent. During a single recessionary year, 100,000 U.S. steelworkers were laid off. But even during a more economically ordinary year, 1979, the auto industry laid off a third of its workforce.

The mid-'70s recession had been triggered by a sudden quadrupling of oil prices by OPEC, the dozen-nation cartel that produced most of the world's petroleum. Yet for Americans, the oil crisis wasn't just about the oil crisis and the higher gasoline and home heating prices—it was routinely called the *Arab* oil crisis. OPEC consisted of *third world* countries, and we were also months away from officially losing our disastrous decade-long war to a third world country, North Vietnam. On multiple fronts, the end of America's twentieth-century invincibility suddenly seemed nigh.

While there was nothing in the 1970s economically comparable to the Depression to trigger an equivalent political about-face, there were several simultaneous and mutually reinforcing narratives about our failing national moxie. The federal government seemed manifestly incompetent *and* weak, both at home *and* abroad, *and*—don't forget Watergate, don't forget the new revelations of FBI and CIA misdeeds—*evil* to boot. *It didn't used to be this way. Why can't things be like they used to be?*

The pivotal year for the energized economic right was 1978. Its dreams were starting to come true. Americans were now more skeptical of government than of big business. At the beginning of the year a CBS News/ *New York Times* survey found that 58 percent of Americans agreed that "the Government has gone too far in regulating business and interfering with the free enterprise system," up from 42 percent during the 1960s.

A critical mass of the people elected to run the government had also been persuaded to give big business what it wanted. Democrats held the presidency and a two-to-one House majority and a historic sixty-two-seat Senate majority. Yet in early 1978, a bill to create a new consumer protection agency was defeated in the House because 101 Democrats voted against it, including a majority of the Democratic freshmen, thanks in large part to lobbying by CEOs from the Business Roundtable.

And 1978 was also a tipping-point year in the economic right's crusade to persuade people that because government now sucked, all taxes paid to all governments by everyone, no matter how wealthy, were way too high and also sucked. The overwhelmingly Democratic Congress overwhelmingly passed and the Democratic president signed into law a huge reduction in taxes on income from selling stocks, capital gains—a definitive turn toward making extra-sure the rich got richer faster. Just five years earlier, when he was governor of California, Ronald Reagan had pushed a ballot initiative to cut and permanently limit various state and local taxes; it was decisively defeated. In 1978 Proposition 13, a California state constitutional amendment to cut property taxes by more than half and permanently limit increases, was decisively approved.

Carter was elected as the sweet, honest anti-Nixon. Ironically, the rapid zeitgeist shift of the 1970s meant that after a Republican who'd governed as a liberal, certainly by the standards ever since, his immediate successor governed as "the most conservative Democratic President since Grover Cleveland," according to the liberal historian Arthur Schlesinger, Jr. But conservatives weren't buying it, any more than liberals had bought Nixon's liberalism. By the summer of 1979, even though he'd presided over no disasters (yet), only about 30 percent of people told pollsters they approved of the job the president was doing, fewer than for any postwar president so far except Nixon in his final Watergate year.

So how did Carter respond? By canceling a big televised Fourth of July Oval Office address at the last minute and spending the next ten days writing a new one. His call to action was austerity, reducing our use of imported oil—not for environmental reasons but because oil had gotten so expensive. The speech, however, was like a scene from a remake of *Mr. Smith Goes to Washington* written by and starring Wallace Shawn. Carter spent the first two-thirds on a half-hour jeremiad about America's "crisis of confidence," wondering "why have we not been able to get together as a nation," bewailing "the growing doubt about the meaning of our own lives" and "a system of government that seems incapable of action"—but it's worse than that, he said, because "all the legislation in the world can't fix what's wrong with America." After this dire diagnosis, he offered no cure except a vague wave back to the wonderful past—somehow restoring "faith in each other" by relying on "all the lessons of our heritage"—and then fired half his cabinet. Because he privately referred to America's *malaise* as he'd prepared the speech—"the President will try to transfer the wide dissatisfaction with his own performance into a 'national malaise,'" the Republican ex-speechwriter Safire previewed in his *Times* column forty-eight hours beforehand—journalists afterward named it "the malaise speech," and that stuck. The president continued with scolding jeremiads for the rest of his term, such as one about high inflation in which he reminded Americans of the "discipline" that they needed to start exercising and the "pain" and "painful steps" they'd be required to suffer.*

Americans wanted to *feel* a jolt of old-fashioned national solidarity, of the kind they remembered or imagined feeling before the late 1960s,

*On its editorial about this speech, *The Boston Globe* accidentally and infamously printed a joke headline—MUSH FROM THE WIMP.

not merely be reminded by Parson Carter they weren't feeling it anymore. One of the points of the 1970s pivot toward the old days was to feel happier about being Americans—*Happy Days* was the name of the TV show—because Vietnam and the rest of the 1960s had made so many people feel ambivalent or worse. Carter was unwilling or unable to indulge the manic performative patriotism that was becoming obligatory for American politicians in the 1970s.

In many senses, America's 1970s were not a repudiation but an extension of the late 1960s. The new norms and habits of mind spread and scaled, became entrenched, and no longer seemed remarkably new. Female and nonwhite people were treated more equally. The anti-Establishment subjectivity and freedom to ignore experts and believe in make-believe that exploded in the '60s was normalized and spread during the '70s and beyond. Freedoms of religion and speech continued to be exercised extravagantly. The signifiers of bohemian nonconformity—long hair, drug use, casual sex, casual clothes, rock music—became ubiquitous, standard, mainstream. A single two-year period in the mid-'70s seems like a hinge moment in this regard: the Vietnam War ended, the oldest baby boomers turned thirty, the youngest baby boomers entered puberty, *Rolling Stone* moved from a hippie dump in San Francisco to a fancy Establishment building in midtown Manhattan, the new president was a Dylan fan, *Saturday Night Live* went on the air, the Apple II was invented, and Microsoft was founded.

In retrospect, Milton Friedman's 1970 manifesto on behalf of shameless greed amounted to a preliminary offer by the philosopher-king of the economic right to forge a grand bargain with the cultural left. Both sides could find common ground concerning ultra-individualism and mistrust of government. And by the end of the 1970s, only the formalities remained to execute the agreement. Going forward, the masses would be permitted as never before to indulge their hedonistic and self-expressive impulses. And capitalists in return would also be unshackled, free to indulge their own animal spirits with fewer and fewer fetters in the forms of regulation, taxes, or social opprobrium. "Do your own thing" is not necessarily so different from "every man for himself." That could mean calling it quits on a marriage more quickly—the divorce rate doubled in the 1970s—or opting out of marriage altogether, or smoking weed, or wearing blue jeans every day, or refusing to agree to gun regulation—or rich people paying themselves as much as they wanted, or banks misleading borrowers and speculating recklessly. Deal? Deal.

So around when Tom Wolfe named it the Me Decade in 1976, the new hyperselfishness expanded beyond personal vanity and self-absorption and extreme religion to encompass the political economy as well. And indispensable to that was the one way the American sensibility definitely *changed* after the 1960s: nostalgia became a mania. With so many Americans so charmed by the cultural past in so many ways, it was easier to persuade them that restoring a version of the economic past would somehow make them happier—the past when the federal government didn't give away so much to the undeserving poor and fought wars they didn't lose.

The great political opportunity at the end of the 1970s was to play to the Me Decade's narcissism by using nostalgia—cynically, smoothly, theatrically—to cut through the despondency. A new majority of Americans were ready to be impressed by a president who convincingly and comfortingly promised to lead them into an American future resembling the American past. *Comfort* was key. Since the early 1960s, the conservatives' political harnessing of backlash against kindly liberalism had been unsmiling and scary, all ferocious contempt. That's why Barry Goldwater lost in a landslide, why George Wallace was a national pariah, why grim Richard Nixon was smart enough not even to try to make the right-wing economic case. A reframing was required. Instead of emphasizing conservative *disgust* with the *new,* somebody had to serve up delicious-looking gobs of the beautiful past.

Ronald Reagan was an ideal figure to take advantage of the moment in every conceivable way.

He didn't just talk about the good old days, he stepped right out of them, as cheerful and easy to like as his genius pal Walt Disney's make-believe Main Street USA. Reagan was an avuncular artifact of Hollywood's golden age, sixty-eight when he announced in 1979 but a very modern American kind of old, sunny and ruddy and energetic and fun, riding the horse, wearing the jeans, doing photo-op chores around his fancy California ranch.* For years he'd been popping up on TV in old movies and an old TV series he hosted, playing generic good guys and war fighters from various old days. He was *familiar,* a charismatic celebrity (like Jack Kennedy) but never such a star that voters couldn't easily accept him in this new role, an old-fashioned midcentury American TV dad who wasn't a weenie or a tool or a crook like his immediate predecessors. Long before Dad Jokes became a meme, Reagan was a chuckling virtuoso of the form who put a fun candy coating on right-wing propaganda: "The nine most terrifying words in the English language," he loved saying, "are 'I'm from the government and I'm here to help.'"

He was also a twinkly quasi-Christian, unlike his authentically Christian sermonizing predecessor. Reagan appealed to America's newly extreme and politicized Protestants, repeatedly affirming his belief in the End Times and the Second Coming. But he did that without any of his Moral Majority allies' angry nostalgia for the old days, which alienated other voters. American Protestants were undergoing their own rapid and extreme theological makeover, from about a third belonging to evangelical churches in the early 1970s to 60 percent by the mid-1980s, and he was the ideal political recruiter for binding them to the reborn party of the old-fashioned hard-core economic right.

But in addition to being in sync with the new post-1960s conditions—extreme individualism, extreme religious belief, a sweeping embrace of nostalgia—Ronald Reagan also found himself at the convergence of three longer-term historical trends. And he possessed the perfect combination of skills and temperament to take political advantage of those as well.

The first was the general national hankering for friendly familiarity and calm following the frenzied circa-1970 finale of the century of nonstop *new,* a conservative reaction that was much more about culture and psychology than economics.

The second was that the natural evolution of the political economy had reached a critical point. Forty years after the cascading flood of

*In addition to being the oldest president until recently, he was the first to have been divorced—just the right dash of louche to suggest that his conservatism wasn't the unpleasant old-fashioned judgmental kind.

change that gushed forth during the 1930s, the New Deal had lost its propulsive power as it widened into a big boring American reservoir on which everyone depended but lately took for granted or held in contempt. That finally gave the New Deal's enemies their chance to undo as much of it as they could. In this effort, they exploited another definitive late-1960s change. Reagan was a conservative but was so far right he came across as a renegade. "The one unifying thing about the baby boomers," a Republican strategist told a reporter back then about that younger generation, "is that they are anti-Establishment and anti-institution," and "the Reagan appeal is to people who don't go for the Establishment and for big institutions."

The third long-term historical trend was the evolution of modern media and celebrity from words to pure images. Thirty years into the TV age, show business and presidential politics became so intertwined that Americans were ready to elect a professional entertainer-in-chief. Ronald Reagan's job from the 1930s through the mid-1960s had been to perform for cameras, reciting words written by other people, so cynics are apt to look no further than that for an explanation of his subsequent political success—good-looking TV dummy, strings pulled by right-wing puppet-masters. But that's not correct.

Reagan was no intellectual, but he'd always been a cheerful, politically engaged ideologue, and by the time he ran for office, he was more fluent in political economics than most politicians. At age thirty-five, after morphing from sincere left-winger to sincere anti-Communist liberal, he continued making political ads decrying corporations' "bigger and bigger profits" and Republican tax cuts for "the higher income brackets alone," and he repeatedly got reelected president of his show business union, the Screen Actors Guild. But before he was fifty, after reading books like Hayek's libertarian manifesto *The Road to Serfdom* and giving hundreds of speeches a year as GE's $1 million–a–year traveling ambassador, he'd turned into a sincere right-winger.

Way before the liberal 1960s, Reagan was a Milton Friedmanite giving speeches about the "stultifying hand of government regulation and interference," the "little intellectual elite in a far-distant capital" that presumed to "plan our lives for us," and—remarkably right-wing—"the immorality and discrimination of the progressive tax." Then in the fall of

1964, there on NBC in prime time was the star of the weekly Western series *Death Valley Days*, but now in a suit and tie, nominally endorsing his pal Barry Goldwater—this was the half-hour ad the campaign *did* run nationwide—but in fact introducing himself to America as a political figure. Because he wasn't running for anything yet, he was free to be blunt, even extreme—in favor of letting the well-to-do opt out of Social Security, declaring that "government does nothing as well . . . as the private sector," warning against Medicare as proof that "it doesn't require expropriation or confiscation of private property or business to impose socialism on a people." One week after his network TV talk, voters repudiated that ultraconservatism decisively—for now. But with Goldwater done, the right had a *new* avatar, another horseback-riding, fifty-something southwesterner who wasn't too stern or scary.

And when he ran for president in 1979 and 1980, Reagan suggested his administration would resemble those of beloved dead *Democrats,* fondly alluding to FDR and Truman and JFK. It was nostalgia for old heroes and for his own younger days—probably sincere but also well played at a time when voters' own nostalgic yearnings had become all-embracing. As he ambled briskly to the presidency, Reagan's ultra-conservative agenda for the political economy was cloaked behind an old-timey, almost nonpartisan scrim.

"Extremism in defense of liberty is no vice," Barry Goldwater had famously said in his speech accepting the Republican nomination. He *owned* it and lost. As the 1980 election cycle got under way, Goldwater marveled in his diary about the normalization of the hard right since then, which was about to permit his fellow traveler to be elected president. "It is interesting to me to watch liberals, moderates and conservatives fighting each other to see who can come out on top the quickest against those matters that I talked so fervently and so much about in 1964"—against regulation and unions and taxes and sharing more of the wealth, against government. "Almost every one of the principles I advocated in 1964 have become the gospel of the whole spread of the spectrum of politics."

In fact, Milton Friedman thought Goldwater had self-sacrificially fought the necessary opening skirmish for the long war that he and the rest of the economic right and big business seriously launched in the 1970s and won. "I do not believe Reagan would have been elected in 1980," Friedman said during his presidency, if Goldwater had not carried out his campaign in 1964. You've got sets of political ideas and values that take a long time to develop and have an enormous momentum. It takes a long time to turn them around. Goldwater was enormously important in providing an impetus to the subsequent move away from New Deal ideas.

8

The 1970s: Neoliberal Useful Idiots

During my first visit to Washington, D.C., in June 1972—on the very evening of the Watergate break-in, as it happened—a mod young federal bureaucrat informed me over dinner that the liberal political era in America was ending. As a seventeen-year-old fresh from Nebraska looking forward to wearing my MCGOVERN FOR PRESIDENT button to a White House reception for a hundred new high school graduates with Vice President Spiro Agnew the next day, this was a shocking revelation.

The guy turned out to be right, of course. And when I started college, I saw firsthand that the youthquake and student movement and greening of America, everything I'd spent the past few years getting stoked about, was palpably, rapidly ending. The U.S. war in Vietnam was winding down and nobody was getting drafted, so fighting the Man started to seem more like a pose than an authentic passion. I was still politically liberal, but the overwhelming focus of my college years was being on the staff of *The Harvard Lampoon*. The highlight of my sophomore year was a public *Lampoon* roast of and raucous private dinner with the right-wing icon John Wayne, who arrived at our headquarters in an armored personnel carrier a year before the U.S. surrender in Vietnam. My senior year I volunteered for the

1976 presidential campaign of Democratic senator Fred Harris, an economic populist from Oklahoma whose campaign catchphrases included "The issue is privilege" and "Take the rich off welfare." He'd been the one member of the Senate to vote against confirming Lewis Powell to the Supreme Court. My senior thesis argued that more and more white-collar jobs, thanks in part to technology, were apt to become more and more proletarian, and it discussed whether workers in such professions might follow the lead of federal air traffic controllers, who'd recently unionized.

I wasn't romantic or enthusiastic about unions the way liberals used to be. The basic college-educated-liberal attitude toward unions was evolving from solidarity to indifference to suspicion, the result of a crackup at that very moment of the old New Deal political coalition. The antiwar movement and counterculture, coming right after the successful civil rights movement, had generated intense mutual contempt between the two main kinds of white Democrats, members of the working class and the expanding New Class. The televised beatings by Chicago police of protesters outside the Democratic convention in 1968—beatings encouraged by Mayor Richard Daley, the principal national white-working-class Democratic power broker—was the most spectacular early episode in the crackup. But a lesser-known instance two years later in New York City was an even more perfectly focused display of that cultural-political fissure in its early stages.

It was 1970, a cool May morning in New York City. Two months earlier a squad of young left-wing bomb-makers had accidentally blown themselves up in a Greenwich Village townhouse owned by their comrade's dad, an ad executive who'd been vacationing on St. Kitts. And in another two months *Joe,* a movie about a factory worker who hates liberals and teams up with a Manhattan ad executive to massacre hippie communards, would become a big hit. On the Monday of that week in May, National Guard troops at Kent State University in Ohio had shot thirteen students in and around an antiwar protest, killing four of them. So that Friday in lower Manhattan on Wall Street, around the statue of George Washington in front of the Federal Hall National Memorial, a thousand people, mostly students, gathered for an antiwar protest and memorial vigil. Not far away at City Hall, the American flag had been lowered to half-mast. New York police were in position around the demonstration.

Suddenly a couple of hundred union construction workers, a lot of them wearing hard hats and carrying tools, swarmed into the crowded intersection, chanting *All the way, U.S.A.* and *Love it or leave it*. "The workers, marching behind a cluster of American flags, swept policemen aside and moved on the students," according to the *Times* account. They beat up scores of protesters as well as random passersby, kicked them, bashed them with hard hats, and struck them with crowbars and pliers. The attack was organized by the leaders of the workers' union; a Wall Street executive told the *Times* he'd watched "two men in gray suits and gray hats 'directing the construction workers with hand motions.'" Then the mob moved north, where some smashed the windows of a college building and pulled down and burned a peace banner. Across the street, others burst into City Hall and raised the lowered flag. After a city official re-lowered it, angry workers bullied a deputy mayor into raising it again.

The Hard Hat Riot got extensive national press attention—as a kid in Nebraska, I watched film of it on TV and read about it in *Time*. Plastic hard hats became a nationalist antiliberal icon. And union workers in New York City kept at it, marching in the streets day after day for nearly two weeks, "vaulting police lines to chase those who raised their fingers in the 'V' peace salute." The mayor had condemned the initial riot, which made him—John Lindsay, handsome prep-school Yale WASP, a liberal Republican for whom "limousine liberal" had been coined one year earlier—a natural target for the marching workers. They carried "signs calling the mayor a rat, a commie rat, a faggot, a leftist, an idiot, a neurotic, an anarchist and a traitor," a news story reported. (The construction workers' union was already in a fight with Lindsay for his executive order requiring them to increase black and Hispanic membership.) Watching a final 100,000-person antiprotester protest march in Manhattan that had been officially organized by the union, a Brooklyn college kid told a reporter, "I'm scared. If this is what the class struggle is all about, there's something wrong."

Beginning right then, in fact, the suspicion and contempt between less-educated white people and the liberal white bourgeoisie *was* what the American class struggle was most visibly and consciously about. And it would define our politics as the economy was reshaped to do better than ever for yuppies and worse and worse for the proles, regardless of their ideologies and cultural tastes.

During the 1960s, liberals had started falling out of love with unions for reasons more directly related to the political economy. It was another side effect of triumphalist liberal complacency, how Americans in general were taking for granted the progress and prosperity that the New Deal had helped make possible. Sure, back in the day unions had been an essential countervailing force to business, but now—having won forty-hour weeks, good healthcare, good pensions, autoworker salaries of $75,000 (in 2020 dollars), OSHA, the EEOC—organized labor was victorious, powerful, the Establishment. "These powerful institutions," the former machinist Irving Kristol astutely wrote at the beginning of 1970, just before publicly moving full right, were "inexorably being drained of meaning, and therefore of legitimacy." As a result, "trade unionism has become that most dangerous of social phenomena: a boring topic," and "none of the younger reporters is interested in spending so much time in the company of trade union officials."

Apart from organized labor's apparently permanent hold on decisive power at the time, another reason people like me found unions kind of boring was that a unionized job was almost by definition a boring job. When I started work as a writer at *Time* in 1981, I joined the union, the Newspaper Guild, but I understood that everything I cared about in that job—good assignments, decent salary increases, titular honorifics—would be entirely at my editors' discretion, not a function of union rules.* A union? Sure, fine. But I was *talent*. I was *creative*. I was an *individual*.† College graduates tend to want to think of themselves that way, younger ones all the more, younger ones starting with baby boomers the most. And the intensified, all-encompassing individualism that blew up during the 1960s and then continued—*I do my thing, and you do your thing. I am not in this world to live up to your expectations*—wasn't a mindset or temperament that necessarily reinforced feelings of solidarity with fellow workers or romantic feelings about unions.

*A bumbling, ineffectual strike by Time Inc.'s one thousand editorial employees, the first ever, had taken place a few years before I got there; its big demand had been that raises be exactly the same for everyone in percentage terms. After editors and managers successfully produced the next issues of the monthlies and three issues of the weeklies on schedule, the strikers gave up. The big problem, according to the head of *Time*'s Newspaper Guild, was the "large number of members new to the idea of a union, let alone a strike."

†I've been an enthusiastic dues-paying and voting member of the Writers Guild, the union for TV and film writers, for three decades.

What happened with organized labor in journalism during the 1970s is an excellent illustration of those early days of the deepening, widening fracture between upper-middle-class and lower-middle-class (white) Americans. It encompasses both the cultural split, yuppies versus yahoos, and the introduction of transformative technology in the workplace.

Between the publication of the Pentagon Papers in 1971 and the end of Watergate in 1974, *The Washington Post* became a celebrated national institution, sexy liberalism incarnate. Following immediately on those two heroic achievements was another milestone episode, neither very celebrated nor heroic but likewise emblematic of the moment. In the spring of 1974, the journalists of the *Post* went out on strike—bumblingly. They didn't even ask the paper's blue-collar unions to join them, they refused their own Newspaper Guild leaders' request to walk a picket line, the paper continued publishing, and after two weeks they gave up and accepted management's offer.

It was a generation before websites and browsers, universal PCs and cellphones, thirty years before print dailies entered their death spiral, but technology was already changing newspapers in a big way—the *manufacturing* part of the operation. Owners were eliminating typographers, who operated obsolete, elephantine *Brazil*–meets–*Willy Wonka* Linotype machines that turned molten lead into blocks of type, and they also wanted to pay fewer workers to operate the printing presses. A large majority of the *Post*'s two thousand employees were those blue-collar guys, and a large majority of them were suddenly redundant. In 1975 the two hundred pressmen wouldn't come to terms and went on strike, and the other blue-collar unions at the *Post* went on strike in solidarity, as unions are supposed to do. On their way out, some of the pressmen sabotaged some of the presses, a major strategic error. Quite a few of the nonunion strikebreakers whom management hired to replace the (white) strikers were black, a brilliant strategic decision.

And absolutely key to how it played out was the behavior of the *Post*'s journalists. Just as the recent exposure of the secret Pentagon report on Vietnam and Nixon's crimes had been game-changing work by journalists with the essential support of management, the crushing of the strike and pressmen's union, also game-changing, was the work of management with the essential support of journalists.

Two-thirds of the *Post*'s unionized editorial employees didn't stop working at all, and a majority voted again and again against striking in solidarity with the pressmen. "What I find ominous is that a number of Guild people don't think they have common cause with craftsmen," a *Post* journalist told a reporter at the time. "They feel professionally superior to guys with dirt under their fingernails." At a guild meeting, a *Post* reporter referred to the striking pressmen as "slack-jawed cretins." Four weeks into the five-month strike, a *Times* article reported that "if a *Post* Guild member is asked why he or she is not supporting the strike," many "say they do not see themselves as ordinary working people. One said, 'We go to the same parties as management. We know Kissinger, too.'" And while probably none of the pressmen knew the secretary of state, their average pay was the equivalent of $111,000, about as much as reporters, which is the excuse one of the paper's reporters gave for crossing the picket line from day one. "If they got slave wages, I'd be out on the line myself," said thirty-two-year-old Bob Woodward, co-author of the second-best-selling nonfiction book of the previous year.

The strike ended just before the release of the film adaptation of *All the President's Men,* a fictionalization that only intensified the love of American liberals and journalists for *The Washington Post,* even though the *Post* pressroom was about to become nonunion and membership in the journalists' union, the Guild, strictly optional. As a *Post* columnist wrote back then in *The New Republic,* "The pressmen's strike was crushed with methods and with a severity that the press in general or the *Post* in particular would not be likely to regard as acceptable from the owners of steel mills. Yet because it was a newspaper management that broke the strike, no other newspaper has touched it properly, or even whimpered a protest."

When I arrived at *Time* a few years later, I went out of my way to produce copy the *modern* way—abandoning my office Selectric to use one of the special computer terminals crammed into a special little room, holed up with a few of the other young writers. That technology presently enabled the company to eliminate the jobs of the people downstairs who were employed to retype our stories. At the time I probably shrugged, like the newspaper reporters who hadn't cared much about the redundant Linotype operators and pressmen.

If I'd been one of those unionized craft workers who were abandoned by my unionized journalist colleagues forty-five years ago, I think that during these last fifteen years, watching journalists get washed away and drowned by the latest wave of technology-induced change, I'd have felt some schadenfreude.

It's a close-to-home example of that spiral of mistrust and resentment that wasn't only cultural, hard hats versus hippies, but about earning a living, the changing political economy. And what happened at newspapers (and magazines) back then also had disproportionate impact on this whole history because once journalists were actively ambivalent about organized labor, that disenchantment spread more contagiously than if it had just been random young professionals disrespecting and badmouthing unions. News stories about labor now tended to be framed *this* way rather than *that* way or were not covered at all. Thus, like Democratic politicians in Washington at the same time, media people became enablers of the national change in perspective from left to right concerning economics.

I'm not claiming that labor unions are always virtuous or aren't frequently annoying. Parochial, shortsighted, and other kinds of misguided, with a rich history of racism, sexism, and corruption—construct your own critique. I heard every criticism growing up as the opposite of a red-diaper baby; my father was a lawyer whose practice was negotiating with unions on behalf of employers.

But they or equivalent vehicles must exist and have serious power. It's a question of achieving a decent balance, a dynamic tension and equilibrium among the various players in the political economy—workers and employers and citizens. The balance this country managed from the 1930s through the 1970s worked and seemed fair. Then over the last few decades, as unions and belief in the premise of organized labor weakened, big business and the wealthy took predatory advantage, and the system became highly unbalanced. It's important to look hard at how liberals were variously complacent and complicit as that unbalancing happened.

During the 1930s and '40s and '50s, the right had derided liberal writers and editors as Communists' "useful idiots," doing soft propaganda work for the extreme left; it looks in retrospect as if starting in the 1970s, a lot of them—of us—became capitalists' useful idiots. Indeed, that's how the former socialist Kristol foresaw the huge new cohort of college-educated liberal professionals being co-opted into the system. "A good part of this process of assimilation," he advised conservatives and capitalists in the

1970s, "will be the education of this 'new class' in the actualities of business and economics—*not* their conversion to 'free enterprise'—so that they can exercise power responsibly. It will be an immense educational task, in which the business community can certainly play an important role."

During the 1960s, the decade of maximum new here in our land of the new, the New Deal had started to seem old, one more thing over thirty not to trust. The institutionalized political left that had grown out of that era was renamed the Old Left, because the younger generation—in some cases more radical, in all cases groovier—was called the New Left. As I've said, at the moment the revolution failed and voters rejected McGovernite ultra-liberalism, Americans of every caste were giving themselves over to romanticizing the past in pop culture and high art. The smart sets were reviving and recycling old forms and styles, not just returning decoration to architecture but melody to classical music and human figures to fine art—all of which felt charmingly old but also unfamiliar, fresh, excitingly . . . new.

In politics and public policy too, the past was being selectively rediscovered. Fancy-college-educated liberals, who like artists and cultural gatekeepers still defined themselves by their openness to the new and challenging, chose not to return to the tired FDR liberalism of the older generations with whom they'd been fighting an internecine war for a decade. Rather, the unfamiliar things they dusted off were pieces of the old conservative critique of New Deal liberalism—which was a bit transgressive, therefore cool. They became the New Democrats, as opposed to the old New Deal Democrats, the *new* new versus the old new.

Fred Dutton was a prominent professional Democrat who'd worked in the Kennedy White House, then for Vice President Humphrey, then for Bobby Kennedy's presidential campaign in 1968. In the summer of 1971, this middle-aged Establishment liberal published a very ahead-of-the-curve book called *Changing Sources of Power* that predicted and advocated for a new species of liberalism geared toward white-collar workers and especially youth. He praised the baby boomers for providing "a severe psychic jolt for traditional liberals, who long ago came to believe that they had an almost exclusive stewardship over the American conscience." In the 1970s, he said, "the greatest shift is the current tipping of the balance of political power from the economic to the psychological, from the stomach and pocketbook to the psyche." In other words, more or less: forget political economics, forget the blue-collar guys, forget unions, it's all about the college kids, we're entering the Me Decade.

One afternoon that same summer, 1971, at age sixteen, I was among 100 or 150 people in Omaha's big central park watching Senator George McGovern deliver a speech. He was the most liberal, most antiwar candidate for the Democratic nomination. I remember nothing of what he said, because I was furtively inching toward and trying to overhear the two men standing near me: thirty-four-year-old Warren Beatty and McGovern's thirty-four-year-old campaign director, Gary Hart, who I also recognized because I was a politics geek and a McGovern volunteer.

McGovern had led the Democratic Party commission that had just democratized the process of nominating presidential candidates, making it a matter of winning citizens' votes in primaries and public caucuses rather than delegates' votes at closed party conventions. Which meant that from then on it was much harder for labor unions to influence the Democrats' choice of nominee—which in turn enabled Hart to help win the 1972 nomination for the hippie-loving antiwar women's lib acid amnesty abortion candidate whom the blue-collar union members tended to despise.

Immediately after the 1972 wipeout, Hart launched his own first political candidacy, for a U.S. Senate seat in Colorado. The Vietnam War and its cultural waves had made leaders and members of unions dislike McGovern, but as a child of the Depression and former history professor, he had totally been on their side concerning the whole point of unions—maximizing worker power versus corporate power in the economy. Hart, on the other hand, was at odds with the working class on both counts, a cool young Yalie who barely pretended to be their economic ally.

"We are not a bunch of little Hubert Humphreys," he said during his 1974 Senate campaign, referring to his party's 1968 presidential candidate, whom McGovern had beaten for the nomination in 1972. Vice President Humphrey had epitomized the compromised passé liberalism hated by the New Left for supporting the Vietnam War, so Hart was playing to that accumulated ill will. But in fact, ideologically, he had jumped overnight from the left of Humphrey and company to their right.

Hart's 1974 Senate campaign stump speech was actually called "The End of the New Deal." He disparaged liberals who thought that "if there is a problem, [you] create an agency and throw money at the problem," who "clung to the Roosevelt model long after it ceased to relate to reality"—and to that he added some sexist shade, calling them "the Eleanor Roosevelt wing" of the party. "The ballyhooed War on Poverty" of the 1960s, the Democratic programs that included Medicaid and food stamps, "succeeded only in raising the expectations, but not the living conditions, of the poor," he said inaccurately. "This nation desperately needs a new breed of thinkers and doers who will question old premises and disregard old alliances." In that first post-Watergate election, Hart beat the Republican incumbent by a landslide and became the very model of a modern major Democrat.

I felt an affinity for this new, youthy, college-educated political wing—as I felt at the time for postmodern architecture and New Wave music. I was in my twenties, so partly it was the sheer hubris of the young, rejecting the older generation because it was old. Hart's Senate campaign slogan was "They had their turn. Now it's our turn."

But more than that, I actually, earnestly considered myself a new breed of thinker questioning old premises and disregarding old alliances. I wanted to be counterintuitive, contrarian, evidence-based, ready to look at everything afresh. Like so many in my generation, I learned from the war in Vietnam and the war on drugs to mistrust the government, so maybe in other ways it had gotten bloated and inefficient, maybe nitpicky regulations were making it too hard to do business, maybe the antitrust approach invented in my great-grandparents' day was outmoded. And weren't labor unions retrograde and lumbering in lots of ways? Why, for instance, couldn't we imagine *new* forms of worker solidarity and security? In the late 1970s, when the government was about to bail out Chrysler and a freshman Democratic senator, Paul Tsongas, proposed guaranteeing the workers $1.1 billion in the form of Chrysler stock rather than wage increases, why didn't that make sense?

And thus a new buzzword that spread like mad during the 1970s and '80s through art and culture, *postmodernism,* acquired a younger sibling in American politics—*neoliberalism*. Back in the 1970s and '80s, at least in the United States, neoliberalism wasn't yet what it is in the twenty-first century, leftists' all-encompassing derogatory term for anything to the right of nationalized-industry socialism.* Rather, it was a term proudly self-applied by a certain kind of wonk. Their wellspring was an intensely reportorial little magazine called *The Washington Monthly* founded in 1969 and run by a cofounder of the Peace Corps, Charlie Peters. It had a circulation of less than 40,000 in the 1970s and early '80s when I subscribed, but during that pivotal political period, it had an outsize influence in reshaping center-left thought and policy.†

All enlightened, open-minded people should "distrust *all* automatic responses, liberal or conservative," Peters said—and who could disagree?—so "the liberal movement has to change and reject the liberal clichés and automatic responses of the past," such as "their old habits of automatically favoring unions and opposing business." There was too much loyalty to the ideological home team, which followed the rules of "Don't say anything bad about the good guys" because "any criticism is only likely to strengthen the hand of their enemies," and "Don't say anything good about the bad guys." Peters's new tendency consisted of "liberals who decided to retain their old goals while abandoning the prejudices that they realized were blinding them to the real nature of many of the nation's problems" that had begun "to cripple the nation"—such as declining productivity and "decaying plants and infrastructure" and "inefficient and unaccountable public agencies." The notion, certainly among many writers and thinkers if not necessarily the politicians, wasn't to pursue centrism or moderation for their own sakes, or cynical political triangulation between left and right, but intellectual rigor and honesty.

*There's a long etymology here. In the 1930s, when anti–New Deal economic libertarians were called liberals, as they still are outside the United States, some became known as "neoliberals." By the 1970s the term was occasionally used to describe the radical New Left, then the wonky-moderate-Democrat self-definition came and went, supplanted around 2000 by today's expansive everyone-from-Milton-Friedman-to-Elizabeth-Warren meaning.

†Outsize influence then and now: a quorum of its writers and editors from the early days remain big-deal journalists and commentators, including Jonathan Alter, James Fallows, David Ignatius, Mickey Kaus, Michael Kinsley, Nicholas Lemann, Joe Nocera, and Walter Shapiro. Other prominent staff from later years include Katherine Boo, Nick Confessore, Gregg Easterbrook, Suzannah Lessard, Josh Marshall, Jon Meacham, Timothy Noah, Nicholas Thompson, Steven Waldman, and Benjamin Wallace-Wells.

The new approach propagated rapidly. The young *Washington Monthly* writer-editor Michael Kinsley took over the main weekly magazine of Washington liberalism, *The New Republic,* and the young *Washington Monthly* writer-editor Jim Fallows became one of President Carter's speechwriters. "There is a legitimate modesty now about intervening in the economy," said the young head of antitrust enforcement in the Carter Justice Department. "The hard-bitten D.A. approach isn't very useful and the people in Justice recognize that."* Soon almost every up-and-coming national Democratic politician was a New Democrat: Hart, Tsongas, Jerry Brown, Bill Bradley, Al Gore, Bob Kerrey, Bill Clinton—all first elected senator or governor between 1974 and 1984 when they were in their thirties, all about to become serious presidential candidates.

For two generations, liberals had been in control of the government *and* the news media *and* the culture, so it seemed as if that hegemony afforded them the luxury of true liberalism—admitting mistakes, cutting some slack for the other side, trying new approaches. For forty-four of the previous forty-eight years Democrats had controlled both houses of Congress, and they had also held the presidency for most of that half-century. The Harvard professor Daniel Moynihan, for instance, served in four straight administrations, two Democratic and two Republican, before becoming an unpredictable Democratic senator from New York in 1977. All through the 1970s, when the GOP had only about a third of Senate seats, a third of those Republicans were bona fide liberals. *Of course* good-faith compromise and consensus between left and right were possible.

At the end of the 1970s, liberal PBS commissioned a ten-episode Friday-night series starring Milton Friedman called *Free to Choose*. Its funders included General Motors, General Mills, and PepsiCo. The executive producer said the show, *airing on the Public Broadcasting Service,* would explain to viewers like you "how we've become puppets of big government." On the show, Friedman explained why federal taxes, the Food and Drug Administration, public schools, and labor unions, among other bêtes noires, were bad for America. "The economic controls that have

*As it happened, his antitrust experience had been entirely in private practice, representing corporations, as an attorney at the law firm of Lewis Powell before and after he wrote the Powell Memo and became a Supreme Court justice.

proliferated in the United States in recent decades," his accompanying bestselling book asserted, "have also affected our freedom of speech, of press, and of religion." Conveniently for the right, the series premiered in early January 1980, just before the first primary elections in which Reagan was one of many major Republican candidates.

But despite the liberal Establishment's openness and the right's new think tanks and foundations and zillionaire donors, it seemed in the 1970s that the antigovernment diehards and libertarian freaks, the Milton Friedmanites and Ayn Randians and *Wall Street Journal* ideologues, would never *really* be allowed to run the show. The American ideological center of gravity was plainly undergoing a rightward shift, but wouldn't the 1980s just turn out to be some kind of modest course correction, like what happened in the late 1940s and '50s, part of the normal endless back-and-forth pendulum swing from center-left to center-right?

We had no idea. Almost nobody foresaw fully the enormity of the sharp turn America was about to take. Nobody knew that we'd keep heading in that direction for half a lifetime, that in the late 1970s big business and the well-to-do were at the start of a forty-year-plus winning streak at the expense of everyone else.

Partly as a result of various kinds of liberal *niceness,* liberals were ill-prepared to appreciate or cope with what was about to happen. The energized economic right was led by corporations and the rich as well as zealots who'd been shut out of real power for decades—whereas liberals found zealotry vulgar and, although they'd been broadly empowered for decades, didn't have big money riding on the outcome. The New Democrats were more like journalists and academics than traditional political types, more inclined to be polite than tough. Modern liberals prided ourselves on *not* being ideologues, on entertaining all sorts of disparate policy ideas for improving the world, whereas the economic right really has one big, simple idea—do everything possible to let the rich stay rich and get richer.

That last difference is the crucial one. Most Americans, even those to the left, have been reluctant to subscribe fully to Marx's basic big idea, that modern society is shaped by an endless struggle between capital and labor, owners and workers, the rich and powerful versus everyone else. Our special American reluctance to go there has several different sources. We've never been a classless society, of course, but at the start we were a lot closer than most of the rest of the world. In 1830 the richest 1 percent of Americans received less than 10 percent of all the income, just half the share taken by Britain's richest 1 percent at the time.* Slavery made factory owners look good compared to Southern plantation owners, and we fought a war to prove the point. The American Dream, in which a plucky individual moved up in the world and even turned from a worker into a boss, actually came true often enough to make people believe it might happen to them. For most of a century, the Soviet Union and the other countries that called themselves Marxist were terrible advertisements for anything from that lineage. For a long time, Americans did a good job using the government and other means—persuasion, threats, shame, honor—to level up workers' and citizens' shares of money and power, and to limit the shares taken by big business and the rich. As the wealth was distributed more equally, it grew faster than ever, which also disinclined most people to think of America as a place run by a minority of greedy, cheating self-dealers at the expense of a large majority.

So most liberals, like most Americans, preferred not to regard capitalists as categorically rapacious and amoral, or to imagine the U.S. political economy as a never-ending class war in which everyone must ultimately choose between two sides. That seemed crude. They didn't vote for Reagan, but most didn't *hate* him, certainly not at first, because in their way they shared his dreamy faith in the 1940s Frank Capra movie vision of America. It was during the 1970s that *It's a Wonderful Life* was rediscovered and made an icon—by liberals. And to some degree, most succumbed, like most Americans, to a new form of economic nostalgia that was being revived and popularized—the notion that market forces are practically natural forces with which we dare not tinker or tamper too much. Finally, upper-middle-class liberals didn't want to think badly of all their friends and neighbors and classmates who happened to work at banks or in real estate or the vicinity of C-suites.

Starting in the 1970s, the Friedman Doctrine and its extrapolations freed and encouraged businesspeople and the rich to go ahead and conform to the left-wing caricatures of them, to be rapacious and amoral

* By the end of the 1970s, we'd gotten the 1 percent's share back down to that egalitarian early American level, but since then it has more than doubled, so U.S. economic unfairness in 2020 is similar to British economic unfairness in 1830.

without shame. Indeed, the new economic right even encouraged them to wage class war—explicitly against the affluent "New Class" of (traitorous white) liberal professionals and the (black) "underclass," more discreetly against the (white) working class they were enlisting as political allies. Meanwhile liberals clung to their strong preference to see both sides, meet halfway, seem reasonable. Such a colossal irony: after socialists and Communists in the 1930s and then the New Left in the 1960s had tried and failed to achieve a radical class-based reordering of the American political economy, the economic far right took its shot at doing that in the 1970s and succeeded beyond anyone's wildest hope or fear.

PART THREE

Wrong Turn

9

The Reagan Revolution

By the time the election came around in 1980—after Iranians took over the U.S. embassy in Tehran and kept fifty-two Americans hostage for a year, and a brief economic recession sealed the deal—it wasn't a big shock when Ronald Reagan won. But exactly what was that election's "mandate" concerning the political economy?

The campaign had run a TV ad with an excellent supply-side-for-dummies voice-over. "Ronald Reagan believes that when you tax something, you get less of it. We're taxing work, savings, and investment like never before. As a result we have less work, less savings, and less invested." See, if *you* pay less in taxes—and *only* if you pay less in taxes—America's economic prosperity and stability will be restored. It's not selfishness, it's *patriotism*. It's not sleight of hand, or what Reagan's vice president had derided during his primary campaign against him as "voodoo economics." It's the miraculous invisible hand of the market.

So what if millionaires would start paying a little less too? So what if big business was relieved of some of the government red tape everybody hates? And as for cutting government programs, people understood that Reagan was only going to get rid of the things that didn't benefit *them*—all the waste and fraud, all the foreign aid, all the giveaways for all the lazy bums and welfare queens.

But the 1980 election was not really a popular mandate to reorient the political economy permanently to give big business and the well-to-do more wealth and power. In fact, in 1980 fewer than 51 percent of the electorate voted for Reagan; a total of 48 percent voted for the moderate Democrat and the liberal ex-Republican third-party candidate John Anderson.

Reagan's *re*election over the dull old-fashioned Democrat Walter Mondale was indeed a massive landslide, 59 to 41 percent. But look at Congress, and compare what happened starting in 1980 to what happened starting in 1930. The Congress elected before the Crash of 1929 consisted of large Republican majorities in both the House and Senate. Six years later, during the Depression, Democrats controlled the Senate by *75 to 17* and the House by *333 to 89*. That was a holy-smokes mandate on a scale unseen since. During the entire 1980s, on the other hand, the most Republican Senate of all was unexceptional, 54 seats out of 100, while the Democrats never got close to losing a majority in the House, and they won back the Senate in 1986.

That meant two things for liberals and Democrats in general. Politically and psychologically, they never felt utterly overwhelmed, the way Republicans felt in the 1930s. Yes, in three presidential elections in a row during the 1980s, Democrats lost thirty-eight states. But every time they had nominated an uninspiring tool, losing twice against the exceptional, probably unbeatable Ronald Reagan, and then against a moderate Republican incumbent vice president, George H. W. Bush.

More fundamentally, continuing Democratic dominance in Congress during the 1980s meant the economic right could use the federal government to remake the political economy only to the extent that Democrats *let* them. As the 1980s approached, even liberal Democrats were already cooperatively moving right—more skeptical of unions and government oversight of business, open to lower taxes on the rich—so when the time came, Democrats definitely did let them. Too many confused the singular appeal of Ronald Reagan personally with massive popular approval of pro-business, pro-rich Reaganism, and their reaction was to cower, essentially disavowing their New Deal social democratic past.

As Reagan settled into office and became *presidential,* liberal dread concerning domestic policy was reduced by the nature of his appointees—who mostly were, like his vice president, moderate Establishment types, normal Republicans, not crazies.* In addition, Democrats had taken their eyes off the ball of the political economy and focused more of their dread of what this old-school anti-Communist president would or could do abroad—fund death squads and counterrevolution in Central America, upset the precarious nuclear balance with the USSR, trigger World War III.

Reagan was also very lucky very quickly in ways that made him more popular. The very day he was inaugurated, Iran released their American hostages. Two months later he was shot by a movie-mad would-be young assassin—and survived, unlike any president who'd ever been shot before. The normal honeymoon period intensified.

Reagan also lucked out right away with the month-to-month, year-to-year economy. As soon as he took office, the tough tight-money regime of the new Federal Reserve chairman—who'd been appointed by Jimmy Carter in 1979—was finally cooling inflation down. A providential global oil glut suddenly and precipitously drove down the price of gasoline and other energy. Americans felt as if Reagan were working magic. A recession kicked in right away, a year of pain that came with bringing down inflation—but that timing was also lucky, politically best to get it over as early as possible.

While the economic turmoil of the previous decade—the high inflation, the quintupling price of oil, the multiple recessions—was seriously unpleasant, as I've said, it didn't come close to Depression-level cataclysm. Throughout the 1970s, however, the economic right had pretended otherwise. "The United States," Jude Wanniski's 1975 article introducing supply-side economics began, "has been passing through an economic nightmare." The new president stuck to that script in the 1980s, telling Americans they'd just barely gotten off the road to dystopia, and that the big bad federal government itself *until the moment he was inaugurated* had been to blame. "In this present crisis," he said in his first inaugural speech, "government is not the solution to our problem; govern-

*The one right-wing fanatic in Reagan's first cabinet was Interior Secretary James Watt, a Pentecostal Christian who'd run the new anti-environmental-regulation law firm funded by Joseph Coors. Watt was forced out after two years for what he said about a federal commission he oversaw, a remark I doubt would have cost him his job in a current Republican administration: "We have every kind of mix you can have. I have a black, I have a woman, two Jews and a cripple."

ment *is* the problem." During his first couple of years, he said on various occasions that "when this administration took office, we found America in the worst economic mess since the days of Franklin Roosevelt," with the "government careening out of control, pushing us toward economic collapse, and quite probably, the end of our way of life," but that already "we've pulled America back from the brink of disaster." *Whew*.

An exaggerated sense among Americans that they'd just barely escaped a death spiral, along with the actual relief of an improving everyday economy, made it easier for Reagan and his comrades to move to the next level in their project of restructuring the political economy and rewriting its premises.

Most of the big corporate titans had not started the 1970s as Reaganites, and even at the end of that first decade of intensified, systematic corporate political activism, their favorite candidates had been the more familiar Establishment guys. Charls Walker, who was one of the best-connected lobbyists of the era and a former deputy treasury secretary, wrote a memo early in the 1980 campaign to the top corporate CEOs granting his imprimatur to Reagan—another history-changing memo to the capitalists! A little later he claimed that he had thereby closed the deal for their support.

> The Business Roundtable didn't know Reagan, and they tend to identify him with right-wing positions and extremism. But the publicity that me and these "moderates" are in there makes them feel a lot better. None of us who started working on [this project] in the early 1970s thought the consensus would come along this fast.

As president, Reagan immediately and totally delivered for the CEOs and the rest of the rich. In addition to Reagan himself, the administration official most important to executing on that was David Stockman. Stockman was Reagan's director of the Office of Management and Budget (OMB), an intellectual two-term congressman in a job previously done by technocrats, economists, business guys. He was neither a crazed New Deal–hating libertarian nor a cynical corporate lobbyist but an idealistic, old-fashioned young conservative who wanted a smaller, cheaper federal government and a balanced budget. He'd gotten into politics in 1970 as a protégé of John Anderson, the moderate who'd just run as a third-party candidate against Reagan.

Stockman didn't entirely buy the supply-side notion—wishful fantasy or disingenuous con?—that giant tax cuts alone would restore golden-age American prosperity. But he played ball. In the movie version of this story, you'd definitely include scenes of the winter day and night he spent in New York City just before he started the big Washington job with the new administration. First he and former NFL quarterback Jack Kemp, a fellow House Republican and the leading supply-sider in Congress, visited the big investment banks for meetings to reassure them. Even after Reagan was elected, the head of the Chamber of Commerce called the first big supply-side proposal, a gigantic 30 percent tax cut, "a most dangerous experiment." That day on Wall Street, according to Kemp, "we told them we weren't for scaring the market. Dave's credibility is extremely important." After reassuring the captains of finance that they and Reagan were not in thrall to some cabal of reckless wing nuts, Stockman and Kemp drove uptown to celebrate victory at the grand old private clubhouse of the Century Association with *the* cabal of supply-side ultras—including *The Wall Street Journal*'s Bartley and Wanniski, Kristol, and Greenspan, whom Reagan would appoint to run the Federal Reserve.

As OMB director, Stockman looked for ways the government might spend less, apart from reducing foreign aid and help for the poor, to accommodate the largest tax cuts in U.S. history. For instance, he suggested saving billions by reducing tax breaks for business and for rich people with mortgage loans, and by increasing fees paid by owners of private planes. The president told him no. During that first year, Stockman gave a series of interviews to the journalist William Greider, who turned them into a long cover story for the *Atlantic*.

When it was published at the end of 1981, the article got enormous attention because the OMB director, who'd been a Harvard theology grad student before he got into politics, was astoundingly honest. The Reagan administration had managed that summer to convince Congress, including the Democratic House, to make the richest Americans' top tax rate lower than it had been anytime in the previous half-century. Stockman admitted in the article that that had really been the entire point. Because politically it would've been "hard to sell 'trickle down,'" he explained, "the supply-side formula was the only way to get" that. The massive cuts were *conceived* cynically, he admitted, "a Trojan horse to bring down the top rate" on the wealthy and taxes on business. As for Laffer's supply-side theory, Greider said Stockman conceded it "was not a new economic theory at all but only new language and argument to conceal a hoary old Republican doctrine." In fact, Stockman told him, "Laffer sold us a bill of goods. . . . Whenever there are great strains or changes in the economic system, it tends to generate crackpot theories, which then find their way into the legislative channels."

Greider said that Stockman was dispirited by the "final frenzy of trading and bargaining" in which he'd just participated—the "special tax concessions for oil-lease holders and real-estate tax shelters, and generous loopholes that virtually eliminated the corporate income tax." This was Reagan's frontline economic main man talking, just nine months into the administration:

> Do you realize the greed that came to the forefront? The hogs were really feeding. The greed level, the level of opportunism, just got out of control. . . . The power of [big business and the rich] turned out to be stronger than I realized. [They] know how to make themselves heard. The problem is, unorganized groups can't play in this game.

Stockman's reaction might seem disingenuous, but the extent and power of organized greed were new in the modern era. In the spring of 1981, three months after Reagan's inauguration, for instance, the first sentence of a *Times* story about lobbyists' salivating excitement referred to "K Street, where the equivalent of a new branch of government is thriving among the glass and steel buildings." *K Street* was about to become the standard metonym for Washington's suddenly huge and growing lobbying establishment.

So in addition to earnest liberals acting in good faith to compromise with conservatives, a few earnest conservatives such as Stockman were also trying to act in good faith and also becoming useful idiots for big business and the rich. Another of them was Martin Feldstein, the conservative Harvard superstar who became the new president's chief economic adviser—but only nominally, because Reagan ignored him. Feldstein actually hated deficits, as true conservatives did, and called his supply-side colleagues "extremists." Stockman's chief economist at the Office of Management and Budget—who left in 1983 to earn a fortune on Wall Street, then become a cocaine addict and TV pundit—said that Feldstein "has failed at making the transition from academic economist to political economist." That was thirty-six-year-old Larry Kudlow, defining *political economist* to mean not an expert on political economics but an economist willing and eager to dissemble and lie to suit his political masters, thirty-five years before he returned to government work as Trump's director of the National Economic Council.

During Reagan's second year in office, the recession ended, and the stock market started booming, beginning its 254 percent rise by the end of the decade—like back in the *good* 1960s. And inflation kept gliding down toward irrelevance—like it too used to be in the early 1960s, before everything went nuts. Thus the lucky Reaganites had the wherewithal to create for the reelection campaign one of the great political advertisements of all time. It managed to make Americans feel something like nostalgia for the *present,* to believe for sixty seconds at least that the president had in three years returned America to the relaxed, neighborly, wonderful way it used to be.

"It's morning again in America," the soothing baritone narrator matter-of-factly explained at the beginning, because interest rates on borrowing and inflation were half what they were four years earlier, and just *look* at all these contented Americans in splendid Sonoma County—a farmer plowing his field, men going to work, other men raising American flags, a wedding, a family moving into a house, a kid on his bike tossing a newspaper onto an old-fashioned porch, everybody happy, just about everybody white, not a single black person, so "it's morning again in America," the narrator repeated at the end.

The ad was a perfectly masterful distillation of the story the right told so successfully all through the 1980s. They understood and managed to harness what had happened over the last decade in American culture, the sweeping nostalgification, to their depiction of the American economy and the reasons it seemed to be humming again. Everything old was new again, yes, but to really work, the message had to seem simultaneously old *and* new, like Bruce Springsteen and brand-new-old-fashioned postmodern buildings. Morning in America was the revival of the nice familiar past, but it was happening *right now,* the way supply-side economics was abracadabra cutting-edge but drawn from ancient wisdom about wealth creation.

The narrator of the Morning in America ad, the bona fide San Francisco ad genius Hal Riney, was also its author and producer, making the gorgeous facsimile of sincerity seem so authentic, like a singer-songwriter performing his own schmaltzy song. The whole Reagan A-team, such as the inventors and promoters of the supply-side policy pitch, were also perfectly cast for this show—the tough financial newspaper opinion editor (Bartley), the fast-and-loose Washington columnist out of Vegas (Wanniski), the ambitious B economist with D.C. experience and something to prove (Laffer), the New York intellectual gadfly (Kristol), and of course, the charming old former Hollywood star.

Reagan, who'd climbed from the lower middle class to a special celebrity-super-upper-middle class and positively radiated fantastical American cheerfulness and confidence, was a perfect salesman for the supply-side fantasy. It was a cousin of the preexisting American economic fable, that we were a society where practically everybody was middle class, a fantasy that still felt plausible, just barely. And Americans' founding attraction to the excitingly untrue had been growing like mad since the 1960s. The early 1980s were thus an ideal moment for selling this new fantasy of *painless* big change in the political economy—that the experts had finally figured out a way to have *no losers at all* and no fights over deciding who gets how much.*

So much was accomplished so quickly! With a right-wing president elected and then reelected, success encouraged the billionaire zealots and the more cautious corporate funders who'd embarked on the long

*Painless victory was also a new principle in geopolitics: less than a decade after we'd slunk and then rushed out of Vietnam in defeat, the Reagan administration managed a restoration of America's sense of military supremacy by invading the tiny Caribbean nation of Grenada (pop. 95,985) and brushing its Communist regime out of existence at the cost of just eighteen U.S. service members' lives.

march in the early 1970s to keep giving and doing more and more for the cause. The new counter-Establishment was full-fledged—the nonprofit think tanks, lobbyists, institutes, law firms, and foundations all devoted to increasing the profits and wealth and power of business and the wealthy—and during the 1980s it grew faster and extended further.

Richard Mellon Scaife and Joe Coors were still handing out tens of millions a year. Although the ammo-and-DDT heir John Olin died in 1982, management of his foundation was taken over by William Simon, a rich summer pal of his from East Hampton, Long Island. Simon had been Ford's button-down Republican treasury secretary, but in the 1980s he let his Mr. Moneybags freak flag fly, returning to Wall Street as a new-style greedhound *and* bumptious right-wing propagandist. In 1985 the counter-Establishment got yet another major financial fountainhead in the Midwest, the suddenly megarich Bradley Foundation of Wisconsin, which joined the Amway founders, the DeVoses of Michigan, in the new right-wing campaign to discredit public education.

In ways that would've been unimaginable a generation earlier, the libertarian right continued to be fully mainstreamed. Nobel Prizes kept being awarded to free-market, antigovernment economists such as James Buchanan, a University of Chicago contemporary of Friedman. Another new think tank funded by usual suspects among the right-wing foundations, the Manhattan Institute, incubated two widely read, very influential books. With Olin money, the institute funded an unknown political scientist named Charles Murray to write *Losing Ground: American Social Policy, 1950–1980,* which argued that federal antipoverty programs actually *caused* poverty by encouraging recipients to be lazy and irresponsible, and that such programs should be scrapped. The other book was written by one of the institute's staff, George Gilder, a well-born New York liberal anti-Goldwater Republican in the 1960s who in the 1970s became a kooky right-winger. His book *Wealth and Poverty,* published just as Reagan took office, is a strange, breezy religious-faith-based sermon in defense of U.S. capitalism, including its supposed prehistoric roots in the customs of indigenous cultures. "The official poor in America have higher incomes and purchasing power than the middle class" had in the 1950s, Gilder wrote. In fact, America's "so-called 'poor' are ruined by the overflow of American prosperity," and instead of more money, "what they need is Christian teaching from the churches." It became a big bestseller and made the economic right-wingers who read it, in business and otherwise, feel *good* about their beliefs and, if they were rich, their riches.

As never before, very conservative politicians and commentators now had a large and rapidly growing body of fresh scholarly argument and research to which they could point to justify and rationalize pro-big-business, antiregulation, antitax, anti-social-welfare instincts and desires. The staff of AEI, the older conservative Washington think tank, having quintupled during the 1970s, grew by another 50 percent between 1980 and 1986—now with as many full-time scholars on staff as a college. During the 1980s the new, further-right Heritage Foundation caught up in size and influence. At the first meeting of his cabinet secretaries, Reagan handed out to each one the Heritage "Mandate for Leadership," a massive programmatic wish list, more than a thousand pages long with more than a thousand detailed proposals. According to one of the two Heritage cofounders, 775 of the proposals were adopted by the administration. By the beginning of the second term, several dozen Heritage people and several dozen more from AEI and the Hoover Institution were serving under Reagan.

In addition to its freestanding think tanks, the economic right established important new outposts within existing academic institutions. The dream and prototype were what the right-wing director and funders of the Hoover Institution had pulled off at Stanford over the previous decade. By then AEI also had hundreds of paid and unpaid affiliated professors on college faculties around the country. And then there was George Mason. In the early 1970s, George Mason College had been a nothing University of Virginia satellite campus in the Washington suburbs. By the 1980s, it was a well-funded research university, still funded by the state of Virginia, now with a specialty in libertarian political economics featuring Buchanan, the new Nobelist. Charles Koch funded two libertarian nonprofits, a think tank that became the Mercatus Center and an academic networking outfit called the Institute for Humane Studies, and transplanted them to George Mason. They've both been influential, Mercatus particularly aggressive and effective in working to hold back federal environmental regulation.

The founder of Mercatus was a libertarian economics Ph.D. student at NYU who first pitched himself to Charles Koch in the late 1970s. His actual name is Rich Fink. In 1980 Rich Fink was installed on the economics faculty of George Mason, and for most of the next four decades, he served as Koch's chief ideological officer, helping to build and oversee his far-flung and constantly expanding propaganda and political enterprises, as well as managing Koch Industries' Washington lobbying operation.

The Kochs and their man Fink also started creating explicitly political organizations, a great variety of them over the years. Some were pop-ups and some endured, some were lobbying groups and some posed as citizen start-ups. They nimbly evolved and built alliances as necessary. In the 1980s the Koch groups started producing papers and articles and advertisements arguing the Koch line—against labor unions, against expanded Medicare and Medicaid, against the findings of climate science about global warming.

And actually writing laws. They helped underwrite and build the American Legislative Exchange Council, a very effective organization that drafts right-wing bills in Washington for right-wing state legislators to introduce and get their states to enact. Although ALEC is ostensibly an association of elected officials, its operations have been funded almost entirely by members of the Business Roundtable and other big corporations. It camouflaged itself well for decades—in the '90s *The New York Times* called it "a bipartisan organization of state legislators."

In 1985, the Kochs created Citizens for a Sound Economy. Which was exactly . . . what? In the press it was seldom to never identified as an entity founded and run by the owners of an oil and coal company. When various *New York Times* articles quoted experts from the group during the 1980s and early '90s, it was described as "a public interest group based in Washington," "a public-interest lobby" with "250,000 members," "a conservative public interest group," and "a Washington research group." Its first chairman was the extreme libertarian Texas congressman Ron Paul, whose ideas were at the time still considered freaky by the Republican mainstream, but Citizens for a Sound Economy was against antitrust enforcement so they got Microsoft, facing serious antitrust scrutiny in the 1990s, to kick in a six-figure donation. The first great victory of this "public interest lobby" was to crush a proposed federal energy tax that Fink said "may have destroyed our [Koch Industries] business." The group kept the Senate from even voting on the bill, despite the Democrats' fifty-seven-seat majority.

Starting in the 1980s as well, the right's project expanded beyond the *Wall Street Journal* editorial pages to genuinely mass media. The Reagan administration did away with the federal Fairness Doctrine, which had been in place since the early broadcast era to prevent radio and TV news programs from having distinct ideological or partisan tilts. With fairness and balance no longer required, Rush Limbaugh led the way, making talk radio practically synonymous with right-wing proselytizing. Rupert Murdoch had started buying U.S. newspapers and magazines in the 1970s, including the *New York Post,* which he turned overnight from politically liberal to right-wing. Jack Kemp said in 1981 that "Rupert Murdoch used the editorial page, the front page and every other page necessary" in the *Post* "to elect Ronald Reagan President." In 1985 Murdoch moved into television, spending the equivalent of $5 billion to buy TV stations in seven of the ten biggest cities. Reagan helped: he fast-tracked Murdoch for U.S. citizenship so that his company could get around the federal law forbidding foreigners from owning stations, then waived the federal rule forbidding anyone from owning a TV station and a newspaper in the same city, as Murdoch suddenly did in New York and Boston. The footings were now in place to build the important final piece of the right's counter-Establishment.

10

Raw Deal: What Happened in the 1980s Didn't Stay in the 1980s

When I first began thinking about this book, before I researched it, my sense of the story both overemphasized and underemphasized 1980, the definitive pivot point of Reagan's election. The overemphasis was because I really hadn't known about all the crucial advance work done by big business and the economic right during the 1970s—the decade of strategizing, funding, propagandizing, mobilizing, lobbying, and institution-building. My initial underemphasis was due to a different kind of ignorance. Because I'd lived through the 1980s and definitely noticed in real time, plain as day, the rapid and widespread uptick in deference to business and the rich and profits and *the market,* I'd neglected afterward to take a close, careful look at the various pieces of that shift. During the 1980s and '90s, my focus as a writer and editor was really on the *cultural* effects of this new America revealing itself—the primacy of selling and celebrity, the mixing of fact and fiction, the shameless ostentation, this ridiculous character Donald Trump. I wasn't thinking hard about the political economy at the time. In fact, after the Cold War ended, it seemed to me, as it did to many people, that what happened in Washington had become a sideshow to the main American action in the private sector.

So many of the impacts of the economic right's crusade to stop and roll back the New Deal and its Great Society extensions showed themselves only gradually, like steadily compounding interest, becoming formidable over a generation. Before and after David Stockman, OMB directors were mostly obscure because the OMB is typical of the guts of government and governance—bureaucratic, abstruse, unexciting. Indeed, that general public obscurity was how most of the transformation of the political economy happened during the 1980s and afterward. For all the back-to-the-good-old-days rhetoric and professions of faith in the free market—Reagan's department—so much of the monumental shift was the result of countless nuts-and-bolts changes so dweeby and tedious, and so often bipartisan, that they appeared inconsequential and were uncontroversial. It's in the nature of tax codes and federal regulations, complicated and esoteric, to permit big change to occur quietly.

Furthermore, an important and even stealthier part of the restructuring were acts of omission, declining to update codes and regulations so that more money and power flowed to businesses and the well-to-do gradually. In their excellent 2010 book *Winner-Take-All Politics,* the political scientists Jacob Hacker of Yale and Paul Pierson of UC Berkeley call this *drift,* the "systematic, prolonged failures of government to respond to the shifting realities of the dynamic economy" that "is a huge and growing part of how policy is actually made." This includes all sorts of essentially invisible but important policies-by-omission, from the willful failure to go after violations of labor and antitrust laws to letting corporations pretend that executives' stock options aren't actually salary to declining to regulate (or even understand) esoteric new financial contrivances. Citizens don't notice this kind of malign neglect, so they don't get angry about it.

Social Security taxes are a prime example of this kind of unnoticeable drift effect, a way that the richest have made out better than everyone else for the last four decades. People's incomes over a certain level aren't taxed to pay for Social Security at all. But from the beginning of the system, Congress regularly and significantly raised that income threshold where that tax-free level begins, so that as the twentieth century rolled on, more and more affluent people were paying more Social Security taxes. But then around 1980 Congress *stopped* raising it—instead, the tax-free threshold has increased according to an automatic formula, pegged to increases not in the cost of living but in average wages. As a result, since average wages haven't increased much since 1980, people with higher incomes have just kept getting more and more of their money shielded from taxation. Today a fifth of all income earned by Americans is free from any Social Security tax, twice as much as in the early 1980s—and that tax break is going only to the richest 6 percent of us, those who earn more than $138,000. Meanwhile, the revenue stream automatically flowing in to fund Social Security has shrunk.

After finishing most of my research, as I looked through my thousands of notes, a pattern showed itself: *this* trend line took off in the 1980s, and this *other* one plummeted; *this* norm began crumbling in the 1980s, and *that* stigma started evaporating; *this* strike was crushed, and *this* financial rule was tweaked in the 1980s; and look over *there* at *that* huge change in the 1980s that hadn't even seemed connected to politics or economics. When I boldfaced all the 1980s dates, it was like a eureka-moment scene from *Good Will Hunting* or *A Beautiful Mind*. The before-and-after changes were so numerous and stark, I realized that the paradigm shift of the 1980s really was equivalent in scale and scope to those of the 1960s and the 1930s. Almost everything changed.

Key intellectual foundations of our legal system were changed. Our long-standing consensus about acceptable and unacceptable conduct by big business was changed. Ideas about selfishness and fairness were changed. The financial industry simultaneously became reckless and more powerful than ever. The liberal establishment began habitually apologizing for and distancing itself from much of what had defined liberal progress. What made America great for centuries, a taste and knack for the culturally new, started to atrophy. Plus much more. And all of what happened in the 1980s definitely didn't stay in the 1980s.

The digital revolution also started in the 1980s, including the invention of PowerPoint, so in that spirit I present this introductory data-point chronicle as a preface to the next several chapters.

The Decade When Everything Changed and Our Present Was Created: 57 Data Points

Some Key Cultural and Technological Changes in the 1980s

- The fraction of women in the paid workforce rises from 47 percent in the late 1960s to 75 percent by the end of the 1980s.
- The fraction of two-income households increases from a small minority to a large majority.
- The immigrant population doubles from its twentieth-century low of fewer than 10 million in 1970 to nearly 20 million in 1990.
- Americans begin staying put, moving to new places less frequently.
- Cable TV takes off, with the number of channels and of homes with cable tripling.
- Twenty-four-hour TV news begins.
- Nostalgia becomes a full-fledged division of the fantasy-industrial complex, further enabled by old movies and shows now watchable on VCRs and cable TV, and by the massive rerelease of old albums on the new CD medium.
- The federal rule that TV and radio broadcasters must present a diversity of views is repealed.
- Personal computers become a mass-market product, and the mass-market Internet is invented.

Some Key Changes in the 1980s Good for Big Business

- Corporate lobbying in Washington and the number of corporate political action committees wildly increase, and the costs of congressional campaigns begin their doubling and tripling over the next thirty years.
- Corporate taxes as a fraction of GDP drop by more than half in just four years from the late 1970s to the early '80s.
- Federal enforcement of antitrust laws to rein in corporate power suddenly shrinks to a fraction of what it has been.
- The deregulation of business by government accelerates.
- Large, dominant companies start charging customers historically higher markups on the products they sell.
- The rate at which entrepreneurs create new firms drops by almost a third.
- After years of scholarly spadework and litigation here and there, the conservative legal and judicial counter-Establishment suddenly booms on its way to dominance.

Some Key Changes in the 1980s Good for the Financial Industry

- Stock prices almost triple (before almost quadrupling again during the 1990s).
- The long-standing federal prohibition on companies buying their own stock, meant to prevent share price manipulation, is repealed.
- The new "shareholder value" movement's redefinition of capitalism makes a company's current stock price essentially the only relevant measure of corporate performance.
- The share of all stocks owned by a few big institutional investors triples (on its way to doubling again in the 1990s).
- Increasingly abstract and untried and unregulated financial bets on other financial bets, derivatives, become normalized and start becoming economically significant.
- Leveraged buyouts, financial firms using frequently excessive debt to take over and often ruin companies, become normalized and significant.
- Wall Street salaries increase by more than 25 percent (before increasing another 50 percent in the 1990s).

- The financial industry's (and real estate industry's) share of the total U.S. national income rises from 14 percent to over 35 percent in less than a decade.

Some Key Changes in the 1980s Good for Rich People in General

- The ratio of CEOs' pay to their employees' pay doubles (before *sextupling* in the 1990s).
- The top income tax rate on the richest is reduced from 70 percent to 28 percent.
- The maximum tax rate on stock profits (capital gains) is reduced from 28 percent to 20 percent.
- Estate taxes on the rich drop more than ever—for instance, the heirs to a $3 million fortune would pay $1 million less in taxes on it.
- The income of the most affluent top fifth increases by 25 percent and that of the richest top 1 percent almost doubles.

Some Key Changes in the 1980s Bad for Americans in General

- The United States experiences the fastest and biggest increase in income inequality between the 1920s and 2020.
- After a century of wages increasing in sync with increases in productivity, that synchronization ends.
- Employees' share of the national income abruptly declines from 62 percent to 56 percent and even more sharply for everyone but the richest tenth.
- Median household income stagnates and median wages decline.
- The share of all wealth owned by the bottom 90 percent peaks and begins to decline.
- The withering of labor unions in companies accelerates dramatically, as public and political sentiment and regulations and laws turn against them.
- Jobs in manufacturing rapidly disappear—by 22 percent during the decade.
- Companies start eliminating fixed pensions for retiring employees.
- The fraction of companies providing employee health insurance peaks and starts to decline.
- The decline in the number of manufacturing jobs and the expansion of the economy's service sector both accelerate.

- Companies begin replacing low-skill, low-wage workers with even-lower-wage workers supplied by outside contractors.
- The federal minimum wage is frozen for the entire decade, longer than ever, which translates to an effective pay cut of one-third for America's lowest-paid workers.
- Consumer credit is deregulated excessively, causing consumer debt suddenly to increase by a third and interest payments to balloon.
- The number of jobs requiring a college degree increases significantly.
- The salary premium for four-year college graduates starts increasing significantly.
- The cost of four-year college and the student debt to pay for it suddenly start increasing significantly.
- The fraction of men who graduate from four-year colleges plateaus.
- The percentage of men working or looking for work begins dropping.
- Inequality in incomes among different regions of the United States begins increasing significantly.
- Home mortgage foreclosures quadruple.
- Personal bankruptcies suddenly increase, more than doubling (before doubling again in the 1990s).
- The up-and-down year-to-year volatility of family incomes starts increasing significantly.
- Upward economic mobility—earning more than one's parents did—begins to become much more unlikely.
- The large-scale movement out of poverty for black men from 1960 to 1980 stops.
- Federal spending on housing programs for low-income people is cut by 75 percent.
- Incarceration of criminals begins its massive increase, doubling (before doubling again in the 1990s), and the first private profit-making prison companies are founded.*
- U.S. healthcare spending and life expectancy both suddenly diverge from the rest of the rich world—heading from about average toward

*In 1982 I reported and wrote a *Time* cover story called "Inmate Nation" about what's now called mass incarceration, because the number of U.S. inmates had just started to increase sharply and, to my editor and me, alarmingly—that year by 43,000 to 412,000. The total number of inmates today is 1.5 million, of whom 130,000 are in privately run prisons.

the top in spending and from about average toward the bottom in life expectancy.

- After the scientific consensus definitively concludes a climate crisis is imminent, the petroleum industry and the political right begin aggressively downplaying and denying it, blocking government regulation to reduce CO_2 emissions.

11

The Rule of Law

The 99 percent of us who weren't lawyers or judges or legal scholars or conservative activists in the 1980s had no clue that the law itself had become an important front in the war to remake the U.S. political economy. In a democracy, the economic right and business couldn't depend on having friendly presidents (and state governors) or compliant Congresses (and state legislatures) forever. To make fundamental and *permanent* change, they also needed to cultivate power in the other, largely *un*elected branch of government, the judiciary. They needed to colonize the legal community and reframe the law itself to make sure they kept getting their way. Instead of litigation almost entirely being used *against* them by antitrust enforcers and class-action troublemakers and environmentalists and Ralph Naders, they needed to reshape fundamental American legal understandings—to make it a toolbox they could use to accumulate more power and wealth for big business and the rich over the long run. People these days throw around the phrase *fundamental structural change* a lot, but what the right did in the legal domain was exactly that, breathtakingly so.

You'll recall the memo that Lewis Powell wrote in 1971 just before he joined the Supreme Court, his confidential call to arms and battle plan for the struggle to save big business and America from the rampaging socialist hordes and their agents embedded throughout the Establishment. "The judiciary is a vast area of opportunity," he wrote, if only the rich and powerful would "provide the funds." In 1980 came another lawyer's call to arms and detailed battle plan for the legal front. It is not widely known. Like the Powell Memo, reading it now is kind of staggering, because we can see how thoroughly and successfully its vision was executed.

Like Powell, Michael Horowitz was a lawyer in private practice commissioned by politicized wealth to produce a report—in his case, by Richard Mellon Scaife's foundation, which was funding right-wing "public interest" law firms. Horowitz's memo runs more than a hundred pages. He had three big recommendations for the embryonic right-wing legal movement of which he was a member. His comrades had to begin the long process of recruiting and forming a network of top students and young graduates from the top law schools. Their ambitions had to extend way beyond an occasional lawsuit here or there against this or that regulation that constrained a particular business. Instead, they needed to adopt and fund a *strategy* that sought a genuine right-wing revolution in the high-end legal profession and the judiciary. And even though the not-for-profit conservative legal movement would inevitably be the servant of big business, he advised that it had to stop *looking* so much like that, to appear more idealistic and philosophical and independent.

The world of mainstream public interest law, Horowitz wrote, considered the new right-wing nonprofit law firms created in the 1970s to be "pretenders . . . largely oriented to and dominated by business interests, a description which is unhappily not wide of the mark for many such firms. . . . All too often, conservative public interest law firms serve as mere conduits by which monies contributed by businessmen and foundations are given to private law firms to assist it in the prosecution of 'its' cases." That is, instead of directly hiring litigators to fight government environmental protections or victims of corporate malfeasance, image-conscious companies were really just laundering money through "public interest" firms who then hired the necessary litigators to do the dirty work. This, remember, wasn't a liberal take but a conservative's critique funded by Scaife, the right-wing billionaire heir to an old banking and oil and aluminum fortune.

Yes, of course, Horowitz admitted, "the need to protect the profitability . . . of the private business sector" was a "significant premise" of "public interest" firms on the right. Nevertheless their movement would "make no substantial mark on the American legal profession or American life as long as it is seen as and is in fact the adjunct of [the] business community." Lawyers in the new right-wing movement had to start *looking* like principled crusaders rather than poorly disguised minions of the greedy rich. "It is critical that the conservative movement seek out and find clients other than large corporations and corporate interests" in order to make itself "intellectually respectable."

Instead of occasional "episodic tactical victories" in lawsuits, it needed permanent, large-scale changes in the legal academy and law and jurisprudence, switching from a focus only on "courts and legislatures to law schools and bar associations." The movement as of 1980, he wrote, consisted of "appallingly mediocre" lawyers, the result of "still-prevailing notions of law students and young attorneys that their career options are largely restricted to serving the public interest (i.e., enhancing governmental power) or 'selling out'" by working *directly* for corporations. Horowitz, a Yale Law School classmate of Gary Hart and Jerry Brown, said the right needed to create a bar "comprised [*sic*] of law review editors, former law clerks and, in no small part, of alumni of national law schools." They needed to infiltrate the judiciary and the rest of government.

Voilà. Just a little over a year later, a handful of law students at Yale, Harvard, and the University of Chicago, sharing an enthusiasm for what one called "free-market concepts," founded the Federalist Society. It turned out to be the monumentally important first step in the plan Horowitz's memo had laid out. The Chicago chapter enlisted a professor at their law school who was also on the payroll of the conservative Washington think tank AEI to be their faculty adviser—Antonin Scalia. The idea behind the society, in addition to hanging with young fellow travelers and organizing campus lectures and symposia, was to create an ongoing national network of like-minded future lawyers and judges, a right-wing but certifiably elite legal fraternity-cum-mafia. At birth the Federalist Society got funding from the new standard roster of right-wing billionaires' foundations—Scaife, Olin, Bradley, the Kochs.

Michael Horowitz, who promptly joined the Reagan administration as David Stockman's chief lawyer, also practiced what he'd just preached, cruising Federalist Society meetings to recruit promising true believers for entry-level administration jobs. Within just a few years of its founding, when Scalia began his tenure as the exemplary right-wing Supreme Court justice for the new legal age, the Federalist Society had two thousand members in seventy law school chapters, and scores of alumni embedded in key venues—working for the Justice Department in Washington and U.S. attorneys' offices around the country, clerking for Scalia and other Reagan appointees in the judiciary. In 1987 Brett Kavanaugh entered Yale Law School, where he joined its Federalist Society chapter (its president, George Conway, had just graduated), and a year later Neil Gorsuch started at Harvard Law School and became a member.

The spectacular rightward swerve of legal thought starting in the 1980s had two freshly cast ideological pillars, one focusing narrowly on the Constitution, the other on more general criteria for determining proper legal outcomes. Each was a movement with its own builders and promoters. As with the rest of the right-wing makeover of the 1970s and '80s that sought to take America back in time, both legal movements amounted to fundamentalisms, radical right turns presented as reassuring returns to original American first principles.

The one concerning the Constitution became known in the 1980s as *originalism*. How flexibly or rigidly the Constitution's provisions should be applied to governance was a debate from the get-go, two centuries ago. In the early 1950s, the moderate Republican president Eisenhower appointed the moderate Republican governor of California, Earl Warren, to be chief justice of the Supreme Court. For a generation his court issued world-changing decisions interpreting the Constitution on behalf of progress—outlawing racial segregation and organized prayer in public schools, requiring that criminal defendants be advised of their basic rights and provided with lawyers, stipulating that contraceptives be freely sold. Reactionaries and other right-wingers castigated the Warren court and other federal judges for being "judicial activists" and called themselves "strict constructionists" who adhered to the plain old meanings of the Constitution. Accusing white liberals in the 1950s and '60s of being constitutionally sloppy was more effective than calling them atheists and coddlers and race traitors. Conservatives figured the more they could get the Constitution to be interpreted narrowly and literally, supposedly the way Americans back in 1789 or the 1860s understood its eternal meanings, the less liberals could use it *now* to justify pieces of modern progress that the conservatives disliked.

By the 1980s that approach had become a respectable movement, and before long the legal scholar Jeffrey Rosen, nowadays president of the National Constitution Center, wrote that "we are all originalists now." He meant that everyone in the legal world acknowledged that the original meanings of the Constitution and its amendments couldn't be ignored. But originalism became a crude and self-justifying meme that the right used, from the 1980s on, simply to serve its own interests and prejudices. Originalism's most important hidden agenda was to keep courts and judges completely out of the business of business, as if what worked for the U.S. economy for its first century, before modern corporations existed, was how things should work today. It was like the Friedman Doctrine, which turned a reasonable capitalist truism (*profits are essential*) into a simple-minded, unhinged, socially destructive monomania (*only profits matter*).

As movements, originalism in the law and libertarianism in economics were fraternal twins. Both were born of extreme nostalgia, fetishizing and distorting bygone America, so both more easily achieved mass appeal in the everything-old-is-new-again 1970s and '80s. Both purported to be based on objective principles that transcended mere politics or special interests, even while both were vehicles for big business and the right to recover, fortify, and expand their economic and political power. And both shared key promoters, of whom probably the single most important was Robert Bork.

Bork was a founder of originalism in the 1970s, and in 1986 he was in the running for an open Supreme Court seat (as he had been in 1981). But Reagan made the safer choice from among the new generation of hard-right ideologues—Antonin Scalia, who as a result came to be the personification of originalism. A year later, however, Reagan finally did nominate Bork to fill the seat of—*perfect*—retiring Justice Lewis Powell. In the trivia-game category Failed Supreme Court Nominees, Bork is the most famous by far. The ascendant right in 1987 figured he would be a shoo-in—the Senate had just confirmed Scalia 98–0. Bork was a right-wing hard-liner but also, as an influential Yale Law School scholar, respected and liked by the liberal legal elite. So they were shocked and disappointed and angry at Bork's bipartisan rejection in the Senate, a last-hurrah victory by Washington's declining liberal-left political machine. What's more, six years into the official right-wing takeover, six *Republican* senators had voted against him. Afterward, thanks to the new counter-Establishment—AEI fellow, George Mason University professor, Federalist Society standing ovations—Bork spent the rest of his life working his postrejection fame, making a second career out of right-wing martyrdom.

He'd joined the Yale faculty at age thirty-five in 1962, and in 1971, that seminal year for the great right-wing counterrevolution, Professor Bork wrote the law review article that became the foundational document for originalism. It remains one of the most frequently cited law review articles of all time.

Given that the notion underlying the movement Bork cofounded is the unchanging word-for-word sacredness of the Constitution, it's very odd that Bork begins that essay by disparaging the Bill of Rights as a cynical political add-on stuck there in 1789 just to get the whole thing passed. Madison and Hamilton and the rest "had no coherent theory of free speech and appear not to have been overly concerned with the subject"—although to the degree the Founders cared at all, he claims, they were often *against* free speech, being "men accustomed to drawing a line, to us often invisible, between freedom and licentiousness."* Because "the law of free speech we know today grows out of the Supreme Court decisions" from the 1900s, Bork wrote, it is "Court-made law" and therefore wrong. He somehow decided that the First Amendment protects *only* "explicitly political" speech in an extremely narrow sense, "speech concerned with governmental behavior, policy or personnel." He actually insisted that apart from opinions about government and politicians, "there is no basis" in the U.S. Constitution for any court or judge "to protect any other form of expression, be it scientific, literary, or that variety of expression we call obscene or pornographic."

Bork's Yale faculty colleague and friend Guido Calabresi, later dean of the law school, said the *early*-1960s Bork was "an aggressive libertarian conservative—that is, 'Keep the Government out of everything.'" But by 1971, when he wrote his famous originalism article, the times had

*LOL. For instance: Alexander Hamilton, confessed adulterer and payer of blackmail to his mistress's husband, and Thomas Jefferson, secret slanderer of his political opponents.

revealed that what Bork called his "generally libertarian commitments" were a sham that really *only* applied to economics, the freedom of businesses to do whatever they wished.*

Except for people in the pornography business. Porn movies were just starting to be mainstreamed, and they loom curiously large in Bork's article. Pornography is "a problem of pollution of the moral and aesthetic atmosphere precisely analogous to smoke pollution" and possibly an even greater danger to public health, so it was okay to outlaw smut. Bork declared elsewhere in the article that the quintessentially political act of burning an American flag shouldn't count as free speech either, because the flag is, you know, *"unique."* Likewise, he wrote that the Supreme Court decision that individuals' rights to privacy included the right to buy contraceptives was "utterly specious" and "unprincipled." Likewise, Bork ruled as a federal judge that the navy could fire a sailor for being gay because there was no explicit "constitutional right to engage in homosexual conduct"—although as a professor he'd also just argued for welcoming employers to Yale who discriminated against gays because Yale simply shouldn't "ratify homosexuality." And likewise, he said that the Constitution's equal protection clause shouldn't prohibit discrimination against women—yet also that *amending* the Constitution to guarantee equal rights for women would be a bad idea. In his later books—*Slouching Towards Gomorrah: Modern Liberalism and American Decline,* and *A Country I Do Not Recognize: The Legal Assault on American Values,* he completely dropped the judicious mask to spew full-strength reactionary bile.

In other words, as Bork spent a career creating and propagating this new doctrine of worshiping the old, his claims of principled impartiality—that he was *all* about adhering to the Constitution as written when it was written, that "nothing in my argument goes to the question of what laws should be enacted," and that it "has nothing to say about the speech we

*More than three decades later, in his book *A Country I Do Not Recognize: The Legal Assault on American Values,* published by the Hoover Institution, Bork was still steamed about the 1960s—even by the Students for a Democratic Society's gentle 1962 manifesto advocating for a "politics of meaning," after which the "counterculture gained traction and further radicalized attitudes among elites," in turn causing the Supreme Court to ruin America by "denigrating the sacred, by abolishing taboos, by announcing the principle of man's radical autonomy." He also said *in 1996* that "rock 'n' roll is a subversive music and in that sense could easily lead to drugs."

like or the speech we hate"—were not just disingenuous but flatly contradicted again and again by his arguments in particular cases.

Even though he lost his great battle in 1987 for a seat on the Court that he might have held until his death in 2012, his side kept winning the war. Just a decade after Bork was dinged, Rosen found it "a little startling to reflect on how dramatically [Scalia] and the movement that he personifies have transformed the terms of constitutional debate." Like Bork, the judicial general of the right wing whom he replaced, Scalia used the supposedly neutral philosophy of originalism as a means to achieve a particular set of right-wing ends. In his 1997 book on the subject, published after a decade on the Court, he made clear he was not actually "a partisan of textualism or originalism, but a partisan of traditionalism," Rosen explained back then, which

> looks a lot like the judge-made law that he claims to abhor. . . . He strives in his jurisprudence to conserve traditional moral values against . . . cultural change. He is exercised not by the methodology of recent Supreme Court decisions, but by the results. His objection to the cases [a males-only public college, an antigay state law] is that they unsettle longstanding traditions that he, as a proud social conservative, wants to keep.

Like almost everyone on the right today, Bork was a very selective, cherry-picking libertarian of convenience—iffy on civil liberties and executive power and even iffier on personal liberty, but unbudging in defense of the rights of business (apart from publishers, especially pornographers) to operate without restraint. In one of his books from the 1990s, he was still complaining about smut—"the pornographic videos," the early Internet erotica site "alt.sex.stories"—and even about people on the right unwilling to outlaw it: "Free market economists are particularly vulnerable to the libertarian virus."

Free-market political economics was where Bork's beliefs were forged back in the day, and where his specific influence, beginning in the 1970s and '80s, remains vast and enduring. Like so many midcentury American right-wing zealots, Bork had been a left-wing zealot in his youth, a teenage nationalize-it-all socialist. Right after World War II, when anti-

Communism suddenly became a national faith, Bork "went to the University of Chicago and came across the Chicago economists" such as "Milton Friedman . . . and they destroyed my dreams of socialism right there." As a graduate student working with Friedman's brother-in-law, another influential right-wing Chicago School economist and antitrust specialist, Bork said he had the equivalent of "a religious conversion," immediately becoming "an avid free-market type." He spent most of the 1950s as a lawyer in private practice in Chicago specializing in antitrust cases for big business defendants, and when he joined the Yale faculty, students joked that he taught "*pro*-trust law."

But the opinionated and cocksure young Bork didn't stay in his lane. Economic libertarianism was also the basis of his argument in 1963 and 1964 against the proposed Civil Rights Act.* At the very moment when Martin Luther King, Jr., was leading the watershed pro-civil-rights March on Washington in August 1963, Bork published an article in *The New Republic* arguing that any law requiring businesses to serve people of all races would be "subversive of free institutions" by "self-righteously impos[ing] upon a minority"—that is, upon racist white businessmen—"the morals of the majority." The Civil Rights Act was based on "a principle of unsurpassed ugliness," Bork explained, that might lead to an even more nightmarish future for businesses—requiring "not merely fair hiring of Negroes in *subordinate* positions, but the choices of *partners or associates* . . . without regard to race" (emphases added). It was these statements that lost him the seat on the Supreme Court.

But apart from that early crusade against civil rights, as a scholar Bork mainly stuck to his actual specialty, antitrust. For almost a century, antitrust laws had been passed and more and more strongly enforced because Americans agreed that when companies became very large, they tended to get too much power, to crush smaller businesses, to scare off entrepreneurial competitors, to charge too much for products, to pay workers too little, to corrupt government. Even regulation-hating right-wingers like Friedman originally made an exception for antitrust laws.

*Around that time, Bork also wrote a seventy-five-page memo for Barry Goldwater, the Party of Lincoln's next presidential nominee, providing constitutional and legal backup for his opposition to a federal civil rights law.

According to Richard Posner, the influential conservative University of Chicago economist and law professor (and former federal court of appeals judge), in the 1950s "business-oriented people and conservative lawyers were troubled by the antitrust jurisprudence" because it was getting too leftish, too anti-big-business. "But they didn't have the vocabulary or conceptual system with which to criticize that jurisprudence" until Posner and his conservative academic comrades started producing it. As antitrust enforcement and Naderite consumer activism got more aggressive in what Posner calls "the collectivist mood of the 60s and 70s," that business-oriented right got acutely nervous. Forced to choose between the principle of maximum competition and their bottom-line wish for unencumbered big business power, the conservative intellectuals chose the latter. Bork was among that select group of "free enterprise radicals" whom Milton Friedman gathered at his 1970 conference in Washington, and according to a historian of antitrust law, he became "concerned the socialists would take over the country through antitrust."

Rather than undertake a doomed quest to repeal those statutes, Bork contrived a brilliant way to neuter their enforcement by getting legal thinkers and judges to reinterpret and redefine the laws in pro-big-business fashion. That is, the great "originalist" opponent of any kind of "judicial activism" adopted *a strategy based entirely on vigorous judicial activism.* He argued that America's evolving, expansive intentions with antitrust laws as they'd been understood, to keep big business from screwing over the rest of us, made that body of law and precedent an impossible muddle. "Antitrust policy cannot be made rational until we are able to give a firm answer to one question," he wrote in his incredibly influential 1978 book on the subject, *The Antitrust Paradox*. "What is the point of the law—what are its goals?" His too-simple answer, true to a too-simple Chicago School free-market vision: maximizing economic efficiency in the system exclusively and by any means necessary.

Bork had been working on the argument for years, but he published his book at just the right moment, when a critical mass of Americans were persuaded that government was terrible and that regulation was terrible—and who really understood or cared about this antitrust gobbledygook anyhow? As Judge Posner says, with characteristic candor, there was now "a respectable body of academic thinking" that big business and economic right-wingers "could use to support their predilections," "a patina of academic respectability" to justify their "instincts."

Although the original U.S. antitrust law in 1890 was intended mainly to keep mighty new corporations from unfairly crushing competitors, and subsequent antitrust statutes had other specific origins and intentions, in his book Bork badly distorts that history by casting the whole long, amorphous body of law strictly as a "consumer welfare prescription" that "Congress designed" in 1890. As another law professor and leading antitrust expert wrote in the 1980s, Bork made the "brilliant but deceptive choice of the term 'consumer welfare' as his talisman, instead of a more honest term like . . . 'total economic efficiency.' After all, who can be against 'consumer welfare'?" Furthermore, Bork declared that the *only* legitimate measures of undesirable and illegal corporate power were improperly high prices. Naderites had just successfully turned *consumer* into a kind of synonym for *citizen,* and *consumer welfare* into the all-American lodestar concerning business, so now Bork flipped it: Who cared how businesses behaved or how large they got as long as they sold their products cheaply?

Exactly one year after Bork's book was published, a pivotal Supreme Court decision quoted its key "consumer welfare" sentence, and since then federal judges have quoted the line in antitrust decisions dozens of times. Just like that, economic efficiency as measured by prices became "the stated goal in antitrust" *exclusively*. "Antitrust was defined by Robert Bork," says the University of Arizona law professor and antitrust specialist Barak Orbach.

> I cannot overstate his influence. Any antitrust person would tell you the same thing. . . . The Court started thinking they should have an economic framework, and they had Chicago's work as very simple ideas they could use. The thing about this is that they were very simple. You read them, you understand them. Any person can understand them. . . . The world is not that simple.

Again and again after that, Supreme Court decisions, relying on Bork's arguments in *The Antitrust Paradox,* legalized behaviors by corporations—

becoming virtual monopolies, stifling competition, and so on—that until 1978 everybody had agreed were violations of federal law and antithetical to fair, healthy free-market capitalism.

What's more, in the 1970s and '80s a whole new field of law emerged out of the theories and ideas that Bork and his fellow Chicago School libertarians had been crafting. Its name is simple and deceptively generic: Law and Economics. Getting lawyers and especially judges more fluent in economic analysis is a good thing, of course. But the animating idea behind Law and Economics was political—that a main point of *the law,* not only of antitrust, is to maximize economic efficiency, that the law's bottom line is the economic bottom line. So if you happen to think it's a good idea for judicial decisions to also consider fairness or moral justice, or other values or versions of social happiness that can't be reduced to simple metrics of efficiency, Law and Economics says you're a fool. Like its brilliantly anodyne name, the equations and other math in Law and Economics texts give it an impartial, scientific sheen. The founders of Law and Economics understood that we do indeed live in a *political* economy, that determining who's entitled to what is the result of all kinds of power struggles and societal choices—so they wanted *their* hard-core free-market politics explicitly encoded into America's underlying legal DNA.

In the mid-1980s, as Law and Economics was taking off, the renowned constitutional law professor Bruce Ackerman, then at Columbia and now at Yale, called it "the most important thing in legal education since the birth of Harvard Law School" in 1817. The speed and effectiveness of the movement's spread was remarkable. Its founders had spent decades laying its groundwork, so how did the 1980s blitz of law schools happen? It was thanks in large part to the Olin Foundation, which gave Harvard Law its biggest donation ever, the equivalent of $44 million, to create the John M. Olin Center for Law, Economics, and Business. It also created Yale Law's Olin Center for Studies in Law, Economics, and Public Policy, Stanford Law's Olin Program in Law and Economics, and the University of Virginia Law's Olin Program in Law and Economics, among others. By the end of the 1980s, more than seventy universities had started Law and Economics programs. They'd become almost obligatory, and then ubiquitous. Victory for the legal right was swift and total.

During the 1980s, that public university that the Kochs and others on the economic right had been taking over in Virginia outside Washington,

D.C., George Mason, hired one of the founders of the Law and Economics movement to create a law school from scratch. The conservative AEI gloated that while "law and economics programs at elite institutions had to adapt to institutional norms," George Mason "was free to launch an Austrian-flavored program"—right-wing libertarian by way of Friedrich Hayek—"free from such constraints."

From 1980 on, Law and Economics arguments powered both the subversion of antitrust enforcement and the new mania for deregulation. It also, for instance, provided the rationales for legal and regulatory changes that were particularly sweet for the telecommunication and financial industries, and for corporate defenses of female pay gaps as being justified by economic efficiency. Law and Economics has shaped other policy as well—it even presumes to reduce marriage and child custody and civil liberties cases to simple questions of economic efficiency—but its primary and profound impact has been to fortify the power of big business to do as it pleases.

So the successful war launched by the economic right in the 1970s and '80s had several theaters, one of which was the law, with two main battlefronts, originalism and Law and Economics. Both were long-haul strategic campaigns effectively camouflaged as impartial philosophical movements. Originalists' deep anger didn't really derive from legal analytics about what Bork called "the Supreme Court's unconstitutional rulings" of the last century. Rather, it was about the progressive *particulars* of what he called "the sustained radicalism of the Warren Court," such as the rulings that guaranteed equal legal rights for blacks and women and every such "attempt to remake society." The common mission of the originalists and of the subtler Law and Economics conservatives has been precisely what they ostensibly oppose, of course—to utterly remake our society and political economy using the legal system, to make both resemble their vision of the American good old days, before the 1960s, before the 1930s, before the twentieth century.

12

The Deregulation Generation

Of all the important subjects about which I knew little before I started this book, government regulation of business was one where my knowledge didn't even count as superficial. The details seemed confusing and tedious and really best left to lawyers and other experts. I think regulation strikes most people that way.

And it was that ignorance and complacency—*leave it to the specialists*—that enabled big business and the right to convince a large majority of Americans during the 1970s and '80s that they were indifferent to regulation if not actively opposed. Back then, as the great regulatory rollback began, not many Americans were consciously, let alone passionately, dedicated to regulating business in general. For the libertarian right, however, reflexive opposition to any and all regulation was a fundamental principle. And since dealing with regulation usually costs money, big business's new shamelessness about maximizing profits turned corporate executives into libertarians of convenience.

The public's turn against regulation also derived from a special case of our confused feelings about the past. The rush to deregulate during the 1970s and '80s was helped along by the intertwined strains of American suspicion toward government: the angry 1960s anti-Establishment fight-the-Man kind, and also the nostalgic kind based on fantasies of a simpler America before all these dang Washington bureaucrats were telling us what we could and couldn't do.* But the vision of the past that Americans bought was a mythical one, consisting of only the nice parts and none of the bad parts—such as brutal and dishonest business practices. Moreover, political conservatives and liberals more or less came to agree in the 1970s that one part of the American past, the New Deal, was obsolete, unworthy of nostalgia. The alphabet soup of regulatory agencies and complicated regimes created in the 1930s and '40s seemed so . . . *antiquated.* As with so much that happened to the political economy in the 1970s and '80s, Americans never had a proper national debate about regulation.

The heart of the right's successful strategy was to turn regulation of business into a simple-minded, single-minded for-or-against binary question. All politics (and most of life) involves simplifying complex issues. But the politicians' and propagandists' oversimplification of this question has been particularly problematic because regulatory policies are so complex, and because there are several distinct *kinds* of regulation that fulfill the basic mission, *serving the public good,* in very different ways.

First are the regulations that help citizens directly, which consist of two basic kinds. There are the ones meant to protect or enhance public health—requiring companies not to poison our water or air or land in the process of making things, and not to make or sell or operate things (foods, drugs, cars, toys, buildings, airliners) that are unnecessarily unhealthy or unsafe. Then there are the regulations that try to make life more fair, like not letting financial firms take advantage of investors and borrowers, and not letting corporate insiders abuse nonpublic information to buy or sell stock in their own companies, and not letting merchandisers lie in their advertising and packaging, and not letting airlines keep you trapped on a plane on a runway for more than three hours.

We're mostly unconscious of the vast web of government regulations and codes on which we depend to make life safer and fairer and otherwise

*In fact, during the 1980s America developed a weirdly bipolar attitude toward regulation: just as we started deciding government should be banished from the free market so that big business could do as it pleased, and that parents didn't have to send their kids to school, and that gun ownership couldn't be regulated, we also started licensing every possible occupation and got hysterical about children being hurt on playgrounds or kidnapped or abused by satanic cults.

better than it would otherwise be. As soon as a rule or regulation solves some problem, we tend to forget about both the problem and the solution. If you were to read the previous paragraph aloud to people before asking them the standard Gallup poll question—"Do you think there's too much, too little or about the right amount of government regulation of business and industry?"—I'm certain that many, many fewer would answer *too much*. In the most recent survey, in fact, 38 percent of people picked that choice, while a large majority, 58 percent, said they want as much or more regulation of business as we have now.*

The other category of business regulation is at least as important, but harder for people to appreciate because it isn't as much about directly improving their lives and preventing disasters and requires some economic understanding. These are all the laws and regulations intended to make our economic system operate as well as it can, to referee the balance between making American economic life both as free *and* as fair as possible, optimizing those two goals in tandem rather than simply maximizing one.

The main part of this other category of business regulation is antitrust, all the evolving rules spun out of our antitrust laws for more than a century—and, crucially, the *interpretation* of those laws by courts and judges, interpretations that Robert Bork and the Law and Economics movement so effectively changed in favor of big business.

The word *antitrust* was coined back in 1890 when Congress passed the first such law. A *trust* was one of the shockingly large new corporations that had effectively eliminated competition by swallowing up competitors (and suppliers) and thereby controlling whole industries. The important point is that antitrust laws were never anticapitalist or antibusiness. They are anti-*big*-business, but only to the extent that particular companies get so big and dominant in their capitalist sectors that the rest of us are cheated in one way or another.

Properly enforced, antitrust laws prevent corporate gangsterism. Giant companies, simply by being rich and dominant, shouldn't be able to kill off competitors because they can afford to set prices artificially low

*The fraction who tell Gallup there's *too much* regulation of business has bobbed up and down in this century in an intriguing pattern: a low of 28 percent during the Bush administration, up to 50 percent during Obama, then back down to 39 percent under Trump. In other words, whenever Americans elect an antiregulation president, they discover they actually want regulation.

temporarily, or to bribe competitors, by acquiring them, to throw the fight. In the 1990s, as Microsoft was extending its quasi-monopoly power over software to the new Internet, the company's chief technology officer actually used a term from loan-sharking (for extortionate interest) and bookmaking (for taking both sides of a bet) to describe their plans—"that Microsoft intended to get a 'vig,' or vigorish, on every transaction over the Internet that uses Microsoft's technology."*

The point of antitrust is to keep capitalism as competitive and sustainable and altogether desirable as possible by making sure prices stay as low *and* salaries as high and innovation as robust as an optimally free market will bear. Antitrust enforcers are thus pro-capitalist the way foresters who cut back trees to make room for new growth and gardeners who fight pests and farmers committed to seed diversity are all pro-agriculture.

I mentioned earlier how Americans, in the middle of the last century, took antitrust enforcement more and more for granted, assuming that the old problem of one or just a few companies dominating an industry had been solved. That was why, for instance, newspapers in the 1960s were publishing fewer and fewer articles that referred to corporate monopolies, and after 1970 references to monopoly in American books dropped by half. That complacency helped pave the way for the swift triumph of Bork and the Law and Economics movement and the rest of the anti-antitrust right. In 1969 the Justice Department had launched an aggressive antitrust case against IBM, when it was still effectively the U.S. (and global) computer monopoly. The case dragged on and on, and in 1979 Bork gloated that it was "the antitrust division's Vietnam."

In the first year of the Reagan administration, the head of antitrust at the Justice Department decided, as he said, that "the only sensible thing to do" was to drop the IBM case, in line with his new approach of "backing off" antitrust enforcement in general. A few months later, he backed off systematically and officially. The Justice Department issued much looser new guidelines for mergers, based on the Law and Economics premise that it was fine for a couple of companies to dominate a business sector as long as efficiency was maximized and prices were low, and

*Fun fact: In the 1990s right after the government busted Microsoft for monopolism, in Microsoft's new Internet magazine, *Slate,* that executive, Nathan Myhrvold, reviewed my novel *Turn of the Century,* a main subplot of which involves hacker characters posting a stock-market-moving fake Internet news story about Bill Gates.

hey, *just don't worry* about the other economic and political downsides of corporate behemoths. Under Reagan, the antitrust staff was cut in half, and consequential mergers—such as the *two dozen* between airlines during the 1980s—were consummated with barely a peep from Justice. "When I became a judge in 1981," the Reagan appointee and conservative anti-antitrust pioneer Richard Posner later confessed, "I thought I had a lot of interesting antitrust cases, and I did—for about three years. And then they started to dry up," and before long "there were virtually no antitrust cases left."

The liberal media were also on board for phasing out antitrust. In the first weeks of the Reagan administration, one of *The New York Times*'s main business reporters wrote an op-ed entitled "Antitrust: Big Business Breathes Easier," explaining why and endorsing the new laissez-faire consensus: "Many economists and legal scholars contend that with productivity sagging, the nation can no longer afford the costs of antitrust actions," so "big is no longer bad." During Reagan's second term, the *Newsweek* business and economic columnist Robert Samuelson went even further, arguing out that antitrust law itself was obsolete, vestigial.

> The antitrust laws reflected the "American fear that concentrated private power could undermine democratic government." When the antitrust laws were enacted, Big Business was dominant. Government checks were narrow and weak. Now the opposite is true. Government regulation is powerful and pervasive.

And so given "the triumph of [antitrust's] central political premise," which was "the subordination of private business to public purpose," we were . . . all done! This take got remarkably little pushback in the 1980s.

The final, most interventionist kind of business regulation is quite different from antitrust. These regulators don't sit and wait to catch a big business violating the law and then sue to stop it. Instead they oversee a given industry closely, constantly, writing and enforcing detailed rules prescribing how each business must conduct itself. For essential utilities like electricity and water that everyone needs, and where the private providers are nearly all local monopolies, or railroads' inherent regional monopolies—in other words, in economic sectors where monopolies are "natural" and inevitable—that kind of tight control of rates and service is obviously necessary.

Extended to other industries, however, it's the kind of regulation that by the 1970s and '80s had often come to be outmoded. As air travel turned into a business in the 1920s and '30s, the federal government came to exercise this sort of tight control over the new industry. Of course, the federal government needs to set and enforce aviation safety rules and operate the air traffic control system, but for decades a federal agency also decided exactly where each particular airline could and couldn't fly, how many flights they could run, and how much they could charge for tickets. This system of regulation eventually became problematic because it created an uncompetitive market. Airlines had their own government-protected quasi-monopolies that let them charge high prices that virtually guaranteed high profits. The rigmarole required to adjust fares up or down or change routes was the opposite of nimble. Starting a new airline was nearly impossible. So who finally made airline deregulation happen in the late 1970s? *Famous liberals,* Senator Ted Kennedy and his aide Stephen Breyer, the future Supreme Court justice, in order to make the carriers really compete on price and service. Airline fares dropped, and new, better airlines got started.*

It was also the Democratic president and Congress in the late 1970s that phased out the old government-set prices for natural gas and shipping freight on railroads. Electric utility monopolies were required to start buying electricity generated by other companies. Federal antitrust enforcers in the liberal Johnson administration began a push that finally led in 1975 to the end of the high government-mandated fees that people had to pay stockbrokers when they bought or sold shares.

Suddenly everyone agreed: *deregulation is great!* The Washington left was tweaking and improving the political economy in good faith, finding common ground with the reasonable good-faith Washington right, which

*But then in the 2000s the more surreptitious and structurally profound form of corporate deregulation, the weakening of antitrust, *reduced* airline competition and undid much of the good. A wave of mergers left just four companies controlling 85 percent of the U.S. market. In addition to providing less service to smaller cities, North American carriers in the last decade became three times as profitable as carriers in Europe, where antitrust rules are more aggressively enforced.

still existed. But the craze for deregulation soon became a spectacular example for liberals of no good deed going unpunished. The new big business right had started caricaturing nearly *all* federal regulation as heavy-handed, job-killing, nanny-statist, *bad*.* *Bureaucrat* became a more and more common term of contempt. And as soon as Republicans won the White House and Senate in 1980, they began a promiscuous deregulation frenzy that, with Democrats' help, extended in every direction for decades.

In case you think *promiscuous deregulation frenzy* might be hyperbole, here's the astounding hard fact: in 1977, companies in highly regulated industries produced 17 percent of America's economic output, but just eleven years later, in 1988, that regulated fraction of our economic output had been cut by nearly two-thirds to just 6.6 percent.

To give a sense of what that meant, let's look more closely at two pieces of the consumer economy with which everybody's familiar—cable television (and now Internet) service and TV commercials for pharmaceuticals. Only if you're middle-aged or older, however, do you remember the time before everyone paid for TV, which was also back when TV ads for prescription drugs didn't exist.

In 1969 fewer than 4 million U.S. households had cable, most of them in rural places beyond normal broadcast coverage. Everyone else watched TV for free. By 1976, there was HBO and exclusive sporting events, so one in six households had gotten cable, which was enough to make businesses launch more programming channels. By 1984 almost half of Americans were wired-up basic cable subscribers.

Because cable had initially been a collection of who-really-cares little local businesses stealing and streaming network shows, the federal government barely bothered to regulate it, leaving that to towns and counties, which set the rates that their local operators could charge. But then in the early 1980s, as cable and TV were about to become synonymous—a utility that almost everyone would pay for, like water and

*I understand how encounters with difficult bureaucrats or stupidly written rules make people suspicious of regulation. In the 1990s the New York state authorities in charge of preserving forests informed my wife and me that we'd have to pay the same large financial penalty whether we clear-cut the plot of rural forest land we'd just bought or only the couple of acres on which we thought we might build a little house. Briefly I was put in touch with my inner Republican.

electricity—the big businesses that were taking over the industry saw an opportunity. They got Washington, in full deregulation mania, to radically deregulate their booming industry—specifically, to make it *illegal* for local authorities to regulate the fees the local cable monopolists could charge local citizens. The Senate passed the bill 87–9, the House on a voice vote, and Reagan signed it into law a week before his landslide reelection in 1984.

Right away the cable operators did what monopolists do: in the first four years after deregulation took effect, the average cost of the most basic cable service rose 61 percent. A generation later, the lucky big businesses that had come to control cable service started offering fast access to the Web as well, making them even luckier—virtually unregulated quasi-monopolists selling one highly desirable utility, TV, and a second, genuinely essential utility, the Internet.

At least cable TV and the Internet were actually new technologies that required us to figure out new ways of regulating them—or, as it happened, declining to regulate them. By contrast, no technological breakthroughs occurred in the 1980s that obliged the government to allow pharmaceutical companies to deluge American citizens with ads for prescription medicines. Rather, two industries consisting of very big businesses, pharma and media, took advantage of free-market mania.

In this case, they took us back in time to the turn of the twentieth century, before Americans decided it wasn't a good idea to let makers of medicines that were unnecessary or dangerous advertise them freely, back when half of newspapers' ad income came from bogus and/or addictive patent medicines. From 1906 to 1962, federal law regulated medicines ever more closely, trying to make sure they were safe and did what they were supposed to do. As new pharmaceuticals proliferated, a federal law in 1951 finally established the legal category of prescription-only drugs. In the industry, they were known as "ethical pharmaceuticals" and "ethical drugs."

And the industry quite effectively self-regulated, ethically, marketing those drugs exclusively to physicians . . . until the 1980s. There was no federal law against advertising prescription drugs directly to consumers in newspapers and magazines and on TV, just sensible norms, observed all over the world, that it was a bad idea. But then in the early 1980s, a couple of pharmaceutical companies began running a few ads on TV, and the FDA asked them to stop, pretty please, for a moratorium. Then in 1985 it lifted the moratorium. Ads on TV popped up, at first without actually naming the drugs, then naming them, then pushing the boundaries more. Pharma quickly became, so to speak, addicted to consumer advertising, as did, of course, advertising-supported media, especially TV networks, which had spent the 1980s encouraging the drug companies to begin consumer advertising and the Republican administrations to give it a green light. After an FDA commissioner tried to hold back the tide, the Republican Speaker of the House, Newt Gingrich, called the agency America's "number one job killer," and the floodgates opened wide. Suddenly in the 1990s such ads were all over the place. In 1991 the pharmaceutical industry's total consumer ad spending was $102 million in today's dollars, a small fraction of it going to television; just seven years later it was twenty times higher, more than $2 billion, $1 billion of that on TV. Since then pharmaceutical ad spending has tripled to more than $6 billion a year.

For the pharmaceutical as well as the media business, allowing consumer ads for prescription drugs, a deregulation that required no laws being debated or passed or repealed, worked splendidly. In 1980 the average American spent the same on prescription drugs as she had in 1970. By 1990 that amount had doubled, then it doubled again before the end of the decade, and since then it has more than doubled again. So we now spend *ten times* on prescription drugs, in real dollars, what we spent in 1970—and not just because drugs are much more expensive, thanks to all the micro-monopolies our big-business-friendly government creates for individual drugs. We see the ads, so we simply take lots more, surely more than we need and more than is healthy. America is exceptional, in this as in so many ways. Only one other country on Earth, New Zealand, allows prescription drugs to be advertised directly to its citizens.* Until the 1990s, we spent around the same per person on prescription drugs as Canadians and western Europeans, but now we spend as much as 200 percent more. By the way, after the 1980s the term *ethical drug* quickly faded from use. That was probably just a coincidence.

*In 2015 the doctors' American Medical Association finally declared itself in favor of a federal ban on mass-market prescription drug advertising.

13

The Culture of Greed Is Good

The public face of American business, in the middle of the twentieth century, was reliable, responsible, deliberately boring. In fiction, Ayn Rand, especially in *Atlas Shrugged* (1957), depicted big businessmen as fuck-you swashbucklers, but the real ones didn't dare come off like that. As late as 1981, when left-wing professor Marshall Berman finished writing *All That Is Solid Melts into Air,* he noted how reticent corporate leaders were, seldom celebrating the intrinsic thrills and chills of capitalism. How ironic, he wrote, that in this modern CEOs, obliged to appear to be reassuring *anti*radicals, had been outdone a century earlier by Karl Marx's enthusiastic depiction of capitalism's "revolutionary energy and audacity, its dynamic creativity, its adventurousness and romance, its capacity to make men not merely more comfortable but more alive." As Berman said of modern American corporate executives:

> Even as they frighten everyone with fantasies of proletarian rapacity and revenge, they themselves, through their inexhaustible dealing and developing, hurtle masses of men, materials and money up and down the earth, and erode or explode the foundations of everyone's lives as they go. Their secret—a secret they have man-

aged to keep even from themselves—is that behind their facades, they are the most violently destructive ruling class in history.

But in fact, after working up to it for a decade, America's capitalists were finally, fully *feeling* the destructive glee and at that very moment coming out of the closet, loud and proud. It's remarkable how well in 1987 a big Hollywood movie—a movie distributed by the studio Rupert Murdoch had recently acquired—dramatized, in real time, the unashamed new money-money-money American zeitgeist that considered capitalism nothing but *awesome*. It wouldn't and couldn't have been made just a dozen years earlier.

The main plot points of Oliver Stone's *Wall Street* were spot on: a superstar financial speculator engages in illegal inside trading, a predatory takeover strips a profitable company of its assets, and unionized workers are bamboozled into going along with a deal that will leave them without their good jobs and pensions. The corporate raider Gordon Gekko, played by Michael Douglas, does get his comeuppance in the end because his stockbroker, the Charlie Sheen character who provided him with the tradable inside information about his mechanic father's airline company, flips on him. But Gekko is the star of the show, the exciting sexy late-model 1980s antihero.

The most memorable scene from *Wall Street* is Gekko's speech to a meeting in a big hotel ballroom in midtown Manhattan of hundreds of shareholders of a paper manufacturer in which he's bought up stock to execute a hostile takeover. The company's stuffy old CEO speaks first, explaining to his investors that he is "fighting the get-rich-quick, short-term-profit, slot-machine mentality of Wall Street." In this new approach to American business, "we are undermining our foundation. This cancer is called *greed*. Greed and speculation have replaced long-term investment. Corporations are being taken apart like Erector Sets, without any consideration of the public good."

Then the smirking, charismatic, sharply dressed Gekko strides onto the podium. "We're not here to indulge in *fantasy*," he says, "but in political and economic *reality*." Then he harks back nostalgically to the good old days of the nineteenth and early twentieth centuries, as the real-life capitalist right actually did and does—

> the days of the free market, when our country was a top industrial power, there was accountability to the stockholder. The Carnegies, the Mellons, the men that built this great industrial empire, made sure of it because it was *their money* at stake. . . . You own the company. That's right—*you,* the stockholder. And you are all being royally screwed over by these, these *bureaucrats*. . . . The new law of evolution in corporate America seems to be survival of the *un*-fittest. . . . I am not a destroyer of companies. I am a *liberator* of them. The point is, ladies and gentlemen, that *greed*—for lack of a better word—is *good*. Greed is *right*. Greed *works*. Greed clarifies, cuts through, and captures the essence of the evolutionary spirit. . . . And *greed*—you mark my words—will not only save Teldar Paper, but that other malfunctioning corporation called the USA!

In just four minutes, Gekko summarized and incarnated the U.S. political economy's new doctrine. It was Libertarian Economics for Dummies, the Friedman Doctrine dramatized, a stump speech for money and its manipulation as the root of all glory.

And in the movie, Gekko's audience responds with wild applause, a standing ovation, the whole crowd ecstatic over his endorsement of single-minded financial marauding. And life imitated art, which was imitating life. Among the millions of Americans watching in theaters and at home on TV were tens or hundreds of thousands of actual and would-be investors and traders and bankers and bloody-minded players of the system who were electrified and inspired, virtually coked up. I've met business guys who can recite Gekko's lines. For them, it was a rousing band-of-brothers speech to the assembled mercenaries in the new war. The Gekko character's commission of felonies was almost incidental, part of the plot because a Hollywood movie requires them, although the crimes also make him seem even more badass.

Lots of *Wall Street* fans also got their ferocious animal spirits ignited by watching and memorizing the most memorable scene from a contemporaneous companion piece, David Mamet's *Glengarry Glen Ross,* where Alec Baldwin's character Blake mysteriously arrives to terrify an office of real estate salesmen. "A-B-C—*A,* always, *B,* be, *C,* closing. *Always be closing,*" "Coffee's for closers only," "Do you think I'm fucking with you? I am *not* fucking with you," "Nice guy? I don't give a shit. Good father? Fuck you, go home and play with your kids," and "What's my name? *Fuck You,* that's my name."* He's like a hellish noncommissioned officer to Gekko's gleefully demonic general in the U.S. capitalist legion as it was then being reconstituted.

In 1987 as well, some Wall Street guys started referring to themselves as Masters of the Universe, thanks to *The Bonfire of the Vanities,* Tom Wolfe's novel inspired, as he said, by "the ambitious young men (there were no women) who, starting with the 1980s, began racking up millions every year—millions!—in performance bonuses at investment banks."

Suddenly in the 1980s the news media were also celebrating and glorifying real-life big businessmen as they hadn't since the 1950s and early '60s—in fact, as they really hadn't since the 1910s and '20s. It was in 1982 that *Forbes* realized it was now acceptable to create an annual ranked list of the four hundred richest people, with estimates of their wealth, and in 1984 some A-list journalists launched a very glossy, stylish national monthly about businesspeople called *Manhattan, inc.*

The most celebrated and glorified were the megalomaniacal loudmouth alpha-male SOBs like Lee Iacocca and Jack Welch, leaders of two of the biggest public companies, Chrysler and General Electric, who barked and swaggered in ways that such leaders hadn't really been allowed to do in the modern age. They were hired managers performing the roles of lovably tough and cantankerous founder-owners. Both companies were big old-fashioned manufacturers from the golden age, each the tenth-largest company in America when Iacocca and Welch took them over in 1979 and 1981, respectively, just as we began realizing we'd entered the twilight of big old-fashioned American manufacturing. Each is a good case study illustrating the breakneck remaking of our political economy, in response to both new technology and globalization, and by decisions that the bosses and financiers and political leaders chose to make.

In the 1970s the U.S. auto industry had responded slowly to ramped-

*An *Evil Geniuses*–themed film festival would include *Wall Street* (1987), *Glengarry Glen Ross* (1992), *The American President* (starring Michael Douglas, 1995), *30 Rock*'s season 4 episode 14 (in which NBC's actual ex-overlord Jack Welch plays himself with Alec Baldwin's fictional NBC executive, 2010), and Baldwin's best several *SNL* performances as Donald Trump (2016–20).

up foreign competition and higher oil prices. Chrysler did worst of all, continuing to manufacture nothing but hulking, unreliable gas-guzzlers on which it lost the equivalent of $1,000 per car. But the company was deemed too big to fail, the first, so Iacocca arranged for a nonbankruptcy bankruptcy, getting the federal government to cosign for billions in bank loans. Meanwhile, he made himself the star of Chrysler TV ads and even flirted with a presidential candidacy in 1988—his campaign slogan was to be "I Like I."

In a 1985 cover profile I wrote for *Time,* I said he was "overbearing," had "a Daffy Duck lisp," and went "hardly a half-minute without mentioning *'guys'*—specific guys or guys in the abstract, guys who build automobiles ('car guys') or sell automobiles or buy them." But I kind of liked him. In our interviews, he slagged Reagan's economic right-wingism.

> The Democrats today are more pragmatic, not so ideological. . . . We are deindustrializing the country. . . . I'm not very popular with the people around the White House anymore. I told them [on trade policy], "Let's make sure we don't get hosed." They don't like that. This Administration sees you either as a protectionist or a free-trader, with no shades in between. And we're going to lose, as a country, for it. . . . Where's Dave Stockman? Every time he tells the truth he gets in trouble. He gives them the hard facts. . . . So who's in charge of economic policy? Who are these people?

Iacocca convinced his unionized workers to agree to be paid the equivalent of $20,000 a year less than GM's and Ford's workers—and then spent the remainder of the 1980s laying half of them off. After retiring in 1992, he returned a few years later as part of a Gekko-like raider's attempted leveraged buyout of Chrysler, which failed and wound up enabling its takeover by a foreign company.*

General Electric, for its part, wasn't in trouble when Welch became CEO. Rather, Welch took advantage of the new rules of the economy to make the company's stock price skyrocket, which had been deemed,

*In the early twenty-first century, as the fantasy-industrial complex continued annexing American life beyond show business, Chrysler hired the eighty-year-old former CEO to be its Colonel Sanders, playing himself in TV ads with Snoop Dogg.

even more than actual profit, the only thing that matters. Like Gekko in *Wall Street* and Blake in *Glengarry,* Welch was known for being brutally candid. In fact, GE made a doctrine out of brutality, codified it as a system that ensured worker insecurity by constantly identifying a quota of doomed losers. Every year, according to Welch's new rule, one out of every ten GE employees were fired, no matter what, because nine other employees were judged by their superiors to be superior. It was called the Vitality Curve, and other big companies were soon instituting dread-inducing worker-culling systems with their own euphemistic names—Personal Business Commitments at IBM, Individual Dignity Entitlement at Motorola. At GE, many were never replaced; during Welch's first five years as CEO, the workforce shrank by a quarter, and he became known as Neutron Jack—ha!—because like a neutron bomb, he evaporated tens of thousands of people without damaging the businesses where they worked. Such corporate "rank-and-yank" systems were just one way that an acute new sense of economic insecurity spiked in the 1980s and then stayed high.

Welch also started turning GE from a manufacturing company into more of a financial services company—just as the abstract and increasingly exotic games of pure financial betting, lending, and otherwise making money by fiddling with money and hypothetical money was sucking up more of America's resources and focus and giving Wall Street ever more influence and control of our economy. In addition to eliminating jobs, the original great American technology company drastically cut back its spending on research and development. As a result, GE's profits increased (for a while) and its stock price went up phenomenally (for a while), and Jack Welch became the superstarriest CEO, worshipfully covered by the media and emulated by corporate executives. He and Iacocca and were both perfectly cast for the hypernostalgic *USA! USA!* moment—John Waynes in suits and ties, straight-talking manly men from working-class families who'd come to the rescue of enervated, simpering corporate America, taking over iconic companies to remake them for a hard-assed new age.

By the way, although American spectators had started doing that "*USA! USA!*" chant with its cheerfully fuck-you edge at international sporting events during the 1970s, it was in the 1980s that it became a national cultural habit, first at the 1980 Winter Olympics in Lake Placid, when Team USA (a new coinage) beat the unbeatable Soviet hockey team, then spreading into professional wrestling and Reagan reelection campaign rallies and finally to any sort of excited mob of Americans who felt like madly *insisting* on our awesomeness, to *perform* feelings of patriotic self-confidence, which used to abide more organically and implicitly. In other words, the *"USA! USA!"* chant was yet another expression of the nostalgia tic, an old-timey barbaric yawp spontaneously invented and then ritually reenacted.

Starting in the 1980s as well, rich Americans were given permission—by Reaganism, by the media, by themselves—to behave more like rich people in the old days, showing off their wealth. Conspicuous consumption had never disappeared, of course, but in the thriving decades that followed the Depression and the war, the big economic winners were really not supposed to flaunt their good fortune, and cultural norms were in place to enforce discretion. When I was growing up in Omaha in the 1960s and '70s, no one there thought it remarkable that our local multimillionaire Warren Buffett lived in a nice normal house on a small lot among other nice normal houses on small lots in a neighborhood that wasn't the fanciest in town. What seemed remarkable, rather, was the twenty-thousand-square-foot house that the founder of Godfather's Pizza built in 1983, by common reckoning the first true *mansion* to go up in Omaha since the 1920s. Those national quiet-wealth norms were crumbling when a Rolls-Royce Owners' Club newsletter morphed into a successful glossy national magazine for and about the wealthy called *The Robb Report* (1976), and they'd evaporated entirely when *Lifestyles of the Rich and Famous* went on the air (1984) to persuade people that the lives of the fictional superrich on *Dallas* (1978) and *Dynasty* (1981) were real—get a load of this *Glengarry*–meets–*Wall Street* Iacocca-Welch impersonator Donald Trump!—and that ostentatious personal wealth was now the only American Dream that mattered.

Our fantasy-industrial complex also reflected and normalized the new old-fashioned laissez-faire rules by making legal gambling ubiquitous, like in the Old West and in old Europe. Until the late 1980s, only two U.S. states allowed commercial casino gambling, but within a decade, legal casinos existed in half the states. Before the 1970s, only two state governments operated lotteries, but most did by the end of the 1980s, a decade states also spent cutting taxes. In addition to the bad odds of winning, the state-run numbers rackets really amount to a crypto-tax, maybe the most regressive ever, since lottery players are disproportionately poor.

I don't think it was coincidence that this happened simultaneously with the U.S. political economy metaphorically turning into a winner-take-all casino economy. The gambling hall replaced the factory floor as our governing economic symbol, a flashy, totally temporary gathering of magical-thinking individual strangers whose fortunes depend overwhelmingly on luck instead of on collective hard work with trusted industrious colleagues day after day. Risk-taking is a good thing, central to much of America's success, but not when the risks are involuntary for everyone except the people near the top, required rather than freely chosen, and when those at the top have arranged things so they don't have much serious downside risk. As Americans were herded into literal casinos, they were simultaneously being herded en masse into our new national economic casino, where the games were rigged in favor of the well-to-do players.

People put up with it, for the same reason that the great mass of people in casinos put up with playing games that the house always wins in the long run. The spectacle of a few ecstatic individual winners at that poker table or the screaming slot machine over there makes the losers envious but not resentful and encourages them to believe that, hey, they too might get lucky and win.

After all, for as long as anyone could remember, Americans shared *proportionately* in the national prosperity, the fractions going to the people at the bottom and the middle and the top all growing at the same rate. In the 1980s it wasn't yet clear to most people that the political economy was being changed from a more or less win-win game to one that was practically zero-sum, that over the next few decades, at least three-quarters of them would be the economic casino's suckers, that their losses and forgone winnings would all go to the luckiest 20 percent, and that thenceforth in America *only* the rich would get much richer.

That's because the successful and comfortable social contract that had been in effect in America from the 1930s was replaced by a new one. Social contracts are unwritten but real, taken seriously but not literally, which is their beauty and their problem. They consist of all the principles and norms governing how members of society are expected to treat one another, the balance between economic rights and responsibilities, between how much freedom is permitted and how much fairness is required. All the formal rules specifying behavioral constraints and responsibilities, the statutes and bureaucratic codes, are distinct from the social contract but overlap with it, because lots of the specific rules—tax rates, minimum wages, environmental regulations, the cost of education—are codifications of the social contract.

Contracts are negotiated, ideally in a way that all the signatories feel fairly treated. In the evolving American social contract, the balance among the competing demands of liberty and equality and solidarity (or *fraternité*) worked pretty well for most of the twentieth century, the arc bending toward justice. But then came the ultra-individualistic frenzy of the 1960s, and during the 1970s and '80s, liberty assumed its powerfully politicized form and eclipsed equality and solidarity among our aspirational values. *Greed is good* meant that selfishness lost its stigma. And that was when we were in trouble.

The best test of a morally legitimate social contract is a thought experiment that the philosopher John Rawls named the Veil of Ignorance in 1971, just as modern American ultra-individualism exploded. The idea is to imagine you know nothing of your actual personal circumstances—wealth, abilities, education, race, ethnicity, gender, age; all those salient facts are *veiled* from you. Would you agree to sign your country's social contract and take your chances for better or worse in the social and political and economic system it governs?

Conservatives and the well-to-do in particular should submit to this test. A central tenet of economic libertarianism is the importance of literal contracts: if people sign a contract freely agreeing to its terms, it's their business and nobody else's what they do for or to one another. But "*social* contracts"? Fuck you, you do-gooders and losers and moochers. Libertarians fantasize that they're action heroes and entirely self-made. They tend to exempt themselves from the truism that there but for the grace of God goes each one of them, because an implicit premise of their ultra-individualism is that anybody in America can make it on their own and that unfair disadvantages either don't exist or can't be helped. I have a hunch that the demographic profile of self-identified libertarians—94 percent white, 68 percent male, 62 percent in their forties or younger—has something to do with those beliefs and fantasies.

14

How Wall Street Ate America

The ugly, confusing word *financialization* was invented in the late 1960s, the period of Peak New, just before America entered the era of extreme financialization. But it didn't really become a common term until we all first experienced one of its spectacularly ugly, confusing, and destructive results, the market crash and meltdown of 2008.

Simply put, financialization is how Wall Street effectively took over the U.S. economy during the fourth quarter of the twentieth century. Our economy's main players and private stewards went from a focus on actual work and production of goods and services to a preoccupation with financial scheming around productive enterprises and the work they do.

It was another paradigm shift. Financialization happening in sync with the other plotlines and big shifts in this book was not a coincidence. The changes were all of a piece and synergistic. Wall Street's new hegemony was first enabled by Milton Friedman's mainstreamed libertarianism and then reinforced it in turn—ditto with financialization and deregulation, the Law and Economics movement, the atrophying of antitrust, the lionization of guys like Jack Welch and Gordon Gekko, the digital revolution, increasingly short-term thinking, only the rich getting richer, and the explosion of corporate lobbying in Washington.*

The Harvard Business School political scientist Gautam Mukunda has a lucid explanation for how extreme financialization happened. "Real power," he wrote recently in the *Harvard Business Review,*

> comes not from forcing people to do what you want but from changing the way people think, so that they *want* to do what you want. . . . The ability of a powerful group to reward those who agree with it and punish those who don't distorts the marketplace of ideas. . . . The result can be an entire society twisted to serve the interests of its most powerful group, further increasing that group's power in a vicious cycle. . . . In the United States . . . it's . . . the financial sector—particularly Wall Street—that has disproportionate power. . . . The financial system is the economy's circulatory system. The large banks that have driven finance's incredible growth are the heart of the financial system. . . . The American economy is suffering from an enlarged heart.

This chapter is the longest in this book. That's partly because its story—a set of interlocking stories, really—is so central to America's wrong turn. It's also long because of some personal stories I've included. But mainly it's because if you aren't deeply familiar with finance, as I wasn't, even a basic understanding of what happened requires some careful unpacking.

Before the 1970s, finance—regular banks, investment banks, stockbrokers, credit card companies—was just another service industry, the one in charge of lending and investing and processing money. It was mostly dull, and not just because WASPs mostly ran it. Sobriety and restraint were the whole point, a point traumatically reinforced by the Crash of 1929, then codified by new federal laws and regulations in the 1930s. For a half-century after that crash, the financial industry's appetite for

*The financial industry spends about half a billion a year on Washington lobbying, about a million dollars per member of Congress. Only the healthcare industry spends more.

risk was low. As the financial journalist and former investment banker William Cohan has written, "Wall Street's ability to manage risk was one of its singular successes." That's why in 1972 a doctoral dissertation I happened across on "Wall Street in the American Novel," for instance, casually stipulated that lately, "fewer novels are written which are based on the marketplace of high finance" because "the excesses and exuberances which made the headlines in an earlier day are now largely prevented from occurring," and "the wide-open frontier quality has disappeared and Wall Street has settled down and become sedate and mundane."

What that Ph.D. candidate and most of us didn't yet realize was that in finance, according to Cohan, "starting in 1970, prudence gave way to pure greed." The culture of Wall Street changed along with the rest of American culture during and after the 1960s. For instance, an exclusive new kind of mutual fund for rich people was proliferating, with managers who invested promiscuously, wildly—not just buying promising stocks but making bets that a stock's price would fall, acquiring real estate, speculating in currencies, and investing with borrowed capital to get returns even higher if you bet right. In 1967 the American Stock Exchange issued a stern warning to its members to "consider carefully" any involvement in these newfangled "hedge funds," to ask the exchange's permission first, and to always obey the existing "prohibitions against excessive dealing"—a gentlemanly catchall term for aggressiveness that would be considered *bad form*.

During the late 1960s in America generally, sobriety and restraint were discredited as square while risk-taking and self-gratification were celebrated. In finance, starting in the 1970s, fusing *if it feels good, do it* with the Friedman Doctrine meant that the pursuit of maximum profit for *oneself* as well as for one's company trumped every other value or motive, so recklessness and corner-cutting became normalized, even obligatory. The last guys who'd been in the business at the time of the 1929 crash retired. Until around then, investment banks were legally partnerships, consisting of people mainly investing their own personal wealth in deals, and thus they were strongly inclined to be prudent—eager to make more money, of course, but as eager as anyone not to lose what they had. But then, Cohan explains,

> one Wall Street partnership after another became a public corporation. The partnership culture gave way to a bonus culture, in which employees felt free to take huge risks with other people's money in order to generate revenue and big bonuses. Risk management on Wall Street [became] a farce, with risk managers being steamrolled by bankers, traders, and executives focused nearly exclusively on maximizing annual profits—and the size of their annual bonuses.

As investment banks and bankers took more risks, managing it often meant persuading—sometimes conning—other people to assume the risks you didn't want. Thus the invention of all sorts of new derivatives. Simple derivatives had been around forever, such as betting on what the price of cotton or oil would be at some date in the future. But then starting in the 1980s, based on work by economists trained at the University of Chicago, ever more complex and abstract bets on bets on interest rates appeared, and bets on those bets.

The financial industry actually coined the astonishingly shameless term of art *incognito leverage* for invisible corporate debt, debt kept off balance sheets, hidden from the clueless chumps among the investors. The "large banks start[ed] acting more like traders" than trustworthy advisers, the journalist Nicholas Dunbar explains in *The Devil's Derivatives,* his history of financial innovation. The result was an "innovation race between ways of transferring risk"—such as the credit default swap, a derivative bought by financial firms that was actually *predicated* on unpaid loans and financial disaster, an invention that "Goldman Sachs quickly moved to exploit and was richly rewarded for its ambition and ruthlessness."

It wasn't just the more adrenalized loosey-goosey culture and going public that made Wall Street greedier to the point of recklessness. From the mid-1970s on, government was also an enabler in various crucial ways. In 1974 a new federal law regulating pension funds literally changed the operative definition of the term *prudent* to mean that henceforth, pension fund managers choosing investments were legally required to be *exclusively* driven by maximizing cash value *now,* by whatever means, even if—catch-22—that required making imprudent investments, or investments that might ultimately wreck their pension beneficiaries' industries or communities.

In 1978 a federal tax law got a new line of code called 401(k), and before long *everyone* was encouraged to set up a 401(k) and funnel money from each paycheck into stocks and other investments for retirement—which amounted to an immediate and immense new revenue stream for Wall Street. Then during Reagan's first year in office, Congress cut the tax on profits from stock sales—capital gains—to its lowest rate since the 1920s. And so after a steady drift downward since 1965, stock prices in 1982 began rising like crazy. The value of shares doubled by 1986 (and despite a one-day crash of 22 percent in 1987, they doubled again twice more by the end of the century).

Finance was *fun* again, as it hadn't been since the mid-1960s. The well-to-do were getting *so* much richer *so* quickly, and without any of that '60s lefty buzzkill to make them feel bad. The casino excitement encouraged still more Wall Street firms to go public and invent still more exotic new investments, and it encouraged government to deregulate more and cut taxes more. "You're a writer," a finance guy I'd just met actually said to me one night in the mid-1980s. "I just realized the other day that *rich* and *risk* are almost the *same word*—that happened on purpose, right, historically?" I told him I didn't think so, but that unlike *team,* they do both contain an *i,* a joke he didn't seem to get.

From the mid-1970s through the '80s, the government began exposing all of us to more risk by empowering financial hustlers in another way. It's a bit complicated and involves a subject I never thought I'd be writing about and that you probably never thought you'd be reading about: bonds. But it's a good place for us to take a closer look under the hood of financialization. And bonds are important because they were a key part of the systemic undermining that eventually led to the financial disaster of 2008.

Issuing and selling bonds are how big corporations (and public entities like cities) borrow huge sums of money. Bonds were always less risky for investors than stocks, because if a company's stock plummets, that's just too bad for the stockholders, whereas the company is supposed to be obliged to pay back in full the people who bought its bonds. Three big American rating agencies rate each bond or other giant chunk of debt from triple A, the best, down through about twenty gradations of risk, more or less the way the big-three credit bureaus rate your and my creditworthiness.

The difference is that you and I have no relationship with the credit bureaus that might incline them to push up our scores improperly to please us and thus let us rack up more debt than we can afford. By contrast, the big-three corporate-debt-rating agencies are all paid by the big corporations and financial firms that are issuing and selling the tranches of debt—and *not* by the investors who want risk ratings that are, you know, objective. That business model, "issuer pays" rather than "subscriber pays," has been standard only since, yes, the 1970s. In other words, while the fox did not start guarding the henhouse, he was definitely now employing and training the guard dogs. At the same time, in 1975, Wall Street's federal regulators, the SEC, made rating bonds an even sweeter insiders' business by deputizing the big three as the U.S. economy's official corporate credit referees, effectively extensions of the government, thereby locking in those businesses as a no-competition triopoly.

Not coincidentally, the late 1970s were also when Wall Street started making fresh billions from a newly conjured type of bond, a financial species called mortgage-backed securities that were illegal at the time in most states. Millions of individual home loans were thrown together, ground up, nicely packaged, and sold to investors in bite-size pieces as financial sausages—nobody really knew what was in any given mortgage-backed security, but they were hot and tasted good. Their main promoter became vice-chairman of Salomon Brothers, the biggest bond-trading firm in the world, who by 1984 was claiming that just that one sausage-extruding part of his firm "made more money than all the rest of Wall Street combined." No wonder he was giddy: a new federal law in 1984 declared by fiat that mortgage-backed securities were now as safe as U.S. government bonds, the ultimate low-risk guarantee, as long as one of those big private rating companies gave the particular sausage its seal of approval. In 1986 another federal law created a specific tax benefit that made mortgage-backed securities even more attractive to investors. For the rating companies, rating all these proliferating debt sausages was fabulous business, eventually generating as much as half their revenue.

At the bottom of this new scheme, of course, were tens of millions of regular Americans paying off their home mortgages every month. Because everyone in the financial industry—investment banks, mortgage lenders, raters, *everybody*—was now profiting in so many new ways from the mortgage boom, they kept making it easier for people to borrow money to buy houses and condos, and got the government to help. During the 1980s, prudent New Deal rules concerning mortgage loans were repealed, allowing people to get home loans with too little money down and interest rates that would "adjust" to unaffordable heights. So during the 1980s, the average price of a house in America doubled.*

Ever easier borrowing was the fundamental change that allowed the financial industry to take over more and more of people's lives and ever more of the economy. "I think we hit the jackpot," President Reagan kvelled in 1982 as he signed one of the first big financial deregulation laws, which the Democratic House had passed by three to one. Because people could easily borrow ever more on their credit cards, they saved less and less, assuming ever more risk, living ever closer to the financial edge. In 1970, only one in six households had a general purpose credit card like Mastercard or Visa; by the late 1980s, a majority of Americans had at least one. Starting then and continuing through the end of the century, Americans' personal debt *excluding* home loans increased twelvefold, after inflation. In 1978 the credit card business became much more attractive thanks to a Supreme Court decision that allowed banks to charge credit card interest rates as high as they wanted, regardless of legal maximums in the state where a cardholder lived, by setting up shop in states that were cool—*free markets,* man—with usury.

That 1980s wave of financial industry laissez-faire helped trigger a disaster immediately: savings and loans, the several thousand local bank-like entities that specialized in lending to local folks—like Bailey Building and Loan in *It's a Wonderful Life*—promptly went a little nuts, making too many loans that were too risky, especially to developers of shopping malls and office buildings. Fully half of America's S&Ls collapsed in less than a decade, and the government had to provide the equivalent of a quarter-trillion dollars to make good on their losses. Yet that crackup did not prompt Washington or Wall Street to sober up and slow down the loose-money craze in finance. The amount of all credit extended to Americans from 1980 to 2007—home mortgages, student debt, car loans,

*It all started going bad for taxpayers and many homeowners when, as of 2007, one of the big three, Moody's, began revising its ratings downward on 83 percent of the approximately $1 trillion worth of mortgage securities to which it had given its very top rating just the year before.

credit cards, and the rest—more than doubled, and the debt owed by the average American *quadrupled*.

Money got easy for people in the middle and toward the bottom, for suckers with credit card and mortgage payments they could barely afford—but also, of course, for people at the top, the financial speculators and middlemen who had other innovating to do.

Such as leveraged buyouts of companies, or LBOs. Until the late 1970s, leveraged buyouts were small-time backwater deals, too skeevy for the old-school Wall Street firms or banks. In the standard version of an LBO, outsiders take over a public company by teaming up with its senior executives, providing a small down payment, and putting up the company's own assets as collateral to borrow the necessary zillions to buy up all the stock and eliminate the pesky shareholders—that is, taking it private. Then for a while they use the company's profits to pay themselves and make payments on the debt they used to buy the company. And then they resell the company ASAP to *new* shareholders by taking it public again. It sounds slightly dodgy but unremarkable. Look a little closer, however, and you see why LBOs so often are, in several ways, caricatures of capitalist rapacity.

Companies are supposed to borrow money in order to grow their businesses—to hire more people and buy more equipment and lease more space to make and sell more and better widgets. The whole point of a modern LBO, however, is quite often not the business as a business at all, making a company better and bigger and profitable for the long haul. Rather, the point is the *financing*, quickly enriching the financiers and top management by means of a scheme with a ridiculous tax dodge at its center. The business, whatever it is, is just a pretext for that fast-in-and-out scheme.

The federal tax provision that makes LBOs work is shockingly simple: income is taxable, but interest payments are deductible on tax returns, so when you start using almost all of the LBO'd company's income to make interest payments, you get to stop paying corporate taxes. Of course, that's a perversion of the tax code, given that Congress makes interest deductible so that businesses can more easily expand and hire and prosper, not so that financiers (and top executives) can enrich themselves. In fact, what often happens with LBO'd companies is the opposite: in order to afford their huge interest payments on their huge new loans, they lay off employees, sell whatever they can, cut research and development, and otherwise hunker down.

That tax-deductibility trick was nothing new, but a couple of new 1980s factors enabled the mainstreaming of the LBO. Both depended on Wall Street's new postprudence shamelessness. One was the up-front fees that investment bankers and the rest of the financial elite were skimming off of LBOs, often several percent of a company's purchase price just for . . . wheedling, advising, pushing paper, attaching their corporate names to the deal—even though they didn't actually care about the "long-term success of the new enterprise," as the Republican treasury secretary admitted at a Senate hearing in the 1980s, a carelessness that he admitted might make LBOs a "financial snipe hunt where the new long-term investors, flashlight in hand, are left holding the bag." *Funny,* the cabinet member overseeing U.S. finance said, *it's a con game!*

But most important to making the formerly disreputable LBO take off was a new way to finance the takeovers—by means of the formerly disreputable junk bond. Junk bonds had been what happened to good bonds when the issuing corporations got into trouble, causing the big rating firms to downgrade the bonds, which meant the corporations had to pay higher interest to people who bought their bonds. But then in the late 1970s, the young Los Angeles investment banker Mike Milken started creating and issuing risky bonds *as* junk bonds, from scratch, thereby creating a white-hot new financial subindustry.* During just the first half of the 1980s, the market for junk bonds grew sixfold, to the equivalent of $94 billion a year, and more than a thousand different junk bonds were issued—half of which wound up defaulting, failing to pay the money due when it was due to the bond owners. Junk bonds are like car manufacturers deciding to start making and marketing lines of brand-new designated lemons—cheaper parts, shoddily manufactured, much more liable to break down or crash, but *so inexpensive*.

*Milken's bank, Drexel Burnham Lambert, paid him the equivalent of $2.3 billion between 1984 and 1987 alone. When he pleaded guilty to securities fraud in 1990, he choked up and said his crimes were "*not* a reflection on the underlying soundness and integrity" of junk bonds. After he snitched, his ten-year prison sentence was reduced to two, and according to *Forbes,* he's still worth $3.7 billion. When President Trump granted him an official pardon in 2020, the White House issued a statement praising "his innovative work" that "democratized corporate finance."

Funded with junk bonds or not, a typical LBO was a conceptually new sort of acquisition, more brazen and shameless in its selfishness and greed—indifferent outsiders offering to make a few executive collaborators very rich as long as they were up for abandoning their fellow employees and the company itself if necessary. Most people agree that short-term thinking has become a chronic problem for business, for the economy, for society—yet unabashed short-termism is the *point* of an LBO, the financiers' optimal outcome being to take over, make a fortune, and disappear as quickly as they can.

One of the godfathers of this fast-and-loose new game was Henry Kravis, whose Manhattan firm Kohlberg Kravis Roberts got the craze going in 1979 by investing a cash down payment equivalent to $4 million to use $1 *billion* in junk bonds and other debt to take over an obscure Fortune 500 company. One of the most spectacular early LBOs was undertaken by former treasury secretary William Simon after he left government to propagandize for the right and the rich, and to get very rich. (By his account, he was still in public service—because, as he'd testified to a Senate committee, "If you really want to help the poor, help the rich.") In 1982 he bought a greeting card company by borrowing the equivalent of $140 million and putting up less than $1 million of his own money. A year later, right after paying himself a special dividend of $1 million from the company's cash, he took the company public again, selling the shares of stock for $800 million, out of which he personally got the equivalent of about $177 million, and bade farewell to the greeting card industry.

The rush was *really* on. The respectable banks and insurance companies were now eagerly in the game. A respectable-sounding new term of art was adopted, *private equity*.* In just five years, 1984 through 1988, the equivalent of almost $400 billion worth of LBO schemes were pulled off, ten times the value of the deals of the previous six years. In 1989 KKR took over the cigarette and snack company RJR Nabisco for the equivalent of more than $50 billion—still the biggest LBO ever, by far. That deal

*Shares of stock that are sold to the public (thus the term *public company*) are also called equities. *Private* equity dealmakers, in addition to buying up all of a public company's shares on the open market (turning that company "private") in order to have their way with it before selling stock to new public shareholders, also invest in privately owned companies that they eventually sell to individual shareholders or all at once to another company.

was the subject of the book (and the TV movie) *Barbarians at the Gate*. Everyone agreed afterward that Kravis and KKR paid way too much. On the other hand, *who cares* when the cash you're putting up is only a few tens of millions, less than one-tenth of one percent of the purchase price? But wait, *that's not all:* just for helping to make the deal happen and advising others snuffling and gulping at the trough, KKR also received in *fees,* up front, the equivalent of more than $800 million. Which was standard, the new normal.

Very full disclosure: I know Henry Kravis. That is, for several years I ridiculed him publicly, and for a couple of years right after that, I insubordinately worked for him. Let me explain.

Spy, the satirical magazine that I cofounded and edited during the late 1980s and early '90s, focused much of our journalism and ridicule on the rich and powerful and celebrated, especially in New York. As it happened, *Spy* never published a feature story about Kravis or KKR, but he was a recurring secondary character. We referred to him variously as "dwarfish takeover maniac Harry Kravis," "overleveraged buyout hustler Henry Kravis," "tiny eighties relic Henry Kravis," and, after he bought Nabisco, "groceries commissar Henry Kravis" and "Shredded Wheat king Henry Kravis," who was willing to "pay billions of dollars for nothing more than a few brand names and some junk food." He was also among the fifty-eight rich people who received $1.11 "refund" checks from *Spy*'s fake National Refund Clearinghouse, and each time they cashed one, received another, smaller check with a new fake explanation; Kravis was one of the thirteen semifinalists who cashed a $0.64 check, but in the final round he failed to cash a $0.13 check.*

Anyhow, shortly after leaving *Spy,* I became editor-in-chief of the weekly *New York* magazine—which Henry Kravis and KKR had recently acquired (from Rupert Murdoch) for their new media company, K-III Communications. I assume that if publication archives had been digitally searchable back then, I wouldn't have been hired.

*The two winners who cashed the final $0.13 checks were Adnan Khashoggi, a shady Saudi wheeler-dealer whose wealth was at that moment shrinking from a few billion to a few million dollars, and Donald Trump, whose first casino bankruptcy occurred a year later.

It's called *New York,* founded to focus on New York City, so naturally we covered Wall Street. Two years into my tenure, we published a great cover story on the internal battles at one of the elite investment banks. It reflected badly on its star executive, who'd talked to the writer quite candidly and was pushed out of his firm not long afterward. When the article appeared, Kravis invited me to breakfast at his enormous Park Avenue apartment. The story had made him very uncomfortable, he said, so now he wanted *New York* to stop covering Wall Street entirely. I explained why that would be unwise and politely declined his request. When I told my actual bosses at the publishing company about it, they told me to "ignore Henry." Which I did. A few months later, we ran a story about the imminent 1996 presidential election featuring a cover photo of the Republican nominee with his eyes closed and the headline BOB DOLE, WAKE UP! Kravis was his campaign's deputy finance chairman, had hosted a birthday fundraiser for him, and had recently donated $250,000 to the GOP, so he was included in a FAT-CAT CATALOGUE sidebar. A week later I was fired.

The subtitle of *Barbarians at the Gate* is *The Fall of RJR Nabisco*: the company wasn't improved by the takeover, it *fell,* got broken up to no particular point, and in the end, apart from those remarkable up-front fees—*unlocked value* is one of the financiers' terms of art that emerged in the 1980s, like when a safe is unlocked in an amazing heist—the deal didn't do well for Kravis and KKR. A problem with leveraged buyouts and other private equity takeovers, and with financialization in general, is that so often the main point isn't to create enterprises of lasting value, enabling particular businesses (or American capitalism or American citizens) to prosper for the long term. It is to obtain those fees, the vigorish, and to score by making *this deal,* and then another deal, and another, because greed is good, kill them all, and let the invisible hand sort it out.

As I was beginning this book in 2017, I noticed that big, familiar retail chains were all going under—Toys "R" Us, Payless, The Limited, Gymboree, and many more. Then I noticed that each of them had been subjected to a leveraged buyout, finally choked and smothered by debt piled on by temporary private equity owners. The list of solid, profitable American companies unnecessarily wrecked this way since then is extremely long.

The story of one familiar company, not yet gone, is illustrative as a capsule history of the evolution of American capitalism from ingenuity and grit and social benefit to passionless, pointless, wasteful, endless financial whoredom in LBO hell. In the late 1800s a tinkerer in Wisconsin named Simmons found a way to mass-produce spring mattresses, then cut costs and prices by 90 percent. His son took over and introduced the Beautyrest brand, then the grandson managed to keep the company going through the Depression, when the stock lost 99.9 percent of its value—and then Simmons thrived again for decades. During the 1970s, along with so much of U.S. manufacturing, things started going a bit south for Simmons Bedding, the great-grandson was purged, the company was sold to the conglomerate Gulf + Western, and then in 1985 it was taken over in an LBO by . . . William Simon, freshly retired from the greeting card racket.

Over the next two decades, Simmons was sold and resold a half-dozen more times, going private and public again and again, accumulating more and more debt, from the equivalent of $300 million in 1991 to the $1.6 billion it owed when it finally entered bankruptcy during the Great Recession. In the course of the 2009 bankruptcy to reorganize the company, a quarter of the workforce was cut loose, more than a thousand employees, and people who'd bought the company's bonds were out hundreds of millions. Then in 2012 Simmons was acquired out of bankruptcy by *another* financial firm, which owned Serta Mattress, and two years after that, yet another financial firm took over the combined company. It didn't quite constitute a monopoly, because there was still one other big mattress company, Sealy, controlled at the time by . . . KKR. Between its first leveraged buyout and its (first) bankruptcy, Simmons's succession of short-term financial-firm owners sucked $1 billion out of the company in fees and profits.

There are plenty of LBO stories worse than this one. Reading the details made me realize that the term *vampire capitalism* is fair enough.

"After a long dry spell," the first line of a breathless *New York Times* business story announced in 1980, "venture capital is booming again." The reporter felt obliged to explain what venture capitalists were, the way articles back then also had to explain what Silicon Valley was. "The last six months has been the hottest we've ever seen," a VC in San Francisco told the reporter. All at once the three hot species of swinging financial firms—revitalized VCs, legitimized hedge funds, overleveraged takeover artists rationalized as private equity investors—were flooded with investment capital from big commercial banks, investment banks, insurance companies, pension funds, and university and foundation endowments. At the same moment that *alternative rock* became a genre, so did these *alternative investments* and *alternative asset managers*. Meanwhile, money from merely well-to-do and solvent individuals was gushing into conventional mass-market mutual funds, turning them into far, far more powerful economic institutions than they'd ever been before.

Looking back now, the scale and speed of the growth of the U.S. financial sector from around 1980 through the turn of the century is freakish. It suddenly began growing twice as fast as it had during the 1950s and '60s and '70s. Back in 1980, the bit of the American economy in the hands of the "alternative alpha" guys—venture capital, private equity and hedge funds, the for-rich-people-only investment firms—was insignificant. *All* the invested venture capital and private equity capital combined was around $22 billion in today's dollars. And all the money in U.S. hedge funds combined was no more than a few tens of billions. By 2007, just before the crash, those sums had grown to the equivalents of $1.4 trillion and $1.8 trillion. The bigger, more familiar business of Wall Street, brokering and advising and being the middlemen between the mass of investors and the plain old stock and bond markets, quintupled as a fraction of the U.S. economy from 1980 to the early 2000s. The growth of mutual funds specifically was even more phenomenal: in 1980 they held the present-day equivalent of about $400 billion in investments, but by 2007 it was $16 trillion, forty times as much.

That has worked out extremely well for people in the money-manipulating professions. Only the people near the top in America have gotten richer, but the well-paid people in finance have led the way. During that one generation, all the fees received by all mutual fund managers increased tenfold, to more than $100 billion a year. As recently as 1990 all the fees that went to all the people running hedge funds and private equity and venture capital firms rounded down to nothing, "near-zero," according to an exhaustive Harvard Business School study of the industry. By the early 2000s, that smallish group was raking in more than $100 billion a year as well.

I've mentioned some of the political choices and government actions (and inactions) starting in the late 1970s and '80s that allowed for these sums—the looser rules about who may borrow and lend, 401(k)s, the rules encouraging debt, the much lower taxes on investment profits. Here's another: the government agrees to pretend that those billions paid each year to people running private equity firms and hedge funds aren't huge salaries but are instead profits on investments—even though those managers don't actually own the investments. That is the "pass-through income" loophole that currently lets them pay taxes of 20 percent instead of the normal top income tax rate of 37 percent.

Within finance, the rich people in charge do let some of their gusher trickle down to their little people. Back in the old days, the early 1900s, the average employee of banks and investment firms earned a lot more than did people of the same education level who worked in other businesses. But then during the half-century following the Depression and New Deal, that pay premium for people in finance evaporated. Then in 1980 it suddenly reappeared, reverting to what it had been in the 1920s. In 1978 the average employee in finance was paid the same as the average employee in every other field—$53,000 in today's dollars. By 2000, that average finance person was paid $92,000 and everybody else just $59,000. The new post-1980s premium for *executives* in finance, however, was considerably larger—they started being paid three and four times what the equivalent executives in other fields got.

As financialization was starting, the Yale economist James Tobin, having just won the Nobel Prize, delivered a lecture called "On the Efficiency of the Financial System." It's remarkable how clearly he saw in 1984 that the financial tail was suddenly, crazily wagging our economic dog. Tobin said that although as an economist he was supposed to be unsentimental about such things, he felt "uneasy" about the change. "We are throwing more and more of our resources, including the cream of our youth, into financial activities remote from the production of goods and services." Before the rest of us were talking about America's refashioned casino economy, Tobin expressed his dismay at the new "casino aspect of our financial markets," because Wall Street was no longer just the house that always wins, it had started winning more off more suckers by rigging it as "a negative-sum game for the general public." Tobin also saw clearly how the digital revolution, barely begun, would enable the financial industry's bookkeeping gimmicks and speculative bets to grow exponentially.

> I suspect that the immense power of the computer is being harnessed to this paper economy, not to do the same transactions more economically but to balloon the quantity and variety of financial exchanges . . . facilitating nth-degree speculation which is short-sighted and inefficient.

I love his phrase *nth-degree speculation*. It covered the range of obsessive-compulsive financial speculation that would be enabled by computers and the Internet, from the mania for derivatives in the late twentieth century to high-speed trading in the twenty-first. With more and more people suddenly in the *business* of buying and selling stocks for a living, digital technology enabled more and more stock to be bought and sold, an order of magnitude increase in the scale of that churn between the 1970s and 2000. "What is clear," Tobin concluded in 1984, "is that very little of the work done by the securities industry" these days "has to do with the financing of real investment in any very direct way."

A decade or so later people had just begun referring excitedly to digital businesses collectively as the New Economy, although there was no Google or Facebook yet. The New Economy was new. In early 1998 I wrote a somewhat skeptical essay in *The New Yorker* called "The Digital Bubble." Among my arguments was that because PCs and the Internet were already essential tools in journalism and finance, early-adopting journalists and finance people might have gotten overexcited about their potential.

In 1999, however, I found myself eager to dive into this New Economy myself, to help make something cool and have fun before it was too late. I cofounded an ambitious online (and eventually print) publication called *Inside* that covered media and entertainment with a special focus on the dawning digital age for both. That experience gave me a spectacular and revelatory first-hand glimpse of the financial industry at the turn of the century.

VCs and Wall Street banks—Chase, Goldman Sachs, and Lehman Brothers, among others—required hardly any convincing to invest. One day in early 2000, an investment banker from Bear Stearns knocked on our door. *Were we financed? Did we need capital?* Incredibly, she was going up and down the grungy halls of the industrial building where we had our office, making cold calls. This, we half-joked, must be a sign of the top of the market. In all, Wall Street and others invested the equivalent of $50 million in our dot-com. That sum, flabbergasting then and even more so now, was only one-twentieth of 1 percent of the capital funneled through the 4,503 VC deals in that peak year of dot-com madness. We finished raising most of that money practically the very day that what I'd called a bubble two years earlier began to pop.

We didn't pay ourselves much, and the journalists of *Inside* did some excellent work, but it lasted only two or three more years. In the end, it was acquired by an established media company, an acquisition that earned me nothing and after which I promptly resigned. The acquirer was called Primedia, the new name for K-III, the media company owned by Henry Kravis's KKR.*

Despite *Inside*'s evanescence, the millions poured into the venture were, contrary to Tobin's warning, the financing of real investment. Indeed, as a result of the extreme growth of the financial industry from 1980 onward, its worldview and interests soon had *everything* to do with real investment, the real economy, and the real lives of Americans in very direct ways.

How did that happen? The short answer: as Wall Street's financial approach became more casino-like, that short-term, jackpot-ASAP focus also became the overriding focus of big business executives, which helped lock in as never before Wall Street's dominance of American business and American life.

*Instead of using excessive debt to buy, dismember, and quickly resell a single existing company, in this instance KKR used excessive debt to acquire publications (and then Internet start-ups) and keep them. Before buying *Inside,* for instance, Primedia bought the site About.com for the equivalent of $1 billion—but two years afterward all of Primedia was worth only a third of that. When KKR finally ditched the whole business in 2011 after two decades, it was one of its biggest disasters.

And now for the longer answer. Like so much of this story, its wellspring is Milton Friedman's 1970 announcement of the new American gospel that maximizing profit was the one and only responsibility of people running any business. In the early 1970s at the University of Rochester, whose right-wing economics program was Avis or Budget to the University of Chicago's Hertz, a libertarian professor specifically commissioned two business school colleagues, both University of Chicago–trained, to write a paper elaborating on the Friedman Doctrine.* That became, when it was finally published in 1976, "Theory of the Firm," which made the new callousness seem scientific and which became the first or second most cited business and economics paper ever. "The modern understanding" of how corporate managers should run companies, a Harvard Business School professor and *Harvard Business Review* editor declared in 2012, "has been defined to a large extent" by that paper. Its authors took a two-hundred-year-old observation of Adam Smith's—that the insufficiently "anxious vigilance" of hired company directors could result in management "negligence"—and extended it to fifty-six pages with impressive-looking equations and language of the "manager's indifference curve is tangent to a line with slope equal to –u" kind.

The argument was that if corporate executives were mere salary-earners, their interests inevitably diverged too far from the interests of the company's owners. Instead of doing their jobs with absolute financial single-mindedness, executives might start being too fair and decent, so they would overspend on "charitable contributions," get lax on "employee discipline," concern themselves too much about "personal relations ('love,' 'respect,' etc.) with employees" and "the attractiveness of the secretarial staff."

The authors' 1983 follow-up to the paper was a much shorter, more accessible one in which they dumped the math and any pretense of scholarly neutrality. "The right of managers to use corporate assets in the interest of stockholders has gradually been eroded away," they wrote, so that "special interest groups thereby transfer wealth from [shareholders] to themselves." Because they provided no examples of "erosion" or plun-

*In 1986 a certain right-wing leveraged-buyout pillager donated enough millions to persuade the university to rename its MBA program the William E. Simon Graduate School of Business.

dering by "special interests," it's unclear if they meant safety or environmental regulations or corporate taxes or what. "Big business has been cast in the role of villain" by "the intellectually unwashed," the "anti-war protesters, consumer advocates, environmentalists, and the like," who "wish to use the power of the state to pervert" the corporate status quo and to spread "the cliché that corporations have 'too much' power." That "attack on the corporation" starting in the 1960s, the two professors asserted without evidence, was the reason for "the poor performance of the stock market" during the decade or two since.

Most consequentially, they posited as a kind of scientific fact that a public company's stock price *right now* was the only meaningful measure of a company's value.* Friedman had said maximizing profits was everything. Profits, at least, are a real, objective measure of a company's success. However, this new, supposedly absolute gauge and guiding star, a stock price, is just the momentary average of all the hunches and biases of a high-strung mob of buyers and sellers, most of whom have a very superficial understanding of the company. Yet it *seems* objective, and in any case is so irresistibly simple. Plus: democracy! Giving the high-strung ill-informed mob absolute power, letting them vote every day—every hour, every minute—was maximum democracy.

By the 1980s this approach had turned into a movement with a new name and mantra: *shareholder value*. Unlike Friedman's contemptuous bah-humbuggery or Gekko's *Greed is good,* it sounded neutral, uncontroversial, practically self-evident—like Law and Economics. Victory for the new dogma was fast and total. Back in 1981, the official scripture of the Business Roundtable, the big business politburo, still held that "corporations have a responsibility, first of all, to make available to the public quality goods and services at fair prices" and to "provide jobs, and build the economy." The term *shareholder value*'s first apparent use in *The New York Times* came the following year. *Boom:* according to an economist

*The co-authors were Michael Jensen and William Meckling. Jensen moved on to Harvard Business School in the 1980s, where he remains. Weirdly and fittingly, since the 2000s he has co-written two dozen scholarly papers about leadership with Werner Erhard, the founder of est, the creepy therapeutic and motivational training business of the 1970s and '80s that trained devotees to be righteously selfish and rude. Erhard's biographer, an est devotee, was another influential right-wing American economist—and co-wrote F. A. Hayek's final book, *The Fatal Conceit: The Errors of Socialism,* in the 1980s.

who specializes in U.S. business history, "no one was talking about 'shareholder value'" in 1984, but then boom, by 1986, "everyone was talking about it." In the 1990s the Business Roundtable doctrine was amended accordingly, professing the new faith that the point of a business enterprise "is to generate economic returns to its owners," period, by being "focused on shareholder value." By then a more pointed and accurate term had been coined for the new stock-price monomania: *shareholder supremacy.*

The most obvious way to make corporate executives obsess more over their stock price was to start paying them in shares of company stock instead of cash. Until the late 1960s only about one in five senior executives at big U.S. corporations were being paid partly, and fairly minimally, in stock options. In the 1970s a new standard accounting rule allowed corporate financial statements to pretend that stock-option pay didn't really count as a corporate expense—free money!—which naturally encouraged the practice. By the 1980s a third of senior executives' pay came from stock and stock options. The IRS code was tweaked in 1993 to encourage it some more—from then on, any *cash* salary over $1 million was no longer tax-deductible at all for companies, but *stock options* remained fully deductible. So by the end of the 1990s, fewer than one in five senior executives *weren't* getting stock options, and stock constituted half their compensation. Recently options and other stock awards amounted to two-thirds of senior executive pay, and for the highest-paid ones even more.

Making executive pay more stock-based at least had a plausible rationale, like putting a shock collar on a dog to make it behave but mainly rewarding it with extra delicious treats when it's a *good* boy, *good* girl. But what's so revealing about this change during and after the 1980s was the sudden growth in America of the *amounts* of that executive pay. For forty years, from the 1940s through the '70s, the compensation of the top three executives of the largest companies had increased modestly, less than 1 percent a year, from the equivalent of $1.4 million on average to $1.8 million. Then it suddenly went crazy, particularly during the 1990s, so that by the early 2000s, those executives were receiving an average of $13 million a year. In the 2010s the average compensation of the five hundred highest-paid executives of public companies was $30 million.

Why did CEOs and other top executives suddenly start getting paid ten and twenty times as much as they'd been paid before, and lots more than their peers in the rest of the rich world? I think the answer is threefold.

First and most simply, greed and shamelessness and shameless greed had been normalized. In American capitalism's upper precincts, a kind of self-justifying orgiastic hysteria took hold, particularly in finance. It's a spectacular illustration of the tacit across-the-board decision then that economic boats would no longer rise together, that it'd be *fine* to increase inequality to staggering new levels.

Just as CEOs' compensation rose steadily but modestly for a half-century, the premiums they got compared to their employees were also more or less steady, reflecting the all-boats-rise norms of the American social contract. From the 1930s through the '80s, the top three executives at the fifty largest U.S. corporations were paid between thirty and sixty times as much as their average employee.

But then in just a dozen years, that ratio quadrupled, so that by 2003 those three top bosses on average were earning 219 times as much as their average employee. The ratio between the pay of the average worker and that of the CEO climbed even higher and remains close to three hundred. Some U.S. CEOs—at Starbucks and Disney, for instance—are paid one thousand times more than their median employee.

Paul Volcker, the former chair of the Federal Reserve and of a Wall Street investment bank, said not long before he died recently that "a kind of contagion [was] at work," the profligacy symptomatic of a mass hysteria emanating from Wall Street.

> Do the CEOs of today's top banks (or other financial institutions) really contribute five to ten times as much (in price-adjusted terms) to the success of their institution, or the economy, as their predecessors did forty or so years ago? I have my doubts. At least, it doesn't show up in the economic growth rate, certainly not in the pay of the average worker, or, more specifically, in an absence of financial crises.

The second factor driving the madness was perverse but more quasi-rational: if the goal of shareholder supremacy was for hired managers to resemble owners psychologically, didn't making executives rich enough to *live* like Scrooge McDucks have a certain sick logic? Furthermore, in the Fortune 500 boardrooms where pay packages are approved, who was going to argue that smart, hardworking people like themselves didn't finally *deserve* to be paid these vast sums? Besides, they could say and sincerely believe starting in the 1980s that "deserve" is totally subjective, that pay is determined and ratified by the *market,* and that market judgments are final . . . even though, as some of them admit privately, with a shrug and a smile, the top-executive job market isn't really a free market but more of a clubby, crony-capitalist cartel practically immune to true market forces.

Third and finally, the extra billions in compensation funneled by Wall Street to managements of all the major corporations starting three decades ago amount to a de facto gargantuan bribe to *obey Wall Street,* thus extending and consolidating Wall Street's power over the entire economy.

That last point is not a conspiracy theory. I'm not suggesting that the 1990s pay increases of 500 percent or 1,000 percent were designed with that in mind, as part of a grand master plan by the financial sector for world domination. But it did work out like that, one more powerful new tether making America more beholden to Wall Street, financialized. Nor was private equity invented by the financial sector in order to give themselves more direct, hands-on control over more and more of the economy, but that was what happened. Until the 1980s, when private equity firms arose, Wall Street bankers were just bankers, middlemen providing capital to companies but not actually presuming to run the companies, let alone remake or dismantle or loot them. Now there are more than two thousand private equity firms in America owning and running businesses worth around $2 trillion.

But finance came to dominate the rest of the corporate economy most profoundly by changing the job of the top executives at America's several thousand public companies. The number one responsibility became not producing better products or satisfying customers or planning five years ahead, but making the stock price get higher *today* and stay high.

My closest personal encounter with this crazed new corporate reality came in 1993. At the time my wife was an executive at the cable channel Nickelodeon, then in its extremely profitable heyday, and she'd just closed an important $30 million home video deal for the company with Sony. Late on the day the deal became public, Sumner Redstone, chairman of Nickelodeon's $11 billion parent company Viacom, phoned her for the first time—not to offer congratulations but to berate and scream at her, irrationally, because the announcement of her deal hadn't made the Viacom stock price move up. Just then he was particularly desperate for a higher stock price in order to acquire the Paramount movie studio more easily with stock. But she says that despite high earnings, that obsession with getting Viacom's share price higher definitely made her and her Nickelodeon colleagues reduce quality and innovation.

That's just one company run by one old guy. But evidence for this new dominance of business by Wall Street since the 1980s is vast and inarguable. For instance, in a survey in the 2000s of four hundred financial officers of public companies, as many as 78 percent of them actually admitted they would cancel projects and forgo investment that they knew would have important long-term economic benefits for their companies rather than risk disappointing Wall Street's every-ninety-days earnings expectations. Another giant irony: precisely that kind of perverse, enterprise-damaging management behavior was what the professor-godfathers of shareholder supremacy in 1976 had warned that purely salaried managers were doing. According to "Theory of the Firm," when an executive's pay isn't a function of the stock price, "his incentive to devote significant effort to creative activities such as searching out new profitable ventures falls. He may in fact avoid such ventures simply because it requires too much trouble or effort" to understand new technologies and use them to innovate. Forty years later, the research provides no consensus that paying executives in stock solves the problems of executive inattention or laziness.

Indeed, now that the overriding goal of the managers of every public company was to get the stock price up, the focus of corporate "innovation" became doing *that,* financially innovating by any means necessary. I remember when I first read in the 1980s about companies buying up masses of their own shares on the stock market as a strategy for jacking up the price—by having fewer shares in circulation, their earnings per share magically rose—it struck me as . . . not a con, maybe, but not exactly kosher. As with almost all the arcane changes going on in the political economy at the time, however, my response was to forget about it and move on. But I've now learned that my natural civilian suspicion of the practice had been encoded in federal securities law since the New Deal: buying back shares of your own stock was tantamount to illegal market manipulation, insider trading in the spirit if not the letter of the law, and it had been essentially outlawed.

But then in 1982, without any real debate and without almost anybody outside finance noticing, the SEC did away with that ban.

At first managements were hesitant to *go for it,* continuing to spend as they always had, trying to use their profits to pay dividends to shareholders and grow their companies rather than concentrating on hacking the stock market. So in 1984 a pair of big-time Wall Street executives wrote a *New York Times* article exhorting companies to take advantage of this fantastic new zone of financial lawlessness. Reagan's giveaways to big business, tax rate cuts of 40 percent, and "tax credits and other benefits for corporations," they wrote, had provided companies "unprecedented" amounts of cash, "one of the biggest cash buildups in corporate history." In this "stunning and strange" new world, conventional capitalist logic had been overthrown. To use company money in the old-fashioned slow-payoff ways, to "reinvest" it in "new capacity," to build for future growth in the actual business, was now a chump's game. Since the bull market for stocks that had started in 1982 had ended and prices were now dropping, these two Wall Street geniuses asked and answered a question: "Who will support stock prices? It could and should be the companies themselves." They also pushed the new American truism that perception *is* reality, that as a display of corporate self-esteem buying your own stock is fabulous PR.

The year that manifesto was published companies bought back only a few billion dollars' worth of their stock, but as the decade ended five years later, the annual average was tens of billions. That's when Jack Welch (Jack Welch!) announced that GE (GE!) was going to buy back the equivalent of $21 billion worth of its own stock because that was so much easier than "going out and taking a wild swing" at developing new technologies or new businesses. It was the biggest single buyback yet. Welch was acting even more like a Wall Street guy, and Wall Street redoubled its love for him. Unquestionably a new party had started.

The largest U.S. companies went from spending 4 percent of their annual profits buying back stock in the early 1980s to 30 percent in the late 1980s, then in the '90s around half. During just the five years leading up to the crash of 2008, the number of buybacks by the biggest companies quadrupled. In 2007, the four hundred biggest companies spent

89 percent of their profits to buy shares of their own stocks, and most corporate earnings are still spent that way. During the last decade, U.S. airlines, for instance, spent 96 percent of their available cash buying back stock to jack up their share prices—shares of which the executives of those airlines personally sold for $1.6 billion during that same period. Buybacks effectively became obligatory in corporate America, done by 85 or 90 percent of big public companies. The cost lately has been around $1 trillion a year, three times what businesses spend on research and development.

Even in a short-term financial sense for investors, it might be a waste. One study published in 2011 for chief financial officers concluded that stock buybacks "may not yield as much value as investing in a company's business." Company executives tend to buy back their shares when the price is excitingly high, and for three-quarters of the companies, the return on investment was subpar. During the period of the study, the stock market was down 19 percent, but the share prices for the 29 companies (out of 461) that *didn't* do buybacks went *up* on average by 40 percent.

How much do companies use buybacks to fool shareholders and the markets about the actual health and prospects of their companies? How much do executives, each being paid with stock and options worth millions and sometimes hundreds of millions, use buybacks simply to enrich themselves? The new SEC rule in 1982 didn't define what might constitute unacceptable deception or fraud when it came to buybacks, so in the thirty-eight years since, no company has been prosecuted for abusing the practice. In 2018 an SEC commissioner who happens to be an NYU law professor specializing in this area did a study of this problem, and he makes a compelling case for systematic abuse. Right after a buyback becomes public, the average executive sells five times as many of his or her shares as usual. "When executives unload significant amounts of stock upon announcing a buyback, they often benefit from short-term price pops at the expense of long-term investors." That is, he found, three months after a buyback is announced, "firms with insider cashouts," as they're called, "*underperform* the other firms . . . by more than 8 percent."

This bizarre new normal is a vivid display and powerful underpinning of the de facto enslavement of the economy to Wall Street and to shareholder supremacy dogma. And speaking of dogma, if the stock market at large isn't correctly valuing a company, thus requiring its CEO to step in and correct that mistake by spending billions on stock purchases, doesn't that cast doubt on our absolute faith in the efficient free market? In this way, massive stock buybacks are like the capitalist version of Christians who shake and scream to prove that the holy spirit is *real* and inhabiting *them.* But if you sincerely think the market is undervaluing your stock because investors just don't *get* your amazing company, then why not buy all of your shares back and go private?

Essentially every CEO now does buybacks because everyone else does them. Their stock-price-based performances will be judged this quarter and this year against all those other CEOs, so it's a mad recursive loop. How is the result not a stock market bubble—an extremely long-lasting bubble but a bubble nevertheless? It's unsustainable: you can take 10 percent of your company's shares out of circulation, then 20 percent, then 30 percent or even (as IBM has done over the last two decades) 60 percent, but you can't keep doing that forever.

For a decade, since before she was in the Senate, Elizabeth Warren has been saying that stock buybacks provide only a "sugar high for companies in the short term." That metaphor seems too benign. It's more like the high—and addiction—produced by cocaine, another craze that swept America in the 1970s and '80s, and that makes addicts neglect their important but mundane duties and long-term health in favor of the next jolt of artificial self-confidence.*

Consider this remarkable fact: from 2010 through 2019, *most of the money* invested in U.S. stocks came not from true investors but from companies buying back their own stocks. If it "makes sense" for corporations to devote such a stupendous fraction of our economic resources to stock buybacks, it's because the rules of our political economy were written—that is, *rewritten*—forty years ago to make it so.†

*Stock buybacks aren't performance-*enhancing* drugs, because those actually make athletes run faster and hit baseballs farther.

†Another epic irony: although Charles Koch is responsible for horrific damage—by promoting right-wing political economics and climate change denial, and by corrupting government with profits from his fossil fuel company—Koch Industries is a model of responsible old-fashioned corporate governance: as a private company, not beholden to Wall Street or investor hysteria, it has no public shares to buy back, so it reinvests almost all its profits in the company and holds on to the companies it acquires.

• • •

When *shareholder value* became a new capitalist article of faith in the 1980s, the word *shareholder* was being imbued with a kind of sacred democratic sheen, like *citizen*. I own stocks, you probably own stocks, half of us are shareholders. But we should all keep in mind that the 90 percent of Americans worth less than $10 million own only 12 percent of all shares. In other words, it probably made personal financial sense for most rich people to support the shareholder supremacy movement. However, for most American shareholders (let alone the half of Americans who don't own stocks at all), maximizing corporate profits at the expense of all other economic and social goals and values now looks like a bad trade-off. What's more, being a shareholder is *really not* like being a citizen. It's temporary. Indeed, as shareholder supremacy was turned into an inviolate American principle, the average shareholder was less and less like a true owner and more like a short-term renter. In the 1970s a given shareholder in a given company owned shares for more than five years on average. By 2000 that average ownership period was only a year, and in the full digital age, with lots of people holding shares for days or hours or fractions of a second, the average period of ownership has shortened to a few months.

The final piece of financialization comes from the enormous growth of the so-called institutional investors, in particular mutual funds. Owning a share of stock isn't the same as being a citizen of a corporate domain, but stock ownership used to be much more directly democratic, and the finance industry didn't run the show. In the 1950s individual Americans directly owned more than 90 percent of shares. My parents kept their paper certificates of the few stocks they owned in a filing cabinet in our house. Even by 1980, only a quarter of Americans' stock holdings were managed by people paid to do that, and the biggest mutual funds held only 4 percent of all shares. But then everything changed. By the 2000s, *most* stock shares were being bought and sold by professional asset managers. The several biggest mutual funds are now the majority shareholders of 90 percent of the four hundred biggest companies, and such institutional investors control 80 percent of all the stock in all U.S. public companies.

It's a huge concentration of economic power. I always imagined *the market* as a vast democratic hive mind producing the self-correcting wisdom of crowds. But for practical purposes, the financial market has been reduced to a small group of people, in the low thousands, who share a mindset.

That's financialization. So in addition to the new power of stock-price obsession over corporate executives, and VCs often effectively running companies they fund, and private equity guys actually running companies they take over, the big mutual funds also now closely meddle in the operations of most big companies, ranging from being backseat drivers to co-pilots sitting on boards. In effect, the managers of the big funds have made themselves corporate America's national shadow management, a kind of upper house of the congress of the capitalist party of the U.S.A.

Mutual fund companies are reincarnated equivalents of the excessively powerful trusts that made us enact antitrust laws in the first place. Economists and others across the ideological spectrum now worry about the effects of this new stratum of command and control. Because mutual funds have controlling interests in the big dominant competitors in almost every major business—food, drugs, airlines, telecommunications, banking, seeds, whatever—they aren't naturally inclined to make those rival companies compete aggressively against one another. As the top dogs in a small, not-very-competitive oligopoly, why wouldn't Fidelity and Vanguard and the others see their comfortably less competitive arrangements as the optimal model for the companies they control? Until 1980 the stock market generally valued smaller companies more highly than big companies. But then as mutual funds gobbled up more and more stock and effectively *became* the market, they overthrew that conventional wisdom. With their new power, institutional investors decided for the rest of us that companies should be as big as possible, regardless of any damage that caused to our economy and society. Because if the stock price is *everything*, whatever got companies to that end—less competition and thus less innovation and lower salaries, draconian cost-cutting—was justified.

• • •

At the end of their exhaustive 2013 paper called "The Growth of Finance," consisting almost entirely of quantitative research, two Harvard Business School professors pose the right question: "Has society benefitted from the recent growth of the financial sector?" Financialization was okay in a couple of ways, they conclude—ubiquitous credit cards allowed people to smooth out the ups and downs of their personal cash flows, people who own stocks sensibly diversified, and newer companies got much easier access to investment capital. But otherwise, not so much. The hysterically expanding credit industry "made it easier for many households to overinvest in housing and consume in excess of sustainable levels." The enormous increase in the number of professional financial people neither made stock prices more rational nor improved corporate management. And they conclude it's also bad, "costly to society," that all the easy money going to the finance industry "lure[s] talented individuals away from potentially more productive sectors" such as science and engineering. In 1965 only 11 percent of new Harvard MBAs went into finance; in 1985, 41 percent did. In the early 1970s, 6 percent of new Harvard College graduates went into finance; by the 2000s, 28 percent did, and that fraction has continued growing.

When the Nobel economist James Tobin gave that lecture in 1984, he described financial professionals' suddenly ballooning pay as "high private rewards disproportionate to social productivity." One of the ways the alliance of the right and the rich and finance was just then managing to change the social contract and transform our political economy was to *disallow* such moral judgments concerning money—to convince enough of the correct people that there *can be no such thing* as disproportionate private rewards in a market economy. They convinced people that the market and only the market must be the supreme authority, that only it can determine what's fair or unfair, right or wrong. Thus began America's radical increase in economic inequality—fully a quarter of which, research shows, might be attributable to just the increased pay and wealth that has gone since the 1980s to the people working in finance.

What's more, all those smart financial professionals' advice and judgments about what stocks and bonds to buy and sell, so-called "active management," apparently don't even make clients more money. In other words, much of this financial priesthood is superfluous, unnecessary. The evidence in study after study is that active management of financial portfolios by professionals "is not directly beneficial to investors on average . . . especially after taking into account fees." In 2016, for instance, two-thirds of the professional portfolio managers buying and selling shares in the four hundred biggest companies did worse for their investors than if the clients had simply bought shares in all those four hundred companies. And of the pros managing investments in smaller companies, 85 *percent* did worse than the untouched-by-human-hands average of those stocks' prices. Of course, that's just their performance in one year; over longer periods of time, they do even worse.* Even hedge funds, asset management for which the rich are so eager to pay such premiums, mainly make investors *feel special,* which all luxury products do: since the mid-1990s, hedge funds on average have basically done about the same as the stock market.

It's ironic that a realm presenting itself as relentlessly quantitative and rational indulges in such magical thinking.

It's ironic that just as we entered an economic era all about eliminating inessential middlemen and corporate bloat, one bloated sector filled with inessential middlemen, finance, has flourished as never before.

It's ironic that one of the rationales for America's 1980s makeover was to revive the heroic American tradition of risk-taking—given that so much of the story has turned out to be about reckless financiers insulating themselves from risk by shifting it to customers and, through the government, to taxpayers.

It's ironic that finance, a service industry created to help business and the rest of us, so bubbly and booming on and on these last four decades, has mainly helped itself. "There is no clear evidence," the chief financial industry regulator of the U.K. and former vice-chairman of Merrill Lynch Europe concluded in 2010, "that the growth in the scale and complexity of the financial system in the rich developed world over the last 20 to 30 years has driven increased growth or stability."

A final disturbing effect of financialization can't be proven with statistics or experts' quotes. It's the damage to the human spirit that comes from making everything everyone is or does literally and strictly reducible to dollars and cents, and how such a cynical system makes everyone in

*Americans have started to realize the fakery, shifting more and more of their investments into funds that simply buy the whole market, but half of stock mutual funds are still under "active" management.

it more cynical. A finance-obsessed society makes us each a little less human, a lot more of an abstraction. An employee of an LBO'd company is *only* a cost that needs to be kept down or eliminated. A shopper is a credit rating. Somebody with a home mortgage is an anonymous revenue stream—and barely that after she's transmogrified into one infinitesimal bit of a mortgage-backed security. In all this, financialization has done what people back in the 1950s and '60s and '70s worried and warned that the Communists would do if they took over: centralize control of the economy, turn Americans into interchangeable cogs serving an inhumane system, and allow only a well-connected elite to live well. Extreme capitalism resembles Communism: yet another whopping irony.

When John Kenneth Galbraith wrote *American Capitalism* in the 1950s, the idea that American capitalism was in any sense run by a financial cabal, Wall Street, seemed like an obsolete cartoon. "As the banker, as a symbol of economic power, passed into the shadows," he wrote, "his place was taken by the giant industrial corporation," which

> was much more plausible. The association of power with the banker had always depended on the somewhat tenuous belief in a "money trust"—in the notion that the means for financing the initiation and expansion of business enterprises was concentrated in the hands of a few men. The ancestry of this idea was in Marx's doctrine of finance capital; it was not susceptible to statistical or other empirical verification at least in the United States.

But what struck this leftish economist in the bright, new, modern American 1950s as a ridiculous, antique caricature of our system came true starting in the 1980s, after the laissez-faire dogma of the old days was revived. It was a kind of systemic time travel: we returned to a level of economic inequality as extreme as it had been in the 1920s and earlier, entered our second Gilded Age, and our second era of unregulated, swashbuckling robber barons creating cartels and monopolies. We've gone back to a political economy closer to the one that existed in the 1870s and '80s, when Marx (with Engels) was finishing up his vision of how industrial capitalism would evolve into a new financial capitalism dominated by trading in the "fictitious capital" of stocks and credit.

In *Capital,* Marx reviled various kinds of capitalist middlemen as "parasites" (as well as "vampires"), and near the end of the final volume, published in the 1890s, he discussed "a new kind of parasite in the guise of company promoters, speculators, and merely nominal directors; an entire system of swindling and cheating with respect to the promotion of companies, issue of shares and share dealings." Blame Marx for the horrors of Communism if you want, but the guy had some prescient insights about the capitalist future.

Until 1980, a more reasonable metaphor than Marx's parasite for our financial industry was the remora. Those are the fish that attach themselves to sharks and whales for the bits of leftover food and the essential oxygen that the free ride provides. Remoras apparently provide benefits to the big sea creatures by eating those hosts' . . . *parasites*. A purely parasitic relationship, on the other hand, "is one in which one organism, the parasite, lives off of another organism, the host, harming it and possibly causing death." A lot of the financial players since the 1970s have indeed evolved into parasites, like tapeworms. Tapeworms live in the gut, to which they attach themselves by "hooks" and "suckers," then "get food by eating the host's partly digested food, depriving the host of nutrients." They can grow hideously large, many feet long, and live inside hosts for decades. Thinking about the future of our political economy, though, I was heartened when I read that "hosts also develop ways of getting rid of or protecting themselves from parasites."

I know that many people in finance think authors and critics and second-guessers like me are parasites. Undoubtedly even more of them consider individual Americans dependent on direct government assistance to be parasites. As William Simon made his midlife career switch in the late 1970s from Wall Street drone and U.S. treasury secretary to right-wing foundation president and leveraged buyout wizard, he was frank on exactly this topic. "The 'ethics' of egalitarianism must be repudiated," he wrote, because "achievers must not be penalized or parasites rewarded."

15

Workers of the New World, You Lose

Not every way in which our political economy has gotten worse for most Americans during the last forty years was entirely the result of swinish policy choices on behalf of finance and big business and the well-to-do. Some changes were global and more or less unstoppable, in particular concerning how and where jobs could be done—that is, workers in poor countries and machines in this country were doing more and more of the work which for a century Americans had been well paid to do.

After the amazingly prosperous three-decade run following World War II, by 1980 the economies of almost every developed country were growing more slowly. During the 1950s and '60s, the U.S. economy had grown by as much as 3 percent per year per person. Then during the 1970s, '80s, and '90s, growth shifted into a slower gear, averaging only 2 percent per person per year. One way of thinking about that change is that after the three postwar decades of exceptional expansion, the rate of growth in America and the rest of the rich world returned to normal, about where it had been for more than a century. At that more ordinary speed, the U.S. economy took twenty-three years to double in size instead of just seventeen—unfortunate but not necessarily disastrous.

Governments elsewhere in the rich world figured out how to adapt, adjust, and share the pain of slower growth in their own globalizing, automating economies. In America, however, as a result of the new right-wing, favor-the-rich, big-business-rules charter, only the well-educated and well-to-do continued to get bigger pieces of our more slowly growing economic pie. And not only did the *size* of the pieces of pie served to the unlucky American majority stop getting bigger, the *quality* of those relatively skimpy pieces got worse: jobs and healthcare and retirements became more insecure, cities and regions were left to wither, college education became much less affordable, and upward mobility was a longer shot than ever.

I've relied on the metaphor of an American economic pie to convey how only the luckiest few kept getting served good, larger pieces as it grew. But that may be another metaphor that's too benign for how the economy changed starting in the 1970s and '80s. It's more like this: after surviving the Depression and winning the war, Americans cruised along together for almost four decades in glorious sunny weather that seemed like it would go on forever—then we hit rough seas, and suddenly the first-class passengers, saying they hoped everyone else could join them later, grabbed all the lifeboats for themselves and sped off to their own private luxury ship anchored in a safe harbor.

Joseph Schumpeter was a brilliant economist at Harvard in the first half of the twentieth century who approved of entrepreneurs but also thought capitalism would eventually be replaced by some kind of democratic socialism—not through workers' uprisings but by means of a subtle, nonviolent process. The "perennial gale of *creative destruction*" would drive this evolution of advanced economic systems, he wrote (without italics) in 1942, right after the Depression, "the same process of industrial mutation—if I may use that biological term—that incessantly revolutionizes the economic structure from within, incessantly destroying the old one, incessantly creating a new one. This process of Creative Destruction is the essential fact about capitalism."

I feel sorry for Schumpeter, who died in 1950, because three decades after his death, with the rise of new-fangled old-fashioned free-market mania, he got famous when that phrase was revived and reduced to a meme, repeated endlessly to explain and justify the sudden obsolescence of blue-collar production workers (and then the lesser white-collar workers). "Creative destruction" was popularized in a way Schumpeter hadn't meant it, as a celebratory sorry-suckers catchphrase for the way rootin'-tootin' Wild West American capitalism permanently *is,* where the rich and tough and lucky win and losers lose hard. In the 1980s the term and its distorted meaning were enthusiastically embraced by the right and accepted with a shrug by college-educated liberals whose livelihoods didn't look likely to be creatively destroyed anytime soon by competition from computers or foreigners.

We liberals had heard of Schumpeter, and we knew a bit about the industrial revolutions at the turns of the previous two centuries. My professor in the 1970s, Daniel Bell, had predicted this difficult turn more than two decades earlier in a book called *Work and Its Discontents: The Cult of Efficiency in America.* Thanks to automation, he said, "many workers, particularly older ones, may find it difficult ever again to find suitable jobs. It is also likely that small geographical pockets of the United States may find themselves becoming 'depressed areas' as old industries fade or are moved away." We college-educateds were instructed to take it as a truism that painful transitions like these were just how history and economic progress inevitably unfolded, and that after a difficult patch—for the actual, you know, *workers,* in what we started calling the Rust Belt—things would eventually sort themselves out.

That long view, however, tended to omit the history that had made the previous industrial revolutions come out okay in America—the countervailing forces that took a century to build, all the laws and rules and unions and other organizations created to protect citizens and workers and keep the system reasonably fair and balanced. It was exactly that web of countervailing forces that, at exactly that moment, was being systematically weakened.

The fraction of all American workers employed in manufacturing peaked in the 1950s, but the actual *number* of those jobs had held steady through the 1960s and '70s. In 1980 manufacturing workers' salaries and benefits still provided the livings for a third of all Americans. But then came this latest wave of creative destruction, and that was that. The collapse of the steel industry came right around 1980—spectacularly, because most of us hadn't seen it coming, and steel plants were so gigantic, and geographically concentrated, each one the economic foundation of a town or city or whole region. Those were well-paid union jobs that had seemed secure. In and around Pittsburgh during the 1980s, unemployment rates at their lingering height—15 percent, 20 percent, 27 percent—were the same as the rates all over America during the Depression of the 1930s (and once again in 2020).

It wasn't just the steel industry that was undone, of course. Almost 3 million U.S. manufacturing jobs disappeared in just three years. In 1980 one of the huge textile company Parkdale Mills's plants in South Carolina employed 2,000 people—but by the 1990s, thanks to more efficient machinery, that factory was producing just as much fabric with only 140 employees, 93 percent fewer workers. That's an extreme case but a microcosm of what was starting to happen throughout manufacturing. By the end of the century, U.S. factories were producing two-thirds more things than they had in 1980, but they were doing so with a third fewer workers.

And when new machines couldn't do the work more cheaply than people, then people in poor countries could become our slavish machine equivalents as never before. Starting in the late 1980s and especially the 1990s, more and more of our manufacturing work was done in China and other poor countries. Between 1990 and the early 2000s, the annual value of things made in China and bought by Americans increased twelvefold. Many millions of U.S. factory jobs were "offshored" during the 1990s and early 2000s, many of them to China. From 1980 until now, the fraction of Americans working in factories shrank by two-thirds, from more than one in four workers to fewer than one in twelve.

The new jobs to which laid-off workers moved, during and after the 1980s, tended to be much worse than the ones they'd had. A massive study by economists of "high-tenure workers laid off then from distressed firms" in Pennsylvania—including steelworkers—found that years after they lost those jobs, their incomes remained much lower. For instance, the average Pennsylvania worker whose job disappeared in early 1982 had been earning the equivalent of $53,000 a year, but six years later he or she was earning only $34,000 in today's dollars. That $19,000-per-year reduction in average earnings was as if they'd all been involuntarily transported back in time to the 1940s, those three decades of accumulated American prosperity instantly erased.

As I explained earlier, for centuries new technologies had kept making it possible for each worker to produce more stuff, and it was that, improving productivity, that allowed economies to grow, and more people to live well. For the last century and a half, from the late 1800s on, productivity in America increased most years by 2 percent or more. There were ups and downs in the trend line, of course—dramatically down during the Great Depression, exceptionally up for some years right after World War II. Along the way, new technologies made some jobs uneconomic and unnecessary. But because of the grand economic bargain we had in America to bring everyone along through those ups and downs and changes, to share the increasing wealth, *everyone's* standard of living increased over time, slower some years, faster other years, but always in sync. During the three postwar decades, U.S. productivity doubled, and the size of the U.S. economy doubled, and the average American's share of the economy doubled. Then, from the late 1970s through the '80s, we experienced a subpar slough, a fifteen-year period when productivity increased by just 1 to 2 percent a year instead of 2 to 3 percent.*

As so many switches flipped, nobody would see the full effects until decades later. The productivity of workers and economic growth both continued going up, albeit more slowly, almost doubling since the 1970s. But for the first time, *most Americans' incomes* essentially flatlined for forty years. Instead of everyone, rich and middle and poor, all becoming more prosperous simultaneously, only the incomes of a lucky top fifth kept rising as they had in the past. Around 1980, the Great Uncoupling of the rich from the rest began.

It wasn't just that serious salary increases started going only to a small group of fortunate workers. The share of money that went to *all employees,* rather than to corporate shareholders and business owners, also became smaller. Until 1980, America's national split of "gross domestic income" was around 60–40 in favor of workers, but then it began dropping and is now approaching 50–50. That change amounts to almost $1 trillion a year, an annual average of around $5,000 that each person with a job *isn't* being paid. Instead, every household in the top 1 percent of earners has been getting $700,000 extra every year. It undoubtedly has been the largest and fastest upward redistribution of wealth in history.

*We entered a similar productivity slough after the Great Recession, which seemed to be ending just before the 2020 recession.

This historic Great Uncoupling, in which America's economy grows but most Americans don't get fair shares of the growth, was the result of the public and private policy choices described in this book and hundreds more. I don't think most of the people who engineered and benefited from the remaking of the political economy consciously intended for most of their fellow citizens' incomes to stagnate forever. Driven variously by ideology and selfishness, big business and the rich wanted more wealth and power for themselves, but surely most wouldn't have *objected* if everyone's boats had kept rising together after 1980, if the middle-of-the-pack family earning $50,000 then was now earning $100,000 instead of $55,000.

But there's the disingenuous rub. It's as if I'd abandoned my wife and children and thereafter gave them as little money as I could get away with legally, but said sincerely that I hadn't *intended* to make their lives so difficult but, you know, *sorry*. Because the major drivers of America's economic transformation after 1980—from low taxes to the laissez-faire unleashing of business to reflexive opposition to new social programs to the crushing of organized labor—guaranteed the massively unfair outcome. And while perhaps the CEOs at the Business Roundtable in the 1970s didn't explicitly say their mission was to make their employees much more insecure and thus more compliant and cowering—by laying off thousands at a time, phasing out pensions, moving factories overseas, and eliminating competitors—that's what happened.

The shocking cataclysm in America's big, iconic heavy industries, steel and cars, along with the longer-term slowing of economic growth generally, created a chronic widespread dread and anxiety about the economic future. The economic right and big business *used* that confusion and fear to get free rein to achieve their larger goals. *Times are tough! Government can't save you! Adapt or die!* But then when the acute crises passed and the economy stabilized in the late 1980s and '90s, and productivity and economic growth returned to their long-term historical norms, the norms of *fairness* were *not* restored. The system that had been reengineered to better serve big business and the rich remained in place.

Because I'm an American who graduated college and as an adult haven't been paid to do physical labor, I've never thought of myself as a *worker*.

It's too bad, I think, because since the 1960s that linguistic distinction has reinforced the divide between people who do white-collar and blue-collar work. We're nearly all workers, rather than people who live off investments. Looking back now, probably the single most significant cause *and* effect of the big 1980s change in our political economy was the disempowerment of workers vis-à-vis employers.

A few years ago when I first read the book *Postcapitalism* by the British business journalist Paul Mason, I came across a paragraph that stopped me short because it seemed so hyperbolic and reductive. But now it seems to me very much closer to true than untrue. In the 1970s and '80s, Mason says, the political leaders from the economic right

> drew a conclusion that has shaped our age: that a modern economy cannot coexist with an organized working class. . . . The destruction of labour's bargaining power . . . was the essence of the entire [conservative] project: it was a means to all the other ends . . . not free markets, not fiscal discipline, not sound money, not privatization and offshoring—not even globalization. All these things were byproducts or weapons of its main endeavor: to remove organized labor from the equation.

As the modern corporation emerged and grew and multiplied starting in the late 1800s, so did unions. In the 1880s fewer than 5 percent of American workers belonged to a union, and in 1930 it was still only around 10 percent. But after the Depression and New Deal and World War II, more than a third of the U.S. private workforce was unionized, and in 1950 a large majority of blue-collar workers in the North belonged to unions. In the late 1950s state laws started changing so that teachers and other public employees could also join unions, and eventually more than a third of them became unionized. As labor unions grew larger and more powerful, negotiating higher salaries, America's wealth was more and more equally shared.

As I've said, by the 1960s and '70s, Americans were taking for granted the benefits and prosperity that organized labor had been crucial in achieving for workers in general, and many were becoming disenchanted with unions. After the unionization of workers at corporations peaked in the 1950s, that overall percentage slid to a quarter by the early 1970s—just when big business and the right started powerfully organizing capital to *really* fight against organized labor.

In 1979 moviegoers, especially liberal moviegoers, made a hit out of the movie *Norma Rae*. Sally Field won an Academy Award for playing the title role. It was based on the true story of a J. P. Stevens textile factory worker in North Carolina who organized a union and a successful strike—which led quickly to the unionization of three thousand textile workers at other plants in the same town. The real events had happened only a few years earlier, so the movie encouraged viewers to imagine, incorrectly, that U.S. labor power wasn't half-dead—yet it simultaneously played as wistful nostalgia.

The political winds had definitely shifted. Also in 1979 public TV producers at WGBH in Boston were developing a ten-episode dramatic series called *Made in USA* about the history of the labor movement. They'd planned on having unions put up a quarter of the budget—but in early 1980, the president of PBS in Washington stepped in to forbid that, because unions had a political agenda. After it was pointed out that Milton Friedman's PBS series *Free to Choose,* airing right then (including the antiunion episode "Who Protects the Worker?"), was funded by corporations and rich people with a political agenda, PBS relented, but after the controversy and then Reagan's election in the fall, that project died.

Consider what happened to political action committees, the tremendous new sources of campaign donations. From 1976 on, another two or three business-funded PACs were created *every week* on average, compared to one union-funded PAC every few months. In the early 1970s, union PACs were still donating *most* of the PAC money going to U.S. Senate and House candidates; by 1980 they were donating not just much less than the business groups but less than a quarter of the total given by all PACs.

In 1977 President Carter declined to work hard for a bill that would've given construction workers greater power to strike, and it was defeated in the House, where Democrats had a two-to-one majority. The next year the same Congress was considering a labor law change that would've made it easier for all workers to unionize. The CEOs of fully unionized GM and GE were disinclined to oppose the bill, but their fellow Business Roundtable member who ran the barely unionized Sears persuaded them to lobby against it—and capitalist solidarity carried the day. It too was defeated. Carter and most Democrats shrugged.

That was a final straw for the president of the United Automobile Workers (and Lee Iacocca's good pal), Douglas Fraser. At the time, the White House regularly convened a semiofficial Labor-Management Group that brought together CEOs, many of them members of the new Roundtable, with union leaders. "I know that some of the business representatives . . . argued inside the Business Roundtable for neutrality" on the bill, Fraser wrote in his letter resigning from the White House group in 1978, "but having lost, they helped to bankroll (through the Roundtable and other organizations) the dishonest and ugly multimillion-dollar [publicity and lobbying] campaign against labor law reform" that "stands as the most vicious, unfair attack upon the labor movement in more than 30 years. Corporate leaders knew it was not the 'power grab by Big Labor' that they portrayed it to be." He went on to deliver an impassioned real-time critique of the axiomatic shift just beginning:

> The leaders of industry, commerce and finance in the United States have broken and discarded the fragile, unwritten compact previously existing during a past period of growth and progress. . . . At virtually every level, I discern a demand by business for docile government and unrestrained corporate individualism. Where industry once yearned for subservient unions, it now wants no unions at all.

If destroying labor's bargaining power was the essence of the project of the economic right, its essential act was performed single-handedly by Ronald Reagan six months into his presidency.

The typical air traffic controller was an archetypal Reagan Democrat—a white man from a working-class background without a college degree but highly skilled and well paid. In the late 1960s, the controllers in New York had started a union, the Professional Air Traffic Controllers Organization (PATCO), which before long almost all controllers in the United States joined. Two weeks before the 1980 election, it was one of the very few unions to endorse Reagan against the preachy, unreliable Democrat in the White House. "You supports them that supports you," one of the top PATCO leaders explained, "and you don't support them that don't support you." That is, when you can't count on Democrats *or* Republicans to support you on your economic issues, you might as well support the ones who agree with you about hippies and professors and welfare recipients.

Two weeks after Reagan became president, his administration began negotiating a new contract with the controllers, who were federal employees. The ultimate leverage any union has, obviously, is the threat that its members will stop working if they and their employers can't come to terms. The same bit of the U.S. criminal code that prohibits any federal employee from advocating the overthrow of the government, enacted in 1955 during the anti-Communist frenzy, also makes it a crime for any of them to go out on strike. A couple of times a year during the 1960s and '70s, groups of federal employees had stopped working to get what they wanted, including a weeklong wildcat strike by a minority of postal workers in 1970, but no federal workers had ever officially threatened to cut off essential services to get a better labor contract. Push had never really come to shove.

PATCO was thus in a singularly powerful and precarious position. No civilian federal employees had more strike-threat leverage than air traffic controllers: all of U.S. aviation and thus the U.S. economy depended on them. Right before their contract expired in the spring of 1981, the brand-new president had survived his assassination attempt, which increased Americans' approval of him to 68 percent. The controllers were already earning the equivalent of $100,000 a year on average and now asked for a 40 percent increase in pay, a four-day work week, and retirement after twenty years. Union leaders agreed to a lesser deal, but then the members rejected it.

Liberals were not in solidarity with PATCO. A *New York Times* editorial headlined BRING THE CONTROLLERS DOWN TO EARTH said that "the Reagan Administration is making a more than reasonable offer" in response to "the union's exorbitant terms," and a later editorial said that if "President Reagan were now to sweeten the deal . . . he would only be inviting other Government employees in key positions to exploit their leverage." In *The Washington Monthly,* twenty-three-year-old Jonathan

Alter, just out of Harvard and not yet a celebrated liberal journalist and author, wrote that the episode "proved" Reagan and the right correct, that the federal government was bloated, "as badly featherbedded as we've feared."

The lead-up to the strike was a big national story for months, then the biggest for some weeks. First thing in the morning on the first Monday in August 1981, when the *Times* ran another anti-PATCO editorial (HOLDING UP AMERICA), the thirteen thousand controllers stopped working. Reagan said they had two days to come back, and on Wednesday the 90 percent who didn't were fired—and prohibited from holding any federal job ever again.* Two months later the fired strikers' replacements took a vote to get rid of the union, and that was that.

The strike-day *Times* editorial said that it was "hard to feel much sympathy for the controllers." Sure. In retrospect, however, it's hard not to feel some sympathy for them, and even more, it's hard not to feel deep regret that so many left-of-center Americans had abandoned the fundamental commitment to the *idea* of unions. The air traffic controllers' strike and the right-wing president's instant, unchallenged destruction of their union was the turning point. Losing that battle, American organized labor effectively lost the war.

As part of the New Deal, a fundamental federal law had been passed guaranteeing employees of businesses the right to organize unions and go on strike. Three years later, in 1938, the Supreme Court ruled that the Mackay Radio & Telegraph Company had broken that law after a strike by refusing specifically to rehire its organizers—but the court's decision also said, in passing, that not only were companies free to hire replacement workers during strikes but that after a strike ended, companies were free to keep employing the strikebreakers. The strikers' only right was to be rehired for any additional jobs that might open up soon. The logic of that Mackay Doctrine, that strikers aren't technically *fired* if they're replaced by scabs, is absurd. Despite that 1938 decision, the American *norm* that emerged out of the New Deal was that for companies to replace striking workers was unacceptably unfair—a norm that remained in force until its spectacular de facto repeal by Reagan during the air traffic controllers' strike.

*After a dozen years, the Clinton administration lifted that ban on federal employment.

In the years right after the 1981 strike, companies all over the country made and remade the point again and again—big strike, strikebreakers brought in, national press attention, strike continued and disastrously failed, unions dissolved or rendered impotent. And the old Mackay Doctrine, which had sat on a back shelf for half a century, let them.

One of the big American mining companies realized that the moment for good-old-days antiunion ferocity had returned: a year after a strike began in Arizona and the company replaced striking copper miners with strikebreakers, its workers all over the Southwest were persuaded to do away with their unions.

A year after that the meat company Hormel demanded that its slaughterhouse workers take a one-quarter cut in wages that hadn't gone up in almost a decade. Workers at a Minnesota plant went on strike, strikebreakers were hired, and most of the strikers never got their jobs back.

International Paper had tripled its profits from 1985 to 1987—but as a recently public company, its 10 percent rate of profit wasn't good enough anymore to satisfy the demands of shareholder supremacy, so its executives decided to end the company's long history of worker-friendliness. In a town in Maine where the International Paper mill was everything, and typical workers earned the equivalent of $87,000 a year, the union made an opening bid to renew their contract with no wage increase at all. The company responded with a plan to lay off 15 percent of them and, for those remaining, do away with extra pay on weekends and holidays. The workers went on strike, the company hired replacements from out of town, a year later the strikers surrendered, and sorry, no job openings, bye.

Hiring strikebreakers, for decades a rarity in corporate America because it had been considered old-fashioned and brutish, was *back,* old-fashioned and tough: during the late 1980s, more than a third of the companies where workers went on strike threatened to replace the strikers, and half of those did.

The deterrent effect was extreme. Strikes very quickly became almost obsolete, like vinyl LPs and rotary-dial telephones. Between World War II and 1980, our great era of prosperity and increasing equality, almost every year there had been at least two hundred strikes involving at least a thousand workers. Some years there were more than four hundred big strikes. Since 1981, there haven't been a hundred big strikes in any year, and in this century there have never been more than twenty-two in a year. As recently as the early 1970s, 2.5 million American workers would go on strike in a given year, but 1979 was the last time that more than a million went out. It doesn't seem like coincidence that the rise and fall of strikes during the twentieth century correlates very closely with the rise and sudden stagnation of U.S. wages.

After the don't-make-scabs-permanent norm was abandoned in the 1980s, Democrats tried to get their act together, kind of, early in the next decade. The House passed a bill to outlaw what was now happening—companies effectively firing strikers for striking. Remember how back in the 1970s *The Washington Post* had hired permanent replacements for its striking pressmen, thus busting that union? Twenty years later, when the bill prohibiting that got to the Senate, the *Post* editorialized against it as "a sop to organized labor" and "bad legislation"—because sometimes "strikers by their behavior forfeit the right of return and companies ought to hire permanent replacements. This newspaper faced such a breach in dealing with one of its unions in the 1970s." Days later, despite a large Democratic majority in the Senate, the prospective law was filibustered to death by the Republican minority.

Labor law isn't only a federal matter. During the New Deal, unions began signing contracts with company managements that required workers to join their unions or at least to pay union dues so there would be no free riders. Soon businesses and the political right started lobbying state legislatures to outlaw such contracts, shrewdly calling the proposed statutes "right-to-work" laws. And then in 1947, during one of just four years between 1933 and 1995 when Republicans controlled both the House and the Senate, Congress amended the National Labor Relations Act to give states permission to enact such antiunion laws. By 1955, seventeen states had done so, mostly in the South. But then the right-to-work movement stalled, and for almost a quarter-century it seemed dead—until the late 1970s and '80s. Today most states have right-to-work laws, all but two of them states that voted Republican in the 2016 presidential election.

Studying America's organized labor history, I noticed a symmetry that seems to show a tipping point: the moment when the fraction of all workers belonging to unions hits 25 percent. During the New Deal, that fraction zoomed from less than 10 percent past 25 percent in a decade. It was still 25 percent in the mid-1970s, but then as the right's Raw Deal forced what had gone up to keep coming down, the percentage plummeted to 10 percent by the 1990s for workers in the private sector, and it kept on shrinking, down to 6 percent today—a level of unionization back to what it was in the very early 1900s. *Most* of the decline in unionization during the last half-century happened just during the 1980s.* Once again, it's remarkable how much the American 1980s amounted to the 1930s in reverse.

Employers in the '80s also started using as never before a clever, quieter way of paying low-wage workers even less and neutering their unions: contracting with private firms to do blue-collar service work. This technique proved especially popular among public and nonprofit entities like colleges and cities, for whom the optics and politics of directly nickel-and-diming laborers and security guards could be awkward.

Harvard, for instance, employed a couple of thousand people as guards, janitors, parking attendants, and cooks, most of them unionized. Then in the 1980s and '90s, the university started outsourcing much of that work to private contractors—contractors that paid lower wages and used nonunion workers. After that the threat of outsourcing still more jobs loomed over all of Harvard's negotiations with its own unionized workers, which persuaded them to accept lower wages: between 1980 and 1996, their pay actually *fell* from the equivalent of $600 or $700 a week to $500 or $600.† Or consider the people paid to schlep baggage onto and off of planes at U.S. airports. In 2002, 75 percent of them were employed directly by airlines; by 2012, 84 percent of them worked for outside contractors, and their average hourly wage had been cut almost in half, to less than twelve dollars.

Until I started researching this book, I'd never thought about this new wrinkle in the economy, let alone understood its scale or impact. Like so many of the hundreds of changes instituted in the 1980s, the practice of replacing staff with contract workers was too arcane and te-

*Because the unionization of *government* workers only happened in the 1960s and '70s, just before the right started its full-bore campaign to turn back time and diminish workers' power, more than a third of public-sector employees were in unions by 1980, and they still are.

†Because it was Harvard, protests and ambient liberalism and an endowment of $18 billion in 2002 persuaded its president—Larry Summers, who'd just served as Clinton's secretary of the treasury—to start paying those service workers good wages after a generation of stiffing them.

dious for many of the rest of us to care or even know about. But imagine the thousands of companies and cities and schools and cultural institutions all over the country that have delegated so much of this kind of work to contractors, thereby making the treatment of all those eleven-dollar-an-hour workers somebody else's problem. According to a 2018 study by five major-university economists, a full *third* of the increase in American income inequality over these last forty years has been the result of just this one new, dehumanizing labor practice.

Another cunning way big businesses began squeezing workers in the 1980s was to become *extremely* big. "The basic idea," explains an economist specializing in markets for labor, "is that if employers don't have to compete with one another for workers, they can pay less, and workers will be stuck without the outside job offers that would enable them to claim higher wages."

As antitrust enforcement was discredited and enfeebled starting in the 1970s, big corporations were able to get so big and dominant in their business or regions that they had ever fewer companies directly competing with them to hire workers. More and more of them became the only games in town. One of the scholars who has helped expose this particular bit of rigging and its unfairness over the last several decades is the influential, idiosyncratic University of Chicago law professor Eric Posner.* As he and his economist co-author Glen Weyl explain, antitrust laws were enacted to make sure that businesses compete in every way—not just as *sellers* setting the prices they charge for products and services, but also as *buyers* of labor setting the salaries they pay. The appeal of antitrust for citizens was to make sure competition kept prices lower and salaries higher. Enforcement of our antitrust laws, however, has come to focus entirely on consumer prices, particularly since the definitive Borking of the field in the late 1970s. The antitrust enforcers at the Department of Justice and Federal Trade Commission, because they rely "on the traditional assumption that labor markets are competitive," and that it wasn't *their* jobs to protect workers anyhow, "have never blocked a merger because of its effect on labor," and they don't even employ experts who

*He's the son of the influential, idiosyncratically conservative University of Chicago law professor, antitrust expert, and former federal judge Richard Posner, who helped transform antitrust and other economic law to help business.

could calculate those effects. If two rival companies made a secret agreement to cap workers' salaries, they could get sued, but since "mergers that dramatically increase [companies'] labor market power are allowed with little objection," the companies can combine and thereby create a salary-squeezing employment monopoly.*

Companies don't even need to merge in order to pay workers less than they'd have to pay in a truly free labor market. I'd assumed only high-end employees were ever required to sign noncompete contracts—an HBO executive prohibited from going to work at Netflix, a coder at Lyft who can't take a job coding for Uber. But no: shockingly, noncompetes have come to be used just as much to prevent a $10-an-hour fry cook at Los Pollos Hermanos from quitting to work for $10.75 at Popeyes. Of all American workers making less than $40,000 a year, one in eight are bound by noncompete agreements. As another way to reduce workers' leverage, three-quarters of fast-food franchise chains have contractually prohibited their restaurant operators from hiring workers away from fellow franchisees.

Starting in the 1980s, the federal government also instituted big, covert structural tilts in favor of business—examples of the sneaky, stealthy "drift" effect I mentioned earlier. Inflation was an important tool for the economic right to get its way—first politically in 1980, when rapidly rising prices helped them get power, and thereafter by letting normal inflation move money from employees to employers by means of a kind of macroeconomic magician's trick. Instead of actually *repealing* two important New Deal laws that had helped workers for four decades, an essentially invisible ad hoc regime of gradual, automatic pay cuts was put in place. One involved overtime pay, time and a half for each hour an employee works over forty a week—which legally goes only to people with salaries below a certain level. The new ploy was to stop raising that salary threshold in the late 1970s, or the '80s, or the '90s—thus letting inflation constantly lower it, thereby continually reducing the number of people who qualified for overtime pay. In 1975, when the threshold was the equivalent of $56,000 a year, a large majority of U.S. workers were eligible; in 2019, after just a single increase since 1975, the overtime line

*Economists' term for markets where there's just one overwhelmingly dominant buyer of labor (or anything else) is a *monopsony.*

was under $24,000, which meant that fewer than 7 percent of American workers qualified.

A similar surreptitious screwing-by-inaction is how the federal minimum wage was dramatically reduced over time. From the mid-1950s until 1980, the minimum wage had been the equivalent of $10 or $12 an hour in today's dollars. As with overtime pay, the minimum wage was never technically *reduced,* but by 1989 inflation had actually reduced it to just over $7, where it remains today. In other words, it has been the federal government's unspoken decision to cut the wages of America's lowest-paid workers by more than a third, a choice first made during the 1980s when it stopped raising the minimum, then ratified again and again by Democratic as well as Republican Congresses. In addition to keeping costs low for the employers of Kroger cashiers and Burger King cooks and Holiday Inn maids, the lower national floor for pay has the invisible-hand effect of pulling down the low wages of people earning more than the legal minimum.

Economic right-wingers have publicly *reveled* in their squashing of workers' power in so many different ways. Federal Reserve chair Alan Greenspan said in a speech in the 2000s that spectacularly firing and replacing all the striking air traffic controllers in 1981 had been "perhaps the most important domestic" accomplishment of the Reagan presidency.

> [It] gave weight to the legal right of *private* employers, previously not fully exercised, to use their own discretion to both hire and discharge workers. There was great consternation among those who feared that an increased ability to lay off workers would amplify the sense of job insecurity. Whether the average level of job insecurity has risen is difficult to judge.

In fact, it began a cascading increase in job insecurity throughout the U.S. economy that wasn't at all difficult to see and feel and measure.

16

Insecurity Is a Feature, Not a Bug

When I was a little kid, whenever we had to play musical chairs in school or at birthday parties, I never enjoyed it. I hated the tense seconds of waiting for each drop of the needle onto the record. Musical chairs made me anxious and made everyone manic and delivered a nasty set of lessons—life is an accelerating competition of one against all for diminishing resources, survival is just a matter of luck and a touch of brute force, and success is a momentary feeling of superiority to the losers who lose before you lose, with just one out of the ten or twenty of us a winner.

Working on this book, I've thought again and again of that game, how the rules of our economy were rewritten as a high-stakes game of musical chairs, with more anxiety and dread and frenzy. In fact, our economy since 1980 has been a particularly sadistic version of the game, where some players are disabled or don't know the rules, and in addition to winning, only the winners get cake and ice cream and rides home.

The crippling of organized labor since 1980—and the increase in automation and relocating work abroad—helped make most American workers more anxious and uncertain and less prosperous. But there are other ways that increasing insecurity and increasing inequality got built into the political economy and became features of the system more than bugs.

The Friedman Doctrine in 1970 begat the shareholder supremacy movement in the 1980s, which begat an unraveling of all the old norms concerning loyalty and decency of businesses toward employees. *Loyalty* implies treating employees better than the law requires, which was at odds with the new mandates of shareholder supremacy. Replacing strikers was a shock-and-awe swerve, outsourcing work to low-wage contractors a less dramatic form of cold-bloodedness. Both were highly effective means of scaring workers in order to reduce their power and keep their pay lower.

But once the norms changed and a higher stock price became every public company's practically exclusive goal, companies that weren't facing strikes or financial problems also embraced the new ruthlessness. In addition to GE and its rank-and-yank corporate copycats continually, automatically firing a fixed quota of employees, profitable corporations began firing workers in bulk simply to please the finance professionals who constitute the stock market. "In the 1980s," says Adam Cobb, a University of Pennsylvania Wharton School business professor who studies this sudden change in norms, "you started to see healthy firms laying off workers, mainly for shareholder value." IBM, for instance, abandoned its proud de facto promise of permanent employment—starting in 1990, it got rid of 41 percent of its workers in five years, at first softly, pensioning off people fifty-five and over, then after that using straight mass firings. Throughout U.S. corporate culture, it was as if a decent civilization abruptly reverted to primitivism, the powers-that-be in suits and ties propitiating the gods with human sacrifice—which in addition to increasing profits had the benefit of making the survivors cower before the ruling elite.

Other corporate norms that prevailed from the New Deal until the 1980s, in particular those providing *nonunion* employees with fixed-benefit pensions and good healthcare, had been enforced indirectly by the power of organized labor. Because "companies were very worried about unions and the possibility of strikes," another Wharton expert on labor relations explains, "they treated their employees well so they wouldn't join a union. But that is no longer the case. Unions are on the decline. It's easy to quash them if they try to organize. So some managers might not care as much about employee loyalty as they used to."

Jacob Hacker, the Yale political scientist, calls this the Great Risk Shift, the ways that starting around 1980, business, in order to reduce current and future costs, dumped more and more risk "back onto workers and their families." As a result, "problems once confined to the working poor—lack of health insurance and access to guaranteed pensions, job insecurity and staggering personal debt, bankruptcy and home foreclosure—have crept up the income ladder to become an increasingly normal part of middle-class life."

Health insurance became a standard part of American jobs starting in the 1940s and '50s, and early on the pioneering, not-for-profit, cover-everyone Blue Cross and Blue Shield associations provided most of that coverage. As commercial insurance companies got into the game, having Blue Cross and Blue Shield as their public interest competitors helped keep the for-profit insurers honest, not unlike how the existence of strong unions tended to make businesses treat nonunion employees better. In 1980 the three-quarters of Americans who had job-based health coverage paid very little in premiums or deductibles or copayments. But it's been all downhill from there, thanks to more mercilessly profit-obsessed employers and insurance companies and healthcare providers. More and more of the healthcare industry consisted of for-profit corporations that were more and more subject to stock price monomania. Since the 1990s in many states, Blue Cross and Blue Shield have become totally commercial for-profit insurance companies that (deceptively) continue to use the venerable nonprofit brand name. Moreover, barely half of Americans these days are covered by insurance provided by a breadwinner's employer. The average amount each American paid for medical expenses out of pocket increased by half during the 1980s alone. In 1980 the average family of four spent the equivalent of about $2,700 a year on medical expenses; today an average family of four—$50,000 income, insurance through the job—spends about $7,500 a year out of pocket.

The other existentially important benefit that American businesses began routinely offering in the 1950s was a fixed pension, a guaranteed monthly income for as long as you lived after you stopped working, which would be paid in addition to Social Security. Companies funded the pensions, and they became standard, like cover-almost-everything company-provided health insurance.

But then came the 1980s. I mentioned earlier how the tax code tweak 401(k), which went into effect in 1980, handed a captive audience of millions of new customers and a revenue bonanza to the financial industry.

But this innovation also provided a cost-cutting financial bonanza to employers. They now had another clever way to execute on the new Scrooge spirit: replacing the pensions they'd funded for decades with individual-worker-funded investment plans—self-reliance! freedom!—cost them less right away and cost them *nothing* once employee number 49732 left the building for good.

In a recent study, Adam Cobb of the Wharton School found that just as CEOs started satisfying their new Wall Street über-headquarters and shareholder supremacy dogma by laying off workers, they started getting rid of pensions for the same reason. At thirteen hundred of the biggest U.S. corporations from 1982 on, the more a company's shares were held by big financial institutions like mutual funds and banks—arm's-length overlords who definitely felt no loyalty to any particular company's employees—the more likely that company was to get rid of pension plans that had guaranteed benefits. On the other hand, companies that employed *any* unionized workers were likelier to continue paying pensions to their nonunion workers as well.

"The great lie is that the 401(k) was capable of replacing the old system of pensions," says the regretful man who was president of the American Society of Pension Actuaries at the time and who had given his strong endorsement to 401(k)s. Without any national conversation or meaningful protest by employees—without a union or a Congress that was prepared to step in, how did you push back?—this crucial clause in the modern American social contract was unilaterally eliminated. In 1980 eight out of ten large and medium-size companies paid a guaranteed monthly sum to retirees for life, and *most* American workers retired with a fixed pension on top of Social Security, which the pension often equaled. Today only one in eight private sector employees are in line to get such a pension, and most American workers don't even have a 401(k) or an IRA or any other retirement account. It's yet another route by which the U.S. political economy made a round trip from 1940 to 1980 and then back again.

I mentioned the libertarian Fed chair Alan Greenspan's remark that it was "difficult to judge" if the "increased ability to lay off workers" starting in the 1980s had structurally, permanently increased Americans' "sense of job insecurity."

I am frequently concerned about being laid off. From 1979 through the 2000s, that statement was posed in a regular survey of employees of four hundred big U.S. corporations, each person asked if they agreed or disagreed. In 1982, early in our new national musical chairs game, during a bad recession with high unemployment, only 14 percent of this large sample of workers said they felt anxious about losing their jobs. The number crept upward during the 1980s, and then in the '90s people finally registered that, uh-oh, our social contract had been completely revamped. By 1995, even though the economic moment looked rosy—strong growth, the stock market rocketing upward—nearly half of Americans employed by big business said they worried a lot about being laid off.

In fact, in 1997, a strange new condition kicked in—pay continued to stagnate for most Americans despite low and dropping unemployment rates. A fundamental principle of free markets was being repudiated: the *supply* of labor could barely keep up with demand, but the *price* of labor, wages, wasn't increasing. Alan Greenspan, as he presented his semi-annual economic report to the Senate Banking Committee, mentioned those survey results and testified that the surprising "softness in compensation growth" was "mainly the consequence of greater worker insecurity" that had arisen since the early 1980s, insecurity that was also responsible, he said, for the continuing "low level of work stoppages" by unionized workers.

In other words, employees of the biggest corporations, whose jobs everyone had considered the most secure, were now too frightened of being jettisoned from those jobs to push hard for more pay or better working conditions.

Those data and their implications must've slipped Greenspan's mind later when he found it "difficult to judge" the effects of insecurity on workers' leverage and pay. And he never mentioned, of course, that it was he and his confederates on the right who'd spent the last decades restructuring our political economy to reduce the power of workers and increase their job insecurity. He did say he thought the curious disconnect in the late 1990s—low unemployment but no pay increases—was a blip, that "the return to more normal patterns may be in process" already. But two decades later it remained the not-so-new normal. The long-standing balance of power between employers and the employed was completely changed.

The impact of suddenly higher insecurity was a cascade of more insecurity. Starting in the late 1980s, as soon as Greenspan's beloved new "ability to lay off workers" took effect, the fraction of Americans who actually lost their jobs each year increased by a third and stayed there. At the same time, individual household incomes started roller-coastering down and up and down as they hadn't before. Soon the household incomes of one in eight Americans, poor and affluent and in between, were dropping by half or more in any given two-year period. Between 1979 and 1991, personal bankruptcies tripled (and then doubled), and the mortgage foreclosure rate quadrupled (and then doubled).

At the same time that economic insecurity grew, new sources of economic inequality were built into our system that made insecurity more chronic and extreme. Scores of public and private choices and changes increased inequality, all shaped by the new governing economic gospel: everybody for themselves, everything's for sale, greed is good, the rich get richer, buyer beware, unfairness can't be helped, nothing but thoughts and prayers for the losers.

What happened with higher education is a prime example. College had been the great American portal to upward economic and social mobility, especially public universities, which give out two-thirds of all four-year undergraduate degrees. But in the 1980s, that portal started becoming much harder to get through financially *and* much more financially vital. Meanwhile the rapidly rising cost of college provided a new business opportunity for the ravenous financial industry, which beset graduates (and people who failed to graduate) with debt that made the chronic new economic insecurity even worse. If omnipotent sadists had set out to take an extremely good, well-functioning piece of our political economy and social structure and make it undemocratic and oppressive, this is what their scheme would've looked like.

When I graduated high school in the 1970s, I could've gone with a plurality of my friends to the University of Nebraska, for which my parents would've paid resident tuition, room, and board equivalent to $10,000 a year. But I got into Harvard, so I went there, which cost the equivalent of $22,000 a year, all in. Those prices were typical at the time. They were also the same as they'd been for public and high-end private colleges a decade earlier.

But then around 1980, under the camouflage of high inflation, private colleges started increasing their prices every year a bit *faster* than inflation. Public colleges soon followed suit, state legislatures started cutting university funding, and that vicious cycle picked up speed. In the 1990s the price of a college education ballooned even faster—especially at public institutions—and never stopped.

Since 1981 states have cut their funding of public colleges and universities by half. The real, inflation-adjusted cost of attending a four-year college has almost tripled. That undergraduate year at the University of Nebraska has gone from the equivalent of $10,000 in the 1970s to $25,000 now. The $22,000 that Harvard charged in the 1970s, which my parents could *just* scratch together, now runs $72,000 a year, all in.

Only a quarter of people graduating from four-year public colleges and universities in the early 1990s had student loan debt; by 2010, two-thirds did. Credit had been deregulated in the 1980s just in time for the business of student loans to explode in the '90s. When I graduated college in 1976, the total amount of money lent to students to pay for higher education each year was the equivalent of $8 billion—but by the first school year of the 1980s, it had jumped to $22 billion, and in 2005 it reached $100 billion. In other words, over those three decades, while the number of students grew by half, the amount of money they borrowed each year increased twelvefold. For the financial industry, a small revenue stream turned into a great roaring river. For the 45 million mostly young and youngish Americans who today carry an average of $35,000 apiece in student debt, it's yet another source of economic insecurity that did not exist before everything changed in the 1980s.

From the decade my parents attended college through the decade I attended college, the percentage of all Americans with four-year degrees more than tripled. But then college became terribly expensive, and that constant, rapid increase in people attending and graduating, hard evidence of the American Dream working, slowed *way* down, especially for men.

I'm fairly sure that an American college education today isn't two or three times as good as it was when I went, even though it's two or three times as expensive. Rather, in the 1980s *everything* in America became more of a commodity valued only by its market price, and a college degree was turned into a kind of luxury good, the way it had been back in my grandparents' day. But it wasn't just status anxiety that drove up the price of college in the 1980s, the decade in which Hermès started selling a certain leather handbag for ten thousand dollars apiece just because it could. A four-year degree simultaneously became an expensive luxury good *and* practically essential to a middle-class life, because the economic value of a degree also wildly increased during the 1980s and '90s.

College graduates had always been paid more on average than people with less education. But that college premium had actually *shrunk* during the twentieth century before 1950, and even after that didn't grow much—until 1980, when it exploded. In the early 1980s college graduates of all ages earned a third more than people who'd only graduated high school. Just a decade later, in 1992, they earned two-thirds more, as they still do. What's worse, for people who don't have college degrees, average real pay has gone *down* since then by 10 or 20 percent. In other words, a college degree became a more essential but also much less affordable ticket to the increasing prosperity that, until 1980, all Americans had enjoyed.

Yet in this century, there's a bait-and-switch lose-lose-lose punchline to the story. Since 2000, with two generations of college graduates having burdened themselves with unprecedented debt to pay for the unprecedented new costs of college, the college-grad income premium basically stopped increasing. Today four out of ten recent American college graduates are employed in jobs that don't even require a college degree. And while college graduates used to accumulate more wealth at younger ages than people without degrees, according to a 2018 Federal Reserve study, the costs of college and of student debt have now erased that wealth premium for younger college-educated Americans.

If the American Dream had one simple definition, it was that hard work led to a better life, materially and otherwise, if not for oneself then for one's children and grandchildren. In the late 1800s, when Horatio Alger published *Ragged Dick* and his other fictional chronicles of upward economic mobility, America's exceptionalism wasn't just a self-flattering myth. Back then a lot more Americans than people elsewhere really did move up the ladder from generation to generation. Our edge over Britain and the rest of Europe was diminishing by the 1950s, but economic mobility remained a real thing in the United States, onward and upward—until 1980.

That change is particularly clear in a recent study conducted by Stanford and Harvard economists. In 1970, they found, almost all thirty-year-old Americans, 92 percent, were earning more than their parents had at that age and older. Among Americans in their early thirties in 2012, however, only half were earning more than their parents had—and for sons compared to fathers, even fewer. That enormous difference over two generations was mainly caused not by slower economic growth, the economists found, but by how American economic growth was shared after 1980. If we'd continued slicing the pie as we'd done from 1940 until 1980, then 80 percent of those Gen-Xers would be earning more money than their Silent Generation parents, instead of only 50 percent.

These days, if you grow up poor in America, you have less than a one-in-four shot of becoming even solidly middle class—one in three if you're white, one in ten if you're black. If you grow up right in the economic middle, the chances are you won't move up at all. On the other hand, if you come from an upper-middle-class or rich household, the odds are strong you'll remain upper middle class or rich as an adult.

When inequality started increasing in the 1980s, separating the fortunate few and the unfortunate majority, it showed up geographically as well: not only were only the rich getting richer, but neighborhoods and cities and regions segregated accordingly. The economist Enrico Moretti calls this the Great Divergence. Before the 1980s, the decade in which gated communities became common, Americans tended to live more democratically. Americans with more money and less money were likelier to live alongside one another.

In 1970 only one in seven Americans lived in a neighborhood that was distinctly richer or poorer than their metropolitan area overall, but that fraction began growing in the 1980s, and by the 2000s it was up to a third. Before the 1980s, two-thirds of Americans lived in middle-income neighborhoods; now a minority of us do, a fact that makes the terms thrown around about the middle class—*disappeared, hollowed out*—seem less metaphorical.*

As the American middle class quickly grew from the 1940s to the '70s, so did economic equality—that is, the income gap between richer

*The good news is that while neighborhoods have gotten more economically homogeneous, they've also become more racially and ethnically diverse. In 1980 the residents of at least a quarter of all U.S. census tracts, each a neighborhood of a few thousand people, were essentially all white and non-Hispanic. Nowadays only 5 percent of white Americans live in such neighborhoods, most of them in rural areas.

and poorer steadily shrank. Interestingly, that same leveling also happened at the same time among *cities,* with wages back then growing faster in poorer places than they did in more affluent ones, allowing people in the laggard cities to catch up. But around 1980 that stopped too. Since then the average salary premiums for jobs in and around economically robust cities have grown to be several times as large as they'd been in the 1970s, tens of thousands of dollars a year more per employee instead of merely thousands. After 1980 college graduates with skills started getting paid less if they lived in and around Cleveland rather than thriving Omaha, or in Stockton rather than thriving San Jose, so they moved.

This Great Divergence is yet another way in which growing economic inequality gets built into the system and becomes self-perpetuating, with residents of richer cities and regions getting even richer while their fellow citizens in unfortunate places fall further behind.

Not only do people who live in Boston or Raleigh or Austin get to choose from better jobs, their wealth also increases more because of real estate prices, which have risen more than twice as fast in cities in general as in rural areas. Superhigh prices for apartments and houses, in turn, mean that it's harder for people from left-behind places to afford to migrate to booming urban areas, which is bad for them and probably for U.S. economic growth too. And people in the booming cities who aren't Internet workers or their masseuses have a much harder time affording to stay. In Seattle in the 1960s, for instance, a typical janitor and a typical lawyer both spent 10 or 15 percent of their incomes to live in an apartment or house they owned or rented; today the Seattle lawyer still pays 15 percent for housing, but the Seattle janitor has to pay around 40 percent.

One of my premises in this book is that a real and mainly good expression of American exceptionalism had been our willingness and eagerness to take on the *new.* That often meant pulling up stakes and hitting the road in search of new work or a new life. To be American was to be venturesome. In the heyday of the so-called American Century, in the 1940s, people were doing that in a big way. The percentage of people who lived in a state other than the one they were born in rose steeply, and it kept rising as the country boomed and became more equal—and then it stopped rising around, yes, 1980. Since then the rate at which people move to a new state or city for a new job has fallen by half, and it is now at the lowest it's been since the government began tracking it. People without college educations are less likely to relocate, and in just the last decade people in their early twenties have suddenly become stationary, a third unlikelier to move than in the 2000s. Is this new geographic immobility more a cause or an effect of our new economic insecurity and inequality and immobility? Like so many spiraling vicious cycles, it's surely all of the above.

As the disappearance of factory jobs made cities like Detroit and Buffalo losers in the Great Divergence, automation and the digital revolution and globalization made certain cities big winners. Cities with tech companies and lots of college graduates were positioned to grow even faster in this postindustrial age. Unlike most of the other economic changes I've discussed, like shareholder supremacy and ending antitrust and defeating organized labor, this wasn't part of the original strategy of big business and the right. But for them it isn't exactly collateral damage either, because it has been a political boon. So far they've brilliantly managed to redirect the anger of most of the (white) left-behinds to keep them voting Republican, by reminding them that they should resent the spoiled college-educated liberal children and grandchildren of the acid amnesty abortion liberal elite who turned on them and their parents and grandparents in the 1970s.

17

Socially Liberal, Fiscally Conservative, Generally Complacent

Back in the 1930s and '40s, there had been very left-wing Democrats with serious national prominence and significant political bases. Franklin Roosevelt's own vice president Henry Wallace was one, as most notably was Senator Huey Long of Louisiana, who introduced bills in the 1930s to enact a 100 percent income tax on earnings over the equivalent of $20 million and a wealth tax of *100 percent* on everything over $1 billion. Which made the president seem moderate when his 1935 "Soak the Rich Act" raised the tax on income over $2 million to 55 percent. "Political equality," FDR said in 1936, is "meaningless in the face of economic inequality." In what he pitched as a Second Bill of Rights, he proposed *guaranteeing* all Americans "the right to earn enough" for "a decent living" and "a decent home" and to have "adequate medical care" paid for with "a tax [on] all unreasonable profits, both individual and corporate." That was 1944, Peak Leftism for Democrats on economics.

After the war, the American economic left existed in a meaningful way only within organized labor. And by the 1980s, unions were reduced to desperate parochial struggles to save jobs in declining heavy industries and, as mistrust of government grew, to unionizing more government employees. Moreover, the left offered no inspiring, politically plausible national economic vision of a future. In response to economic Reaganism, the national liberals were committed to preserving the social welfare status quo for old people and the (deserving) poor, and to convincing America that Democrats were now modern and pragmatic, not wasteful bleeding-heart suckers or childish protesters or comsymp fools. Very few believed anymore that *unreasonable profits* could even be a thing.

Against a triumphant Republican Party high on right-wing ideology, liberals' new selling point was their lack of any ideology at all. The faction that was now dominant in the Democratic Party had been pushing for a more centrist economic and social welfare policy since the 1970s, but the Republican Party after 1980 had no comparable moderating faction—which in a two-party system meant that Democrats kept moving toward a center that kept moving to the right.

The traumatic Republican landslide in the presidential election of 1972 persuaded generations of Democrats that they must tack toward the center no matter what. The *don't go left* lesson was only reinforced during the 1980s, when three quite *center*-left presidential candidates in a row lost. In the 1984 Democratic primary, Gary Hart was still the neoliberal apostate, running against the supposed mustiness of the New Deal and the Great Society *and* government *and* the Establishment. "The fault line of the party," he said then, "is now between those who have been in office for 20 or 25 years and those who have come into office in the last 10 years, and who are less tied to the arrangements dating to [Franklin] Roosevelt." That was because "the solutions of the thirties will not solve the problems of the eighties."

In fact, as the political journalist and author Richard Reeves wrote in 1984 of "Democratic liberalism's traumatic break with organized labor," the party's neoliberal cutting edge considered unions not just "the solution of the 1930's" but "the *problem* of the 80's," an obsolete obstacle in the way of "a socially liberal, high-technology, high-growth America. . . . We're not going to go down with the crew. Sorry, guys!"

In other words, the New Democrat avatar Hart was telling receptive twenty-something liberal yuppies like me that it was passé to fret about big businesses getting too big or Wall Street speculating too wildly or unions and unionism being definitively defeated, and that it was folly to think of Social Security and Medicare as models for any kind of expanded social democracy. And he was effectively persuading everyone, particularly people who had blue-collar jobs and who used to vote Democratic *because* of all those arrangements dating to Roosevelt, that the two parties did not really disagree about economics.

Rather than offering a distinct programmatic vision for the political economy apart from the adjective *new,* Hart was selling sauciness and smartness and cool, cleverly exploiting the generation gap a generation after it had become a thing, just as the youngest boomers could vote and the oldest ones were about to enter middle age. He himself was approaching fifty, only eight years younger than his primary opponent, former vice president Walter Mondale, whom he nevertheless caricatured as an old fogey. Of the youth of 1984, Hart said in a perfect soft-pedal pander, "You're dealing here with very sophisticated people. They don't want a messiah. They don't want me to personalize an entire generation's yearnings—just to be the vehicle of its expression. I see this campaign as a liberating vehicle." In his campaign stump speech, he would repeat the phrase "new generation" a dozen times.

It nearly worked. I was pleased when he ran a close second in Iowa, finished first in New Hampshire a week later, and after that won a majority of states. I remember being in a Des Moines hotel room covering the Democratic caucuses for *Time,* feeling so state-of-the-art to be filing a story about Hart, a so-called Atari Democrat, through a twenty-eight-pound portable computer connected to a shoebox-size dial-up modem to which we'd docked a curly-corded desktop telephone handset.

Just a few weeks earlier, in January 1984, Apple had introduced the Macintosh. Its famous Super Bowl ad, based on George Orwell's *Nineteen Eighty-four,* featured a heroine smashing the tyrants' huge telescreen, a lone nonconformist underdog spectacularly defying the oppressive Establishment. It suited the moment and digital early adopters who were politically aware but not actually, specifically political, in a stylish little allegory with which everyone from Ayn Rand fans to Hart fans to Deadheads might identify.

Steve Jobs, not yet thirty, had just become the sort of emblematic generational avatar that Gary Hart pretended he wasn't desperate to be. In a 1984 interview, Jobs bragged about his vast wealth—"at 23, I had a net worth of over a million . . . and at 25, it was over $100 million"—and about his indifference to it: "I'm the only person I know that's lost a quarter of a billion dollars in one year." Jobs didn't mind coming across as a jerk, just not a standard *business* jerk—because he was "well-grounded in the . . . sociological traditions of the '60s," like other Silicon Valley baby boomers.

"There's something going on here," he said, "there's something that is changing the world and this is the epicenter. It's probably closest to Washington during the Kennedy era or something like that. Now I start sounding like Gary Hart."

"You don't like him?" the interviewer asked.

"Hart? I don't dislike him. I met him about a year ago and my impression was that there was not a great deal of substance there."

"So who *do* you want to see—"

"I've never voted for a presidential candidate. I've never voted in my whole life." Meaning he'd chosen not to vote against Ronald Reagan in 1980.

Jobs was extreme—in devotion to his work, in arrogance and self-satisfaction, in wealth, in lack of interest in electoral politics or sympathy for the unfortunate—but he was also archetypal. For a decade, politics and social policy had been the passionate and unavoidable topic A in America because of the struggles over racial justice and the Vietnam War, but once those problems were addressed and solved, respectively, only politics geeks remained fully engaged. For the remainder of the century, the issues that aroused liberal and left passions in a major way—nuclear weapons, civil wars in Central American countries, the AIDS epidemic—were intermittent and never directly concerned the U.S. political economy.

People like Steve Jobs, or at least people like me, who did vote, always for Democrats, weren't *anti*union or *anti*welfare or *anti*government. The probability that elected Democrats would tend to increase my taxes wasn't a reason I voted for them, but my indifference to the financial hit—like Steve Jobs!—felt virtuous, low-end noblesse oblige. However, even after the right got its way on the political economy, many people like me weren't viscerally, actively skeptical of business or Wall Street either. Big business—in my case, various media and entertainment companies—paid me well and treated me fine, which probably didn't sharpen my skepticism toward a political economy that was being reordered to help big business (and people like me). When it came to the millions of losers, I felt . . . grateful that *my* work couldn't be automated or offshored or outsourced, and I figured, *Creative destruction, invisible hand, it'll work itself out,* and voted for liberal politicians who said we should retrain steelworkers to become computer programmers. In *Spy,* we didn't avoid politics—we published Washington-themed issues and an investigative piece about Paul Manafort and Roger Stone called "Publicists of the Damned" and a cover story called "1,000 Reasons Not to Vote for George Bush"—but it wasn't the magazine's main focus.

Very few people I knew voted for Reagan, but given that he didn't do anything *crazy* and started making peace with the Soviet Union, affluent college-educated people, liberals and otherwise, didn't disagree very ferociously about politics in the 1980s and '90s, and certainly not about economics. In retrospect, that rough consensus looks like the beginning of an unspoken class solidarity among the bourgeoisie—nearly everyone suspicious of economic populism, but some among us, the Republicans, more suspicious than the rest. Affluent college-educated people, Democrats as well as Republicans, began using the phrase *socially liberal but fiscally conservative* to describe their politics, which meant low taxes in return for tolerance of . . . *whatever,* as long it didn't cost affluent people anything.* It was a libertarianism lite that kept everything nice and clubbable and, unlike Republican conservatism, at least had the virtue of ideological consistency.

To their great credit, the New Democrats took the lead early to start making people aware of CO_2-induced global warming. In 1980, Senator Paul Tsongas conducted the first congressional hearing on the subject, and Congressman Al Gore convened the next in 1981. It was a wonky *new* problem that required *new* solutions. Of course, back then, briefly, it also had the New Democrat appeal of not seeming anticapitalist. And if the Democrats' union allies warned that policies to reduce CO_2 might be bad for industrial jobs, they were just being their shortsighted uneducated-palooka selves.

When Hart ran a second time for president in 1988, one of his tax policy advisers was Arthur Laffer, the inventor of supply-side econom-

*The earliest use of the phrase *socially liberal but fiscally conservative* in all 5 million books and other publications digitized by Google was in 1978, in Charles Koch's magazine *Inquiry: A Libertarian Review,* to refer to the new ideological territory that Massachusetts governor Michael Dukakis and President Carter were both trying to claim.

ics. When Jerry Brown ran for the 1992 Democratic nomination, he also sought Laffer's help to devise some kind of tax scheme "that was clear and easy to articulate," and Laffer himself says he voted for Bill Clinton.

Clinton was one of the founders in 1985 of the Democratic Leadership Council. It was an attempt by an endangered species, white Southern Democratic politicians, to remain relevant twenty years after their die-off had begun. It also became a think-tankish anchor for Democrats who didn't disagree with Republicans that the *only* acceptable new solutions to *any* social problem were market-based.

For the remainder of the century, no candidate from the Democratic left became a plausible finalist for the nomination. In the 1988 primary, Jesse Jackson ran as a full-on leftist, calling for single-payer healthcare, free community college, a big federal jobs program, and the cancellation of Reagan's tax cuts for the rich—and by sweeping the black South and winning everywhere among voters under thirty, he beat Joe Biden and Gore and came in second to Dukakis, but . . . he was never going to be nominated. A Vermont mayor who'd endorsed him, Bernie Sanders, was elected to the House in 1990 as a *socialist,* cute, but really, so what? He was a quirky retro figure, some Ben & Jerry's guy who didn't realize the 1960s were over and was channeling Eugene Debs and Norman Thomas from the '20s and '30s. In 1992, when Clinton won the nomination, his only serious competitors were two fellow New Democrats, Brown and Tsongas. Democrats had settled into their role as America's economically center-right party. There was no organized, viable national economic left in the vicinity of power.

18

The Permanent Reagan Revolution

As the right marched on victoriously through the end of the 1980s and into the 1990s, even what appeared to be occasional reversals weren't really setbacks for the *economic* right. For instance, just after rejecting Bork, the same Democratic-majority Senate promptly and unanimously confirmed Reagan's choice of Anthony Kennedy for that Supreme Court seat. Justice Kennedy is known today as a moderate because of his liberal votes on abortion and gay rights, but on *economic* questions—concerning unions, campaign spending, regulation—he was for thirty years an absolutely reliable hard-line supporter of big business.

And even though the Democrats controlled the House with huge majorities throughout the 1980s and early '90s and won the Senate back for six years, the federal government consistently treated business and the rich spectacularly well. The top income tax rate for the wealthiest was cut from 70 to 50 percent in 1982. It would've been prudent to stop there for a while and see how that worked out. But no: in the second Reagan term, the top rate was cut again to 38.5 percent, then once more to 28 percent—along with a large reduction of the income threshold for the highest bracket, which meant that somebody making $1 million or

$10 million a year would now be taxed at the same rate that a teacher or plumber was taxed on everything they earned above the equivalent of $40,000. The cut in the top tax rate on profits from selling stocks was also cut in half between 1976 and 1982, another enormous boon to the rich, since three-quarters of those gains go to the wealthiest 5 percent of Americans. As it started its second decade of existence, the Business Roundtable successfully lobbied to make sure corporate taxes were significantly cut as well.

But the strategists on the right understood the downside of success, the dangers of complacency and backsliding. For their long war, the counter-Establishment needed to expand to fight specialized campaigns and to retain its ferocity even as it became the Establishment. Many essential subcommandants made the right's permanent revolution, but three in particular are worth a closer look. Each concentrated on a different constituency and area of focus, and each had a different temperament, but all were unwavering zealots.

If tax rates could be cut as easily as they'd been in the 1980s, the rich right and big business knew, those rates could just as easily be raised back to where they'd been for the preceding half-century. The surge of popular antitax anger in the 1970s that led to Reagan's election mainly concerned *local* taxes and could dissipate unless it was somehow specifically institutionalized, with its own campaign and fighters in the long war. A preference for relatively lower taxes and smaller government budgets had been a Republican tenet for generations, along with a wish for a somewhat lighter regulatory hand, but only in the 1980s and '90s did taxes—REGULATION BAD, TAXES *WORSE*—turn into the prime doctrinal phobia and bond for the American right. It didn't happen by accident.

More than any other single person, Grover Norquist is to blame. Like me, he was an upper-middle-class suburbanite who became a Nixon campaign volunteer around the time he hit puberty and attended Harvard College in the 1970s. Unlike me, he never decided that "adolescent libertarianism" was redundant and moved on. Moreover, he settled on taxation as his lifelong libertarian single-issue obsession at just the right moment and stuck with it forever. After college he ran a conservative Washington antitax group, and in the 1980s he created his own more extreme version,

Americans for Tax Reform (ATR), funded over the years by the familiar (Koch, Olin, Scaife) right-wing foundations.

Norquist's stroke of evil genius was to dream up at age twenty-nine the Taxpayer Protection Pledge, which in 1986 made the Republicans' antitax fixation official. It's a document that obliges legislators (and governors) who sign it to "oppose net tax increases," "any and all" of them, for as long as they're in office. Because it's, you know, a *solemn oath,* it must be cosigned by two witnesses, and the group's FAQ answer (in 2020) to the question, "Can the language of the Pledge be altered to allow exceptions?" is "No. There are no exceptions to the Pledge." Fortunately for Ronald Reagan, the pledge didn't exist during his first five years in office, when he signed into law six major tax increases amounting to the equivalent of $300 billion. Soon swearing fealty to Norquist's demand was practically required of congressional Republicans, and three decades later 85 percent of the Republicans in the House and Senate still feel obliged to sign it.

The simplicity and absolutism of the pledge are both its genius and its evil. In addition, Norquist remained single-minded about promoting and enforcing it and avoiding mission creep. It made him among the most influential leaders of the right, libertarian economics division. He was a close adviser to Newt Gingrich before Gingrich became Speaker of the House in 1995. For more than a quarter century, he has presided at the so-called Wednesday Meeting, a weekly gathering of Washington right-wingers at his offices. ATR has been as effective as the NRA (on whose board Norquist served for eighteen years) as an ideological enforcer of hard-right orthodoxy among Republicans in Washington, possibly as responsible for unnecessary U.S. government dysfunction as the NRA is for unnecessary American gun deaths.

Since the pledge began, the top federal income tax rate has never again crept higher than it was before 1932. Yet by Norquist's own measure—the fraction of the economy funneled through the federal government—he and his group have failed. For the thirty-odd years before Americans for Tax Reform began, that government percentage-of-GDP floated up and down between 13 and 19 percent, and for the thirty-odd years since it has floated up and down between 14 and 20 percent. In 1985 it was between 16 and 17 percent, exactly where it was at the beginning of 2020. Instead, what's changed enormously due to the right's antitax phobia is the size of the federal *debt* as a percentage of GDP. After bottoming out in the 1970s, when Democrats controlled Congress and the presidency, that total debt number increased by half during the Reagan administration alone.

This history illustrates the true relative importance of the right's goals concerning fiscal policy and the political economy. Their overriding mission, at which they've succeeded smashingly, is to make sure the rich get richer (and big business bigger), and the most direct, unambiguous, universal way of doing that is by keeping their taxes low, no matter the costs. The old Republican goal of budgetary prudence, trying to balance federal revenues and spending, became vestigial. *Fiscal responsibility* rhetorically pops back to life for Republicans only when they're out of power in Washington, and only as an argument for achieving their secondary goals of reducing Social Security and Medicare benefits and preventing any major expansion of health or education or other social programs.

Norquist is known for his jokey line about his wish to make the federal government smaller—"to shrink it down to the size where we can drown it in the bathtub." But he and the Washington right are really not joking about their dream of repealing a century of progress enacted in Washington. Norquist has said in all seriousness that he envisions a government the size of "where we were at the turn of the [twentieth] century," "up until Teddy Roosevelt"—Roosevelt became president in 1901—"when the socialists took over," before "the income tax, the death tax, regulation, all that." Getting more specific, he definitely wants a federal budget no larger than it was eighty years ago—in other words, a third of what it is today. If the Republicans were to pursue that goal openly, in earnest, in Congress, it would be political suicide, of course, so they don't, and instead they take solace in having maximized the wealth of the well-to-do and the power of big business at the expense of everyone else. Beyond shoveling more money to their allies and benefactors and making big new social programs difficult to enact, the blunt tool of the right's zero-tolerance antitax obsession has had ancillary effects that also serve particular interests, such as making it even harder to tax carbon in order to reduce carbon dioxide emissions. Which might explain, for instance, why the main oil industry lobbying organization is a major funder of Americans for Tax Reform.

• • •

The economic right had won. Impossible dreams of the early 1970s had come true in the '80s and '90s. Taxes on the rich and on business were low. Businessmen were heroes again. Deregulation of big business and indifference to excessively big businesses had become a bipartisan fad. During the 1980s, federal antitrust enforcement budgets and cases were cut back to the levels of thirty and fifty years earlier. A true libertarian OG who wanted to privatize Social Security, Greenspan became Federal Reserve chairman in 1987 (and stayed in the job into the new century). Democratic presidents now governed like liberal Republicans, instructing Americans that "all the legislation in the world can't fix what's wrong with America" (Carter) and that "the era of big government is over" (Clinton). What's more, the genuine menaces that Republicans had demagogued so successfully for generations—the Soviet Union, inflation, rising crime—rather miraculously ceased to be problems as well, and during the 1990s the economy grew by more than 4 percent a year for four straight years.

Happier days were here again, again. But not, at least publicly, according to the right, who turned out to be, as the terrific libertarian journalist Jack Shafer put it back then, "the sorest winners ever recorded in history." As the twentieth century ended, he wrote, the ideological commissars at *The Wall Street Journal* editorial page "continued to posture as if welfare-statist Democrats . . . were the ultimate source of political evil," indulging the "ongoing delusion" that pro-rich-people, pro-business right-wingers were "a downtrodden minority even after the conservative victories."

In part, the right had been so totally on the outs for so long, and their victories had been so thorough and swift, they worried it might all be reversed if they let their guard down. And some right-wingers were temperamentally such fanatics and outsiders that they found it hard or impossible to adapt to having real governing power. From the 1970s, liberals had been cruising toward the ideological center and beyond, eager to compromise, reasonableness and intellectual flexibility central to their self-identities—which made people on the right who were wingers by temperament feel obliged to keep moving further right.

Paul Weyrich, the cofounder of the Heritage Foundation who loved identifying as a radical, was that kind of diehard, one of the sorest winners. Like Norquist, he was an important ideological warlord. Like Norquist, he teamed up early with Gingrich, in the 1980s making himself the center of a right-wing Washington politburo he assembled for lunches every week—on Wednesdays, before Norquist copied even that from his playbook. Unlike Norquist, Weyrich was not jolly or snarky, and he wasn't narrowly focused on serving the interests of business and the rich but instead spread his zealotry across the whole array of new right-wing obsessions, especially those of his fellow Christian extremists.

In the 1990s, with Republicans controlling Congress for the first time since the early '50s and in Clinton a moderate Democratic president who'd just cut taxes and public assistance for the poorest, Weyrich was nevertheless dissatisfied and distraught. He thought the conservative Republican leaders in Congress were capitulators, compromisers, heretics who should be purged. "This is a bitter turn for me," he said then. "I have spent thirty years of my life working in Washington, working on the premise that if we simply got our people into leadership that it would make a difference. . . . And yet we are getting the same policies from them that we got from their [liberal] Republican predecessors."

Weyrich's prominence and personal power-brokering diminished over the rest of his life, even as the revolution he'd helped launch endured through another two-term Republican presidency and beyond. "Most of the successes of the conservative movement since the 1970s," Norquist said of Weyrich when he died in 2008, "flowed from structures, organizations, and coalitions he started, created or nurtured." But beyond being a founder and über-bureaucrat of the right-wing counter-Establishment that eventually swallowed and replaced the old GOP, Weyrich was the very personification of the new right-wing masses decades before the Tea Party and MAGA. He was a true believer who needed to keep feeling the rage, for whom politics as well as religion was a fundamentalist crusade where compromise was an abomination, an archetypal Fox News viewer before Fox News existed.* He wasn't one of the cynics and operators. Nor was he a consistent libertarian like Norquist, one of the overgrown boys who hated taxes as much as they loved Burning Man and themselves. Rather, Weyrich was the ultimate late-stage Republican because he madly dreamed of returning America to the past in all ways, both the

*In fact, three years before Fox News launched, he'd started a right-wing cable channel called National Empowerment Television that had an anti-immigration show, an NRA show, a Cato Institute show, an antigay show called *Straight Talk*, and a show called *The Progress Report* starring Gingrich.

political economy and the culture. He sincerely wanted business unregulated and the rich untaxed and government minimized, *and* he sincerely pined for an explicitly Christian culture bordering on theocracy where women didn't have equal rights and racial segregation was considered okay.*

The surname Sununu is familiar today mainly because of a pair of recent New Hampshire politicians, a governor and a U.S. senator, but the most significant Sununu was their father, John H. Sununu, himself a former New Hampshire governor and the first President Bush's first chief of staff. In several important ways, he was another prototypical Republican for the new age: an asshole personally, a conservative hard-liner, and a critical figure in turning the party away from reason and science and common sense toward full-bore denial of climate change.

In 1980, concerning the greenhouse effect, as it was then called, the "main scientific questions were settled beyond debate," Nathaniel Rich writes in his book *Losing Earth: A Recent History*. "As the 1980s began, attention turned from diagnosis of the problem to refinement of the predicted consequences" to solutions, how to reduce carbon emissions. In 1981 a study by NASA scientists confirming this consensus was front-page news, recommending that the United States continue burning oil and gas and coal only "as necessary." At a symposium the following year organized by James Hansen, the NASA scientist who'd led the study, Exxon's president of research declared that "capitalism's blind faith in the wisdom of the free market was 'less than satisfying' when it came to the greenhouse effect." In a speech to energy executives, Reagan's environment czar said "there can be no more important or conservative concern than the protection of the globe itself."

Two things happened in 1983 that started us toward the disastrous wrong turn on climate change by the end of the decade. One was what happened when another big federal study was published, this one called "Changing Climate" and conducted by a presidential commission under

*Weyrich died the month after Obama was elected president; the month after the 2016 election, his Heritage Foundation cofounder Edwin Feulner was put in charge of finding people to run domestic policy for the Trump administration.

the auspices of the National Academy of Sciences. Its findings confirmed the dire scientific consensus about the nature of the problem—carbon dioxide levels were doubling, warming was continuing, polar ice was melting, and sea levels were rising disastrously.

But that's not how it was spun by the Reagan administration, or by the political ally whom the president had appointed to oversee the commission. In a front-page *Times* story (HASTE OF GLOBAL WARMING TREND OPPOSED), that Reaganite physicist-turned-oceanographer told everyone to calm down, that climate change was no big deal, and that "we have 20 years to examine options before we have to make drastic plans." Exxon quietly decided that capitalism's blind faith in the free market was good by them and there were indeed more important concerns than researching how to protect the planet from carbon emissions, and the American Petroleum Institute ended its research into CO_2-induced climate change.

The other critical 1983 event was the election of a nobody libertarian college teacher as governor of New Hampshire, turning him into a national Republican figure. John Sununu was an engineering professor son of an engineering professor who radiated the conviction that he was the smartest person in every room, certainly when the subject was science—and now concerning the new science of climate change.

But during the 1980s, Sununu's pooh-poohing remained a fringe position even among Republicans. In 1988 alone, dozens of bipartisan bills to deal with global warming were introduced in Congress, and forty-two senators, almost as many Republicans as Democrats, formally asked Reagan to start working toward some kind of international climate treaty—which he agreed to do. Early that summer Hansen, the NASA scientist, testified at a big Senate hearing, and the issue got more public attention than ever—GLOBAL WARMING HAS BEGUN, EXPERT TELLS SENATE was the *Times*'s page-one headline.

The fossil fuel industry freaked out. Global warming was becoming the obverse of a motherhood-and-apple-pie issue—everybody believed in it and hated it. Big business in general had been getting its way for a decade, but on this subject, the oil and gas and coal guys saw that Republicans weren't standing up for *their* business at all. Before the summer was over, Exxon's "manager of science and strategy development" was circulating a confidential memo arguing they must now go to Plan B—that is, to "emphasize the uncertainty in scientific conclusions," even though there was no uncertainty concerning the problem. The rest of the industry signed on, and the lobbyists and the think-tank scholars and the rest of the right's counter-Establishment were recruited for a new mission of casting doubt on science.

Still, at that very moment in 1988, the dangers of the greenhouse effect, and the decisive use of government to stop it, was one of George H. W. Bush's big presidential campaign talking points. Ten days after his inauguration, his secretary of state, James Baker—a smooth former Houston oil and gas lawyer who had also been his campaign manager—gave a speech about global warming. Baker apparently hadn't gotten the memo, because he argued for urgently reducing CO_2 emissions, reforestation, the works. "We can probably not afford to wait" to act, he said, "until all of the uncertainties about global climate change have been resolved."

The White House chief of staff promptly went to see the secretary of state. "Leave the science to the scientists," Sununu told Baker, according to Rich's *Losing Earth*. "Stay clear of this greenhouse-effect nonsense. You don't know what you're talking about."

Baker did as he was told, and Sununu kept riding his hobbyhorse. During a meeting with the head of the EPA and an Energy Department bureaucrat, a staff member made the mistake of referring to a climate change initiative to discourage the use of fossil fuels. "Why in the world would you need to reduce fossil-fuel use?" Sununu snapped at her. "I don't want anyone in this administration without a scientific background using 'climate change' or 'global warming' ever again." By the end of the first year of that first Bush presidency, Sununu had almost single-handedly halted the political momentum in Washington, turned climate change into a partisan issue, and put denial of the science on its way toward Republican orthodoxy.*

• • •

*Right after Sununu lost his job for being a jerk (and for using military jets and government limos for personal travel), but before he physically left the White House, a *Spy* writer phoned him there, posing as a corporate headhunter looking to fill an oil company CEO position. Sununu talked and talked. "Most of what I've been putting together as packages," he told our writer, "start at three and a half million." As it turned out, none of those hypothetical $3.5 million jobs came to fruition.

As the 1990s began, the right stayed angry and upset and kept growing in size and power thanks to the primitives, the bigots, the Protestant fundamentalists and cowboy commando conspiracy fantasists. But the *grown-ups* on the right, the economic right, corporate leaders and the rest of the rich, kept their eye on the prize—less taxation, less regulation of business, greed is good—and they maintained control of the party. The rabble's candidates (Pat Buchanan and Pat Robertson in the 1990s, Ron Paul and Mike Huckabee in the 2000s) never got more than a quarter of the primary vote, and even as the party kept moving right, it kept nominating country-clubby Mr. Respectables for president, from the first Bush through Mitt Romney.

When the economic right and the populist rabble first formed their coalition in the 1970s, they shared enough common ground—whiteness, resentment of the smart set—to make it work, but it was always an alliance of convenience. Lots of the right's sophisticates and true libertarians weren't enthusiastic about the cultural agendas of their partners. (In her seventies in the 1990s, for instance, my mother in Nebraska, who'd always called herself a conservative Republican, started voting only for Democrats.) But to nonredneck Republicans, that was the price of making markets free and the rich richer.* The economic right was shrewd enough to understand that the issues *they* didn't care much about—abortion, gay rights, creationism—*did* matter to liberals, and that those culture wars drew off political energy from the left that might otherwise have fueled complaints and demands about the reconstructed political economy. And Establishment Republicans could keep reassuring themselves that when push came to shove, their culture-warrior political partners didn't ever actually *win*, that abortion was still legal, gay and lesbian rights expanded, creationism kept out of public school curricula.

The *Official Preppy Handbook* president who followed Reagan was probably sincere, in his Kennebunkport way, when he said he wanted to build "a kinder and gentler nation." But Sununu was his chief of staff, and in the 1990s the triumphal economic right didn't kick back or loosen up.

*It's analogous to the cynical bargain that liberal Democrats made with the Southern segregationists in their coalition from the 1930s through the '60s—essentially the same rabble, in fact, that the Republicans brought into their coalition right afterward. Except that to the Democrats' credit back then, they made their devil's bargain in order to help the (white) working and middle-class majority, not the rich.

The *un*-Bushian new counter-Establishment remained vigilant and hard-line, hair-trigger happy to bully heretics and to push for more power, more wealth, less regulation, less social spending. Meanwhile, Democrats continued to show up at the gunfights with knives, and blades that weren't very sharp. And they came without an economic vision apart from continuing to rebrand themselves as chastened, business-friendly moderates.

19

The 1990s: Restrained and Reckless

When Bill Clinton was running for president in 1992, he seemed to have the right idea, at least rhetorically. In the national campaign headquarters in an old building in downtown Little Rock, his strategist James Carville taped to a wall his sign with their message reduced to three points.

> CHANGE VS. MORE OF THE SAME
>
> THE ECONOMY, STUPID
>
> DON'T FORGET HEALTHCARE

BIG GOVERNMENT DOES NOT HAVE ALL THE ANSWERS and THE ERA OF BIG GOVERNMENT IS OVER were not numbers four and five. Yet once he became president, a generation after Jimmy Carter sang that same song, Clinton still felt obliged to continue disavowing belief in government as a vehicle for improving American life, to pledge fealty to the new economic code, and to grant most of the wishes of big business. "We know big government does not have all the answers," he said in a State of the

Union speech in his first term. "We know there's not a program for every problem. . . . The era of big government is over."

As the compensation of CEOs at big companies increased crazily during the 1990s, the president initially thought the government might discourage it with stiff penalties, but the Business Roundtable talked sense into him. And so on. As Nixon had admitted, thirty-odd years after the New Deal, *We're all Keynesians now,* thirty-odd years after that, when Clinton took office, he was saying, *None of us are New Dealers anymore*.

It's worth comparing the New Democrat positioning to that of one older Washington Democrat, whose take was ridiculed as old-fashioned and out of touch. In the 1960s and '70s, Daniel Moynihan had been pigeonholed as a moderate or a conservative, but as a U.S. senator during the 1990s, when the rest of his party went Republicanesque on the political economy, Moynihan was a kind of heroic last left-winger standing.*

At the start of his presidency, Clinton tried to legislate an expansion of the private U.S. health insurance system to make it cover more people. "Mr. Clinton and his allies," a *Times* analysis explained in 1994, "were trying hard to redefine the Democratic Party away from traditionally liberal approaches to domestic policy; they were almost inevitably drawn to the ideas of managed competition. Though still largely theoretical, the concept relies on market forces, not government, to hold down costs and expand access to health insurance." That is, Clinton tried and failed to pass a version of Obamacare sixteen years before Obama succeeded.

One of the many congressional committees that held hearings on the Clinton healthcare plan was Senate Finance, chaired by Moynihan. His chief of staff was Lawrence O'Donnell, who later became an MSNBC anchor. "At the end of the last of two dozen hearings on the indescribably complex Clinton healthcare bill," O'Donnell told me, "I'm sitting behind Chairman Moynihan, and he puts his hand over his microphone and turns over his shoulder and whispers to me, 'Why don't we just delete the words 'age 65' from the Medicare statute?'"

So a quarter-century ago the respected sixty-seven-year-old chair of

*In addition to being a true social democrat on healthcare and helping the poor, Moynihan shared organized labor's skepticism of Clinton's gung-ho free trade policies. He was also one of only fourteen senators who voted against the 1996 bill that prohibited national recognition of legal same-sex marriage, which Clinton signed into law.

the Senate Finance Committee offhandedly suggested a radical overhaul that would have made healthcare a universal entitlement, what we now call Medicare for All. Was Moynihan serious?

"Totally serious," O'Donnell says. "It took twenty-four hearings studying every detail of healthcare policy for him to arrive there. He was a very careful juror who waited until he heard every word of testimony. It was literally while the last witness was finishing that he gave me his verdict. He hated unnecessary government complexity," and the Clinton plan, O'Donnell says, was complex and hard to explain (as Obamacare would be as well). Also, Moynihan "could see the 'reform' policies" proposed by Clinton would "not perform as promised."

As these hearings and negotiations went on for the first eighteen months of the Clinton administration, Democrats had large majorities in both the Senate and House. The main labor union federation, the AFL-CIO, had broached the idea of a single-payer healthcare system. But the Clinton plan was the plan, and it died.

In Clinton's speech accepting the Democratic nomination in 1992, he had promised to "end welfare as we know it." *Welfare* really meant one rather modest program that had been in existence since the New Deal as an add-on to the law creating Social Security. It provided a monthly cash floor to the poorest families with young children. In the 1990s fewer than 5 percent of Americans were getting those benefits, which since the beginning of the right turn in 1976 had been cut by a quarter to around $100 or $150 per family per week in today's dollars, and which in the 1990s cost the federal government the equivalent of $18 billion a year, a fraction of one percent of the budget.

The right-wing-billionaire-funded academic Charles Murray, who'd become a star in the 1980s, was still making the case that we'd be doing poor people a favor if the government stopped providing them with aid. In Clinton's first year as president, he read an article by Murray in *The Wall Street Journal* proposing that any unmarried mother on welfare who gave birth to another child should be punished by being cut off from nearly all federal assistance, not just the monthly cash but also food stamps and housing subsidies. In an interview on *NBC Nightly News* between Thanksgiving and Christmas 1993, the president said Murray had done "the country a great service. . . . I think his analysis is essentially right. Now, whether [Murray's] prescription is right, I question." You could argue the morality, he said, but "there's no question that that would *work*. . . . There is no question."

In other words, Clinton accepted and promoted as fact the basic premise that poor mothers were moochers who *chose* to luxuriate on a hundred dollars a week rather than take advantage of all the good jobs and childcare services available to them. Before long, that belief was the basis for one of the right's main legislative proposals—a bill that Senator Moynihan called a "brutal act of social policy" and a "disgrace" that was "not a negotiable item" and "not my idea of legislating." But it was called welfare *reform*. And in 1996, with a Democratic president's support and the votes of half the Democrats in Congress, that sixty-one-year-old New Deal entitlement was scrapped.

I'm not suggesting this particular program should've been immune from revision. The changes in the law did indeed push some mothers into the workforce—although research suggests that maybe half of that effect was the result of spending much *more* on a different federal financial cushion, expanding income tax credits that helped lower-middle-class people as well as the poor. Most of the many millions of very poor children and their mothers who were denied those few extra dollars a day after 1996 did manage to get by. However, it's another illustration of how thoroughly the right's ideas became the governing consensus, and of how liberals fell down on the job by accepting—or at least not forthrightly rejecting—the instinct to blame the losers, in our extreme free-market society, for being losers, and by disclaiming social responsibility for properly helping them.

Looking back now, it's hard not to conclude that the anxious nominal party of the economic left, Democrats, was magnificently played by the committed and confident economic right, Republicans, for forty years. I'm not saying the shift in popular sentiment wasn't partly organic. But Democrats, after the Republican presidential landslides of 1972 and 1984, remained too dazed and confused and scared for too long. For a decade or two before the rise of right-wing radio and Fox News, Democrats began believing and behaving as if there were a mandate for *everything* that the *entire* right wanted, the elite economic right as well as the reactionary rabble—for giving more and more advantages to big business and the well-to-do in our political economy at the expense of not just the poor but everyone else, for tossing out a social contract that had tried hard to balance the demands of economic liberty and economic equality. Sometime in the 1980s, liberals passed through the stages of political denial and anger and depression, and during the '90s, they settled into modest bargaining and acceptance for the long haul.

How the right played the left for suckers becomes especially clear in looking at the 1990s, when after twelve years of Republican presidents, a Democrat was running the federal government. The bad habit that liberals and other Democrats had learned was this: be *restrained* when it comes to spending to help the less fortunate but simultaneously be *reckless* when it comes to helping business and the rich.

During the 1980s and early '90s, under Reagan and the first Bush, the annual federal budget deficit was much larger than it had been at any time since World War II, $350 billion to $550 billion a year in today's dollars. During Clinton's first year in office, he and a Congress with large Democratic majorities enacted the biggest deficit-reduction plan in history and stuck to it, achieving a budget *surplus* four years in a row for the first time since 1930. As soon as the surplus money began pouring in, Republicans immediately proposed to funnel the equivalent of $1 trillion of it to business via tax cuts over the next decade.

After his reelection, Clinton wanted to demonstrate even more heroic, historic restraint by reducing Social Security benefits over the long term. He secretly negotiated a deal to do that with the right-wing Speaker of the House, Gingrich, but was apparently prevented from announcing it only by the exposure of his extramarital Oval Office sexual liaison. At the beginning of the scandal, Hillary Clinton complained of the "vast right-wing conspiracy that has been conspiring against my husband since the day he announced for president." Fair enough, I suppose, but it is ironic how nicely he'd played with the economic sector of that conspiracy. Which didn't stop the welfare-ending, capital-gains-tax-cutting, budget-balancing Democratic president from being impeached by Gingrich and the bad-faith, bloody-minded Republicans.

As soon as Clinton left office, the new Republican president and Congresses, thanks to their antitax fixation (and the war in Iraq two years later), promptly took us from a budget surplus equivalent to $365 billion to a budget deficit of $534 billion, a reckless and unnecessary trillion-dollar swing in three years.

Irving Kristol, that mastermind and key promoter of remaking the political economy, had candidly *announced* this new strategy of the right—right-wing fiscal recklessness, forcing the left into defensive restraint—in a *Wall Street Journal* column back in 1980, months before Reagan's election. In the 1930s and the 1960s, Kristol wrote, "when in office the liberals (or social-democrats, as they should more properly be called) spen[t] generously, regardless of budgetary considerations, until the public permit[ted] the conservatives an interregnum in which to clean up the mess" in the late 1940s and '50s and '70s,

> but with the liberals retaining their status as the activist party. . . . The neo-conservatives have decided that two can play at this game—and must since it is the only game in town. . . . What if the traditionalist-conservatives are right and a [huge] tax cut, without corresponding cuts in expenditures, also leaves us with a fiscal problem? The neo-conservative is willing to leave those problems to be coped with by liberal interregnums. He wants to shape the future, and will leave it up to his opponents to tidy up afterwards.

From then on the right would be activists, and their generous government giveaways would go to business and the rich, and the liberals—as it turned out, Clinton in the 1990s—would obligingly tidy up the mess. The economic right had done its paradigm-shifting work so well during the 1970s and '80s that this new generation of ruling Democrats were no longer really their opponents concerning the political economy. The Clintonians rewrote the old rules and wrote new rules that built in excess and recklessness on behalf of the monied class.

In 1998 Brooksley Born, the federal official who was running the agency overseeing financial derivatives, got worried about the accelerating flurry of trading in new sorts of derivatives, in particular one called credit default swaps—which the rest of us would learn about a decade later, during the crash of 2008. But she was only one member of the official presidential task force that oversees the financial markets. By law, the other three are the Federal Reserve chair, a job to which Clinton had just reappointed Alan Greenspan; the treasury secretary, who was Bob Rubin, previously cochairman of Goldman Sachs; and the SEC chair, who'd also spent his pregovernment career working on Wall Street. The head of the SEC said later he'd been warned in advance that Born was "difficult" and "unreasonable." When she argued at a meeting—in a "strident" way, Rubin recalled—that these new derivatives and the systemic risks they posed needed urgent scrutiny and possible regulations, the three men were appalled, particularly Greenspan, and they told her to calm down.

Restrain Wall Street? Bah. Regulation? This was the great new age of *deregulation,* freer and freer markets, big business and finance unbound! But Born persisted, publicly announcing an inquiry into derivatives and their risks—prompting her fellow task force members to put out a joint statement that they had "grave concerns" about her rogue regulatory inquiry. Rubin's deputy Lawrence Summers, soon to replace him as secretary of the treasury, warned Congress that by suggesting official skepticism of this latest financial innovation, Born had cast "a shadow of regulatory uncertainty over an otherwise thriving market."

She lost and resigned. The guys won and joined with the Republicans running Congress to write two big new laws, a kind of final grand spasm of the deregulation mania that allowed the financial industry to get even wilder and crazier. The first of those Modernization Acts eliminated the rule, instituted after the 1929 Crash, that prohibited regular banks from investing citizens' money in the riskier ways that Wall Street firms did. For years, the financial industry had lobbied for that change, and the former Fed chair Paul Volcker had fought it, but in 1999 only seven of forty-five Democratic senators and a single Republican voted against it. The other Modernization Act explicitly outlawed proper regulation of derivatives such as credit default swaps. The House in 2000 passed that one 377 to 4, and the Senate didn't even bother to take a roll call vote.

In other words, Clinton's Wall Street–bred economic brain trust helped encode into the system the increased recklessness that Wall Street demanded and that would keep feeding inequality and insecurity and soon lead to the financial meltdown and Wall Street bailout and Great Recession. Congratulations, modern bipartisan Democrats!

To be fair begins this next section, inevitably.

To be fair, when Microsoft executives said they were looking to get their vig from every interaction on the Internet, the Clinton Justice Department filed an antitrust suit against the company for trying to rig and dominate the new Internet business. Antitrust enforcement did briefly spring back to life under Clinton: the number of actions tripled, criminal fines increased from $27 million to $1.1 billion in three years, many big mergers were blocked, and some executives even went to prison for price-fixing.

And to be fair, the 1990s were in so many ways a decade of blithe good times that it was easy for people on the reasonable, rational, responsible, respectable, realistic center-left to consent to the rich and the right continuing to redesign and ravish the political economy. Starting in the 1980s but especially the '90s, Americans used and internalized the phrase *Laissez les bons temps rouler,* with which they could justify almost any sort of indiscipline and selfishness. After a quick recession at the start, America's general prosperity felt pretty good through the 1990s, especially but not only to the prosperous. Americans' median household income, more or less flat during the 1970s and '80s, really popped between 1993 and 1999, finally rising from the equivalent of $55,000 to $63,000. Cellphones appeared and proliferated, and the masses were invited onto the Internet, which was still an entirely thrilling and useful thing, not yet an omnipresent, inescapable, often sinister big-business-controlled leviathan. The spectacle of young technologists starting start-ups and getting rich overnight by being *creative* had the effect of further ratifying the virtue of the free market among affluent liberals and cosmopolitans. A generation after *creative destruction* became the aren't-we-awesome catchphrase of the economically and professionally comfortable, it got its digital updating: a Harvard Business School professor's 1995 article about the tech industry coined the phrase *disruptive technologies* and thereby made the digital *disruption* of any and every industry the supposed goal of every capitalist hotshot.

To more and more Americans in the 1990s as in the '80s, what was going on in Silicon Valley—and in Seattle and Boston, in Los Angeles and New York, for better or worse in action-packed *business*—seemed more interesting and important than anything that might happen in Washington, D.C., particularly after the Cold War ended. The collapse of the Soviet Union and Communism at the beginning of the decade was very good news, but it had the unfortunate effect of making almost *any* left critique of America's new hypercapitalism seem not just quixotic but kind of corny.

Sudden victory in the apparently unwinnable and endless Cold War after forty-four years—USA! USA!—unfortunately pushed America's reborn self-congratulatory instinct deeper into complacency and hubris. It was not hard in the 1990s to believe that the United States and its allies were not just the champions of the world in this latest round, but that this was the *final* round, game over, we won. As the millennium approached, invented-in-America political and economic freedom was triumphing globally and for good, because—in the words of an unknown Reagan State Department dweeb in 1989—we'd arrived at "the end point of mankind's ideological evolution and the universalization of Western liberal democracy as the final form of human government." Francis Fukuyama turned his essay into a bestselling and enormously influential book, *The End of History,* in 1992.

It was a moment of supreme self-satisfaction for America's educated upper middle class in particular. One of their own, a Rhodes Scholar who'd graduated from Yale Law School, was about to be elected president. As the Harvard political philosophy professor (and baby boom Rhodes Scholar) Michael Sandel puts it, "Meritocracies . . . produce morally unattractive attitudes among those who make it to the top. The more we believe that our success is our own doing, the less likely we are to feel indebted to, and therefore obligated to, our fellow citizens."

The zeitgeist was the zeitgeist, but not everybody in the chattering class in the 1990s was sanguine about the emerging future, or as oblivious as I still was to the unfairness that had been built into the economy since 1980, or as complacent as I was about the millions of Americans losing out in the go-go globalizing digitizing frenzy.

One was the late Michael Elliott, an extremely smart journalist who'd expatriated from Britain to America in the 1980s as a correspondent for *The Economist*. In *The Day Before Yesterday* in 1996, he argued that the extraordinary thirty years after World War II had been an anomaly, and instead of moping nostalgically, we needed to accept that it was over and carry on. I read Mike's book just a decade ago, at his suggestion, after I'd described some of my embryonic notions for this book. I was struck by his ahead-of-the-curve clarity, a quarter-century ago, about what was happening to America.

> Between 1973 and 1993 median family income saw virtually no growth at all. Moreover, such gains as were made after 1970 were

skewed toward the rich. The working class started to get left behind. Those who were left in declining industries and declining areas would start blaming anyone in sight. Playing off blacks, foreign competition, and immigrants, a degree of class and racial resentment would eventually develop in the white working class. After the 1994 election, it became briefly fashionable to note the rage and alienation of the "angry white male."

Briefly fashionable. Around that same time in 1996, a lead editorial in *The New York Times,* not a bastion of economic leftism, warned that Republican presidential candidates needed to understand that

> America is bedeviled by growing economic inequality in the midst of plenty. The efficient, post-industrial economy is brutal in the way it separates winners from losers. The bulk of the population, which has less than a college education, is falling further and further behind. . . . When people are worried about being laid off from their jobs, losing their health care or not being able to give their children a better future, every statistic that shows the economy doing well makes them feel worse.

Even earlier in the 1990s, the conservative Charles Murray, of all people, published an essay in the conservative *National Review,* of all places, about the specter of inequality haunting America. It was clear-eyed and prescient. "The numbers of the rich will grow more rapidly in the coming years," Murray wrote.

> Real wages for low-skilled jobs will increase more slowly, if at all. . . . I fear the potential for producing something like a caste society, with the implication of utter social separation. . . . All the forces which I can discern will push American conservatism toward the Latin American model. . . . The Left has been complaining for years that the rich have too much power. They ain't seen nothing yet.

Right around then a forty-seven-year-old law school professor and bankruptcy expert, until recently a registered Republican who'd been affiliated in the late 1970s with the conservatives' Law and Economics movement, began to see the light. Elizabeth Warren said in a recent interview that she didn't vote for Reagan but realized only in the '90s that

> starting in the '80s, the cops were taken off the beat in financial services. . . . I was with the GOP for a while because I really thought that it was a party that was principled in its conservative approach to economics and to markets. And I feel like the GOP party just left that. They moved to a party that said, *No, it's not about a level playing field*. . . . And they really stood up for the big financial institutions when the big financial institutions are just hammering middle class American families.

One reason I like Warren is because I identify with her middle-aged illumination concerning the political economy, and with her shift leftward around the turn of the century. I find it telling and amusing that as recently as 2004, in her book *The Two-Income Trap: Why Middle-Class Mothers and Fathers Are Going Broke,* she scrupled to point out that she wasn't suggesting anything very *left-wing,* like "that the United States should build a quasi-socialist safety net to rival the European model."

I'm betting that at the end of 1999, Warren didn't feel complete solidarity with the thousands of demonstrators in Seattle outside the biannual World Trade Organization meeting. Their grievances were various—from AFL-CIO folks pissed off about U.S. companies manufacturing more and more things overseas to anarchists smashing store windows and otherwise acting out their hatred for The System. A few days before the anti-WTO rioting, I'd published an unconnected *Times* op-ed envisioning the new century in which I said that complacent Americans were now "bask[ing] happily and stupidly in the glow of our absolute capitalist triumph," but I was also probably rolling my eyes at the Gen-X kids in Seattle chaining themselves together and getting off on the tear gas; at their lack of a feasible agenda or nuance or even coherence; and at the belief of so many of them in a shadowy, multitentacled conspiracy of the omnipotent elite to tyrannize the little people and subvert democracy.

Yet around the same time, a private meeting was held in Chicago that looks in retrospect an awful lot like a prime node of the conspiracy of the elite economic right committed to subverting democracy. Except it was not shadowy, because a transcript of their conversation was soon published in *The University of Chicago Law Review*. The group consisted of some of the principal founders of Law and Economics, the movement that was busy encoding the preferences of the economic right into the legal and judicial system. (Not present was Robert Bork's Yale Law School pal Guido Calabresi, another founder of the movement who'd just become a federal appeals court judge appointed by . . . President Clinton.*) This supremely august group of conservative legal scholars had assembled in a room at the law school for a conversation about all that their little group had accomplished during the previous couple of decades, and about what remained to be done in the future. The gathering had a distinctly celebratory air.

One of the five, the Nobel Prize–winning economist Gary Becker—whose mentor Milton Friedman considered him "the greatest social scientist" of the late twentieth century, and who was in turn a mentor to the junk bond felon Mike Milken—fretted that victory was not yet total. In particular, he was peeved by some new federal rules that made it a bit easier for employees who'd been fired or forced to quit to claim discrimination.

But his fellow pioneer Richard Posner, a judge on the federal appeals court based in Chicago, told his comrade to relax. With the indiscriminate deregulation of big business, they'd helped enable "the near collapse of the labor movement," and "the effect of these developments has been to make this a freer country than it was in the 60s. These [new] labor laws are in the category of annoyances."

At this, according to the transcript, the eminent old men actually *laughed,* just as sinister suit-and-tie conspirators gathered in a wood-paneled room in a movie would do.

The digital revolution notwithstanding, as 2000 approached, the American political economy was looking more and more like that of the previous fin de siècle, the good old days of the 1890s. Any last-ditch Democratic efforts now to reempower workers, Judge Posner told his compatriots, would be merely "irritants that good lawyers reduce to where there is only a very minor impact."

*His nephew Steven Calabresi, by the way, was a cofounder of the Federalist Society and clerked for both Judge Bork and Justice Scalia. In 2019 he co-wrote an article called "Why Robert Mueller's Appointment as Special Counsel Was Unlawful."

PART FOUR

Same Old Same Old

20

Rewind, Pause, Stop: The End of the New

W*ow, it's actually happening, the year 2000, a* new century! *A* new *millennium! Computers, videophones! The future!*

But on second thought? Let's try as hard as we can to make sure everything else, the culture and the economy, doesn't change at all.

The earliest work of American fiction that's still famous, published exactly two hundred years ago, is a story of how quickly and radically everything can change in America. In Washington Irving's "Rip van Winkle," the eponymous hero is kind of a hippie—"a simple, good-natured fellow" with an "insuperable aversion to all kinds of profitable labor"—who lives in upstate New York near Woodstock in the early 1770s. Fantastical Hobbitish creatures he meets in the woods give him a magical druggy drink that puts him to sleep for twenty years, until the 1790s. He wakes up to find that the British colonies are now the United States of America and that "the very character of the people seemed changed"—more politically polarized, working too hard, noisier, a bit manic.

As I've written this book, I've kept thinking of that story. And I imagined a modern reboot about a descendant of Rip van Winkle's who slips into a recreational-drug-induced coma in the early 1970s and awakes from her two-decade sleep in the *1990*s, confused and amazed by the transfigured America. Except in the modern version, while this Rip is struck by all the new gadgetry—cellphones, PCs, the Internet—she's even more freaked out by how America had also somehow *gone back in time.* It is life in the early 1900s redux—organized labor impotent, big business and Wall Street idolized, wealth flaunted, taxes on the rich low, Washington corruption rampant and shameless again. (Plus there is a new venereal disease more fatal than any had been before penicillin, our immigrant population is growing again to early 1900s levels, and primitive Christianity is as loud and angry and even bigger that it was back then.)

Neo-Rip in the 1990s is likewise astonished to discover that the yesteryear schticks that emerged just before she passed out—the Beatles' Olde England outfits and lyrics, the Old West evocations of the Band and the Dead, Sha Na Na's nostalgia act at Woodstock—have turned out to be the prototypes and harbingers for the whole cultural future, that every medium and genre is now filled with reiterations and permutations of the familiar past. And *Ronald Reagan* from *Death Valley Days* was elected and reelected *president of the United States*?

In 1988 in *Spy,* we published a love-hate cover story mock-celebrating the bygone 1970s, subtitled "A Return to the Decade of Mood Rings, Ultrasuede, Sideburns and Disco Sex-Machine Tony Orlando." One of its comedic premises was that the new compulsive nostalgia had gotten so out of control that people might start feeling nostalgic for a decade that had ended only a hundred months before. In the 1989 *Spy* essay I mentioned earlier, we wrote about the new phenomenon of our curated, air-quoting, stylishly nostalgia-centric lives. We imagined a couple named Bob and Betty who lived a 1980s everything-old-is-new-again *lifestyle,* the first hipsters, a decade before anyone used that word the way it's used now:

> Bob is wearing a hibiscus-y Hawaiian shirt that he purchased at a "vintage" clothing boutique for approximately six times the garment's original 1952 price. He also carries his lunch in a tackle box and wears a Gumby wristwatch, Converse high-tops and baggy khakis. Bob describes his look as "Harry Truman mixed with early Jerry Mathers." Bob assumes we know that Mathers played the title role on *Leave It to Beaver*. Betty wears Capri pants, ballet

flats and a man's oversized white shirt, along with a multi-zippered black leather motorcycle jacket imprinted with Cyrillic letters. She is "Audrey Hepburn by way of Patty Duke as James Dean's girlfriend waiting on the dragstrip."

Betty and Bob have a child, a two-year-old who they call "Kitten." The child is probably too young to catch the reference to *Father Knows Best,* even though she sits with her parents when they watch Nick at Nite, the [new] cable TV service devoted almost entirely to the isn't-it-ironic recapitulations of shows from the early 1960s. The invitations to Betty and Bob's wedding were printed with sketches of jitterbugging couples; for their honeymoon they rented a station wagon and drove south, visiting Graceland, Cypress Gardens, and the Texas School Book Depository. Betty and Bob buy souvenirs from the 1964 Worlds Fair and "atomic" furniture from the 50s—"real *Jetsons* stuff." Bob has taught the family mutt, Spot, to do the Twist. Bob works in advertising, "like Darren on *Bewitched.*"

In other words, by the 1990s, a generation after the first widespread outbreaks, nostalgia and cultural recycling were fully industrialized. Hollywood never used to remake old TV shows, let alone produce feature films based on them. Most Broadway musicals would now be revivals or a kind of reproduction pseudo-revival that stitched together old songs—*jukebox musicals,* even the name was from an obsolete old-timey machine. The one genuinely new pop cultural genre, hip-hop, made an explicit, unapologetic point of quoting old songs. Science fiction, the cultural genre that is all about imagining the future, got a new subgenre in the 1990s that was considered supercool because it was set in the past—steampunk. And commercialized futurism also became oddly familiar and nostalgic. Apple devices of the twenty-first century and glassy, supersleek Apple stores feel "contemporary" in the sense that they're like props and back-on-Earth sets from *2001: A Space Odyssey,* the 2000s as they were envisioned in the '60s, the moment before nostalgia took over everything.

The nostalgia division of the fantasy-industrial complex began merchandising in precincts beyond entertainment, from fake-old cars like Miatas and PT Cruisers to retail chains like Restoration Hardware selling stylish fake-old things. "Lurking in our collective unconscious, among images of Ike, Donna Reed, and George Bailey," the promotional video for Restoration Hardware's initial public offering of stock in 1998 explained to investors, "is the very clear sense that things were once better made, that they mattered a little more."

Americans were finally so immersed in nostalgia, they stopped registering it as nostalgia. The frequency of the word *nostalgia* in American books steadily increased during the twentieth century, spiked in the late 1980s, then peaked and began a steep decline in 1999. A century ago engines made horses economically useless in the United States and reduced their number by 90 percent. But nostalgia (and wealth) have caused their remarkable comeback: since the 1990s, America's horse population has doubled to 10 million, growing faster than anywhere else on Earth.

The Bob and Betty hipsters who brought back vinyl records at the turn of this century consider it an act of authenticity and audiophilia, not *nostalgia,* God forbid. From 1980 to the early 2000s, annual vinyl album sales decreased by 99.7 percent to just a few hundred thousand. But these days they're selling 20 million a year, a sixth of all albums sold—two per American horse. It's a nostalgic medium for nostalgic music: in 2018 nine of the top-ten vinyl albums consisted of pop songs from ten, thirty, or fifty years earlier. The term *reboot,* borrowed from digital technology, replaced *remake* and *revival* to disguise the fact that stylish young people were now indulging in what used to be the exclusive pastime of uncool old people.

Toward the end of the 1990s, I had my very first inkling that we were entering the curious next phase of cultural time-warping. After the big shift to feasting on the reassuringly familiar *past,* the arts and entertainment and design now seemed to be shutting down production of almost anything that was truly, startlingly *new,* that might usefully nudge us into some uncharted, unknowable *future*. Stasis had begun.

In an article in *The New Yorker* about a show of the late Keith Haring's work, I wrote that the exhibit might *seem* to be heralding "an eighties revival"—because an artist who typified the previous decade was getting a retrospective at "the Whitney Museum, an ur-eighties cultural institution." However, I concluded by suggesting that in fact, we weren't experiencing "an eighties '*revival,*'" but rather that the supposedly quieter, compassionate "early nineties were just a hiatus" and that in fact, "*the eighties never ended.*"

I was half-joking, but from then on I occasionally noticed signs that the 1980s, unlike previous decades, were just . . . continuing. I'd lived through several American decades—the 1950s, '60s, '70s, and '80s—and each of those earlier ones, like the ones before I was alive, had its highly distinct cultural character, identifiable as a stereotype even before it was finished. In that *New Yorker* article in 1997, I'd defined the character of the American 1980s as "manic, moneyed, celebrity-obsessed, shameless." None of that really changed in the 1990s or in the 2000s or in the 2010s.

Yes, of course, the September 11, 2001, attacks and the financial and economic meltdown of 2008 were traumatizing, and right after each, I thought obviously *this* will finally change *everything*, and that I'd finally have to stop pointing out to family and friends every new bit of evidence that the 1980s never ended. Instead, immediately after 9/11, the president instructed us all to *shop* and to have fun as if nothing had happened, get over it, which we quickly did; apart from airport security and a disastrous war and a new focus for bigotry, the main lasting result was to amplify the overcompensating *"USA! USA!"* belligerence that had swelled up in the 1980s. In 2009 I imagined that the near-death economic experience of the crash and recession might scare us straight, prompt us to reform the reckless laissez-faire casino economy, as our forebears did after the Roaring '20s. I even published a hopeful little manifesto to that effect. But no, instead we were like a nation of Wile E. Coyotes: having sped off a cliff into midair after the 1980s, looking down for a reality check, and plummeting to Earth in 2008, we then returned to crazed business as usual on Wall Street, which continued to dominate the economy. Not much really changed.

Sure, technology was changing everyday life around the edges, at least for the first decade of the new century—the Internet scaled, and new world-changing devices (iPod, iPhone, Kindle) and platforms (Netflix, iTunes, Facebook, YouTube, Spotify, Twitter, Grindr) appeared. But the digital revolution had very clearly *started* in the 1980s, when every yuppie bought a personal computer, and many of us, by means of CompuServe or The WELL, got on the Internet, and some early adopters even had mobile phones. When Pixar's short *Luxo Jr.* appeared in 1986, I realized I was seeing the future of movies. And by the mid-1990s, when we'd all seen *Toy Story* and had cellphones and a browsable, searchable Web, on which we were buying books on Amazon and cool *old* things on eBay, the digital revolution was a done deal.

Around the time I first read one of my novels as an e-book and looked forward to buying my first iPhone, I had that wrinkle-in-time epiphany I mentioned in the introduction—how after three decades marinating in nostalgia, something even weirder had happened to Americans and American culture. Reading the *Times* one morning in 2007, I came across the revelatory photograph in an article about Ian Schrager and Steve Rubell, the supreme New York discotheque impresarios who then became inventors of the boutique hotel. The picture was from twenty-two years earlier, 1985, when they'd posed with some of the young staff at Morgans, their cool old-fashioned-but-cutting-edge Manhattan prototype.

Schrager's collarless dress shirt looked somewhat retro, but I was otherwise struck by the fact that none of the dozen people in this very old picture appeared obviously, amusingly *dated,* not their clothes, not their hairstyles, not the women's makeup. If any of them had walked by me on the street that afternoon, I wouldn't have given him or her a second look. They could've all passed for contemporary people. Which as I thought about it seemed very weird, particularly given that they were all professionally required to appear cool and au courant—and weren't short shelf lives intrinsic to fashion and style?

I kept thinking about it. I imagined the stylistic changes that would have appeared over any comparable chunk of historical time. Suppose in 1997 I'd looked at a similar photo taken in 1975, or watched a 1970s movie or TV show . . . the jangly music, the luxuriant sideburns and hair, the bell-bottoms and leisure suits, the cigarettes and avocado-colored refrigerators and AMC Matadors and Gremlins—everything and everyone would have looked so different, so dated. Or if back in 1975 I'd looked at images or shows or movies from twenty-two years before then, 1953, before rock and roll and Vietnam and the Pill, when both sexes wore hats, and only women had long hair, and no adult wore jeans or sneakers in public, and cars were massive and bulbous; again, unmistakably different. Rewind back another generation, from 1953 to 1931, absolutely distinct looks and style . . . and again, 1931 versus 1909, ditto. A man or woman on the street dressed and groomed in the characteristic manner of somebody from twenty-two years earlier would look very odd. A twenty-two-year-old car always looked *old*.

No more. Now people drove new Nissans and Infinitis that looked practically identical to the Nissans and Infinitis from a generation earlier. They sat in new Aeron chairs exactly like the new Aeron chairs people had sat in twenty years earlier.

I conducted taste tests among people my age and in their forties and thirties and twenties. I played them new pop songs that weren't big hits and showed them clips of unfamiliar new movies and photos of recent buildings and cars, asking when they thought each had been created. Almost nobody could definitively say that things from 2007 weren't from 1997 or 1987. Weren't Lady Gaga and Adele and Josh Ritter, all new phenoms at the time, more or less Madonna and Mariah Carey and Bob Dylan redux? Hip-hop had broken through to the mainstream in the late 1980s and early '90s, but in the 2000s it was just . . . continuing to be mainstream, no longer excitingly *new*.

I started culling through old images and recordings, hundreds of them from the twentieth century and back in the nineteenth century, comparing era to era, decade to decade, the differences in clothes and hairstyles and cars, music and movies and advertising, architecture and product design and graphics, all of it.

In the past, over the course of any and every two-decade period, the look and sound of life changed dramatically. New York's famous new architecture of the 1930s (the Chrysler Building, the Empire State Building) looks nothing like the famous new architecture that appeared twenty years earlier (the Flatiron Building, Grand Central Terminal, the Woolworth Building) or twenty years later (the Seagram Building, the UN Headquarters, the Guggenheim Museum). Anyone can instantly identify a 1950s movie (*On the Waterfront, The Bridge on the River Kwai*) versus one from twenty years before (*Grand Hotel, It Happened One Night*) or twenty years after (*Klute, A Clockwork Orange*) and tell the difference between hit songs from 1992 (Sir Mix-a-Lot) and 1972 (Neil Young) and 1952 (Patti Page) and 1932 (Duke Ellington).

That unmistakable ceaseless stylistic change was the nature of life for most of the history of the United States. But after the 1980s, cultural time slowed down and in many ways stopped. The 1990s looked and sounded extremely different than the 1970s, but by comparison, the 2010s were almost indistinguishable from the 1990s, as 2020 is almost indistinguishable from 2000.

In any year during the twentieth century, if somebody on an American city street were dressed and groomed in the manner of someone from twenty or twenty-five years earlier, they would've looked like an actor in costume or a time traveler. Whereas if every second pedestrian you passed today actually *was* a time traveler fresh from 2000, you'd really have no clue, even if one of them were speaking on her (cool vintage) cellphone.

Jeans and T-shirts and sneakers remain today a standard American uniform for all ages, as they were in 2000, 1990, and the 1980s. There are now more yoga pants and other "athleisure wear," which is really just tighter, thinner sweat clothes.

Pop music was a truly modern cultural form because by its nature it changed so quickly, its stylistic evolutionary speed resulting from a century of new technologies, first recordings and radio, then TV and cable TV. This makes music worth a slightly deeper case study, because that process of abandoning real novelty as a guiding principle is so apparent. Along with the rest of pop and high culture, music plunged into self-conscious nostalgia in the 1970s, which listeners at first *heard* nostalgically—such as *Born to Run*—and then proceeded into automatic recycling and stasis, with listeners more and more unaware that more and more of ostensibly "new" music was being recycled from musical history.

I started nailing down this phenomenon in an essay in *Vanity Fair* a decade ago, around the time Simon Reynolds published *Retromania,* his great book-length history of the decline and fall of the new in pop music, showing how startlingly new sounds had disappeared in favor of "revivals, reissues, remakes, reenactments" and "rampant recycling." I was delighted to have my theory validated in the musical sphere by somebody with far greater knowledge. The 1960s had "set the bar impossibly high" for breaking new ground, writes Reynolds, who was only six at the end of the '60s, and then as

> the eighties rolled into the nineties, increasingly music began to be talked about only in terms of other music; creativity became reduced to taste games. What changed from the mid-80s onwards was the level of acclaim that blatantly derivative groups began to receive. Retro-styled groups had generally been a niche market, for people unhealthily obsessed with a bygone past. But now these heavily indebted bands [such as] The Stone Roses, Oasis, [and] The White Stripes, could become "central." In the 2000s the pop

> present became ever more crowded out by the past, [with] bygone genres revived and renovated, vintage sonic material reprocessed and recombined. There has never been a society in human history so obsessed with the cultural artifacts of *its own immediate past*.

Reynolds documents how the new pop musical stars of the twenty-first century, even the best artists among them, continue doing cover versions, de facto when not literally, of soul and rock from the 1960s, punk and rap and synth pop from the '70s and '80s. "Is nostalgia stopping our culture's ability to surge forward," he asks, "or are we nostalgic precisely because our culture has stopped moving forward and so we inevitably look back to more momentous and dynamic times?" I'm pretty sure it's both, as it tends to be with big, diffuse causes and effects.

Thirty years have passed since the last two genuinely new pop genres of significance had their golden ages—rap and hip-hop, and techno and house and rave. In 1990 the former was about to be mainstreamed and still endures, while the latter, with its self-consciously futuristic *newness* from the early digital age, now seems . . . quaint. I asked Reynolds if any new musical forms had emerged during the 2010s that inclined him to modify his theory of the case. He mentioned the "digital maximalism" of "electronic producers whose music is very processed sounding and smeared in terms of both its textures and its pitch." Right. In other words, not really. "You could say with much of this stuff, it's an extension of what was going on in the nineties, just with even more fiddly production and tiny sonic events per bar."

In fact, it is ironic how digital technology—newness incarnate, the essence of the present and future—has reinforced our fixed backward stare and helped mesmerize us into cultural stasis. Starting in the 1990s, Internet search (as well as cable TV) provided access to old pictures and sounds that we'd never had before, and then all at once, from 2005 to 2007, comprehensive new digital archives of the old opened up and transfixed us—first the astounding YouTube, then the endless streams of Pandora, Spotify, and online Netflix. When the future arrived, it let us sink further and further into uncanny dreams of the past.

As Reynolds writes, "We've become so used to this convenient access" to old music and images "that it is a struggle to recall that life wasn't always like this, that relatively recently one lived most of the time in a cultural present tense, with the past confined to specific zones, trapped in particular objects and locations." If you're young, and have grown up only since the Internet has been dissolving the distinctions between past and present and old and new, the sci-fi writer and futurist William Gibson says, "I suspect that you inhabit a sort of endless digital Now, a state of atemporality enabled by our increasingly efficient communal prosthetic memory." What's more, I think digital technology has made it so easy for anybody to create and distribute songs and pictures and videos and stories, and for everyone to consume them, that the resulting democratic flood of stuff—each of the 100 million cover versions and impersonations and fan fictions that are *nominally* brand new—can fool us into thinking the culture is more fertile and vibrant than it is.

A slightly different expression of the stasis that descended in the 1990s was the disappearance of musical diversity among the most popular pop songs. A 2018 study, by two young data journalists, of the summer hits every year from 1970 to 2015 algorithmically derived each song's "fingerprint" not from its genre or style but from its underlying sonic components—valence, loudness, energy, and so on. By those measures, from the 1970s through the '80s and into the '90s, the hits were extremely different from one another, such as the 1988 songs the researchers deconstructed by Cheap Trick, INXS, and Def Leppard. But then suddenly, in the late 1990s, they discovered, the hits were no longer diverse, and they haven't been since. Now even when hit songs *seem* fairly different—such as those by Katy Perry, Eminem, and Lady Gaga in the summer of 2010—their deeper sonic traits (valence, loudness, energy) are actually quite similar. So it isn't that the most popular new songs now all sound like *old* songs, but that they all fundamentally sound the *same*, like one another, thus satisfying the deeper need driving nostalgia—for reassuring *familiarity*, nothing too strange or challenging.

Genre by genre and medium by medium, we could debate whether *this* or *that* show or song or design or work of art counts as a truly new cultural species. Obviously the last twenty years have been an exceptional time for television drama—few to no series as great as *The Sopranos, The Wire, Breaking Bad, Black Mirror, Atlanta, Fleabag,* or *Succession* existed on American TV during its first fifty years. However, this golden age mainly resulted not from deep changes in culture and sensibility but rather from changes in the technology of distribution and the business models of entertainment: cable and Internet broadband allowed for a great migration of creative talent and ambition and risk-taking and rule-breaking from one distribution channel to another, from movie theaters to TV sets and computer screens. It's like how Amazon hasn't changed the things we buy, just how we can buy them and how they're delivered to us.

Plus ça change, plus c'est la même chose always meant that the constant novelty and flux of modern life is superficial, that the underlying essences endure unchanged. But that saying now has an alternative and nearly opposite meaning: the more that underlying structures change for real (technology, the political economy), the more the surfaces (style, entertainment) remain the same.

In the early 1990s, Francis Fukuyama published his argument that all societies were inexorably arriving at the same evolutionary end point—the glorious finale of political economic history. Such folly. Yet in the arts and entertainment and style, what happened then, at the moment when both *The End of History* and the film *Groundhog Day* came out, does feel like an end of cultural history. Or at least, and I'm still hoping, an extremely long pause.

So to recap: the national nostalgia reflex was triggered in the first place in the 1970s by fatigue from all the warp-drive cultural changes of the '60s. It's as if the whole culture, finally too stoned to stand up and lift the stylus on an LP that was skipping, just let it go on playing the same track over and over and over. That was indulged and encouraged by impresarios and marketers and, in the digital age, by new archival technology. We entered a Been There Done That Mashup Age, in which our culture's primary MO came to consist of endlessly recycling and reviving old forms, or in any case steering clear of the unfamiliar. After two or three decades of compulsively pressing SEARCH and REWIND on the culture machine, which was now equipped with the practically infinite Alexandrian library of YouTube, we'd found a STOP NEW OUTPUT button and pressed that too.

But *why*? Why did we allow a taste for old or otherwise familiar forms and styles to spread and congeal into a general cultural stasis?

Because, I think, the economic changes of the 1980s, while not as immediately or spectacularly obvious as those of the '60s, were in their ways at least as profound. The 1960s had triggered that first nostalgia wave as a soothing counterreaction. A generation later the unpleasant economic changes of the 1980s and '90s made us retreat even deeper into our havens of the recycled and reassuringly old as a kind of national cultural self-medication. The *unavoidable* newness disoriented many people—the brutal winners-take-all economy and PCs evolving to supercomputers in every pocket all connected to one another, the easily graspable Cold War replaced by the confusing rise of China and militant Islamism, the influx of immigrants—take your pick.

Just as Americans who came of age from the 1960s and after tended to be Peter Pans, fearing or resisting adulthood like no previous generations, trying to stay forever young, we also started fearing the future and resisting the new in general. Again, the writer J. G. Ballard delivered a kind of early-warning prophecy. "The year 2000 will come," he wrote in the early 1990s, "but I have a feeling that some time over the next 10 or 20 years, there is going to be a major break of human continuity. One of the reasons we've turned our backs against the future at present is that people may well perceive unconsciously that the future is going to be a very dangerous place."

Since the 1990s, people able to make good livings in technology have reveled in innovation and disruption and remain devoted to the quest for the new in some ways, but many more Americans have been clinging ever more desperately to the tried and true and familiar, wherever and however they can, comforted by a world that at least still looks and sounds more or less the way it looked and sounded last year, or last century.

There are now also pockets of wistfulness for the time just before cultural stagnation took full effect. In 2019 I talked with Liz Phair, the singer-songwriter whose first album made her famous in 1993, and asked her about all the new young singer-songwriters emulating her musical style from a quarter-century ago. It derives from a specific nostalgia, she thinks, for "the last time before the Internet."

> It's the last time that we weren't all isolated and connected in this isolated way, connected but not really connecting. It was the last time that people had to walk to the record store and pick up something or go to the show and stand there and meet people and make friends that way. It was the last period before we became hooked up to the wires. I think that's what it is.

Research by academic psychologists has confirmed that disconcerting changes do indeed make people seek the old and familiar for reassurance. As one of those scholars recently summarized the corpus of studies and experiments, the more that change "makes people anxious about the world and their place in it" and causes "major disruptions and uncertainties in their lives," then "the more they longed nostalgically . . . for the comparative safety and security of a perceived past."

The general default to nostalgia that started in the 1970s helped soften the ground for the right's project. Fronted by a make-believe cowboy and make-believe war hero from old movies, they built a reproduction-old-days political economy—extremely high regard and low taxation and few constraints for big business and the rich, spectacular selfishness rebranded as healthy American individualism.

But I think the cultural *stagnation* that followed has also served the interests of the right and the rich. Progress, creating and adapting to the new—these had been defining American ideals. The deliberate political and economic and social changes from 1900 to 1970—Progressivism, the New Deal, greater economic equality, greater legal equality—coincided both with accelerating technological change and with accelerating changes in cultural styles, how the surfaces and sounds of life were remade every decade or two, all reaching maximum velocity at the end of the 1960s. Those brief stylistic shelf lives trained us to register artifacts even from the recent past as old-fashioned, and to keep moving forward. America's pursuit of the new and improved, political and economic over here and culture over there, operated in sync.

But that ended at the end of the twentieth century, and we locked ourselves in a vicious cycle of mutually reinforcing status quos—culturally, politically, and economically. As the changes in music and design and fashion and the rest slowed or stopped, I think that served to reinforce people's fatalism and resignation, the sense that *major* changes in the political economy also wouldn't or couldn't happen anymore. Since the stage set and soundtrack of life had remained weirdly the same for a quarter-century and counting, it made some kind of dreadful sense that salaries also remained weirdly stagnant, and that more Americans stay put in the states and the economic classes where they happened to be born. With each passing year of stagnation, every kind of stagnation seemed less strange, more natural. *It is what it is,* everyone started saying in the

1990s. A cultural diet of reboots and revivals on an endless loop habituates people to expect and put up with the same old same old forever and to lose their appetite for the new, for change, for progress.

Once again, just to be clear, I'm not suggesting that the evil geniuses who pulled off the remarkable political and economic transformation from the 1970s through the '90s also planned or executed our cultural U-turn. In this respect, they were mainly just shrewd and lucky. Rather, it's like when two different chronic illnesses tend to appear in the same people at the same time—like arthritis and heart disease, or depressive disorders and anxiety disorders, or COVID-19 and type 2 diabetes. The medical term of art is *comorbidity*. The outbreak of mass nostalgia in the 1970s that then developed into a general cultural listlessness, in other words, is comorbid with what happened to our political economy. One illness didn't exactly cause the other illness, but each made the other more serious, and harder to cure.

21

The Politics of Nostalgia and Stagnation Since the 1990s

The economics professor (and author and blogger and podcaster) Tyler Cowen has written intelligently about our national stagnation and "the growing number of people in our society who accept, welcome, or even enforce a resistance to things new, different, or challenging." He also thinks we reached a tipping point on this score in the 1990s. "Americans are in fact working much harder than before to postpone change," he wrote in his 2017 book *The Complacent Class,*

> or to avoid it altogether, and this is true whether we're talking about corporate competition, changing residences or jobs, or building things. In an age when it is easier than ever before to dig in, the psychological resistance to change has become progressively stronger. On top of that, information technology, for all the disruption it has wrought, allows us to organize more effectively to confront things that are new or different, in a manageable and comfortable way, and sometimes to keep them at bay altogether.

He predicts that "eventually stasis will prove insufficient," given the "ongoing collapse of the middle class" and because our political economic "structures are not ultimately sustainable for the broader majority of the population" to improve their lives, so "big changes will have to come, whether we like it or not." Cowen shakes his head at "people's willingness to just put up with things" and "settle for the status quo" and "not really agitate for very urgent change."

However, he doesn't say that the resistance to change and enervation and political complacency mainly serve the interests of the right and the rich. Nor does he acknowledge that the increase in economic insecurity and inequality and immobility that began around 1980 was caused or exacerbated by our historic right turn just then. That's probably because Cowen is a product and promoter of that turn—incubated as a student at George Mason University in the early 1980s just as the libertarian right turned it into a headquarters. He is now a George Mason professor and director of its Mercatus Center, the think tank created by Charles Koch, with whom he has a mutual admiration society.*

Cowen correctly points to many *symptoms* of the disease he calls the Great Stagnation, but he's evidently too ideologically blindered to specify all its causes and comorbidities or to recommend emergency treatment. His free-market faith obliges him to conclude that the only real problem is the slower rate of economic growth for most of the last half-century. Furthermore, he thinks the long American economic heyday from the late 1800s through the 1970s came to its natural conclusion because we'd picked and eaten all "the low-hanging fruit" that produced easy growth—cheap land, fossil fuels, new technologies, mass education. Thus it was *only* from World War II through the 1970s, in Cowen's view, that America could *afford* to be so generous—that is, to make the political economy fair for all its citizens—because the GDP per person was growing by almost 3 percent per year, as opposed to 2 percent or less afterward.

The end of that marvelous century-long boom time was nobody's fault, couldn't really be helped, he thinks. So likewise now: while it's *too bad* that since 1980 only the prosperous have continued getting more prosperous and feeling secure, the people refusing to put up with that status quo and agitating to change it politically are indulging in misguided . . .

*Cowen dedicated his short 2011 book *The Great Stagnation* to Peter Thiel, who he calls "one of the greatest and most important public intellectuals of our entire time. Throughout the course of history, he will be recognized as such." Thiel is the libertarian billionaire cofounder of PayPal who donated $1.25 million to the 2016 Trump campaign.

nostalgia. Cowen says it's "nostalgia for aspects of the economic world of the 1950s" that leads economists on the left to push for "some very particular features of the 1950s: high marginal tax rates, high rates of unionization, and a relatively egalitarian distribution of income and wealth."*

LOL and touché, clever contemporary conservative, for using *nostalgia* as a political pejorative, the way liberals have always done, the way a lot of us got into the bad habit of doing in the 1970s and '80s about FDR and organized labor and antitrust and thereby became useful idiots for you and the evil geniuses of the right.

Yet why shouldn't Americans feel nostalgic for the time before 1980 when we had a more equal distribution of income and wealth and all boats rose together? If "Make America Great Again" hadn't already been taken, it could've worked extremely well as a 2020 Democratic presidential campaign slogan.

Nostalgia is not always wrong or all bad. Almost all of us are nostalgic for something, if only for our childhoods. Almost everyone likes new things as well as old and familiar things, each of us choosing different combinations from the menu. For instance, a lot of habitués of those supermodern Apple stores, shopping for an iPhone 12 or AirPods and adoring their regular visits to the high-production-value future promised in the past, go home to make-believe-old-fashioned lives—a new gingerbread cottage or an apartment in a renovated former factory, beer gardens, greenmarkets, local agriculture, flea markets, tattoos, lace-up boots, suspenders, beards, mustaches, artisanal everything, all the neo-nineteenth-century signifiers of state-of-the-art American cool.

Beyond the charming surfaces and styles of the past, it's essential as well to look at history carefully for deeper lessons and models, inspirations and cautionary tales for the present and future. Nostalgia starts getting problematic only when it becomes reflexive and total, congealing into an automatic antagonism to the new or unfamiliar. Nostalgia is problematic when it becomes the fuel for a politics based on fantastical or irrecoverable or unsupportable parts of the past. And that current American political movement, consisting of pathological nostalgias centered on

*To his credit, in his 2018 book *Stubborn Attachments,* Cowen grants that his libertarianism is nondoctrinaire enough to allow that a few problems, such as the climate crisis, do require massive government action.

race and ethnicity and religion and gender and sexuality, Trumpism, has as its avatar a quintessentially 1980s creature, living proof of my '90s theory that the decade never did end.

Misguided resistance to the new isn't limited to the right. *Leftist reactionary* is not an oxymoron. For instance, I think of liberals I know who want to outlaw GMOs and charter schools and allow kindergarteners to go unvaccinated, to make it harder to build affordable housing and easier to prevent disagreeable public speech. Conversely, some people on the left reflexively dismiss almost *any* fondness for the past because so much about the past was *bad*. During a recent panel discussion about the history and future of the news media, I made the point that before the 1980s and '90s, editors and producers did a better job of keeping outright falsehoods and delusions from circulating widely—and the panelists, friends of mine, immediately pounced because it seemed to them I was implicitly excusing the paucity of women and nonwhite people in journalism back then.

But of course, opposing the new has also always been and remains a defining trait of conservatism, and nostalgia-based reactionary politics are thus much more common on the right. Apart from purely technological progress, the important changes of the last century that make the American present preferable to the American past—universal pensions and guaranteed medical care for old people, more freedom and fairness for women and black people and queer people, cleaner air and water for everyone—were opposed by the right. So it's no surprise that today's most explicitly nostalgia-driven politics, all about fearing and loathing the new, are on the conservative side.

One astonishing and unambiguously great new American condition since the early 1990s is how murder and other violent crime rates have dropped by half, and in many places by much more—by more than 80 percent in New York City, for instance. Like all good news, it was soon forgotten and ignored, but politicians on the right go even further, actually *denying* that this remarkable social improvement happened, because it doesn't fit well into their racist or nativist or otherwise fear-mongering political narrative. Donald Trump began his presidency by saying "the murder rate in our country is the highest it's been in forty-seven years," which is the very opposite of the truth. Of course, he'd launched his campaign in Trump Tower by portraying Mexican immigrants as rapists and drug dealers, even though immigrants are *less* likely than native-born Americans to commit crimes.

In addition to these dangerous falsehoods portraying the present as worse than the past, most of the important new social facts on which American politics have hinged lately are no longer actually new. We just haven't managed to address them honestly or seriously or effectively as a nation. Economic growth slowed forty years ago, when the downsides of automation and globalization started becoming obvious—and when experts also agreed that global warming was becoming a crisis. A quarter-century ago the digital revolution was in full swing, and people paying attention saw that economic inequality and insecurity were rapidly increasing. The number of immigrants to the United States started soaring back in the late 1960s, and the increase in our foreign-born population was already leveling off by 2000, and a dozen years ago the undocumented population started decreasing.* So much of the "new" is old.

More and more of our politics has devolved into battles *among* nostalgias, fights over which parts of the past should or shouldn't and can or can't be recycled or restored. Each of the particular nostalgias tends to be more red or more blue, but they all fall on a spectrum from reasonable to understandable to foolish to malignant.

By *reasonable,* I mean both desirable and feasible. It's reasonable to seek to return somehow to something like the economic fairness and opportunity and security we enjoyed before 1980. It's reasonable to want to recover the skepticism our parents and grandparents and great-grandparents had about huge corporations exercising unfair economic and political power, especially companies that provide essential goods and services such as energy or information. It's reasonable to be nostalgic for faster economic growth, although our ability to achieve that by government action is limited.

It's understandable nostalgia, but verging on foolish, to think that the old norms of reality-based discourse or bipartisan Washington cooperation will return anytime soon. It's foolish verging on malignant for leaders

*Likewise, *Roe v. Wade* invalidated laws against abortion almost half a century ago—and by the way, the rate of U.S. abortions is now half what it was at its peak in 1981, and less than it was before *Roe v. Wade*.

to promote a U.S. economic future in which coal mining and steel milling are central features.*

And then there's nostalgia for a strong and widespread sense of national solidarity. A historically important source of that feeling—actual solidarity, not rueful pining to feel it again—was the shared experience of World War II. A related social benefit of the war, and the New Deal before it, was the universal understanding that a strong federal government was crucial as well as basically competent. The American bond from having survived the war (and the Depression before it) lasted a couple of decades—until around 1965, when the sense of national solidarity began its long decay, accelerated by a disastrous imperial war in which most Americans had no personal stake. By 1998, the year Tom Brokaw's book *The Greatest Generation* and Steven Spielberg's film *Saving Private Ryan* came out, the iffy us-against-them bonding provided by the Cold War was over, and World War II was practically fossilized nostalgia.

As recently as the 2000s, it seemed quite reasonable to strive for national solidarity. The 9/11 attacks produced a jolt of it, and three years later it became the premise for the instant rise of an Illinois state senator ("The 'Blue States' . . . the 'Red States' . . . We are *one* people") to superstardom. As a form of nostalgia, the wish for greater national solidarity is understandable, but it lately has felt impossible to achieve and therefore somewhat foolish.

The biggest (but not only) reason for national disunity the last dozen years or more is that a quarter or third of Americans and one political party have explicitly given themselves over to malignant nostalgia—nostalgia for a country with much larger and more dominant majorities of white and native-born and Christian people, and for a time when people who weren't white or male or straight had fewer rights and less stature. That's a lost cause for them—the United States will never be as white or Christian as it was, nor a country where women and people of color are oppressed like they were when I was young.

That nostalgia is also a revival of the Lost Cause from a century and

*"We on Team Trump," Peter Navarro, the president's director of manufacturing policy, said in 2018, "are astonished by the argument that America's future is in the services sector, and [that] Americans don't want 'dirty' jobs in steel furnaces."

a half ago—post–Civil War white Southerners' self-pitying, self-flattering nostalgia for the wonderful Old South (which happened to include the enslavement of black people) and the Civil War they started and fought to preserve it.

Our twenty-first-century political fight over immigration is a case of dueling nostalgias over the same subject. It's *Build the wall* nostalgia for the mid-twentieth century, when our foreign-born population shrank to less than 5 percent, versus Ken Burnsian nostalgia for a half-century or century earlier, huddled masses sailing in to breathe free, become new Americans, and continue the building of a new nation. Back in 1855, when young Walt Whitman described us as "not merely a nation but a teeming nation of nations," America's foreign-born population had exploded since he was a boy from 2 percent to more than 13 percent, where it remained through the 1920s. Since we reopened the gates in the late 1960s, our immigrant fraction has tripled, reaching nearly 15 percent, back to what it was when the Statue of Liberty and Ellis Island were new.

There was always plenty of bigotry against immigrants—for being Catholic, Jewish, poor, foreign, swarthy—but historically a negligible fraction of immigrants were not white. Indeed, in the late nineteenth century, 98 percent of Americans outside the South were white. For all of America's defining embrace and embodiment of the new, for more than two centuries our society was *unchanging* in its basic racial makeup—overwhelmingly white and very consistently so. From the first census in 1790 through the one in 1970, the national population was 85 percent white and non-Hispanic, give or take a couple of percentage points from decade to decade, and it was still at 80 percent in 1980. But as a result of the latest immigrant influx from Latin America and Asia, today barely 60 percent of us are non-Hispanic white people.

It is an unprecedented American metamorphosis. As a white person delighted to live in a thriving city with low crime rates where white people became a minority just after I arrived forty years ago and the foreign-born population has since doubled, I say: *Good job, United States!* Obviously not all my fellow white Americans agree, especially not my fellow white men, and more especially my fellow old white men, many of whom also feel diminished by the simultaneous rise of women. Those transformations of American society have reduced some of their privileges.

To me, the most striking metric of female empowerment concerns women's higher education: in the early 1970s, almost twice as many men as women in America had graduated from college, but today more women than men have B.A.s, and they earn most of the advanced degrees as well.

The large social and political consequences of lots more people having college degrees extend beyond equality for women. In 1970, when the hard hats and other angry blue-collar patriots were hating and beating on uppity college-kid protesters, only a small minority of American adults, 11 percent, were college graduates. Back then, 88 percent of Americans were white and 95 percent were not Hispanic *and* 89 percent lacked a college degree—in other words, non-Hispanic white people who had no more than a high school diploma made up three-quarters of Americans. (And if their kids wanted to go to college, it cost a fraction of what it costs now.) That majority, naturally, felt as if in every way they *ruled*.

Since the 1970s the giant U.S. supermajority of white people without college degrees has shrunk by more than half, down to about 35 percent. They constitute a shrinking fraction that's now the same size as the fraction of college graduates and the fraction of people of color, both of which are growing. Thus a lot of less-educated white people, especially older ones, feel nostalgic for the old days. Yet while it's understandable that such nostalgia zeroes in on race and ethnicity, it's inexcusable when it's politicized—and by my moral calculus, even more so for affluent white people with no screwed-by-a-rigged-system economic excuse for resentment and racism.*

Since the 2016 presidential election, scholars and journalists have debated which type of unhappiness more importantly drove a majority of white people to support Donald Trump. Was it all about America's new racial and ethnic character, or was it all about America's new economic character? Was it nostalgia for a whiter, more sexist society or for more fairly shared prosperity, security, and economic mobility or for the time before America was awash in the meritocratic hubris of the liberal social

*In the 1960s, just a few states had white populations of less than 70 percent: Mississippi, South Carolina, Louisiana, and Alabama. Today the size of the white majority in the whole United States is down to what it was only in the Deep South back then—which I think helps explain why so many white Americans outside the South turned into crypto-Southerners during the last fifty years. As their communities got more racially and ethnically diverse, they got more *consciously* white and defensive and racist.

winners? Of course it was all of those different versions of nostalgia for the past and of resistance to the new. It's another clear case of social and political and economic comorbidity: different chronic conditions with intertwined causes and symptoms that make both more debilitating and harder to treat.

But in fact, most white people have voted for the Republican presidential candidate ever since 1968—that is, ever since the first election after the new federal civil rights laws came fully into force and after several consecutive summers of large black urban riots-cum-uprisings. And now for nine presidential elections, including 2020, the overall white vote has been quite consistent: an average of 56 percent voted for the Republican candidates (except when quasi-Republican Ross Perot ran in the 1990s), and an average of 41 percent voted for the Democratic candidates. In 2016 Trump actually did worse among white voters than the average modern Republican candidate, and his margin among them in 2020 was three points smaller than in 2016. Even among whites without college degrees, Trump did six points worse in 2020 than in 2016. A study of thousands of election precincts in six big swing states found that in white-majority neighborhoods that had had influxes of Hispanics and immigrants, the same fractions of white people voted for Trump in 2016 as had voted for each of the three previous Republican nominees—in other words, all the new foreign-born and nonwhite neighbors didn't make them more Trumpist. And in *poorer* white neighborhoods that had Hispanic influxes, Trump did *worse* than his Republican predecessors.*

So to the degree that white people began voting for Republicans and against Democrats out of racial animus or fear or solidarity, that started a half-century ago and apparently hasn't changed much since. What's new is that unlike the Republican candidates and presidents before him, Trump doesn't stick to innuendo and codes and dog whistles; his heart was obviously in it, even more so since 2016, which meant that the white people who voted for him in 2020 were unquestionably ratifying racism.

But the scholars and others who emphasize bigotry as the only meaningful factor tend to define the economics—that is, voters' "economic

*A different study by political scientists found that Trump's anti-immigrant ravings actually inspired more white people to vote against him than it did white MAGAs to vote for him.

anxiety"—way too narrowly as acute distress rather than as structural malaise. Because voting for Trump didn't correlate in surveys with a "drop in income in the previous year" or concern about losing jobs or making the rent or paying for healthcare *right now,* researchers conclude that Trumpism is entirely about feeling racial hatred or defensiveness. Some analysts also argue that support for Trump by prosperous people discredits the importance of economics to his appeal, but prosperous Republican voters reflexively support Republican candidates as a safe bet on lower taxes—even Trump, especially after his four years of strictly adhering to the Republican line on business and the rich.

How better to nail down the kind of chronic economic unhappiness and anxiety I'm talking about? Measuring the actual conditions of whole communities over time seems like a good idea. The authors of one study divided all 3,138 U.S. counties into two groups, Opportunity-Falling and Opportunity-Rising America, depending on whether each county lost or gained businesses between 2005 and 2015. In the two-thirds of counties that were Opportunity-Falling during that decade before the 2016 election, Trump won the two-party vote by 53 to 47 percent, while in the Opportunity-Rising counties he lost by 55 to 45 percent.

I have a different way of dividing America that amounts to the same thing: Dollar General–Dollar Tree–Family Dollar America versus Starbucks–Target–Whole Foods America. All six of those chains started or exploded in the 1980s as we began making the political economy more unfair and unequal. In 2016 Trump won all 9 states where the density of dollar stores is highest, and 10 of the next 13 on the chart; Clinton won 15 of the 25 states that have the relatively fewest dollar stores. *Of course* most people in Dollar Store America responded to the candidate who sounded in 2016 like a Democrat of a very old-fashioned kind—rough, tough, promising to spend billions building new roads and bridges and never to cut and possibly to improve Medicare and Social Security, telling them that "big business and major donors are lining up behind the campaign of my opponent because they know she will keep our rigged system in place."

Then there are those fascinating, problematic 8 or 10 million people who voted for Obama, then Trump. People are confused—and so often *encouraged* to be confused by political actors—about which kinds of new they should or shouldn't want or have no choice but to accept. After the

2016 presidential election, experts couldn't reckon with the large fraction of the reactionary white racist candidate's voters, as many as one in six, who had *also* voted for the cool liberal black ex-professor. But it made sense to me as a kind of desperate independent grassroots political yearning for *some kind of new*. Those Obama-Trump voters may be ideologically inconsistent—like most people—but they were clearly desperate for *new and different,* 8 or 10 million people who repeatedly chose the most unlikely and unconventional candidate on the ballot.

America has become new.

Racially and socially, it is not at all what it was forty or fifty years ago, and it won't be ever again, the whole United States as white as Oregon or Wyoming. I hope and think we're reaching peak nostalgia for the old superwhite (and superstraight) American monoculture. As white people who grew up back then die off, we can hope that particular nostalgia will proceed to be extinguished as a powerful political force.

America is no longer what it was economically, either, and it won't be again. Nostalgia for a manufacturing-based economy is absurd, and the takeover of more and more human work by computers is going to proceed apace and probably accelerate. Yet in fundamental ways, we actually *can* restore our political economy to something like what it was, with fairness a goal as important as growth, all boats rising together.

We Americans will keep screaming back and forth about which aspects of America's past should or shouldn't be missed or celebrated or restored. Today's unhinged right, however, even when it isn't *explicitly* fetishizing the past, is also overrun by a de facto nostalgia for the scientific ignorance of the old days. Resistance to new social norms or demographics always defined conservatism, but now it also includes resistance to newly discovered *facts* that aren't even new. For instance, creationist rejection of evolutionary biology, which has become Republican orthodoxy, amounts to nostalgia for life before 1859, the year Darwin published *On the Origin of Species*.

And by means of the denial of science, we return to the main subject, the excessive power granted to big business starting in the 1970s. Since then, at the behest of the fossil fuel industry, the right has developed a de facto nostalgia for the blissfully ignorant time when almost nobody outside climate science was aware of the CO_2 crisis and its potentially catastrophic effects. Climate change is an absolutely new challenge for which the past provides no models to cope. Will we finally summon the will to stop this willful self-destruction? With our government in the corrupting grip of big business and the rich as it was more than a century ago, America—the land of the new, past master at meeting unprecedented challenges—would prefer not to.

22

Ruthless Beats Reasonable

If not for what happened in the 1980s, when we liberated business to do almost anything it wished no matter what, there's a good chance we'd now be well on our way to ending the climate crisis. Instead, as I described earlier, our new laissez-faire economic model permitted a couple of well-placed right-wingers—the presidential commission chairman and the White House chief of staff—to turn the uncontroversial scientific consensus about global warming into a fake-controversial partisan issue.

Remember the Powell Memo of 1971 prescribing the comeback strategy big business and the superrich right would follow, how it reads like a fictional document in a novel that's a bit too on the nose? In 1998 an even more blatantly sinister memo laid out a plan to protect the fossil fuel industry from climate change regulation. It was drafted and circulated by the American Petroleum Institute, the oil and gas trade association, along with the CEOs' Business Roundtable, Grover Norquist's powerful antitax group, and a think tank cofounded by that global warming commission chairman under Reagan who spun the findings to deny it was a looming crisis.

"Environmental groups essentially have had the field to themselves," the memo complained, and—based on an overwhelming scientific consensus—"have conducted an effective public relations program to convince the American public that the climate is changing, we humans are at fault, and we must do something about it before calamity strikes."

Legitimate arguments against regulation (or pandemic lockdowns) usually focus on economic costs, that some rule or law is too expensive given its benefits. But opposing emission limits "solely on economic grounds" isn't enough, the memo explained, because that "makes it too easy for others to portray the United States as putting preservation of its own lifestyle above the greater concerns of mankind."

Rather, the fossil fuel business and its political allies needed to make civilians believe there was serious "scientific uncertainty" in order "to build a case against precipitous action on climate change." This it would do by means of a "national media relations program" promoting the supposed "uncertainties in climate science" as well as "a direct outreach program to educate members of Congress and school teachers/students about uncertainties in climate science."

The memo defined "victory" as making "uncertainties in climate science part of the conventional wisdom for average citizens" and "promoters of curbs on fossil fuel emissions seen as 'out of touch with reality,'" to the point where "'climate change' becomes a non-issue and"—Dr. Evil had just been invented—"there are no further initiatives to thwart the threat of climate change."

Thus a generation after the big 1980 victory and a decade after John Sununu did his crucial dirty work in Washington, the Establishment right moved definitively beyond legitimate policy argument to a dangerous new bad-faith zone. As Senator Moynihan had started saying at the time about political discourse in general, they decided they were entitled not just to their own opinions about policies for addressing climate change, but to their own facts concerning its existence and causes and possible impacts.

Four years later, in 2002, yet another influential memo about denying climate science circulated among Republicans, this one by the prominent strategist and pollster Frank Luntz. He advised them that so far their decade of climate-change-denial propaganda had been effective, but they needed to redouble it. "Voters believe there is no consensus about global warming within the scientific community," he wrote. "Should the public come to believe that the scientific issues are settled, their views about global warming will change accordingly. Therefore, you need to continue to make the lack of scientific certainty a primary issue," and continue to "challenge the science." Luntz recommended as well that Republican politicians use the term *climate change* rather than *global warming,* because "global warming has catastrophic communications attached to it," whereas "climate change sounds [like] a more controllable and less emotional challenge."

Al Gore's documentary *An Inconvenient Truth* came out in 2006, won an Oscar, and brought the issue to the full attention of millions of people, including me. Which is probably a reason why, at the same time, the oil and coal billionaires Charles and David Koch, together with ExxonMobil and more than a hundred right-wing foundations, were funneling hundreds of millions a year to organizations working against the mitigation of global warming. Before long, full-on climate change denialism was Republican orthodoxy. As recently as 2008, their national party platform had respectfully mentioned "climate change" thirteen times, stipulating that it was indeed caused by "human economic activity" and committing Republicans to "decreasing the long term demand for oil." At the next convention, the platform mentioned "climate change" just once, in scare quotes, only to disparage concern about it.

Beyond their successful work to prevent "initiatives to thwart the threat of climate change," in the early 2000s the Kochs and big business kept expanding what they'd begun in the 1970s and '80s, giving more money to the think tanks and nonprofits and Washington lobbyists promoting their other political economic interests. The Kochs started holding biannual meetings of their new confederacy of right-wing billionaire political donors, the active core of whom had made their fortunes in fossil fuels and finance. A new national right-wing financial organization called DonorsTrust enabled donors to remain anonymous and keep their fingerprints off their $1.1 billion in contributions (so far) to hundreds of groups dedicated to "advancing liberty."

The most recent annual ranking of think tanks' influence (by policy specialists and journalists for the University of Pennsylvania) lists the Heritage Foundation as the eighth most influential on Earth, and the

Cato Institute as the fifteenth. Among the thousand or so U.S. think tanks with a principal focus on political economics and other domestic issues, Heritage is at number two, Cato at number five. Other think tanks that the right created in the 1970s and '80s, such as Charles Koch's Mercatus Center and the Manhattan Institute, are not far behind.

Charles Koch remained closely involved in George Mason University and his quasi-independent institutes there as a major funder, board member, and ideological overseer of faculty for the economics and law programs. George Mason's custom-fabricated right-wing law school was renamed the Antonin Scalia Law School, thanks to an anonymous $20 million donation for which the Federalist Society was the intermediary. But having built that permanent fiefdom inside an established institution, which is now Virginia's largest public university, the Koch operation leveled up and went national. It endows and otherwise subsidizes libertarian economic and legal programs and classes and one-off conferences and a thousand professors at more than three hundred public and private colleges and universities, including every member of the Ivy League and MIT, NYU, Wesleyan, Amherst, Wellesley, Georgetown, Northwestern, Stanford, and most of the University of California system. In the early 2000s, the Kochs' spending on U.S. academia increased to around $30 million a year, and since 2017 it has been $100 million a year.

Most of the right-wing counter-Establishment that was dreamed up and built in the 1970s and '80s is now simply the Establishment, none of its pieces more remarkably or importantly so than those in the law. Back in 1985, three years after the Federalist Society was founded, the young director of its Washington, D.C., branch modestly told a reporter that "the society hopes to continue growing quite a bit." Such a long game: thirty-five years later, that guy is president of the Federalist Society, which has chapters at almost every law school as well as in a hundred cities for lawyers and judges and other assorted rightists, seventy thousand members in all.

Back at that same mid-1980s moment, the Federalist Society's godfather Michael Horowitz, who wrote the seminal memo telling right-wing law how and why it needed to step up its game, was more confident, like Babe Ruth pointing to the fence before he hit his World Series home run. "Twenty years from now," Horowitz promised a reporter, "we will see our federal justices coming from the Federalist Society"—and precisely twenty years later two members of that first generation, Brett Kavanaugh and Neil Gorsuch, became federal appeals court judges.

In fact, a large fraction of all federal judges today are or have been Federalist Society members, including the entire Supreme Court majority. At the level just below the Supreme Court, the 179 federal appeals court judges all over the country, almost 30 percent have been appointed since 2017, and more than 80 percent of those Trump appointees are Federalist alumni or members. These newest appellate judges are almost twice as likely to have Federalist ties as those appointed by Bush in the 2000s, and they are much more likely to have political rather than strictly legal backgrounds. Before he was even nominated for president in 2016, Trump asked the Federalist Society to give him short lists of approved candidates for the Supreme Court from which he agreed to make all his nominations; that is one promise he has absolutely kept.

Certainly for big business, this part of the long war has paid off. One measure of that is how the Supreme Court has decided cases in which the U.S. Chamber of Commerce takes a side. In the early 1980s, decisions in those cases went their way four times out of ten, but since 2006 it's been seven of ten.

The money spent by the economic right on universities and think tanks and the legal profession goes to propagate ideology and change public policy and judicial understandings over the long term. The money they spend on lobbyists is to get Congress and administrations to enact or stop specific laws and policies *now*. In just a decade, from 1999 to 2008, expenditures on Washington lobbying more than doubled to over $3 billion. Of the 100 groups that spend the most, 95 mainly represent business interests, and of the 20 biggest spenders of all, 19 are corporations or business groups, dominated by finance and healthcare. None are unions. The ugly, corrupting frenzy that the Reagan administration unleashed in 1981 and that ostensibly stunned its budget director—*"Do you realize the greed that came to the forefront? The hogs were really feeding. The greed level just got out of control"*—never stopped.

In addition to vastly expanding the scale of their inside work in the intellectual and lobbying worlds, around the turn of the century the rich right's project expanded in scope as well to a whole new realm. Instead of funding mainly behind-the-scenes players, the wheedlers and geeks, the strategy now encompassed far more public operations. In 1980,

David Koch ran for vice president to Reagan's right on the Libertarian platform that then seemed crazily extreme—abolish the EPA and OSHA, privatize Social Security, repeal campaign finance laws—and his brother Charles worried about the reaction if the general public were to learn of their "radically different" views. But a generation later in the mid-1990s, what had once been beyond the fringe was the mass-marketable conservative mainstream. The Kochian economic right had become a tight-knit shadow national political party affiliated with and dominating the nominally independent GOP.

It was perfect synchrony that the Kochs and some of their rich comrades began their direct involvement in electoral and protest politics just as the first right-wing mass media platforms were being launched.

In 1993, just as right-wing talk radio had become huge, Roger Ailes partnered up with Rush Limbaugh to executive-produce and co-own his year-old daily half-hour syndicated TV show. Ailes had also just become the head of NBC's two cable news channels, CNBC and another called America's Talking.

That fall I was working on a cover story for *Time* that was partly about Limbaugh. Out of the blue one day I got a phone call at the magazine's offices from Ailes, with whom I'd never had any communication. Assuming I might trash his boy Rush in *Time,* he was phoning not to be interviewed but simply to snarl and bluster and try to intimidate me preemptively.

The second time he referred to me as "a socialist," I chuckled. There was a pause. "How would you like it," he said then, "if I sent a camera crew to your kids' school?" At the time my daughters were three and five, and NBC was owned by GE. "Wow," I replied. "I'll bet Jack Welch would love to find out that his new news executive was threatening to use his employees to stalk toddlers." That pissed Ailes off. "Are *you*," he asked, "*threatening* me?"

I figured he was speaking from a hundred yards away, 30 Rockefeller Plaza, just across Sixth Avenue from the Time-Life Building. "If the millions of Americans fanatically devoted to Rush Limbaugh have one major common hypothesis about the way the world works," I wrote in my *Time* story, imagining how New York City itself must stoke Ailes's nonstop right-wing anger, "it is that a rich and powerful elite, congregated in Manhattan, sits in posh salons sipping cocktails and smugly denigrating them and their unorthodox heroes. And they're right."

Three years later America's Talking morphed without Ailes into MSNBC, and Rupert Murdoch hired him to create Fox News. Republican elected officials continued helping their great media pooh-bah. The first Bush administration had suspended the federal antitrust rule forbidding networks from also owning the shows they aired, then New York's Mayor Rudy Giuliani successfully pressured the local cable operator, owned by Time Warner, to carry Fox News. Soon Murdoch also had conservative media's high end covered with *The Weekly Standard,* cofounded by Irving Kristol's son, Bill. In 2007, Murdoch added *The Wall Street Journal* to his portfolio and *Breitbart News* launched, funded by the financial billionaire (and Koch associate) Robert Mercer. The elite would be conscripted (and coopted) at scale on college campuses and in Washington, but now through every medium the rabble would be roused as well, 24/7.

Around 1980, donations by business PACs to candidates for Congress started exceeding those made by unions, but never by more than half until 2000, after which the corporate sums were twice those of organized labor, then more than triple. The Club for Growth, a group of the extreme economic right founded in 1999 to oppose regulation and taxes, promptly became one of the largest sources of campaign money for Republican congressional candidates. After Mitt Romney, as a candidate in the presidential primaries in 2011, made the mistake of saying, "I believe based on what I read that the world is getting warmer, and I believe that humans contribute to that," the club led the right-wing attacks on "his support of 'global warming' policies."

At the same time, the Kochs and their gang spent more time and money on their new political dominion, organizations that run attack TV ads against insufficiently right-wing candidates, operate impressive propaganda sites, and mobilize angry citizens to agitate on behalf of the anti-government economic agenda—a kind of grassroots politics funded and coordinated from Washington that had just come to be known as Astroturfing. In addition to the funding by right-wing billionaire coordinators, large corporations—oil, pharmaceuticals, insurance, tobacco—also chip in. The groups evolve and split and merge and dissolve and reconfigure, but the two most significant, both Koch creations, have been FreedomWorks ("Lower Taxes, Less Government, More Freedom") and Americans for Prosperity. Without them—money, planning, talking points, facilities, transportation, almost everything—the Tea Party movement, despite its authentic financial-crash-and-black-president-induced hysteria, might have fizzled out quickly and accomplished little.

Instead, the aroused and properly coordinated Tea Party was crucial to hobbling the Obama presidency. A year after the movement arose, the Affordable Care Act was passed—but barely, thanks to full-bore work by the economic right's hydra-headed political operation. Even though the new law wouldn't go into effect for four years—and would enable 20 million more Americans to have health coverage, nearly half of them as new customers of private insurance companies—the political operation nevertheless convinced millions of Americans to be frightened of the prospect, to *hate Obamacare*. That project was helped, as if providentially, by a signature success of the right's judicial long game: at the beginning of the year, the Supreme Court issued its *Citizens United v. Federal Election Commission* decision, effectively prohibiting serious election finance laws and giving big business (and unions, *as if*) free rein to spend money on campaigns.* And in that fall of 2010, Democrats lost their large majorities in both the Senate and House.

Extremely reasonable, extremely *center*-left Obama horrified the Kochs and their friends, in particular his successful passage of the Affordable Care Act after a year in office. When the Republicans won back Congress—that is, saved America from Obama—Charles told a reporter that while "I'm not saying he's a Marxist, he's internalized some Marxist models—that is, that business tends to be successful by exploiting its customers and workers." In the same article, his brother called Obama "the most radical president we've ever had as a nation" who, in less than two years, had "done more damage to the free enterprise system and long-term prosperity than any president we've ever had." A billionaire member of their political network (and resident of David Koch's Park Avenue apartment building) was also apoplectic about the president's mere suggestion that private equity guys like him should pay taxes on their incomes at an

*The founder of Citizens United, a right-wing political group, became Trump's deputy campaign manager in 2016 and has been credibly accused of operating a scam to rip off MAGA donors. A right-wing legal group that for a decade laid important groundwork for the *Citizens United* case was the James Madison Center, founded in 1997 by Senator Mitch McConnell with funds provided by Betsy DeVos.

income tax rate of 35 percent, as it was then, instead of the capital gains rate of 15 percent. "It's a war," Stephen Schwarzman remarked. "It's like when Hitler invaded Poland in 1939."

David Koch died in 2019, but Charles remains overseer of the interconnected political operations, which are spending $100 million to $200 million a year, mainly on election campaigns. From his personal foundation's assets of nearly $1 billion, he spends an additional $100 million a year promoting the political interests of the rich and big business.

More than that of most rich right-wingers, Charles Koch's ideological zeal seems genuine, as if he'd probably be a screw-the-unfortunate, screw-the-environment libertarian even if he didn't own oil refineries, if he had a net worth of $43,000 instead of $43 billion. But ideologically sincere versus monstrously greedy is a distinction without a difference here. As Koch and his associates reengineered the American system and ways of thinking over the last half-century, his own fortune doubled in the 1980s, then tripled in the '90s and 2000s, then tripled again during the last decade. In other words, his wealth after inflation is twenty times greater than it was forty years ago. The wealth of all affluent Americans, the top fifth, has more than doubled since the early 1980s. Meanwhile the median wealth of all Americans is just about exactly the same today as it was back before the wrong turn.

And the problem isn't just the spectacle of enormous wealth and the gratuitous economic inequality and insecurity. It's also the corruption of our system of government, ruining democracy. Beginning in the 1980s, big business and the rich achieved the political power to tilt our system—legislatures, executive branches, judiciaries, media, academia—much more in their favor. Thus they become even richer, which permitted them to buy more political leverage to tilt the system more excessively, further entrenching their wealth and political power. And so on and on. As the Nobel Prize–winning economist Joseph Stiglitz puts it, we're "converting higher economic inequality into greater political inequality. Political inequality, in its turn, gives rise to more economic inequality." It's another cascading vicious cycle, maybe the most disturbing of all.

It's also another remarkable historical rhyme with America of 100 and 150 years ago, another way we've gone back in time. Our original megacapitalists—John D. Rockefeller in oil, Andrew Carnegie in steel, J. P. Morgan in banking (and steel and railroads and electricity), and Richard Mellon Scaife's great-uncle Andrew Mellon in almost everything—had been a small, coherent, effective group who usually got what they needed out of Washington, thank you. In the early 1900s, when Morgan found out that the new progressive government of his fellow Manhattan patrician Theodore Roosevelt was planning to file suit against a monopolizing railroad he controlled, he went to the White House. "If we have done anything wrong," he told Teddy, "send your man to my man, and they can fix it up." The president's man was the U.S. attorney general, there at the meeting with them.

In the modern age, no country as economically advanced as ours has regressed to an earlier stage of development, not yet. In their epic world history *Why Nations Fail,* an MIT economist and a University of Chicago political scientist explore what has distinguished, over aeons, the poor countries that stay poor from the ones that become fully developed. The basic conclusion is that successful countries keep their greedy elites from exercising too much control of their economies and governments. Likewise, in the recent book *How Democracy Ends,* a political scientist explains that for individual citizens "the appeal of modern democracy is essentially twofold." There's the "dignity" of being able to freely vote for one's leaders, but also the essential "long-term benefits" that democracy needs to provide, the fair "sharing in the material advantages of stability, prosperity and peace." The former without the latter becomes a pointless charade, as FDR said in 1936.

Alan Greenspan has concerns about extreme economic inequality for that same reason, but in a somewhat different spirit. In the 2000s he was asked about the problem. "Inequality is increasing," he said. "You cannot have the benefits of capitalist market growth without the support of a significant proportion and indeed virtually all the people, and if you have an increasing sense that the rewards of capitalism are being distributed unjustly, the system will not stand."

For Greenspan, however, the problem isn't extreme inequality per se, or the newly extreme inequality between the great majority and the rich, but rather the *envy* of the *poor* for the *middle class*. And his proposed solution to that, honest to God, was to contrive to pay middle-class workers even less, to bring their incomes down closer to those of the poor.

> We pay the highest skilled-labor wages in the world. If we would open up our borders to skilled labor far more than we do, we would . . . suppress the wage levels of the skilled. . . . If we bring in a number of workers to suppress the level of wages [of the skilled] relative to the lesser-skilled, we will reduce the degree of inequality.

After Democrats shifted the political and economic paradigm in the 1930s, they moved left in many ways over the next forty years, but never really on economics. The ultra-liberal George McGovern was not to the left of FDR. On the other hand, after the right's triumphal paradigm shift in the 1980s, it never stopped moving further right and trying to bring the country with it, never settled into a permanent posture of compromise on economics. And the Democrats for forty years never stopped trying to reach a middle ground with Republicans, even as the old middle was continuously redefined as too far left and the formerly too-far-right as plenty moderate. In 2005 George W. Bush, the compassionate conservative, tried to turn Social Security into a titanic 401(k), to make people's benefits dependent on the stock market's performance. In 2010 the Obamacare provision most effectively demonized by the right, the very small annual tax penalty that uninsured people would have to start paying, had been designed twenty years earlier as a central mechanism in the big healthcare reform proposal of . . . the Heritage Foundation.

As a candidate running for the Democratic nomination in 2008, Obama delivered an excellent speech in New York City about the political economy that got completely eclipsed by his excellent speech in Philadelphia around the same time. "A free market was never meant to be a free license to take whatever you can get, however you can get it," he said in the same hall where Abraham Lincoln had given a speech when he was about to run for president.

> That's why we've put in place rules of the road . . . Each American does better when all Americans do better. . . . We've lost some of that sense of shared prosperity. Now, this loss has not happened by accident. It's because of decisions made in boardrooms, on trad-

> ing floors and in Washington. . . . Instead of establishing a 21st century regulatory framework, we simply dismantled the old one, aided by a legal but corrupt bargain in which campaign money all too often shaped policy and watered down oversight. In doing so we encouraged a winner take all, anything goes environment. . . . The future cannot be shaped by the best-connected lobbyists with the best record of raising money for campaigns.

That fall, as Wall Street crashed and the financial system teetered and Obama was elected president partly as a result, he hired the House leader Rahm Emanuel as his chief of staff, who immediately made his most famous pronouncement, concerning the crash,

> You never want a serious crisis to go to waste. . . . This crisis provides . . . the opportunity to do things that you could not do before. The good news, I suppose, if you want to see a silver lining, is the problems are big enough that they lend themselves to ideas from both parties for the solution.

He said that at an annual conference of CEOs staged by *The Wall Street Journal*. Alas, that crisis mostly went to waste.

The Obama administration immediately fell into the modern Democratic role of being the restrained tidiers-up after "conservative" recklessness—in this case, the disastrous $2 trillion war in Iraq as well as the disastrous Wall Street crash. The brand-new administration was consumed for a while with the work of preventing a collapse of the financial system and the onset of a depression.

The opposition party in Washington and its Astroturfed Tea Partiers around the country could focus strictly on assigning blame for the disaster. At the direction of the field marshals of the rich right in Washington, the Tea Party was angry about the federal bailout of the banks rather than at the banks themselves. Unfortunately, the Obama administration—restraint!—didn't blame the banks or bankers either. Instead of quoting himself from the year before and taking real political advantage—*We must end this winner-take-all environment, reverse the decisions made in boardrooms and on trading floors, the corrupt bargain in which campaign money and the best-connected lobbyists shape policy*—Obama rescued the financial industry and then neither really castigated nor prosecuted any of its obvious villains.

It was too bad, politically and substantively, that Obama's economic team, official and unofficial, was overstuffed with people who had a distinctly Wall Street view of the economy and life. Moreover, it's probably too bad that both the financial industry and so much of the Democratic Establishment are clustered together in and around New York City. The cozy intertribal mixing can't help but be a bit corrupting when it comes to writing and enforcing the economic and financial rules of the road. During the decade leading up to the 2008 crisis, the five members of Congress who raised the most from people in the financial sector were Chuck Schumer, Hillary Clinton, Chris Dodd, Joe Lieberman, and John Kerry—five senators representing New York and two of its rich-banker-laden neighboring states, all of whom but the future Senate minority leader were running for president. One doubts, for instance, that Schumer would have been such an important, full-throated defender of the inexcusable super-low "pass-through" tax rate on private equity and hedge fund managers' incomes if he didn't literally represent Wall Street.

Given the power balance in Washington during Obama's first two years, it's hard not to feel that his and other Democrats' habitual restraint, manners, and economic centrism got the best of them. In addition to a president who had been elected with a mandate for CHANGE (as well as HOPE and bipartisanship), the Democrats had historically huge majorities of seats in both houses of Congress. The House majority was the Democrats' largest in years—and larger than any the Republicans have held since 1931. In the Senate, Democrats had 59 of 100 seats (and for six months a filibuster-proof 60), more than they'd held since 1979—and larger than any Republican majority since 1923.

But they really didn't act like it. Take healthcare reform. The Affordable Care Act was a difficult and important achievement. However, the administration and the Democratic congressional leadership seem to have punted when it came to pushing for a law that included a "public option," some form of Medicare-for-anybody coverage that people could buy as an alternative to private insurance. For his first few months in office, Obama seemed to be all for it, as did all the Democratic chairs of all the congressional committees that would create the reform law. But the insurance industry and the physicians' trade group, the American Medical Association, were against it. The most conservative Democrats in the House, the Blue Dog Coalition, were iffy, but only a dozen of those fifty would be required to pass a bill. Over the summer, however, Obama got publicly wobbly on the public option—as Paul Krugman wrote at the time, "weirdly unable to show passion on the issue, weirdly diffident even about the blatant lies from the right"—and by Labor Day, the Democrats surrendered.

That same summer of 2009, Democrats also gave in to big business in an important showdown with organized labor. A bill was moving through Congress that had a provision to make unionization easier—instead of winning a secret-ballot referendum in a workplace, labor organizers would just have to convince a majority of the workers face-to-face to sign up. The Business Roundtable lobbied hard against it. A few moderate Democratic senators were persuaded—and without their votes the forty Senate Republicans could kill the whole bill by sticking together and filibustering it, so despite the (theoretically) filibuster-proof majority, it got dropped. A year later big business was still making sure that the measure stayed dead: on Business Roundtable letterhead, the CEOs of Verizon and Caterpillar warned Obama's budget director that any such change remained "foremost among our companies' labor concerns" because it would have "a devastating impact on business" and "significantly and negatively impact global competitiveness, job creation and economic recovery." As it happened, six weeks after he got that letter, the OMB director left the administration and soon went to work for a member of the Business Roundtable, the CEO of Citigroup, as his vice-chairman of corporate and investment banking.

It was very expensive for the government to save Wall Street and the economy after the crash and during the Great Recession, requiring a trillion dollars more per year in extra federal debt for a few years. So of course Republicans and corporate figures and many Democrats framed that hysterically as *the new crisis,* which queered any hopes of creating any large new government programs. To lower those deficits, superresponsible Obama and the superresponsible congressional Democrats did manage to enact a serious spike in the average tax paid by millionaires—up to 34 percent, as it had been under Clinton in the 1990s.

Tax rates for the well-to-do and the tax code in general are fundamental to the story of this book: they are the most direct, large-scale way in which economic fairness or unfairness is built into the system. And for the last forty years, the story of the tax code has been the same back and forth and back again, Republicans radically lowering rates on business and the rich, then Democrats nudging them back up, not mainly to expand social programs or redistribute wealth but to reduce budget deficits. And true to form, in 2017, with Republicans once again in control of both the White House and Congress, the average income tax paid by millionaires was radically cut once again—all the way down to 27 percent, the lowest rate since the Reagan 1980s.

Some Democrats' moves on economics in the late 2010s were often said to amount to a "lurch" to the left. It strikes me rather as a long-overdue ideological correction, people finally standing up, after decades in a defensive crouch that made them resemble the last living liberal Republicans.

23

Winners and Losers in the Class War

A majority of Americans were persuaded to agree to a makeover of our political economy in the 1970s and '80s, to turn it into a brand-new old-fashioned version of itself. By radically reducing taxes on the rich, regarding markets as infallible and government as irrelevant or worse, indulging business at every turn, and letting creative destruction run wild, *everybody* would make out great.

It hasn't worked out that way.

The original supply-side idea of the 1970s and '80s was that low tax *rates* would make people work more and earn lots more and thus generate just as much tax *revenue* for the government. The other half of the Reagan promise was that all the billions and trillions in tax savings going to the investor class and business would make America boom again as it had in the 1950s and '60s—trickling down to regular people—by providing everybody with good jobs and a fair share of the new economic bounty.

A supply-side premise—that tax rates at some very high level tend to persuade people to work less—is true. "Of course," a pair of prominent left economists from UC Berkeley and MIT wrote recently, "increasing upper income tax rates can discourage economic activity . . . and potentially reduce tax collections." Yet as Krugman says, "the optimal tax rate on people with very high incomes is the rate that raises the maximum possible revenue." Economic research shows convincingly that the self-defeating level of taxation is *much* higher than our highest federal income tax rate has been for the last forty years—apparently the disincentive effect doesn't kick in until you get up to a top marginal rate of at least 48 percent and maybe not until 76 percent or higher. Meanwhile, in real life since 1980, the supply-side low-tax pay-for-itself magic has repeatedly failed to do the trick: the federal government is negligibly smaller, but the federal debt has more than tripled in real terms.*

Nor has our post-1980 rich-right tax regime produced the job-creating or other sustained economic good news that it has always promised. Plenty of comparable countries with much higher taxes and much larger social spending have grown as much as we have, and according to *The Wall Street Journal,* "there is no clear correlation between economic growth since the 1970s and top tax-rate cuts" in the world's twenty-five most developed countries. Focusing only on our American experience, when you compare what happened after federal taxes on the well-to-do were raised (by Clinton and Obama in their first terms) or cut (by George W. Bush), the result seems to have been the *opposite*—more overall growth and jobs after taxes went up, no trickle-down benefits after they went down.

We've now had four decades to judge the failure of laissez-faire supply-side trickle-down economics for most Americans, yet the right sticks to its story, unrevised. As Republicans rewrote the tax code in 2017—cutting the tax rate on all income above half a million dollars significantly, cutting the effective tax rate on corporations by half—they insisted, just as they had all the previous times, that despite appearances, the rewrite was really *all about* helping ordinary people, creating jobs, and raising the incomes of the majority of Americans who, as even the Republican Speaker of the House admitted then, "live paycheck to paycheck" with "a lot of economic anxiety." The Trump administration claimed that the new tax law would generate such explosive growth that the average family would soon earn $4,000 or maybe $7,000 more per year. While

*When I refer to the smaller federal budget and the tripled federal debt since 1980, I mean as percentages of our whole economy, the GDP. Incidentally, by far the largest increases in the debt took place under the two two-term Republican presidents, Reagan and George W. Bush.

average people would all get that "pay raise," "the rich will not be gaining at all," the president lied. What's more, the $2 trillion tax cut over this next decade, his treasury secretary promised, would "not only pay for itself, but it will pay down [government] debt" because . . . *supply side,* all the extra tax revenue from all the extra income that rich people and businesses will be earning.

That really wasn't happening in 2018 and 2019. In fact, until the spring of 2020, U.S. economic growth had been steady as she goes for the decade since the Great Recession, not amazing, not terrible, averaging closer to 2 percent a year than 3 percent—and actually a bit slower in 2019 than in the years before.

What clearly and immediately did change after the 2017 tax cut, however, was the flow of money to the well-to-do and big business. They received two-thirds of the benefit through early 2020, and under the law, that fraction was to continue increasing for the rest of the decade. And the gift to big business was an even worse bait-and-switch scam than it looked like originally. In return for slashing the corporate tax rate from 35 to 21 percent, the law included provisions that were supposed to force companies to pay hundreds of billions in taxes, finally, on the trillions in profits they pretend or contrive to earn outside the United States. But that was just for show.

Instead, starting in 2018 the familiar Business Roundtable members (including GE, United Technologies, Bank of America, IBM, ConocoPhillips) and lobbyists from other companies (such as AIG, the giant financial firm that U.S. taxpayers bailed out in 2008) descended on the Trump treasury bureaucrats writing the nuts-and-bolts rules, who cooperatively, promptly made company-by-company carve-outs that gutted the law's untaxed-foreign-hoard provisions.

One of the designers of those tax cuts was Stephen Moore, a poor man's Arthur Laffer who'd joined up early with candidate Trump. Moore is a pure creature of the right-wing counter-Establishment—M.A. (but no Ph.D.) from George Mason, cofounder and former president of the Club for Growth, Cato Institute, *Wall Street Journal* editorial board, Heritage Foundation. "Capitalism," he said a decade ago, "is a lot more important than democracy." A year after Trump's 2017 tax cut was enacted he published a *Journal* piece headlined "The Corporate Tax Cut Is Paying for Itself," but that simply wasn't true. In 2018 the United States had the largest percentage reduction in tax revenues of any developed country on Earth. In fact, in the first three full years of the Trump administration—*before* COVID-19 and the trillions spent to sustain people's lives and the economy—the federal debt increased by $1.5 trillion more than it had in Obama's final three years.

It's hard for me to believe anyone knowledgeable among the right and the rich still believes their rationales when they argue that a robust American economy absolutely *requires* low taxes on millionaires and billionaires. Surely they know that the latest new federal innovations to help business—exempting millions more workers from overtime, minimum wage, and other labor laws, leaving it to employers to report their own violations of those laws, reducing workplace safety inspections, and so on—only help business and overwhelmingly hurt workers.

I said earlier that financialized America is like the specter of a Communist America they used to warn us about. Our economic rightists also remind me of the Soviet party leaders and propagandists who publicly insisted till the end, despite all the miserable realities of their society, that Communism would presently work out *just fine* for the masses. And given how the cynical leaders of our own ruling party have felt obliged for several years to make excuses for the former Soviet intelligence officer who now runs Russia, the irony is extreme.

It was during the Russian Revolution a century ago, in fact, that Americans first became familiar with the term *class war*. Usage in this country peaked during the Depression, then declined after the New Deal was enacted and the huge, thriving economic middle grew and grew. By the late 1970s, *class war* seemed like an overwrought antique word, obsolete and unattractive, unwelcome for use in polite society except in descriptions of the past or of foreign countries or as a kind of jokey figure of speech.

So in 1978, when that UAW president's cri de coeur letter of resignation from President Carter's unions-and-corporations working group included the phrase, people noticed. "I believe leaders of the business community, with few exceptions, have chosen to wage a one-sided class war today in this country—a war against working people," Douglas Fraser wrote, "and even [against] many in the middle class of our society." People on the *New York Times* editorial board were vexed, *alarmed* that "one of the nation's most enlightened labor figures" who thank goodness wasn't a "man of wild temperament . . . talks now about a 'class war' allegedly directed against the big unions by big business." And the following year, in its profile of the presidential heir apparent of the AFL-CIO, the *Times* was so struck by *his* use of the term in a speech to businessmen—"Now, [it] seems class warfare has been launched by the most privileged and powerful in our society"—that they led with it. News is man bites dog—or in this case, a mention of class warfare by a "low-key" labor leader who "hardly seems the sort to man the barricades of a class war" given his "taste for contemporary art."

In fact, for the next three decades, Americans generally used the phrase *class war* and its associated tropes only to dismiss as stupidly old-fashioned or dangerously un-American almost any serious complaint about the unfairness of our economic system or the greed of rich people. For instance, right after the crash of 2008, when we agreed to put up $200 billion to bail out AIG, AIG announced it was paying a *half-billion dollars in bonuses* to its employees who were most directly responsible for the disaster that wrecked their company and nearly wrecked our financial system. The very rich new CEO the Obama administration hired to run the company complained that the resulting public brouhaha over the bonuses had been "intended to stir public anger, to get everybody out there with their pitch forks and their hangman nooses, and all that—sort of like what we did in the Deep South, and I think it was just as bad and just as wrong." He and his rich Wall Street executives were being lynched! *Class war!*

So naturally, attention was also paid in the 2000s, when the world's second-richest man and most beloved American billionaire—beloved because he's both low-key and plainspoken—admitted that those labor leaders in the late 1970s had been right, that the privileged and powerful had launched a one-sided war against working people and the middle class.

"There's class warfare, all right," Warren Buffett said, and "it's *my* class, the rich class, that's making war, and we're winning"—and we "shouldn't be."

Forbes had published its very first list of the richest people in 1982, estimating Buffett's wealth then to be the equivalent today of almost $700 million. Two decades later, when he talked about the rich waging and winning class war, his fortune had grown to $58 billion. His fortune is now $85 billion, 130 times what it was at the beginning of America's—his phrase—class war.

As in actual wars, not all the impacts can be quantified—the winners' glorious victories and sense of their own brilliance validated, the losers' chronic insecurities, diminished hopes, sense of having been mistreated or plundered. But relevant statistics are still necessary and illuminating.

For instance, the experts' standard measurement of inequality, the Gini index, reduces all the disparities of income or wealth in any country (or city or state) to a number between 0 and 100—in a place rated 100, one resident would have all the money, and in a place rated 0, everyone would have an equal share. Back in 1979, America's Gini index for income put us around where Canada is today—in the more admirable and highly developed half of nations, although not up with the super-high-equality countries of northern Europe. Our extreme income disparities these days, however, make us the most unequal rich country on Earth, with a Gini number considerably worse than those of western Europe or Canada, down among developing countries. America is slightly more equal than Uruguay and Congo, a little less equal than Haiti and Morocco.

But that's still a bit of a bloodless abstraction for conveying the effects of the forty-year war. And along with how it has affected the *average* among us versus the average Dane or Japanese, we need to look at how it worked out for the small fraction of American winners compared to our large majority of losers.

So it's time for another synopsis and highlight reel of information I've culled, this one depicting from several angles how the slicing of the economic pie has changed. I suggest you read slowly, in order to savor each one.

Nobody but the Rich (and Nearly Rich) Got Richer: 27 Ways the Pie Is Cut Differently Now

Tax Bonanzas for Rich People

- In 1980 income above $700,000 (in today's dollars) was taxed at 70 percent by the federal government, but today the top rate is 37 percent. And the richest Americans, who back in the day paid an average of 51 percent in federal, state, and local income taxes combined, now pay just 33 percent.
- The richest 0.01 percent of Americans, the one in ten thousand families worth an average of $500 million, pay an effective federal income tax rate half what it was in the 1970s.
- Profits from selling stocks (almost all of which go to rich people) are generally taxed at 20 percent, about half the rate they were taxed in the late 1970s.
- Stock dividends (half of which go to the richest 1 percent) used to be taxed like salary income, but in 2003 they began getting special treatment—and today the tax on dividend income for the rich is 22 percent, instead of the normal income tax rate of 37 percent.
- In 1976 one in twelve American heirs—basically anyone inheriting the equivalent of $1 million or more—paid federal estate taxes, and the maximum rate on the largest of those estates was 77 percent.

Heirs today get the first *$11 million* tax-free, and the tax on everything above that is just 40 percent. In 1976 taxes were paid on the estates of the 139,000 richest Americans who died; these days fewer than 2,000 estates each year get taxed at all.

Bonanzas for Big Business

- During the 1980s, the amount of corporate income tax paid as a fraction of the whole U.S. economy was cut by more than half, and in the years since, that fraction has been kept at half what it was before 1980.
- Since 2000, corporate profits as a fraction of the economy have been 50 or 100 percent higher than they'd been for the previous five decades.

The Rich Are Different: Income

- Before 1980, all Americans' incomes grew at the same basic rate as the overall economy. Since 1980, the only people whose incomes have increased at that rate are people with household incomes in the range today of $180,000 to $450,000. People with incomes higher than that, the top 1 percent, have gotten increases much bigger than overall economic growth. (Meanwhile 90 percent of Americans have done worse than the economy overall.)
- Since 2000, the salaries of the extremely well-paid ($150,000 or more) have increased twice as fast as the salaries of the well-paid ($100,000 to $150,000).
- Since 1980, the income of the wealthiest 1 percent of Americans has almost tripled.
- During the 1990s and 2000s, most of the increase in Americans' income went to the richest 1 percent—and in the years just before and after the Great Recession, they got *95 percent* of the income increases.
- The share of all income going to the ultra-rich—families making $9 million or more per year—is now 5 percent of the total, *ten times* what it was in the 1970s.
- During the 2010s, the majority of all personal income in America went to just the top 10 percent, people with household incomes higher than $180,000.

The Rich Are Different: Wealth

- Of all the stocks and bonds and mutual funds and houses and cars and boats and art and everything else that counts as wealth, the richest fifth of Americans, people with a net worth of about $500,000 or more, now own about four-fifths of it, a much larger share than they owned before the 1980s.
- The unambiguously rich 1 percent—the million and a half households with a net worth of roughly $10 million or more—own 39 percent of all the wealth, almost twice as large a share as they had in 1980. Since the late 1980s, that wealthiest 1 percent have become $21 trillion wealthier, an average increase of about $12 million per household.
- That top 1 percent own an even larger share of all the stock owned by Americans—56 percent, a quarter more of the total than they had in the late 1980s.
- Of the wealth owned by the top 1 percent, more than half is owned by just the richest tenth of them. That is, the top 0.1 percent, one in a thousand American families, worth an average of $100 million apiece, own 22 percent of all the wealth—a share more than three times larger than it was in the 1970s.

Survivors and Losers: Income

- During the grand decades between World War II and 1980, when U.S. median household income more than doubled, 70 percent of all increases in Americans' income went to the bottom 90 percent. Since 1980, nobody's income has doubled except for the richest 1 percent, and the incomes of the entire nonrich 90 percent of Americans have gone up by only one-quarter.
- The average monthly Social Security retirement benefit more than tripled from 1950 to 1980, adjusted for inflation, but it has increased by just half in the four decades since.
- During the last forty years, the median weekly pay for Americans working full time has increased by an average of just one-tenth of one percent a year—and for men has actually gone down 4 percent.
- For the four-fifths of all private sector workers who don't boss anybody, the average wage today is $23.70 an hour. In 1973, it was $24.29.
- Forty years ago, a typical high school graduate working full time could

earn an income of twice the poverty level, the equivalent of $56,000, enough to support a spouse and two children. Today the four in ten adults who have no more than a high school diploma and work full time earn a median salary of $39,000.

- In 1980, 20 percent of all income went to the less prosperous half of Americans; by 2012, that share had shrunk to 12 percent.
- In the 1980s the comfortably middle and upper middle class, the two-fifths of Americans with household incomes that put them below the wealthy top tenth but above the bottom half, earned 37 percent of all the income—almost exactly what their share would be in a perfectly equal society. By 2014, that share had shrunk to 27 percent.

Survivors and Losers: Wealth

- The upper middle class of the 1980s, people who had a nice house and some savings, the 30 percent just below the top 10 percent, owned 29 percent of all the wealth—once again, almost exactly their share in a perfectly equal society. Today that same comfortable 30 percent own only 17 percent of all the wealth.
- In 1987 the least-wealthy 60 percent of Americans owned 6 percent of all U.S. wealth. Today that same large majority—people in the middle and the lower-middle and below, households worth less than $175,000—own a third as much, just 2 percent of all the wealth.
- The combined wealth ($2.5 trillion) of that same large U.S. majority, the 200 million Americans from just above the middle all the way down to the bottom, is less than that of the 607 U.S. billionaires ($3.1 trillion). Therefore a single average American billionaire owns the same as 400,000 average members of the un-wealthy majority, an entire big city's worth of Americans.

Not *all* the conditions of the U.S. economy are uglier and harder for most Americans today than they were before the 1980s. Although the real costs of most of the most essential things we need to buy—housing, education, healthcare—have increased by 50 to 200 percent, since 1981 we haven't had high inflation, when the prices of *everything* go up noticeably from season to season and even month to month. *It's too bad your wages haven't gone up for forty years,* goes one common argument from the right and well-to-do concerning the economic condition of the American majority, *and that pensions and unions and millions of good jobs disappeared, but, hey, haven't we let you eat cake?* That is, they say, in all seriousness, that income inequality isn't as bad as it looks because some things, like milk and eggs, are actually less expensive now, and TVs are gigantic *and* inexpensive, and all the other stuff at the Walmarts and dollar stores is *so cheap,* thanks to Chinese imports. As two influential papers by a pair of University of Chicago economists put it in 2009, the "prices of low-quality products" that "poorer consumers buy" such as "'cosmetics,' 'toys and sporting goods,' . . . 'wrapping materials and bags,'" and "squid frozen filets," fell during the 1990s and 2000s.*

Yet even that booby-prize rationale for the post-1980s social contract—*most pay won't go up, but some costs won't either!*—is no longer operative. The prices Americans now pay for various basic goods and especially services have gone way up thanks to one big change in the political economy made by the right and big business.

I've talked about the legal right's struggle from the 1960s through the '80s—Robert Bork, the Law and Economics movement—to narrow and undermine antitrust, how they weakened the underpinnings and enforcement of the laws against excessive corporate economic power. They also helped transform the conventional wisdom about antitrust, to make people think setting and enforcing limits on such power was outmoded, too cumbersome for the age of Google and Facebook, and even to recast monopolistic domination of an industry as the unabashed corporate *goal,* the dream, a measure of ultimate success. Since 2000 that very long anti-antitrust game by the economic right has been paying off fantastically for big business in America. It's a different, subtler theater of the class war.

The overall trend line in the number of Justice Department antitrust cases has sloped downward since the 1980s, and in 2018 the lawyers there initiated only a small fraction of what they had been doing even as recently as the early 2000s, the fewest since 1972. Thanks to this permissive approach, it became easier and easier for large companies to grow extremely large, making for many fewer and much larger corporations.

*Shortly after publishing those papers, one of the economists left academia for finance, where he specializes in managing hedge fund investments.

In 1995 about half the profits earned by public companies went to the hundred biggest ones; in 2015 the hundred biggest are *much* bigger and took in 84 percent of the profits.

Except for Google, Facebook, and Intel, cable TV and high-speed Internet providers, and Monsanto in much of agribusiness—a very large *except*—few of the resulting corporate giants are literal monopolies, one company absolutely dominating a given sector. Instead, most major American industries have rapidly turned into oligopolies, where two or three or four big companies run their show and tend not to compete fiercely. It's like how smart mob families peacefully coexist.

During the 1990s and 2000s, three-quarters of all U.S. industries became more concentrated, and their average level of concentration doubled. Oligopoly is now the American way in mobile and landline phone service, airlines, credit cards, meat and poultry, beer and soft drinks, breakfast cereal, and more. In the 1990s the six biggest banks held only one-sixth of all Americans' financial assets, but by 2013, five years after the crash, that share had grown to 58 percent—the year the Democratic U.S. attorney general said that while he'd *wanted* to prosecute big banks for their role in the crash, he didn't dare because, in addition to their being too big to fail, the legal trouble might have had "a negative impact on the national economy."

And so even if we're still able to buy low-quality cosmetics and toys and frozen squid cheaply, we're now definitely paying more than we should for more essential things. As a result of looser, lavishly big-business-friendly government policies, every piece of the U.S. medical-industrial complex became much more concentrated during the 1990s and 2000s—hospitals, health insurance companies, large physicians' groups—and prices increased as a result of the greater market power. A conservative estimate is that since 1980, government policy changes have caused Americans to spend an extra $130 billion every year for healthcare. For instance, why are prescription drug prices routinely two and three times as expensive in the United States as in other countries? A big reason is that in the 1980s and afterward, Congress and federal antitrust enforcers gave away the store to pharmaceutical companies by letting them control patents longer and set minimum prices.

Study after study has found conclusively that mergers and fewer companies result in higher prices in every business. The average price for U.S. cable TV service, paid in most places to a literal monopoly, rose by half just between 2010 and 2018. "The evidence strongly suggests," the NYU economist and Federal Reserve Bank adviser Thomas Philippon wrote in 2019, "that increasing concentration in the U.S. is responsible for an excessive increase in prices." He estimates that "this very new era of oligopoly costs each typical American household more than $5,000 a year."

It's really pretty simple: effectively extinguishing antitrust allowed companies to become excessively large and powerful, which relieved them of pressure to compete on price, which has in turn made them more profitable than ever. The public justification for merger mania, of course, is efficiency, economies of scale—that because bigger companies can negotiate better deals from their vendors, and because after mergers they can get rid of their employees doing redundant jobs, corporate earnings increase. But the scholarly research suggests that's mainly bullshit.

During the 1990s, as U.S. banks merged and acquired, their number was reduced by almost a third—yet according to Philippon, there's "little evidence of cost efficiency improvement." A recent study by economists at Princeton and University College London traces this rigging directly back to the 1980s. From 1950 until 1980, they found, American companies' ability to set prices, their market power, was steady—in 1980, they were marking up sales prices by an average of 18 percent over their costs. But then came the 1980s, and so today, amazingly, the average markup by U.S. companies is a *sweet* 67 percent.

Another recent paper by three finance professors found that when a U.S. industry becomes lots more concentrated, the fewer, bigger remaining companies' efficiency does increase by 6 percent. But their profit margins go up by *142 percent,* mainly as a result of charging higher prices because, without so much competition . . . they can. In addition, oligopoly breeds oligopoly because investors approve of it. Money's all green, and higher profits based on unfairly (or illegally) higher prices make stock prices rise even more in more concentrated industries.

Simply put, those unnecessary thousands of dollars you now pay each year to companies with unfair market power are making the shareholders of those companies, mostly rich people, richer. Which is how this postmodern class war has worked.

• • •

After Warren Buffett first called it a class war fifteen years ago, he was not immediately joined by a throng of fellow famous billionaires and thousands of the superrich in a great public display of blunt candor and contrition about having been on the winning side of America's new Raw Deal.

But in this Fantasyland age, with its accelerating denial of undeniable facts by people with power, I welcome on this subject any honesty and clarity and wisps of apology from the rich and from people who were, it could be said, American capitalism's leading apparatchiks and propagandists in the early decades of the class war. "I don't see a relationship between the extremes of income now and the performance of the economy," said Paul Volcker in 2007, for instance, after a decade serving as chairman of a Wall Street investment bank and for a decade before that as Fed chair. In his memoir the year before he died, Volcker wrote that in the 1980s and '90s he and his fellow lords of the political economy "failed to recognize the costs of open markets and rapid innovation to sizable fractions of our own citizenry. We came to think that inventive financial markets could discipline themselves." A son of one of the original evil geniuses who went into the family business, Bill Kristol is still a conservative, but has turned on his lifelong associates of the elite right who've stuck with Trump simply out of greed because they're permitted to continue maximizing their wealth and power. It is they, Kristol says, "business leaders, big donors, and the *Wall Street Journal* editorial page," who should have and "might have rebelled" if they hadn't been kept on board by a key evil genius, Mitch McConnell.

Even Richard Posner, the pioneering conservative scholar and senior federal judge who we last saw celebrating the right's economic victory with some of his fellow masterminds just before the turn of the century, admitted in 2017 that it has all gone too far. During a conference on corporate concentration at the University of Chicago, he was his bracingly candid self. As a member of Congress, he said, "you are a slave to the donors. They own you. That's [the] real corruption, the ownership of Congress by the rich." And the Supreme Court's *Citizens United* decision in 2010, the conservative majority's view that "there's no such thing as spending too much money to support a political candidate, because your money is actually speech—that's all nonsense," but as a result, apart from passing a constitutional amendment, "there isn't anything the government can do [about regulating campaign finance] now."

Then there's the remarkable apostasy of the neoconservative political economist and Reagan administration official Francis Fukuyama. *The End of History* and its celebration of the permanent global triumph of U.S.-style capitalism in the 1990s got him an endowed public policy professorship at George Mason University, the Koch academic headquarters, and although he moved on to Stanford, he remains conservative in some ways. But when he was asked recently what he thought of the apparent new U.S. vogue for social democracy, even *socialism,* he said, "It all depends on what you mean by socialism," and then he went off.

> If you mean redistributive programs that try to redress this big imbalance in both incomes and wealth that has emerged then, yes, I think it ought to come back. This extended period, which started with Reagan, in which a certain set of ideas about the benefits of unregulated markets took hold, in many ways it's had a disastrous effect. It's led to a weakening of labor unions, of the bargaining power of ordinary workers, the rise of an oligarchic class that then exerts undue political power. In terms of the role of finance, if there's anything we learned from the financial crisis it's that you've got to regulate the sector like hell because they'll make everyone else pay. It seems to me that certain things Karl Marx said are turning out to be true . . . that workers would be impoverished.

Earlier in this chapter I referred a couple of times to a "perfectly equal society," an imaginary United States with a Gini index of zero, in which every adult citizen had exactly the same income and/or exactly the same wealth. That's an impossible dream. I'm not even sure it's a desirable dream. But I wondered how that hypothetical America would look.

The absolutely middle American economically, somebody with more than the poorer half of Americans and less than the richer half, lives in a household where the earners earn $64,000 a year and have a net worth of $100,000.

In a U.S. society of perfect economic equality, all the money would instead be divided equally among Americans—the total income of $19 trillion (according to the Bureau of Economic Analysis) *and* the U.S. personal wealth of about $100 trillion (according to the Federal Reserve), all parceled out equally to each of the 129 million U.S. households.

In this imaginary America 2, every household has a net worth of $800,000 and an annual income from all sources of $140,000.

Those numbers shocked me. They shocked me so much I had a long correspondence with a Harvard economics professor about them to make sure I wasn't misunderstanding something.*

In this leveled-out America 2 not only would nobody be poor (or rich), but *everyone would be upper middle class.* Everyone would have an income and net worth that would put them, in today's actual America, well within the most affluent top fifth of the population. It would almost be as if the American Dream tagline of the fictional town in *A Prairie Home Companion,* "all the children above average," came true for the whole country economically.

I've referred to America's evolving social contracts—the versions we had until the early 1900s, the new, improved version we had until 1980, and the current Raw Deal version. And I mentioned the Veil of Ignorance ethical standard—the idea that any social contract of any society is legitimate only if people would agree to it knowing nothing of their personal attributes or family situation, that regardless of their possible handicaps or advantages under that contract, they'd be willing to take the luck of the draw as a random resident.

So imagine that thought experiment applied here. Veiled in ignorance, you have the option of signing either of two social contracts. You can accept the revamped version, America 2, with the clause guaranteeing your household a six-figure income and nearly a million dollars in wealth.

*Weirdly, when it comes to calculating Americans' total income, the government uses very different sets of books kept by two different divisions of the Commerce Department. Back in 1980, the two figures were close, but now one pegged it at about $11 trillion in 2019 and the other at about $19 trillion. When you divide up the smaller number into equal shares, the average household gets $90,000 instead of $140,000. Among other things, the larger number includes the value of employees' fringe benefits, private pensions, Medicare, Medicaid, and other government payments and tax credits, as well as an estimate for hundreds of billions of off-the-books income. For this exercise, I used the larger figure, because it seems to reflect reality better. Of course, in any real-life version of this fantasy, payments would be adjusted up and down depending on the size of the household and how many adults and children each one had, and so on. *It's an illustration of how rich the country is, not a plan.*

Or you can sign our actual current circa-1980 social contract, obliging you to be a random American with a one-in-five chance of making out financially as well or better as you would in America 2 but with a *four-in-five* chance of doing worse, including a serious possibility of being impoverished forever—but in real America you would get to keep your lottery ticket that gives you a 1-in-100,000 shot at becoming a billionaire or a member of his family.

Choose, and be honest.

24

American Exceptionalism

During a Democratic primary debate in 2015, with Hillary Clinton and Bernie Sanders the only Democrats who had a chance, Sanders was asked by the moderator if calling himself a socialist was politically wise. Well, he replied, he thought the United States "should look to countries like Denmark, like Sweden and Norway, and learn from what they have accomplished" with their economies.

In response, Clinton made the excellent point that "what we have to do every so often in America is save capitalism from itself" and "rein in the excesses of capitalism so that it doesn't run amok and doesn't cause the kind of inequities we're seeing in our economic system." Unfortunately she also took a cheap and effective rhetorical shot that became the night's memorable line: "We are not Denmark. I love Denmark. We are the United States of America."

I think political arguments concerning the definition of socialism are mostly a waste of time. And given both the confusion over the word and its baggage—the USSR was the Union of Soviet *Socialist* Republics, Venezuela is run by its United *Socialist* Party—I do think it is unwise for a U.S. presidential candidate to call himself a socialist.

But nobody that night five years ago pointed out the key fact: Denmark and Sweden and Norway are all thriving *free-market capitalist economies.** The citizens of each have saved capitalism from itself by reining in the natural systemic excesses so that it doesn't run amok and cause extreme inequities—just as they've also saved socialism from itself so that it doesn't run amok and smother individualism and entrepreneurial energy.

Of course the United States differs from the Nordic countries, it's vastly more populous and ethnically diverse, but that doesn't mean their versions of capitalism don't offer excellent models. We are not Denmark—but nor are we Turkey, Mexico, Costa Rica, Chile, or South Africa, the only more economically unequal societies than the United States in the OECD, the organization of the world's three dozen most developed countries. We're also not Canada or the other countries of western Europe that practice capitalisms that are plainly superior to our current model.

So far I've explained how we screwed up our system by badly rejiggering the decent one we had, giving much bigger shares of America's wealth and power to the rich and big business. But to complete the case, I need to provide some glimpses of real-world paths not taken. American exceptionalism is an idea usually used by Americans to congratulate ourselves for a history that makes us *special,* better than anyone. But the transformation of our political economy the last few decades makes us differently exceptional, a city upon a hill in Bizarro World.

From the 1970s through the '90s, all developed countries faced basically the same big new economic conditions—slower economic growth, products manufactured much more cheaply by workers in poorer countries, especially China, and things produced more efficiently using much better, smarter machines. The age-old historical pattern of wages rising right along with productivity got out of sync in other countries as well as the United States. Inequality got worse all over the rich world—but at the end of the day only a *bit* worse everywhere except America. Because

*In fact, all the Nordic governments are certified non-socialist-oppressors. According to the annual ranking of countries by the conservative Property Rights Alliance, a spinoff of Grover Norquist's Americans for Tax Reform, Finland ranks first, Sweden seventh, Norway eighth, the United States twelfth, and Denmark thirteenth. And on the Heritage Foundation's Index of Economic Freedom, all the Nordics and the United States are clustered between eleventh and twentieth.

in most other rich countries, the people used politics to soften the blows, share the pain, adapt together. They governed themselves responsibly.

As the Nobel economist Joseph Stiglitz says, although "since the mid-1970s the rules of the economic game have been rewritten" all over the world to "advantage the rich and disadvantage the rest," the rules went much "further in this perverse direction in the U.S. than in other developed countries—even though the rules in the U.S. were already less favorable to workers."

In the late 1970s and '80s, the rest of the developed world pulled into a right lane, but mostly kept heading in the same basic direction on the same modern highway we'd all been traveling together since the Great Depression and World War II, course-correcting as they proceeded. America, however, badly oversteered, beginning in the 1980s, and took a very sharp right turn. As a result, we've been forced to bump along a crappy and dangerous old road, ruining our car and injuring most of the passengers and veering off farther and farther from the main highway.

From 1980 to 2015 in western Europe, the share of national income that went to the half of people below the median dipped from 24 to 22 percent—while in America the share going to the nonrich half has plummeted from 20 to 12 percent. Meanwhile the income share going to the richest western Europeans, the top 1 percent, has crept up from 10 to 12 percent—while in America it doubled to around 20 percent. In a recent cover story by the reasonable British conservatives at *The Economist* questioning the extent of the global rise in inequality, they stipulated that they were giving a pass only to Europe and the U.K., not the United States—that in exceptional America, workers have indeed been screwed and wealth inequality has indeed become extreme.

I described how it's become harder than it ever used to be for Americans who grow up on the lower economic rungs to climb upward. It's also now lots harder in the United States than it is in other rich countries—and also even unlikelier for children born into wealth in America to slide downward as adults. A study from 2010 of social mobility, using as a metric sons' incomes compared to their fathers' in eight western European countries and Australia and North America, found that Denmark, Norway, Finland, and Canada are the most mobile by a lot; the United States was third from the bottom. A 2018 World Bank study ranked each of the world's countries by its fraction of younger citizens who are Ragged Dicks—that is, Horatio Alger types born into the economic lower half who made it to the top quarter before they're old. Among the fifty countries at the bottom of the two hundred, those with the least economic mobility, are forty-six developing countries and, between Indonesia and Brazil, the United States. American society has half the economic mobility of the countries near the top.

The U.S. economy since 1980 has grown as much as or more than those of most of our rich-country peers, although not all—Sweden, for instance, has continuously grown faster than America for the last thirty years. But while the *average* U.S. income and GDP per capita have risen as fast as or faster than incomes in Europe's economies, in exceptional America the more real-life-relevant *median* income—the amount of money going to the person who earns more than the poor half and less than the rich half—has hardly budged for decades. Meanwhile, since 2000 in Canada and the U.K., for instance, the median income has gone up 20 percent or more, and by similar amounts in Europe. Whether this or that country's economy has grown faster or slower than America's, they have *shared* their national prosperity. Boats have risen together.

In Denmark the share of all household income that goes to the top quintile of citizens, the upper-middle class and the rich, is about 60 percent of what their American counterparts get, while the share going to the poorest fifth is 60 percent more than the poorest Americans get. The poverty rate in the United States is half again as high as in Canada and the U.K., twice as high as in the Netherlands and France, and three times as high as in Finland, Iceland, and the-country-we-are-not, Denmark.

Then, of course, there's healthcare. In this area, we are absolutely exceptional. The other highly developed countries have a wide mix of systems—privately and/or publicly employed doctors and hospitals, public and/or private insurance—but in all those other countries, *everyone* gets covered, coverage isn't linked to particular jobs, most of the costs are paid by government, and the total costs are considerably lower. Until the 1980s, healthcare spending in those countries and in the United States were in the same ballpark, but now most of them spend only half or even a third as much per person as we do. In every international ranking of healthcare quality, the United States is low, from twenty-eighth to thirty-seventh place. Until the 1980s too, life expectancies for people in all the rich countries were increasing right in line, but now people in the other countries live three to five years longer on average than Americans.* According to the health-efficiency index compiled by *Bloomberg News,* which combines longevity and healthcare spending into a single metric for almost every country, the United States is second from the bottom, better only than Bulgaria.

Unlike with healthcare, public colleges and universities in the other rich countries probably don't provide better educations than those in the United States. But just as with healthcare, they spend half as much as we do, and the tuitions they charge are a fraction of the U.S. average or—in a third of the countries, including the Nordics—free.

They manage to afford all that; we could afford it, too, especially given our higher GDP per person. The United States spends less on ourselves through government at all levels than do 90 percent of the most developed countries—only Chile, Mexico, and Ireland spend less than we do. And a main way they manage this is by doing something else that the United States doesn't do: taxing the *sale* of all goods and services—not just a sales tax paid by consumers at the checkout counter, but a tax collected at each step along the way, from the bauxite mine to the aluminum smelter to the Foxconn iPhone factory to Apple to you, as each buyer adds value to the product-in-progress and sells it. Every developed country except the United States collects such a value-added tax. If we were to impose a VAT even at the low Swiss rate, which is only half or a third of the rates charged elsewhere in Europe, it would generate around $500 billion a year for us to spend however we wanted.

But it's not just that these other countries tax and spend quite a bit more to increase fairness and enable their citizens to live better, longer lives. They've also stuck to various norms and principles concerning business that we began to abandon forty years ago. In the 1980s and '90s, following the U.S. lead, most rich countries liberalized their economies, selling off government-owned railroads, airlines, energy, and telephone companies to private owners. However, they also kept a reasonable balance between fair and laissez-faire in the ways that America abandoned.

*By the way, even controlling for other exceptional U.S. facts like obesity and guns, people in other rich countries are living longer than Americans, and life expectancy for nonwhite Americans has been increasing *faster* than for whites.

The U.S.-spawned dogma of shareholder supremacy, requiring executives to obsess over stock prices to the exclusion of almost everything else, is less extreme in Europe. The ratios of CEO pay to the pay of average workers in other countries are more reasonable—in Canada and Germany, for instance, they are half what they are in the United States. Moreover, the balance of power between workers and employers elsewhere is much more like it was in America before the 1980s. For starters, because people in other countries don't get their health insurance through their employers, the employers have less leverage over them. Every developed country but one also requires employers to give new parents paid leave that ranges from a few months to a year or more, an essential adaptation to the modern era of working women that America hasn't made.

And in other developed countries, organized labor has not been crushed. In Canada almost a third of workers are represented by trade unions, the same as in all developed countries on average—fewer than in the 1970s but equal now to the fraction in America back then, before the crushing, and three times the U.S. unionization level now. This is another way we are not Denmark or Sweden or Finland, where *two-thirds* of workers are represented by unions. The flip side of Denmark's very comfortable social welfare cushion, however, is its very light government regulation of firings and layoffs. The Nordic social contracts more or less guarantee jobs but no *particular* job. For an average Danish family of four with a single breadwinner who loses their job, the household income six months later is 90 percent back to what it was before the job loss. Their American counterparts six months later have an income only 30 percent of what it had been.

Then there's antitrust. In his 2019 book *The Reversal: How America Gave Up on Free Markets,* the NYU economist Thomas Philippon, who emigrated to the United States from France in 1999, tells a remarkable *Freaky Friday* story of transatlantic political economics since then. As I described in the last chapter, we let our big businesses get *too* big, let them use their size and power to kill off competition and raise prices excessively. Meanwhile Europe by the turn of this century remade itself economically to be more like the United States used to be, enforcing robust competition to make prices lower and service better. "Because the EU has adopted the US playbook," including antitrust enforcement, "which the US itself has abandoned," Philippon writes, the "prices for the same goods and services" have become much lower in Europe. Mobile phone and Internet service, for instance, cost Europeans half as much as they cost Americans.

In fact, the reversal between Europe and the United States extends beyond antitrust enforcement and what companies get away with charging people to use the Internet. And so, inevitably, we must consult Tocqueville. Decades before big modern corporations were invented, prompting American democrats to invent antitrust law to restrain them, back at a time when income was divvied up much more equally in the United States than in Europe, he noted that while "there are rich men," in America, "the *class* of rich men does not exist; for these rich individuals have no feelings or purposes in common." In the 1830s there were "members, but no body" of the American wealthy, and furthermore "money does not lead those who possess it to political power." A century and a half later, of course, we have the Business Roundtable and Charles Koch's network of power-seeking billionaires and a Congress that our capitalist class lavishly underwrites.

In the same chapter, near the end of *Democracy in America,* Tocqueville worried that "the manufacturing aristocracy which is growing up under our eyes is one of the harshest which ever existed in the world," and that America's new capitalist apparatus "impoverishes and debases the men who serve it, and then abandons them." He issued a warning:

> The friends of democracy should keep their eyes anxiously fixed in this direction; for if ever a permanent inequality of conditions and aristocracy again penetrate into the world, it may be predicted that this is the channel by which they will enter.

PART FIVE

Make America New Again

"For things to remain the same, everything must change."
—Giuseppe di Lampedusa

This book is subtitled *A Recent History.* So far I've focused mainly on the last fifty years, and on how we let a powerful clique and its enablers turn a quintessentially modern and reasonably fair political economy that led the world into a freakishly old-fashioned and unfair one.

But what now? What happens *next* to the rules of how Americans work and earn a living and help (or ignore) one another, during the next few years and over the next few decades? How should the United States be fixed? Will it be fixed? Can it be fixed?

This final section looks forward, anxiously and hopefully. The continuing transformation of work (and life) by artificial intelligence and automation is an absolute given, for better or worse—potentially much better or much worse, depending on whether we choose to use technology for the benefit of most of us or only a few of us. Technological progress and social progress are two different things. As always, how or if the former leads to the latter will be for politics to determine.

When I started this book, I worried that my strong sense that we'd arrived at a historic crossroads equivalent to the 1770s or 1860s or 1930s, America's Fourth Testing, might seem like a stretch. By the end, I was no longer concerned about overstatement, particularly after the pandemic arrived—a new virus requiring new behaviors and policies, work and life suddenly more than ever dependent on the Internet, government failure by leaders ideologically dedicated to undermining government, maximizing corporate profit at all costs, and an American hyperindividualism whipped up by the right that makes a huge common problem harder to solve.

So here we are, abruptly shoved into a new age, no longer merely on the threshold of a strange future but altogether *in* it. The year 2020 will become one of those dates ripe with significance, like 1945 or 1914. We don't yet know exactly what era is ending and what is beginning. I think we could prevent America from turning into a permanent dystopian horror show. We might even manage to make it better than it was before the evil geniuses destroyed so much. Either way, we're never returning to normal, life just the way it ever was. And the future is going to be outlandish.

25

Winners and Losers (So Far) in the Digital Revolution

Scholars and journalists and politicians debate whether, after 1980, automation or overseas manufacturing was more responsible for eliminating U.S. jobs and keeping wages lower. It's certainly easier psychologically and politically to *blame* foreign workers (and immigrants) and foreign trade deals than to blame computers and other machines. But the question is now mostly academic.

Starting in the 1990s, technology and globalization worked as a kind of job-killing tag team. When cheaper foreign goods came flooding into the United States, one way U.S. manufacturers lowered their costs to compete was by automating, but the Internet also made foreign trade and overseas manufacturing much easier. In any case, the large-scale replacement of U.S. workers and jobs with cheaper workers abroad essentially finished a decade ago, when the fraction of Americans working in factories dropped below 10 percent and for practical purposes there were hardly any more jobs to offshore. Likewise, starting in the 1990s, white-collar work was moved overseas (such as customer service jobs in call centers) but also increasingly rendered obsolete by digital technology, as the careers for Americans in music and newspapers and travel booking and tax preparation and video rental and other retail businesses came to dead ends. Economic efficiency wins, by whatever means. In the first decade of the new century, another 5 million U.S. manufacturing jobs went *pfffft* even though more stuff was actually being manufactured in the United States. Unlike the way things were set up before the 1980s, all that increasing efficiency and productivity benefited investors and high-end professionals, not most workers.

In the early 1980s, when the outsourcing and offshoring of American jobs had barely started and those terms were just being coined, one esteemed economist suggested that this economic dislocation would be a temporary phase. But he didn't mean in a good way. Back then, Chinese factory workers were paid the equivalent of two dollars a day. As China and other developing countries developed and started paying higher wages, he predicted, the automation of manufacturing would accelerate, meaning that work would "tend to move back to the advanced industrialized countries." And so it is several decades later, now that the average Chinese manufacturing worker makes $11,000 a year, approaching the U.S. minimum wage. For now, there are still cheaper workers in poorer countries. But as the cost of overseas labor keeps catching up with (stagnant) U.S. wages, the logic of efficiency dictates the next phase: just as American workers were replaced by foreign workers who could be paid less and treated worse, now foreign workers will be replaced by unfeeling, uncomplaining machines.

Wassily Leontief was stunningly prescient in that 1983 paper about the future of technology and work, which he wrote ten years after he won the Nobel Prize for economics.* Back in 1949, the middle-aged Leontief had started using one of the earliest computers for his research at Harvard. While early "computerization and automation" had helped increase wages and "labor's total share in the national income," he wrote in 1983, he predicted that before long those same forces "are likely to begin to operate in the opposite direction"—which was exactly what proceeded to happen.

Back in the early 1980s, the share of the U.S. economy devoted to providing services rather than making (or mining or growing) physical

*Throughout his life, Leontief was ahead of his time, not just intellectually. He emigrated from the USSR to Germany right before Stalin took over, and from Germany to the United States right before Hitler took over. In 1975, at sixty-nine, he became so "disenchanted" with the Harvard economics department's paucity of female and nonwhite and leftist faculty—although he was none of those—that he quit and moved to New York University.

things was still just a bit more than half, but "after 60, 70, or even 90 percent of total output is provided by service industries"—it's now hitting 80 percent—Leontief predicted that "continued computerization and automation will ultimately prevail" and push down wages for service workers as well as manufacturing workers. And so it has. What's more, because "any worker who now performs his task by following specific instructions can, in principle, be replaced by a machine," that was bound to happen and accelerate, so "labor will become less and less important. I do not see that the new industries can employ everybody who wants a job."

For a few years, Leontief had refrained from publicly sharing his dark analogy about the inevitable process he foresaw, but with the mass computer age arriving—10 percent of Americans owned a PC and 1 percent were on the Internet in 1983—he decided on candor. What happened to horses in America during his lifetime, he wrote, when we went from owning 26 million in 1915 to owning 3 million in 1960, would happen to human workers as we entered the twenty-first century. "A reduction of oats rations allocated to horses could delay their replacement by tractors," he said of horses in the old days. "But in the case of human rations, or wages," that would work "only in the short run" because

> in the long run, technology will always be introduced, whether quickly or slowly. . . . Had horses had an opportunity to vote and join the Republican or Democratic Party, that solution would've been very different from what it actually was. Had we for instance wished to maintain the 20 million unemployed horses by putting them to pasture we certainly could've done so.
>
> The proposition that the worker who loses his job in one industry will necessarily be able to find employment, possibly after appropriate retraining, in some other industry, is as invalid as would be the assertion that horses who lost their jobs in transportation and agriculture could necessarily have been put to another economically productive use.

In the thirty-seven years since Leontief wrote that, of course, America has indeed put increasingly uneconomic workers on short rations. And although there's still a lot of optimistic, hand-waving conventional wisdom about the future of jobs in the new AI era, a national conversation about putting workers out to pasture with universal basic incomes has begun.

Automation and computers replace human workers in all kinds of ways, some more obvious and visible than others, but the process of actual robots taking over the jobs of Americans is still in its early days. Maybe a million U.S. workers—machinists and welders and the like—have already been replaced by robots. But beyond those direct replacements of skilled workers, two MIT economists recently found that during the first wave of industrial robots in the 1990s and 2000s, each robot installed led to the loss of a half-dozen jobs. The cost of robots is dropping, and the number installed in American factories has been doubling every few years and has passed a quarter-million. But our "robot density" is still less than a third of South Korea's and is also much less than that of Japan and the advanced European countries. At the end of 2019, there were still millions of U.S. manufacturing jobs waiting to be automated out of existence by robots and other machines.

The easy summary of what's afflicted our political economy the last forty years is economic inequality and insecurity, fortunate people at and near the top getting paid more and more and remaining highly employable, but no such luck for almost everyone else. Underlying the growing differences in income and wealth and security are more complicated changes in *how* Americans are able to earn livings.

The central problem is that since the 1980s, jobs with good salaries and benefits in the great big *middle,* both blue-collar and white-collar—machine operators, mechanics, clerks, assistants, bookkeepers, salespeople—have disappeared ever faster. And 90 percent of those jobs, according to a new study, disappeared right after recessions, each recession the prod or pretext for businesses not only to get rid of some current employees but also to eliminate those positions permanently. (Watch for that to happen again in 2021 and 2022.) That sloughing of routine jobs has been accelerated by computers. The impact of automation so far hasn't much reduced the overall *number* of American jobs, but it has forced redundant millions into *worse* jobs—jobs that require fewer skills and pay less, like a person I know who went from being a skilled printer to working as a shopping cart wrangler. According to a 2018 study by the MIT technology and labor economist David Autor, "over the last 40 years, jobs have fallen in every single industry that introduced technologies to enhance productivity," and "automation pushes workers to the less productive parts of the economy." That is, they're pushed out of well-paid factory and office occupations into work that can't (yet) easily be automated, jobs such as security guards and hospital orderlies, waiters at Outback and cart guys at Home Depot.

Meanwhile, however, at each *end* of the economic ladder, the six-figure marketing executives and engineers and seven-figure bankers *and* their full-time and part-time servants and attendants, still have work aplenty and get increases in pay. This is what people mean when they talk about the job market having been "hollowed out."

In particular the *automators,* the college-educated workforce employed by digital companies that didn't exist until recently, are doing fabulously. At Facebook, Google, Netflix, and thirty or thirty-five other companies among the largest five hundred corporations, the *median* pay is now over $150,000. The problem for everyone else who needs a job is that most digital companies are so phenomenally efficient they don't require many workers.

I was amazed when I compared the revenues and workforces of two of the biggest companies with those of two of their goliath predecessors back in the day, General Motors and AT&T. In 1962, when GM made most of the cars sold in America and AT&T manufactured and operated all the telephones, the two together employed more than a million people, one out of sixty American workers, each of whom generated revenues for the companies equivalent to $170,000. Today Apple and Google have revenues *and* profit margins twice as high as GM and AT&T had in 1962, but together employ only a quarter-million people, just one out of six hundred American workers. Thus those newer companies, in constant dollars, collect twelve times as much revenue per employee, and they earn twenty times as much profit in all. The market value of Apple, Google, Facebook, and Microsoft combined is nearly 10 percent of the value of all public companies, yet those four employ only a small fraction of one percent of the U.S. workforce.

Some commentators and scholars have ventured a glass-half-full take on these new small but well-paid digital workforces—that the affluent employees effectively create lots of jobs by living so lifestylishly. According to one estimate, each job at a tech company results in five additional jobs elsewhere—two financial advisers or architects or therapists and the like, plus three nannies and housekeepers and gardeners and dog walkers. There are now more than 4 million of these so-called "wealth workers" in the United States, which doesn't even include the additional millions of drivers or waiters and bartenders who, except during pandemics, also service the well-to-do.

It's another way our political economy and society have been dragged back in time. Not only have we let economic inequality and insecurity revert to the levels of a century ago, we've also shrunk the middle class down to the size it was in the old days *and* reconstituted a vestigial caste to make life even easier for the well-to-do. A century after it began disappearing in America, the servant class is back.

Speaking of Google, as a result of Europe's successful adoption of good old-fashioned mid-twentieth-century-U.S.-style scrutiny of big companies, the antitrust enforcers of the E.U. in three separate actions from 2017 to 2019 fined Google $9 billion for anticompetitive practices. If Google finally loses its appeals and pays all those fines, it would be a serious hit for the company, about a tenth of its annual profits for those three years.

In America, meanwhile, we've only just begun imagining how we might make Google and the other new digital mammoths serve the U.S. public interest. Google and Facebook are exactly the kinds of monopolistic enterprises for which America began enacting antitrust laws at the end of the nineteenth century.

But as I've said, over the last half-century, antitrust violations were redefined to mean *only* corporate actions specifically intended to raise prices for consumers. Most of Google's billions of users pay nothing directly to Google for its services (although like me, millions have surrendered to the monopoly and recently started paying twenty-five dollars a year for extra email storage). So Google's economic power is a new, befuddling kind—*everyone* is a user, but their real paying customers are all other businesses. According to the legal scholar Eric Posner and the economist Glen Weyl, both free-market superenthusiasts, "antitrust authorities are accustomed to worrying about competition [only] within existing, well-defined, and easily measurable markets"—that is, not within the new market of digital advertising, which now constitutes *most* advertising. Back in the pre-Internet, pre-cable day, the closest equivalents were the three (highly regulated) TV networks, which together took in maybe 12 percent of all U.S. ad spending. Google and Facebook get almost *two-thirds* of all digital ad revenue, which is why those two companies alone are worth $1.5 trillion.

Our antitrust authorities have gotten out of the habit of being aggressive. As it happens, the last epic antitrust case was one brought twenty-two years ago to stop the newest computer monopolist at the time from crushing smaller competitors in its quest to dominate the suddenly commercializing Internet.

In the months right after the government filed that antitrust case, *United States v. Microsoft,* Microsoft and the tiny Menlo Park start-up Google had both launched search engines, Amazon announced it would start selling things other than books—and Charles Koch's libertarian Cato Institute held a conference in San Jose called "Washington, D.C., vs. Silicon Valley." Eighty-six-year-old Milton Friedman was a featured speaker.

"When I started in this business," Friedman told the attendees, "as a believer in competition, I was a great supporter of antitrust laws. I thought enforcing them was one of the few desirable things that the government could do to promote more competition." But Friedman said his "views about the antitrust laws have changed greatly over time" because, he claimed, the government had never enforced them aggressively enough. So disingenuous, and so typical of libertarians who really don't believe in competition as much as in disapproving of government and letting big business have its way. "I have gradually come to the conclusion that antitrust laws do far more harm than good and that we would be better off if we didn't have them at all, if we could get rid of them."

Then Friedman turned to the pending federal case whose outcome meant everything to the venture capitalists and entrepreneurs in that audience in 1998. Most and possibly all of them were rooting for Microsoft to lose.

> Is it really in the self-interest of Silicon Valley to set the government on Microsoft? Your industry, the computer industry, moves so much more rapidly than the legal process, that by the time this

> suit is over, who knows what the shape of the industry will be. Here again is a case that seems to me to illustrate the suicidal impulse of the business community.

Three decades after his Friedman Doctrine condemned decent executives for indulging a "suicidal impulse" by pledging their companies would try to serve the public good, he was still at it: businesspeople who were on the side of fairness, whether voluntary or required by government, were by definition enemies of capitalism. In fact, that Microsoft case did not drag on too long—in 2001 the new Republican administration settled it. The company got to keep its huge existing software monopolies (operating systems, word processing, spreadsheets), but it was required to refrain from killing off rival Internet browsers and other online competitors.

Thanks to that timely government intervention at the turn of this century, Internet start-ups flourished freely. MSN Search and its successor Bing didn't crush its superior rival Google, and Microsoft's partner MySpace didn't crush its superior rival Facebook. And yet thanks to the government's permissive, hands-off attitude after that and ever since, Google and Facebook have become anticompetitive monopolies far more ubiquitous, momentous, unorthodox, and problematic than Microsoft ever got to be.

The thing is, while the premise of capitalism is that fresh competition always drives innovation which drives endless creative destruction, the last thing a successful entrenched capitalist wants is innovative competition that might make *his* business the next one creatively destroyed. In order to maintain their monopolies and absolute market power, Google and Facebook buy up their competitors and potential competitors, the earlier the better. Google acquired YouTube when it was only a year old, and since 2010 it has bought some other company every month, on average. Consider Google's history with one competitor over the last decade: At first it paid Yelp to feature its reviews, then tried but failed to acquire the company. Then it swiped Yelp's content for its own listings until it agreed with federal regulators to stop—but then, according to Yelp, it resumed its systematic thievery. The government gave a pass to Facebook to buy Instagram and WhatsApp in the 2010s, which was as if they'd let CBS buy NBC and ABC in the 1940s. The several Facebook social media brands have five times as many American users as the biggest platform it doesn't own, Twitter. Google does more than 90 percent of all Internet searches, forty times as many as its closest competitor. As far as venture capitalists are concerned, digital start-ups looking to compete with the Internet colossi, no matter how amazing their new technology or service or vision, ultimately have two alternatives: to be acquired by Google or Facebook, or to be destroyed by Google or Facebook. If the latter seems likelier—being in the "kill zone," in the Valley term of art—the VCs tend not to invest in the first place.

So now Google and Facebook occupy a dreamy capitalist nirvana, previously unimaginable, good for them but not ultimately for the rest of us or for capitalism. They are utilities, but unlike their forerunners—natural monopolies like water, gas, and electric companies—they're completely private as well as almost entirely unregulated, and the markets they monopolize are national (and global). Still more remarkably, Google and Facebook are also ad-supported media companies that are vastly larger and more profitable than any media company ever. Like broadcasters in the last century and most media companies today, they provide things to viewers and listeners and readers for free—but unlike other such companies, they're allowed to disclaim all responsibility for what they publish and actually *get* most of what they publish for free themselves.*

That is, for "free," because somebody is always paying.

"On the one hand," the great countercultural and early-computer-world figure Stewart Brand said on a stage in 1984 at a Marin County computer conference he'd organized,

> information wants to be expensive, because it's so valuable. The right information in the right place just changes your life. On the

*Although Amazon is Internet-based and very powerful, it is not a new corporate species like Google and Facebook. Antitrust enforcers of the old school—and maybe those of a new school opening soon—would have kept companies like Amazon (and Apple and Netflix) from *making* products that competed directly with the ones made by other companies that they only distributed. But Amazon really just does what Sears started doing in the 1890s (and Walmart in the 1960s), except with an electronic mail-order catalog. For now, online remains a small fraction of all retail, and even Amazon's share of online retail, around 40 percent, is a fraction of Google's and Facebook's market shares in search and social media and digital advertising.

> other hand, information wants to be free, because the cost of getting it out is getting lower and lower all the time. So you have these two fighting against each other.

It was a brilliant insight, at a time when almost nobody except a few geeks even knew of the Internet. But the enduring takeaway from Brand's talk was just the five-word meme, *Information wants to be free.* It was swiftly turned from a lovely philosophical idea into a utopian demand, and then, as the whole world went online, a universal literal expectation that nobody should have to pay for information, or to read or watch or listen to anything on a computer screen.

Information does indeed want to be free, thanks to computers and the Internet and software. But information *started* wanting to be free five hundred years ago, when an early machine, the printing press, made cheap books possible, then made newspapers possible. Three hundred years later, steam-powered printing presses made much cheaper books and cheaper newspapers possible, and two hundred years after that, with digital technology, the cost approached zero, de facto free.

So the larger truth here is that *machines* want information to be free.

But of course, it wasn't just printing and information. The industrial revolution was about powered machines enabling people to produce more and more things more quickly and cheaply, over the last two centuries enabling a remarkable, continual increase in prosperity (and, with luck and political will, social progress).

So if *information wants to be free,* that's just a particular digital-age instance of *machines want everything to be free*—including the cost of every kind of work. Machines want to do all the jobs.

In this century, as computers and AI become ever more powerful and ever cheaper, we're seeing machines get ever closer to their goal, so to speak, of doing all the jobs. We've already moved from the exurbs to the outskirts of that science fiction destination. So the 64-quadrillion-dollar question now is, what happens after the machines' mission is accomplished, and most of us are economically redundant? What is the machines' ultimate goal? Do they want to enrich all of us, or to immiserate most of us? To be our willing slaves or to enslave us? Of course, it isn't actually up to the machines. It's up to us.

26

How the Future Will Work

"For generations they've been built up to worship competition and the market, productivity and economic usefulness, and the envy of their fellow men," a character in the superautomated future says about his fellow Americans in Kurt Vonnegut's 1952 novel *Player Piano*. "And boom! It's all yanked out from under them. They can't participate, can't be useful any more. Their whole culture's been shot to hell."

AI-powered technologies will surely continue to reduce the number of jobs it makes economic sense for Americans to do; the question is how fast that happens. Predicting the impacts of technology on work and prosperity and general contentment isn't a strictly technological question. It's an interlaced set of technological *and* economic *and* political *and* cultural questions—because yes, our economy, like every economy, is a political economy, continually shaped both by the available technologies and by the changing political and cultural climate.

During the last twenty years, for instance, new technology enabled but did not require a global digital-information duopoly consisting of Google and Facebook. As consumers and citizens, we and our governments let it happen. Over the next twenty years, we will, for instance, *choose* at what rate and to what extent driverless vehicles eliminate the jobs of the millions of Americans who drive trucks and cars and other vehicles for a living. How technology is used and whose well-being it improves and wealth it increases doesn't just happen, like acts of God. Societies choose. Might the experiences of 2020 transform Americans' understanding of what government is for, as the Great Depression and New Deal did? Won't social distancing and fear of the next novel virus accelerate the automation and general digitalization of work?

In any event, what we know is that going forward, "the choice isn't between automation and non-automation," says Erik Brynjolfsson, one of the MIT economists focused on digital technology and work. "It's between whether you use the technology in a way that creates shared prosperity, or more concentration of wealth." We will presumably have an economy that keeps growing overall—that could start growing faster, maybe much faster—with people doing less and less of the necessary work. If and when "machines make human labor superfluous, we would have vast aggregate wealth," the MIT economist David Autor has written, "but a serious challenge in determining who owns it and how to share it. Our chief economic problem will be one of distribution, not scarcity."

So just where American society winds up on the spectrum between dystopia and utopia is on us, on how we adapt politically and culturally starting now. We'll either allow the fundamental choices to be made privately, by and for big business and the rich, or else we'll struggle our way through to progress, adapting our economic system to optimize the bounty—things and services and free time—for all Americans.

Here's the basic menu, with five options ranging from worst to bad to better to best.

POSSIBLE AMERICAN FUTURES

	winners take all	**share the wealth**
familiar technology & current growth	BAD	BETTER like the Nordics now *or* WORSE like Venezuela now
AI-boosted prosperity	WORSE	BEST

After recovering from the Pandemic Recession (or Depression), if the United States drifts along as it had been, sometimes growing 2 percent or more a year, no game-changing new industrial technologies, no fundamental changes in the political economy, we will get the future of the top-left quadrant—familiar, grim, *bad,* like *Minority Report,* or Pottersville with Ernie the cab driver replaced by a self-driving Uber.

The option on the uppermost right is the necessary—but immensely challenging—option for a much *better* future. We continue with the same slow-to-moderate economic growth that we (and the rest of the developed world) have had for decades, but we *re*-reengineer our economy to make it more like those elsewhere in the developed world—that is, restoring or improving upon the fairer sharing of national wealth we had in America before 1980, emulating Canada and the Nordics.

But then there's the other, probably equally plausible, but terrible option in that same corner: if we fail to reform our government and economy along sensible democratic lines, we might well experience a large-scale populist spasm involving pitchforks and hangman nooses, as that AIG CEO put it, America the first large modern society to go from fully developed to failing.

Another possible awful American future is the lower-left quadrant, where quantum computing and robots and miraculous nanotech molecular assembly *are* doing and making nearly everything, but inequality of income and wealth and power become even more extreme than they are now—a small ruling elite presiding over what the historian and futurist Yuval Noah Harari calls the "useless class," what the Silicon Valley entrepreneur and investor Martin Ford calls "digital feudalism," *Elysium* without that movie's happy ending.

And finally, there's the best of all plausible worlds—amazing machines, more than enough stuff that our new, optimal social democracy divides fairly, more or less Earth as on *Star Trek* or in the redemptive finale of *WALL-E*.

In 1930—just after the word *robot* was invented, just as Aldous Huxley was imagining the dystopia of *Brave New World* and just before H. G. Wells depicted the utopia of *The Shape of Things to Come*—their friend John Maynard Keynes saw the economic future.* "We are being afflicted

*Such a cozy English intellectual elite it was: Wells turned Keynes into an offstage character in a novel in 1926, then did the same with Huxley in 1937 in *The Shape of Things to Come.*

with a new disease," he wrote in a speculative essay called "Economic Possibilities for Our Grandchildren," a disease of which "readers will hear a great deal in the years to come—namely, *technological unemployment*. This means unemployment due to our discovery of means of economizing the use of labor outrunning the pace at which we can find new uses for labor." It would become a bigger and bigger problem, the founder of macroeconomics warned, and in about a century—that is, around 2030—it would finally require a major rethink of how we organize economies.

As I've said, plenty of intelligent people today have taken it on faith that as the postindustrial age keeps rolling, the problem of disappearing jobs will somehow sort itself out. They point out that good new jobs replaced the ones rendered economically moot by steam in the 1800s, and good new jobs replaced the ones rendered economically moot for much of the 1900s, and now history will repeat, because free markets, the invisible hand, well-paying new jobs we can't even imagine, blah blah blah blah blah. It's pretty to think so, but it seems unlikely. I've not seen a single plausible same-as-it-ever-was scenario with the particulars of how that might happen this time, absent fundamental changes in our political economy. Nor do Americans buy it: a 2017 Pew survey asked people if, in a near future where "robots and computers perform many of the jobs currently done by humans," they thought that "the economy will create many new, better-paying human jobs," and by 75 to 25 percent they said they did not.

The expert consensus is striking. Among the several MIT professors who lead the field studying the effects of automation on work is Daron Acemoglu, an economist and political historian. "In the standard economic canon," he said recently, "the proposition that you can increase productivity and harm labor is bunkum." But "this time is different," he says, because "unlike previous transformations of the economy, the demand for labor is not rising fast enough."

"Exponential progress is now pushing us toward the endgame" of the last two centuries, writes Martin Ford in *The Rise of the Robots: Technology and the Threat of a Jobless Future*. "Emerging industries will rarely, if ever, be highly labor-intensive. In other words, the economy is likely on a path toward a tipping point where job creation will begin to fall consistently short of what is required to fully employ the workforce."

Even Larry Summers—supermainstream economist, enthusiastic

Wall Street deregulator in the 1990s, former treasury secretary, ultimate neoliberal—has thought for a while that we've entered a whole new zone, not the end of economic history but definitely the beginning of an unprecedented economic future. When he delivered the annual Martin Feldstein Lecture at Harvard for economists in 2013, he called his talk "Economic Possibilities for Our Children," playing off Keynes's 1930 essay. "When I was an MIT undergraduate in the early 1970s," he said, every

> economics student was exposed to the debate about automation. There were two factions in those debates. . . . The stupid people thought that automation was going to make all the jobs go away and there wasn't going to be any work to do. And the smart people understood that when more was produced, there would be more income and therefore there would be more demand. It wasn't possible that all the jobs would go away, so automation was a blessing. . . . I'm not so completely certain now.

To Summers, "the prodigious change" in the political economy wrought by computers and the way we use them looks "qualitatively different from past technological change." From here on out, "the economic challenge will not be producing enough. It will be providing enough good jobs." And soon "it may well be that some categories of labor will not be able to earn a subsistence income."

One of his key facts referred to the fraction of American men between twenty-five and fifty-four, prime working age, who weren't doing paid work and weren't looking for work—a percentage at the beginning of 2020 about three times as large as it was when those fifty-four-year-olds were born. Before the troubles of 2020, the fraction of men without college degrees who weren't working or looking for work had doubled just since the 1990s, to 20 percent. Half said they had some disabling condition, one of the most common being "difficulty concentrating, remembering, or making decisions."

In 2019 about 7 million prime-age American men had opted out of the labor force. Only a third of them were among the nearly 9 million young and nonelderly former workers getting monthly disability payments from the government. The number of workers on disability tripled in just two decades, from the early 1990s to the early 2010s, especially among the middle-aged, not as a result of looser eligibility rules but simply, it seems, because there are so few jobs for people who have neither youth nor education nor any other way to make ends meet until they hit sixty-six and can collect regular Social Security. So disabled or "disabled," they receive $15,000 a year on average, the equivalent of a full-time minimum-wage job. Of all the Americans in their fifties who have only a high school degree or not even that, between 10 and 20 percent now receive these nonuniversal basic incomes. The government officially calls them disability "awards."* Not coincidentally, this is the same American cohort who, over the same period of time, started killing themselves more than ever before, deliberately and otherwise, with liquor, drugs, guns. Among white people in their forties and fifties without college degrees, such "deaths of despair" increased by 150 percent from 2000 to 2017.

Lately, the people running big corporations have been admitting, almost accidentally, that the shape of things to come includes next to no workers. "I think the longer-term solution to addressing a lot of these labor costs," the chief financial officer of Nike said in 2013, just before he retired and joined the board of the San Francisco tech company Dropbox, "has really been *engineering the labor out of the product,* and that really is with technology and innovation" (emphasis added).

A few years ago the founder and operator of the annual weeklong convocation of masters of the universe known as the World Economic Forum in Davos, Switzerland, started using "the Fourth Industrial Revolution" to describe what's happening. It stuck, and in 2019 at Davos it was a main topic for the three thousand CEOs and bankers (and government officials and consultants and academics and journalists), a third of them American. The technology reporter Kevin Roose wrote a bracingly honest account in *The New York Times* called "The Hidden Automation Agenda of the Davos Elite." In the public panel discussions and on-the-record interviews, he wrote,

*The federal standard for what qualifies as an "impairment" that renders you "unable to perform substantial gainful activity" is vague and can include back pain or anxiety, for instance, depending on how a local doctor here or a local judge there feels about it or you. Of the 2 million Americans who apply for disability insurance each year and have worked enough years to qualify, about half make the cut and win an award.

> executives wring their hands over the negative consequences that artificial intelligence and automation could have for workers. . . . But in private settings . . . these executives tell a different story: They are racing to automate their own work forces to stay ahead of the competition, with little regard for the impact on workers. . . . They crave the fat profit margins automation can deliver, and they see A.I. as a golden ticket to savings, perhaps by letting them whittle departments with thousands of workers down to just a few dozen.

The president of Infosys, a big global technology services and consulting company, told Roose at Davos that their corporate clients used to have "incremental, 5 to 10 percent goals in reducing their work force," in other words shrinking them by half or more over the next decade. "Now they're saying" about their near futures, "'Why can't we do it with 1 percent of the people we have?'"

There's a whole new subdiscipline of technologists and economists predicting and debating what work can or can't be automated partly or entirely and, depending on the cost, what jobs will or won't be done mainly by smart machines by what year in the twenty-first century.

Even discounting for digital enthusiasts' habitual overoptimism, the recent rate of progress in AI and robotics has been astounding. The exponential growth of digital data and cheapening of computer power reached a point in the last decade that allowed so-called deep learning on so-called neural networks—extremely smart machines—to achieve remarkable technical feat after remarkable technical feat. A common task in creating AI software, for instance, is training a system to recognize and classify millions of images. In the fall of 2017 that task typically took engineers three hours to do, but by the summer of 2019 it took only eighty-eight seconds and thus cost 99 percent less. AI can now do decent translations, carry on complicated conversations, beat anyone at Go and the most challenging video games, recognize faces as accurately as people can, and diagnose some cancers better than doctors. To me one of the most interesting recent accomplishments is an AI that designed new AI software as well as or better than engineers could design it. All of that is why the funding of AI start-ups quadrupled just between 2015 and 2018, to $40 billion, and why the total investment put into in AI businesses in 2019 reached $70 billion.

The debate among technologists tends to focus on when they'll manage to create artificial *general* intelligence, machines able to figure out any problem and carry out any cognitive task that a person can. People at Facebook and Google and Stanford and elsewhere say they'll do it by the mid-2020s, that they'll then have machines "better than human level at all of the primary human senses" and "general cognition" (Zuckerberg), true "human-level A.I." (the head of Google's DeepMind). The state of the art right now is "narrow AI" or "weak AI," software that can merely beat human champions at *Jeopardy* or predict the shapes of cellular proteins or drive cars. But most jobs are fairly "narrow" and don't require a lot of high-level creative problem-solving. I used to hire freelance transcribers and translators, but in the last few years I've replaced them with software that does the work a little roughly but well enough to serve my needs. The first industrial revolution took off around 1800 when steam technology improved from impractical to okay after James Watt designed an engine that captured 3 percent of the energy of the coal it burned instead of his forerunners' 1 percent. (Two centuries later the giant steam engines that still generate most of our electricity still operate at less than 40 percent efficiency.) The good enough beats the perfect.

As for when and how many particular jobs will be taken over by machines, either disembodied AI or robots, the estimates range widely, but pre-pandemic most predicted that between 15 and 30 percent of current jobs in the United States and the rest of the developed world will be eliminated during the next ten to twenty years, with many more "at risk."

A survey conducted of Davos celebrants of the Fourth Industrial Revolution gives a more focused sense of the remarkable speed of the rise of the machines in the immediate future. The Davos researchers asked the relevant executives at three hundred big corporations employing 15 million people about the impact of automation on their companies' work and workers. In 2018, machines were doing 29 percent of all the work at all those companies combined, the "total task hours"; just four years later, in 2022, the executives collectively forecast, it would be up to 42 percent. They expected that even the parts of jobs "that have thus far remained overwhelmingly human," such as "communicating and interacting," "managing and advising," and "reasoning and decisionmaking," would go from an average of 20 percent automated to 29 percent automated by 2022. No wonder the executives at half those companies also said they were planning to shrink their full-time workforces during those same four years. The Davos report euphemistically admitted that the survivors' jobs would keep getting iffier because, on top of accelerating automation, the companies were making a "significant shift in the quality, location, format and permanency of new roles" and would "expand their use of contractors" and "workers in more flexible arrangements."

The hopeful spin by some experts, even some scholars, has been that the machines will be our *helpmates,* not our replacements. Mostly. For the time being. But Martin Ford, the Silicon Valley investor, says beware of assurances that the "jobs of the future will involve collaborating with the machines," because "if you find yourself working with, or under the direction of, a smart software system, it's probably a pretty good bet that you are also training the software to ultimately replace you." The authors of *What to Do When Machines Do Everything*—three executives at the huge digital services and consulting firm Cognizant, whose whole business is about enabling corporations to shrink their workforces—absurdly promise that while some jobs will "be 'automated away' in the coming years . . . for the vast majority of professions, the new machine will actually enhance and protect employment."

Walmart, which employs more Americans by far than any other company, leans hard on that enhance-and-protect line. "Every hero needs a sidekick," said its cute 2019 press release headlined #SquadGoals, "and some of the best have been automated. Think R2D2, Optimus Prime and Robot from *Lost in Space*." In about half of its several thousand American supercenters Walmart had just installed three thousand actual autonomous robot workers—one breed called the FAST Unloader takes merchandise off trucks and sorts it, another perpetually roams the store neatening shelves and notifying the FAST Unloader which items are missing, and a third cleans the floors. "Just like Will Robinson and Luke Skywalker, having the right kind of support helps our associates succeed at their jobs." Of course, the new era of viral disease might eliminate lots of associates' jobs more quickly, because robots don't get sick, or sicken customers easily.

Walmart's main competitor, Amazon, has been introducing machines to replace its tens of thousands of warehouse workers who pack orders. Humans can pack two or three a minute, but the current robots can do ten or twelve a minute. Like Walmart, Amazon accentuates the positive:

because the job is crappy, turnover is high, so instead of laying off packers to bring in more robots, the bosses were saying, pre-pandemic, they'll just "one day refrain from refilling packing roles." Similarly, a small Massachusetts manufacturer of medical and aerospace parts, Micron Products, suggests it did a favor for the employees it recently replaced with robots. Yes, buying the robots made economic sense, because they cost only what the twenty-dollar-an-hour assembly-line workers were paid every seven months, but—win-win—the head of business development says "this was the worst job in the plant. They"—the people replaced—"had to work at a furious pace."

Fast-food restaurants employ about 4 million Americans, almost half again as many as they did a decade ago. A sleek, groovy new hamburger place called Creator, in San Francisco's SoMa neighborhood, has very, very few employees, although Creator's messaging is all hospitably first-person-plural. "Food is communal," the website says. "We love hanging out at the store, creating burgers. Our space is your space; we want you to feel at home eating here with people you care about." The six-dollar hamburgers, quite good, are made entirely by a robotic system that has been in development for years. In fact, the restaurant is actually just the public showroom of a Google Ventures–funded technology company whose founder and CEO forthrightly admits that its mission is not "to make employees more efficient" at the fast-food chains to which they want to sell their technology, but rather "to completely obviate them."

Among those fast-food workers are some of the 3.4 million American cashiers, who are officially distinct from the 4.1 million American retail sales workers—and obviously the great majority of all of them are replaceable sooner rather than later by e-commerce and improved self-checkout machines, known in the industry as "semi-attended customer-activated terminals." Starting now, retail chains will have a public health argument for replacing workers behind the counters with machines. The most common American job, however, has been driver—the 4 or 5 million FedEx and UPS and tractor-trailer and bus drivers, and the maybe 2 million taxi and Uber and Lyft drivers. During this decade, autonomous vehicles will begin making the 6 or 7 million (potentially infectious) people doing those jobs redundant as well.

That debate over whether to blame automation or cheap labor for eliminating U.S. jobs and suppressing wages is continuing to become moot, because robots are replacing foreign workers as well, both here and abroad. Starting in the 1990s, for instance, American customer service operators were replaced by cheaper ones in India and the Philippines and elsewhere—and now the humans abroad and in the United States are being replaced by AI chatbots. The Taiwan-based company Foxconn is by far the largest manufacturer of consumer electronics on Earth—TVs, gaming consoles, iPhones, iPads, Kindles—in factories all over the developing world. And its chairman said at Davos in 2019 that Foxconn intended to replace 80 percent of its 1 million employees with robots during the 2020s.

Back during the period when America massively offshored manufacturing and other jobs to Foxconn and other foreign companies, we were also massively onshoring workers from foreign countries to the United States by means of immigration. We more than doubled the foreign-born fraction of our workforce between 1980 and 2007, when it stopped increasing.

Take agriculture. Three-quarters of the million-plus people paid to work on U.S. farms were born in Mexico and countries to its south. Now that the influx of new immigrants has mostly stopped and seems highly unlikely to increase anytime soon, there's upward pressure on farmworkers' wages, which means the economics argue more strongly for replacing farmworkers with machines. At the California company Taylor Farms, the largest supplier of cut vegetables in the United States (and the world), robots already harvest most of the lettuce, cabbage, and celery, because they can do it twice as fast as people. Soon robots will be picking fruit, a more delicate operation. For instance, a robot made by a company in Florida that can harvest eight acres of strawberries in a day, the work of thirty people, is just about good to go. And if farmers and growers buying robots make themselves feel better because they're relieving people of tedious, backbreaking labor, they've got a point.

Machines want to do all our work. We're letting them. We will keep letting them. And the right turn we made forty years ago has made our political economy and government particularly ill-equipped to deal with the transformation.

Most jobs probably won't become superfluous for a couple of decades, but that's not the distant future unless you consider the 1990s or early 2000s the distant past. Of his coinage *useless class* for the eventual majority of humankind, all those whom AI will make economically obsolete, Harari says he

> chose this very upsetting term . . . to highlight the fact that we are talking about useless from the viewpoint of the economic and political system, not from a moral viewpoint. . . . I'm aware that these kinds of forecasts have been around . . . from the beginning of the [first] industrial revolution and they never came true so far. It's basically the boy who cried wolf. But in the original story of the boy who cried wolf, in the end, the wolf actually comes, and I think that is true this time.

It will be a terrifically difficult transition to navigate, and essential to avoid turning people whose economic boats have already stopped rising, the majority of Americans, into a pathetic or contemptible useless class. Not only are the changes required economic *and* political *and* cultural, but some are urgent and some aren't. Two basic goals will seem contradictory: we want everyone with talent or passion for their work to keep working, and all employees to be treated with fairness and respect *now,* but for the long term we need to start making self-respect and usefulness more independent of employment, to educate and enable and encourage Americans to be and feel engaged and useful and respected regardless of how they receive their fair share of the national wealth.

One of the main challenges will be changing what Harari calls the moral viewpoint. We need to think of his scary wolf, AI and robots, not *necessarily* as a terrifying predator. Instead, they can be like the gray wolves that we tamed thousands of years ago and turned into humans' best friend—dogs. Technological unemployment and its approaching endgame are indeed an existential threat, but they're also a potentially grand existential opportunity. And taking advantage will first require a shift by the United States to some kind of economic democracy, taking the power away from big business and the rich to write all the rules only to serve themselves.

There will be political and cultural problems at every step of the way, no question, but we need to keep our eye on the prize: it's all about solving the one overriding problem—what economists call *the economic problem,* how people decide how to use the available resources to survive and, beyond mere survival, to enjoy life.

In that 1930 essay about the future, as the Great Depression was just descending, Keynes asked his readers to imagine "that a hundred years hence we are all of us, on the average, eight times better off in the economic sense than we are today." America's GDP per person at that time was $8,221 in today's dollars, and at the end of 2019 it was $62,853—exactly 7.6 times better off in the economic sense, right on track to meet Keynes's eight-times-better-off deadline, with a decade left to go. So around 2030, he speculated, "the economic problem may be solved, or be at least within sight of solution." But once that ancient problem is solved, and people can work less and less to live comfortably, the next problem arises.

> We have been expressly evolved . . . for the purpose of solving the economic problem. If the economic problem is solved, mankind will be deprived of its traditional purpose. . . . Thus for the first time since his creation, man will be faced with his real, his permanent problem—how to use his freedom from pressing economic cares, how to occupy the leisure, to live wisely and agreeably and well. . . . [T]here is no country and no people, I think, who can look forward to the age of leisure and of abundance without a dread. For we have been trained too long to strive and not to enjoy. It is a fearful problem for the ordinary person . . . to occupy himself.

But Keynes thought we'd manage it.* Learning to live well after solving the economic problem is literally the ultimate First World Prob-

*"The love of money as a *possession,*" Keynes wrote in that witty essay, "will be recognized for what it is, a somewhat disgusting morbidity, one of those semi-criminal, semi-pathological propensities which one hands over with a shudder to the specialists in mental disease. All kinds of social customs and economic practices . . . which we now maintain at all costs, however distasteful and unjust they may be in themselves, because they are tremendously useful in promoting the accumulation of capital, we shall then be free, at last, to discard."

lem. There's obviously no fixed financial marker for when the economic problem is solved. During the last two centuries, especially the last one, we've built a political economy and an accompanying culture that really do encourage us to be insatiable, to keep always wanting more, specifically to *buy* more. Remember that in hypothetical America 2, if our present national income and wealth were divided equally, every household would earn $140,000 or so and have a net worth approaching $1 million. Going forward, if our economy grows only as fast as it has for the *meh* last quarter-century, then a quarter-century from now, it'll still be 50 percent bigger—which should boost those annual incomes in America 2 toward $200,000 per household. Won't we have solved the economic problem *then*? Of course, as we get close to solving the economic problem, politics aside, it becomes primarily a cultural and psychological problem that people must *decide* is solved and declare victory.

"The Puritan work ethic," Leontief wrote in the 1980s about machines taking on more and more of the work, "will have to yield gradually to a somewhat different attitude toward life. Those who ask what the average working man and woman could do with so much free time forget that in Victorian England the 'upper classes' did not seem to have been demoralized by their idleness." Back in Victorian England, the very productive upper-class writer Oscar Wilde created a Russian prince character who said that "in a good democracy, every man should be an aristocrat." It was a joke in 1880, but it's less of a joke now that the average U.S. household income is by the most conservative reckoning nearly six figures, and nonrich Americans spend endless hours on passionate amateur pursuits—noble, delightful, eccentric, stupid—in the way that only aristocrats used to be able to do.

College degrees make it much easier for people to earn enough money, but higher education is also supposed to make it easier for people to keep educating and amusing and occupying *themselves*, like aristocrats, and to help others, like aristocrats with a sense of noblesse oblige. Again, as the future first Baron Keynes predicted in 1930 about 2030: "We shall do more things for ourselves than is usual with the rich today, only too glad to have small duties and tasks and routines."

Beyond aristocrats and the well-to-do, there are other relevant models for Americans finding a sense of self-worth without the structure of a job to fill half their waking hours. A century ago, after working an average of sixty or seventy hours a week, American workers quickly adapted to forty hours and even less. Today when one lucky person in a couple earns enough from a job to support the household comfortably, a partner who decides against taking a paying job can usually figure out how to be useful and lead a satisfying life. I know contented former firefighters and military veterans who left those jobs after twenty years with pensions that equal or exceed the average annual U.S. salary. In my Brooklyn neighborhood, a large number of middle-aged and now elderly men have been leading relaxed boulevardier lives ever since I arrived thirty years ago: they'd been longshoremen on the nearby East River docks until container ships and automation changed everything—and in the 1970s, when they were young, their powerful union got them pensioned off comfortably. As of 2019, almost 10 percent of Americans leave their paying jobs by age fifty, a quarter by fifty-five, and *most*—thanks to the wealth accumulated by the lucky few but mainly to long-lasting marriages and the socialism of Social Security and Medicare—retire no later than their early sixties.

But the economic problem won't be solved if the abundance is not fairly shared, which explains why most Americans are not sanguine about their ability to enjoy a future where intelligent machines are doing more and more of the work. According to a 2017 Pew survey, they believe by three to one that an AI-dominated America is going to make "inequality between rich and poor much worse than today," which is surely correct if our political economy remains as it is now. That's why by three to one Americans also say they're "worried" about a "future where robots and computers can do many jobs."* They're so worried that in supposedly antiregulation free-market America, 58 percent support legal limits on how many jobs a business may automate, majorities of Republicans as well as Democrats. The big difference of opinion on this question is between those more and those less likely to be replaced by machines: people with only high school educations are strongly in favor (70 percent) of legally

*The survey respondents who said they'd "heard a lot" about the AI-robot future were just as likely to be "worried," but *most* of them *also* said they were "enthusiastic" about it. To me, that ambivalence seems reasonable.

reserving jobs for humans, and people with college degrees are strongly against (59 percent).

And then on the other hand there are, once again, the 27 million people of the Nordic countries. They've built their successful free-market social democracies, they act on the knowledge that work isn't everything, and both of those things make them optimistic about a future in which machines do more and more of the work. When the European Union conducted a survey in 2017 about attitudes toward robots and AI, specifically asking if they're "a good thing for society" because they "help" with jobs, the people of Finland, Sweden, and especially Denmark were consistently among the several most enthusiastic of all twenty-eight countries, between 71 and 86 percent welcoming their robot-overlord liberators.

According to the same survey, one in seven Danes have already worked alongside robots, remarkably, and the Finns (one in eleven) are tied for second place. Sweden's powerful unions cooperate with companies as they automate everything from journalism (okaying software that writes hundreds of stories a week about sports events that weren't previously covered at all) to zinc mining. "In Sweden," the left-wing minister of employment says, "if you ask a union leader, 'Are you afraid of new technology?' they will answer, 'No, I'm afraid of *old* technology.' The jobs disappear, and then we train people for new jobs. We won't protect jobs. But we will protect workers."

The average Nordic person generates less economic output than the average American, 15 percent less in Denmark and Sweden—but they *get* more of the wealth they generate, on average. Moreover, Paul Krugman says analysis of those differences between our economy and theirs shows that "much of the gap represents a choice" and "in the case of Denmark, all of it." That is, they work a little less on purpose.* Between laws requiring employers to give everyone five weeks for vacation and a year of paid leave to new parents, as well as the general cultural sanity concerning work, the average Nordic spends 20 percent less time on the job than the average American, giving them three to four hundred extra hours each year to do

*On the other hand, compared to Americans, many *fewer* Danes decide for whatever reason not to work at all. In fact, of the three dozen most developed countries, as of 2016 the United States had a lower percentage of prime-age men in the labor force than any country but Italy.

whatever they please. Since they don't rack up college debt or pay onerous amounts for healthcare, they're also able to put more away: the Danes save money at a rate more than three times that of Americans. They systematically chill and systematically share, embracing the inevitable new on the road to the future. Alas, we are not Denmark. Yet.

27

This Strategic Inflection Point

Forty years ago the script flipped. The rational right, as opposed to its religious and other non-reality-based allies, sold the country a vision of a political economy that they promised would make life more like it used to be. *Used to be in 1962* or *used to be in 1948* was the vision, a bouncy neighborly prosperity without government mucking things up, America as Norman Rockwell and Frank Capra had depicted it.

What we got instead is a return to the grimness of the *much* older days, as things were in 1919 or 1883—fashion-mad party-hearty prosperity (and stature and power) for the few, hardscrabble insecurity for the rest, everybody for themselves without even the consoling expectation, reasonable in the actual old days, of a better tomorrow. As Americans in the 1970s and afterward slid into a pleasant warm bath of cultural nostalgia that then grew into a weird stagnant lake, they learned to equate *new* with *probably worse* across the board—the new downgraded social contract (with newly underpaid and impotent workers, new self-funded pensions, newly exorbitant college costs), new socially-liberal-but-fiscally-conservative Democrats who didn't seem so different from Republicans, newly corrupted politics, new technologies and a new world order that wiped out jobs and local shops.

America was created and built to pursue and embody the new, which accounts for a lot of the country's exceptional success. But too many of us have lost our appetite for the new. And that's very bad timing, because right now we're obliged to come to terms with all kinds of daunting new conditions—the pandemic and its aftermath for a while, but two others *entirely* new, existential, man-made and ongoing: the global climate we're self-destructively heating up, and an economy we've made self-destructively unfair and primitive just as the intelligent-machine future arrives. We may or may not be up to summoning the old-fashioned grit and gumption necessary to persevere and thrive in this *new* new world.

Some of the large new challenges aren't exclusively within Americans' power to manage or overcome, most pressingly the climate crisis. The slower economic growth of the last few decades in the United States and the rest of the rich world may just be a permanent return to the historical average following a few decades of exceptionally fast growth—and we can't know for sure the net result of a massive effort to deal with the climate, whether it would slow growth further or speed it up for a decades-long new boom. The creative destruction of large chunks of our economy by globalization since 1980 is probably pretty much finished, those jobs gone: it was in the 1980s and '90s that we doubled the foreign fractions of cars and clothes we buy, and in the 1990s and early 2000s that our imports from China went from tiny to massive. But total global trade, as a percentage of the world's GDP, peaked more than a decade ago.

The other strikingly new American condition due to globalization during the late twentieth century is the influx of people as well as goods from foreign places—the genuinely *new* part being that for the first time in U.S. history, most of the immigrants are people of color. The resulting outbursts of nativist and racist sentiment won't end quickly. As we have seen, bad political leaders can always exacerbate fear and loathing of the new even after it's no longer new and when it's pointless to resist, but good political leaders can't easily make that resistance end.

However, unlike the other big challenges, I think this one will tend to solve itself with the passage of time. As with the offshoring of jobs, the big change from before to after is already done, and it's now slowing way down. There are a quarter fewer unauthorized Mexican immigrants in the United States than there were just a decade ago. Over the last half-century the immigrant fraction of Americans shot up from less than 5 percent to 14 percent, but over the next half-century it's projected to inch up only to 18 percent. Notwithstanding a ferociously anti-immigrant president, overall antagonism toward immigrants and immigration has significantly *decreased* over the last decade. In its annual questions about the issue, the Gallup poll in 2019 found that 76 percent of people think "immigration is a good thing for this country today" and only 19 percent "a bad thing." Ten years ago half of the Americans surveyed wanted immigration levels decreased, but now just a third do. After the youngest boomer finally turns sixty-five at the end of the 2020s, the percentage of olds in America, and their political power, will finally level off. Already in all but four of America's biggest metropolitan areas (Seattle, Phoenix, Boston, and Palm Beach) non-Hispanic white people are minorities. I hope and believe by the time the whole country gets there in the 2040s, the significant outbreaks of white racial panic will have subsided.*

But the other big problem—the decisive power grab by the right and big business and the rich, the redrafted social contract of the Raw Deal for most people, the unmaking of modern America—will absolutely not just sort itself out. Fixing that requires government, politics, and a collective will to bend the moral arc hard toward justice. And the *new* part of that challenge, the digital transformation of work and the economy still in its early stages, adds a high-stakes double-or-nothing dimension to America's near future as machines take over more and more of the work—very possibly worse or possibly, if democracy wins, much better.

Earlier I referred to the rich conservative big businessman Jack Welch, the archetypal American CEO of the 1980s and '90s, as a megalomaniacal loudmouth alpha-male SOB. But he was also very smart and, I think, had an excellent understanding of one of my subjects here—stagnation versus change, the ways cultures cling to the familiar or leap for the new. At GE his operating motto was *Change or die,* and in his last annual report as CEO, in 2000, he returned to that idea.

> When the rate of change inside an institution becomes slower than the rate of change outside, the end is in sight. The only ques-

*The Census Bureau predicts that 2045 is the year the U.S. non-Hispanic white population will dip below 50 percent and cease being the majority. If I'm still around, I look forward to attending the celebrations. However, in the most recent census, more than half of Americans who said they were Hispanic also said they were white—so if that remains the case at midcentury, the United States will in fact still be more than 60 percent white.

> tion is when. Learning to love change is an unnatural act in any century-old institution.

Businesses are entirely different species from democratic societies, but here we are, with our almost two-and-a-half-century-old country, variously terrified of change and desperate for it. The other reigning philosopher-king of corporate change in Welch's time was Andy Grove—immigrant, engineer, Intel cofounder, cocreator of the personal computer industry.* In the 1990s, he famously took *inflection point,* the mathematical term for when a curve turns definitively up or down, and popularized it as a metaphor for pivotal moments in the history of any business or organization or industry.

But it really applies to all trajectories, those of individuals or of whole societies. Unlike *paradigm shift,* the related term that I've used to describe the changes in our political economy in the 1970s and '80s, it means not just a profound change in basic thinking but also dramatically changed and changing facts, and in particular the choices people make and actions they take in response to new facts. "A strategic inflection point," Grove wrote in his 1996 book *Only the Paranoid Survive,* is when

> fundamentals are about to change. . . . Strategic inflection points can be caused by technological change but they are more than technological change. . . . They are full-scale changes. . . . They build up so insidiously so you may have a hard time even putting a finger on what has changed, but you know that something *has*. . . . The change can mean an opportunity to rise to new heights. But it may just as likely signal the beginning of the end.

Our last national inflection point came as a result of the epochal social changes of the 1960s and the global economic changes of the '70s. Big business and the self-righteous rich used the opportunity to put the

*When he was a business journalist, my friend Strat Sherman came to know Grove and Welch quite well. He introduced them to each other in the mid-1990s moments before he conducted a joint interview at a *Fortune* conference of CEOs. "They disliked each other at first sight," he says. "Once our public conversation began, it became obvious that each regarded himself as the *premier* leader of change." They were "hissing like cats, asserting supremacy and putting each other down."

United States on a course that served themselves—almost exclusively themselves, even if that wasn't the original and entire intention. We're now at another strategic inflection point. The pandemic and its consequences have simply made it more obvious. The axioms adopted around 1980—market value is the only value, keep democracy out of economics, government is useless or worse, nothing but thoughts and prayers for the victims—can and must be undone, the political economy renovated, new technologies properly embraced in order to start solving the economic problem for everybody. But this will require a patient political long game on behalf of the economic majority—like the class war launched in the 1970s and brilliantly waged ever since by and for the economic elite.

It could mean an opportunity to rise to new heights, or it could be the beginning of the end. A century ago Argentina was the tenth-richest country on Earth, more prosperous than Canada or Australia. When the inflection point of the Great Depression came, Argentines began making bad political choices and never stopped, and now their GDP per person is down somewhere around that of Mauritius and Gabon. Korea arrived at its inflection point after World War II, the country was split in half, and now the per capita economic output of South Korea is more than twenty times North Korea's.

In my lifetime, the most remarkable strategic inflection point on the upside has been China's, which it reached exactly when we reached ours, in the late 1970s, and proceeded to rise to extraordinary new heights—a per capita GDP today ten or fifteen times higher than it was then. Indeed, I think what's required of the United States now is a transformative pivot almost as radical for us as the one China made back then was for them.

China achieved its phenomenal growth by sticking with its undemocratic political system but swapping dysfunctional, decadent command-and-control *economics* for a state-guided market economy—"socialism with Chinese characteristics." Here and now in America, we need to stick with (and seriously reform) our political system, but to swap our dysfunctional, decadent out-of-whack capitalism for a much more democratic and sustainable one—capitalism with American social democratic characteristics. That may seem like a long shot, but what the U.S. right achieved in the 1980s certainly seemed as improbable a decade before it happened. The epic turn we managed a half-century before that with the New Deal didn't seem likely in the 1920s.

At the right's moment of victory in 1982, Milton Friedman published a new edition of *Capitalism and Freedom,* his book that had taken the movement into beta (on its way to launch) in 1962, with a new preface. The default condition in any society is "a tyranny of the status quo," he wrote. "Only a crisis—actual," like in the 1930s, "or perceived," like in the 1970s—"produces real change." Note the tell: a *perceived* crisis will do. "When that crisis occurs, the actions that are taken depend on the ideas that are lying around," so you have "to develop alternatives to existing policies, to keep them alive and available until the politically impossible becomes the politically inevitable."

In the 1990s one of Friedman's adherents expanded on this in a pitch to prospective donors for the new libertarian think tank where he worked. Radical ideas properly framed and promoted by intellectuals, young Joseph Overton explained, thereby get traction and eventually move from beyond the pale toward the center and change the world. Not long afterward, he died a very American-individualist death (his one-man ultralight aircraft crashed), but the Overton Window is now shorthand for that process of normalizing the ideologically wild-and-crazy. A century before Overton or Friedman, however, Anthony Trollope nailed it in *Phineas Finn,* his novel about British politics. After losing a vote in Parliament to give more rights to Irish sharecroppers, a leftist MP character explains to his young protégé how they'll get their way in the long run:

> Many who before regarded legislation on the subject as chimerical will now fancy that it is only dangerous, or perhaps not more than difficult. And so in time it will come to be looked on as among the things possible, then among the things probable; and so at last it will be ranged in the list of those few measures which the country requires as being absolutely needed. That is the way in which public opinion is made.

By the way, *Phineas Finn* was published in 1868. Three years earlier in America, the U.S. government ended slavery once and for all even though, just a decade before, emancipation and abolition were ideas on the American fringe, political pipe dreams. But the Trollope-Friedman-Overton Window opened.

What has been happening with the economic left in America lately could be a historical rhyme with what happened with the right in the 1970s after its forty years in the wilderness. It had had its celebrated lodestars for decades—popularizers like William F. Buckley and Barry Goldwater and Ronald Reagan in the 1950s and '60s, increasingly well-known economists for the cognoscenti (the Austrian Friedrich Hayek) and the masses (Milton Friedman) who both got Nobels in the mid-1970s as credible right-wing think tanks appeared. Then in 1980 the empire struck back, and victory was theirs.

The economic left, during its decades in the wilderness, produced its own new think tanks (such as the Economic Policy Institute in the 1980s and the American Antitrust Institute in the '90s) and its celebrated promoters: Buckley equivalents (Thomas Frank, Naomi Klein) as well as the Friedmanesque popular economists Joseph Stiglitz and Paul Krugman, with their Nobels in the 2000s. In the very same week at the beginning of 2011, the centrist Democratic Leadership Council disbanded and the Occupy Wall Street protest was announced. At that moment as well, the star economist Thomas Piketty, French rather than Austrian, was starting to focus people's attention on the very rich—"transforming the economic discourse," Krugman has said, especially after his remarkable 2014 best-seller *Capital in the Twenty-first Century.* In the 1970s the right coined (and still repeats endlessly) the genius term *unelected bureaucrats* to focus populist antigovernment blame. The economic left did something similar with *the 1 percent* (and *unelected billionaires*) in the 2010s. In 2016 Bernie Sanders came close to winning the Democratic nomination, and in 2019 the CEOs of the Business Roundtable felt obliged to issue a new "Statement on the Purpose of a Corporation," more or less disavowing their adoption of the Friedman Doctrine decades before. The force awakened. And now? Perhaps the pandemic and/or the resulting recession and/or the protests against racist policing will become triggering crises. We'll see if someone eventually becomes the left's Reagan in this historical rhyme scheme. It is a long game.

28

What Is to Be Done?

I wrote this book to figure out how our economy and society got so messed up, why America took such a wrong turn around 1980, and why we Americans then found ourselves confused and frightened and feeling trapped, unable to move forward. We've reached a crossroads. It's up to our politics and actual policy experts to determine exactly how (and if) we fix ourselves. But I have a few thoughts.

Can enough Americans be persuaded that large changes, in some cases scary changes, are necessary to restore a fairer balance of political and economic power? Will they understand that some kind of organized labor renaissance is one of the essential changes? Can people be convinced to trust the government to do much of what needs doing? Will Democrats stop cowering? Are universal basic incomes nuts or inevitable? And so on.

Here are six short chapters-within-a-chapter that could be useful, a few overriding thoughts and underlying principles concerning politics and policy as we try to get America back on track, headed toward a decent future.

1.
Mistrust of the federal government is an effect of conservative politics as much as its cause.

During the 1960s and early '70s, Americans en masse developed a bipartisan outbreak of mistrust of the government—Vietnam, Watergate, inflation, overreach by law enforcement and intelligence agencies, incompetence, left or right or countercultural, pick your reason. In 1964 more than three-quarters of Americans said they trusted the federal government most of the time. By the time Reagan was elected president sixteen years later, only one-quarter felt that trust.

"Our federal government is overgrown and overweight," Reagan had said as a candidate, and then in his first moments as president he said that "government *is* the problem," reinforcing a new conventional wisdom. From then on, his political side has made hating the federal government a prime directive.

However, that the government became overgrown and overweight is a myth, because it has simply grown along with the economy. During the three decades before Reagan was elected and in the four decades since, federal taxes and spending have been constant as percentages of GDP. A lot of politicians still call themselves small-government conservatives, but at this point that's a purely ritual genuflection, because government hasn't shrunk, and that's lucky for them because it means they've not had to pay any political price.

Obviously, rising antigovernment sentiment from the late 1960s through the '70s eased the way for the economic right's main project—letting big business and the rich become much richer and much more powerful. But the neat gimmick has been that by stopping any possible grand and costly *new* federal projects and programs (successors to beloved Social Security, the GI Bill, interstate highways, the space program, Medicare), the evil geniuses since 1980 have also kept citizens skeptical that Washington can improve their lives because *what has it done for them lately?* Out of that vicious cycle came much of the enormous difference between Americans' confidence in our national government and citizens of other developed countries' confidence in theirs: according to a 2018 Gallup World poll, it's 30 percent in the United States, near the bottom, and between 50 and 70 percent in Canada, the Nordics, Germany, and the Netherlands.

Our chronic, festering antigovernment feelings of the last four decades are like the unhappiness in a bad marriage—a marriage where divorce is impossible, yet one party to the marriage, in this case the Republicans, has become invested in *keeping* it unhappy. Fixing America requires reminding Americans how much they depend on government already and convincing them to give it a chance to return to its glory days, to prove it's the *only* possible provider of solutions to some problems, especially the messed-up political economy and climate. Ask what you can do for your country, John Kennedy famously said at his inauguration, and these days the first thing to do for your country is ask and know and tell other people what your country can do for you and does already.

Back in the 1930s, before Social Security was enacted, and in the '60s, before Medicare was enacted, conservatives called both proposals socialism. When we took our economic right turn in 1980, Americans had been getting Medicare for only fourteen years and collecting decent Social Security benefits for only twenty-five or so. But now those two socialist pillars of the American Way have been in place for most of a century, pleasing several generations of citizen recipients. The 88 percent of Americans who get running water and the 30 percent who get (mostly cheaper) electricity from publicly owned utilities do not, I'm pretty sure, begrudge those forms of socialism, either. Nor have many of the people and businesses receiving their shares of the trillions in financial assistance in 2020 complained about the socialist federal government handing out free stuff.

Every time people on the right say that centrists like Barack Obama are socialists, or that "our public education system is a socialist institution" (Milton Friedman, 1999), or that "the state university system is as close to a socialist program as we have" (a *National Review* conservative in 2018), it actually reduces the stigma of the word and helps redefine social democracy as familiar and desirable. We can argue whether and how some proposed big new social program is or isn't affordable or wise, but the instantly demonizing power of calling it socialism is weaker than it has been in nearly all our lifetimes, especially among people who didn't grow up when the two huge countries that called themselves socialist were dysfunctional nuclear-armed tyrannies.

Most people don't realize, for instance, that for more than a half-century, the U.S. government and its funding have been the indispensable investor in new U.S. technology, essential to the development of everything from solar-energy technologies to Tesla, and from computer touch screens to most of the most innovative pharmaceuticals. Instead, as the economist and innovation specialist Mariana Mazzucato explains, "the dominant view, which originated in the backlash against government in the 1980s, fundamentally affects how our government sees itself: hesitant, cautious, careful not to overstep in case it should be accused of crowding out innovation, or accused of favoritism, 'picking winners.'" Moreover, the government-funded private winners get almost all the public credit and the profits, while the government takes financial losses and gets the political blame for the inevitable losers—in other words, Mazzucato writes, "risks in the innovation economy are socialized, while the rewards are privatized."

Americans seem to be coming back around to believing that they can and must use government to make America a better place to live. Since 1995, the *Wall Street Journal*/NBC News poll has repeatedly asked people whether they believed "government is doing too many things better left to businesses and individuals" or, instead, that "government should do more to solve problems and help meet the needs of people." The first time it asked this question, twenty-five years ago, people said, by 62 to 32 percent, that government was doing too much already. But when it asked the question in 2018, the numbers had flipped—58 percent now want the government to do more to help people, a larger majority than ever before in this poll, and only 38 percent want to leave the big-problem-solving to businesses and individuals. Among people under forty, two-thirds or more think we should, through government, be doing more to solve our big problems.

2.

On economics, Americans have been leaning pretty left.

"America today is not a center-right country," the Princeton sociologist Paul Starr wrote in 2018, but rather "a country with a center-right economic elite" that has dominated both political parties for a long time, "and a polarized electorate torn between parties on the far right and center left." I think that's correct. More specifically, I think the leftist UC Berkeley economist Emmanuel Saez was correct when he said in a 2016 lecture that "in America, people do not have a strong view against inequality per se, as long as inequality is *fair,*" meaning that "individual income and wealth reflect the value of what people produce or otherwise contribute to the economic system." On that basic question of how much economic inequality Americans consider fair, people really are further to the left than either conventional wisdom or they themselves realize. In fact, most of them are socialists, by the standard Republican reckoning.

One of the many ways we know this is an ingenious and elaborate survey of a randomized sample of 5,522 Americans conducted by the Duke psychology professor Dan Ariely and the Harvard Business School professor Michael Norton—in 2005, before economic inequality became a prime national issue. For starters, they found that Americans were unaware of the extent of U.S. inequality. They asked the respondents, how much of our wealth is owned by the richest fifth? The average estimate was 59 percent; the correct answer then was 84 percent. (In a survey around the same time conducted by the University of Connecticut, the respondents' median estimate of the income of a "CEO of a large national corporation" was $500,000, when in fact it was about $12 million.) Ariely and Norton then asked each member of their sample to create their own ideal distribution for the United States, to decide how much of the total wealth each fifth of the citizenry ought to own. On average, people gave a larger share to those in the bottom half and a smaller share to the top fifth than either actually has, and Republicans were nearly as egalitarian as Democrats. Then everybody was shown pie charts of the distributions of money in two hypothetical countries—which were actually the United States and Sweden—and were asked in which country they'd prefer to live. "In considering this question," the veil-of-ignorance instruction stipulated, "imagine that if you joined this nation you would be randomly assigned to a place in the distribution, so you could end up anywhere in this distribution, from the very richest to the very poorest." Unsurprisingly, 92 percent of Americans chose to become citizens of the unnamed Sweden.

More conventional surveys have studied Americans' changing attitudes about the political economy over the years. Several ask, are poor people poor because they're "not doing enough to help themselves" or because of "circumstances beyond their control"? In 1995, Americans by two to one said it was mostly poor people's fault. In the early 2000s, two different polls found that respondents were almost split evenly, and in 2018, in a survey by the conservative American Enterprise Institute, a solid majority,

55 percent, said that "circumstances beyond their control cause people to be poor." A 2018 Gallup poll asked people if "the fact that some people in the United States are rich and others are poor needs to be fixed or is acceptable," and a similar solid majority, 57 percent, said we need to reduce inequality.

Polls in 2019 found that by huge margins, three to one, Americans want more government regulation of Wall Street banks and believe that corporations pay too little in taxes. And three different polls in 2019, by *The New York Times* and *Politico,* asked people what they thought of proposals to impose a wealth tax on the extremely rich—a tax of 2 percent a year on all wealth between $50 million and $1 billion, 3 percent a year on everything over $1 billion. All three polls found that nearly two-thirds of Americans are in favor of such wealth taxes—including large majorities of *Republicans.*

If more Americans were to learn of the large body of research showing that higher inequality in rich countries isn't just unfair but actually slows down economic growth—by a fifth since the 1980s, according to a 2014 study by the OECD—the remarkable strong support for Robin Hoodism might get even stronger.

3.

Resetting the balance of power in a big way in favor of the majority—citizens and employees versus big business and the rich—must be the overriding goal.

In a book about America on the social and political brink, a young journalist, not a leftist at all, frets about organized labor's powerlessness. With unionized workers making up only "about one-tenth" of the workforce, he writes, "unionism has a gigantic problem. There seems to be no limit to the methods by which [labor] organization is thwarted. You think of the powerful organizations ready to combat every sign of unionism, of the congestion of immigrants in the labor market, of the hostility" of the media and conservative courts.

> The odds seem to be overwhelming. . . . They have not yet won a living wage, they have not yet won anything like security of employment . . . [or] the right to be consulted as to the conditions under which they work. . . . Until labor is powerful enough to compel [respect], it cannot trust . . . the benevolence of its masters. . . . I don't

> pretend for one moment that labor unions are far-seeing, intelligent, or wise in their tactics . . . [but] their failure will be a tragedy.

That's a quote from 1914, *Drift and Mastery: An Attempt to Diagnose the Current Unrest,* the first book by twenty-four-year-old Walter Lippmann, before he became the most celebrated political columnist of the twentieth century. And here we are again. The question is whether and how American workers and citizens can find ways to reorganize and regain power to negotiate and enforce a fairer social contract, like the one drafted and adopted during Lippmann's lifetime.

The U.S. economy in which unions flourished and wielded real power is obviously different from today's U.S. economy. But over the last few decades, as other rich countries have changed in the same ways—less manufacturing, more automation and international competition—they've maintained their massively and powerfully unionized labor forces. The withering of workers' power in the United States since the 1970s was mainly the result of the right's brilliant, relentless crusade to minimize and where possible eliminate it.

There are no silver bullets, and I have no detailed master plan, just two strong convictions: that without effective counterweights to the power of big business and the rich, the United States will continue morphing into a superautomated plutocracy, and that how people work and get paid needs to become a primary subject of our politics. As the 2018 manifesto of a new Washington think tank put it,

> You don't need a theory of the perfect shoe to feel where your shoe pinches, and you don't need a theory of perfect justice to grasp the injustice of the boot on your neck. We can make real headway toward a better society by spotting and rectifying the most obvious and egregious injustices. We don't need to know what awaits on the mountain's summit as long as we can tell the difference between "down" and "up."

Barely a sixth of the economy still consists of livings earned by manufacturing or mining or growing things, rather than by coding, selling, researching, managing, cleaning, designing, fixing, administering, driving, explaining, sorting, performing, caregiving (or writing). As that second category of workers grew from a minority to the overwhelming majority during the last half of the last century, relatively few of them remained or became successfully unionized—that was left mainly to employees of state and local government, hospitals, hotels, casinos, and show business. As workplaces became smaller and employees more dispersed—or transformed into pseudo-nonemployees, like at Uber and Lyft—the work of organizing workers got harder.

But along with the public's reviving wish for big government to tackle big problems and projects, the organized labor tide may be turning as well. Answering Gallup's regular binary question in 2019 about approval or disapproval of unions, people were pro-labor by two to one; only a decade ago, the split was about even. And to another annual question about levels of confidence in organized labor, the fraction of Americans with "a great deal" or "quite a lot" is higher today than it's been in all but one year since the 1980s. Business and the right are still lobbying and campaigning hard state by state to pass right-to-work laws to make life harder for unions—West Virginia and Kentucky were the latest to enact them in 2016 and 2017. But then in 2018 in a Missouri referendum, voters by two to one overruled the Republican state legislature and governor to repeal the new right-to-work law there.

The basic case for unionization ought to be pretty compelling to people. Since the rise of labor unions seventy-five years ago and still today, organized workers are consistently paid one-quarter more than comparable nonunion workers, an average premium of $200 per week or more. Nearly all unionized workers in America get healthcare through their jobs. Among workers at private companies, two-thirds of unionized employees are still covered by old-fashioned pensions with fixed retirement payments, a benefit that only 13 percent of nonunion employees get.

Lately too, American workers have been feeling confident enough to go on strike as they haven't for years. Nearly a half-million went out in both 2018 and 2019, more in each of those years than in the previous six combined, more than any time since 1986. The biggest 2019 strike shut down dozens of General Motors factories for weeks, costing the company $4 billion, and a separate simultaneous strike by workers at Mack Truck factories was their first since the 1980s.

And then there are journalists, who mostly abandoned their obsolete blue-collar colleagues and unionism itself back in the fat-and-happy day.

I date Peak Media Smugness in this regard to the first Wednesday in May 2000. *New York* magazine and the briefly, astoundingly successful *Industry Standard,* a newsweekly covering the new digital industry, staged a fancy conference, the Media Summit, at the Museum of Modern Art in midtown Manhattan. The (first) Internet financial bubble had in just the previous few weeks begun to burst, although nobody knew that yet. Because I was part of the team about to launch the news site *Inside,* I'd agreed to appear on a panel with the publisher of *The New York Times* and the editor-in-chief of Time Inc. to discuss what the Internet portended for journalism.*

As it turned out that day, however, the museum's unionized workers were on strike and picketing; thus I decided not to attend. "Some of the best-known liberals in New York crossed picket lines at the Museum of Modern Art yesterday," just "breezed past striking workers," Murdoch's *New York Post* was delighted to report. The summit cohost and panel moderator Michael Wolff, a writer for *New York* at the time, was pissed and explained my absence to the crowd mockingly: "While *Henry Louis Gates* was able to come" to the conference despite the picketing strikers, he said of the Harvard African American studies professor, "that great working man Kurt Andersen couldn't bring himself to cross the picket line."

I think such an episode would play out quite differently these days, fifty years after Irving Kristol announced with a smile that "unionism has become . . . a boring topic" in which "none of the younger reporters is interested" and a generation after digital technology enabled the creative destruction of newspapers and magazines. Digital-indigenous media have in the last few years unionized like crazy, including *BuzzFeed, Quartz, Guardian US, Vox, HuffPost, Slate, Salon,* and *The Intercept,* as well as Gimlet podcasts and Vice Media. In addition, for the first time in their histories, the *Los Angeles Times,* the *Chicago Tribune, The New Republic, New York,* and *The New Yorker* are suddenly union shops. With only a few thousand workers in all, the economic impact is negligible. But the news media's new generation deciding en masse to form and join unions, indi-

*During the panel discussion, Norm Pearlstine of Time Inc.—who now runs the freshly unionized *Los Angeles Times*—said he wasn't too worried by the Internet: "I don't think long-form journalism is much threatened," he said.

vidual aspirations to become *brands* and *stars* notwithstanding, is a leading zeitgeist indicator and will surely have an outsize impact on coverage and public attitudes, as the media do.

In addition to the long slog of union organizing, there are other political means to empower workers. A minimum wage and overtime pay and standard forty-hour workweeks, for instance, all came into being by passing federal laws eighty years ago. Over the last five or six years, as a result of popular protest ("Fight for $15") and lobbying, most states have increased their minimum wages, most have set them higher than federal law—several now reaching fifteen dollars an hour—and many cities have set legal minimums higher than their states require.* In 2018 that shift in public opinion, as well as employees murmuring about organizing a union, persuaded Amazon to adopt a fifteen-dollar-an-hour minimum for its hundreds of thousands of workers. It reminded me of Henry Ford, who in 1914 doubled his factory workers' pay and got an avalanche of positive publicity—and who also, only after the New Deal gave unions more power two decades later, was finally forced to sign a contract with the autoworkers' union.

4.

Left-of-center Americans let themselves get played for too long by the economic right.

Permit me to repeat: forty years ago in a *Wall Street Journal* column, the pioneering modern right-wing intellectual *announced* a main part of that cynical plan, presenting it as a defining fuck-you-chumps feature of the conservatives' new approach: if tax cuts for the rich and big business "leave us with a fiscal problem," Irving Kristol wrote, again with a smile, mammoth government debt is *fine,* because from now on "the neoconservative" would force "his opponents to tidy up afterwards."

Ever since, the liberals' political role on economics and deficits has been to disprove the circa-1960s tax-and-spend caricature, to prove that they are responsible grown-ups, sensible Goldilocks moderates, conser-

*States without any legal minimum wage, or with one below the federal minimum, are Alabama, Georgia, Louisiana, Mississippi, South Carolina, Tennessee, and Wyoming.

vative the way conservatives used to be. As college-educated professionals became a more and more important Democratic constituency, the general reluctance on the left to try anything *too crazy* also grew. In the 1970s and '80s that was understandable, but the left learned the lesson too well, and by the '90s it became a very bad habit, especially unattractive as a default posture among the liberal well-to-do—*restraint* helping out the less-lucky majority but *reckless* on big business and the rich getting their way.

In the spring of 2020 we urgently increased the total federal debt by 13 percent. Watch: if Democrats get more power in Washington anytime soon, there will be a new Republican outbreak of mock fiscal panic and insistence on restraint—hysterical in both senses, overwrought as well as darkly funny. It's past time to resist that trap, to dial back the excessive liberal aversion to risk, where habitual fear of political counterreaction to transformative new policies and programs prevents them from even having a chance at getting popular and enacted. Knee-jerk centrism, splitting the difference *from the get-go* between themselves and the official right, with the goal of upsetting nobody very much, has been a terrible Democratic reflex on economics. For a while going forward, our forty-year-long tyranny of the status quo may make doing some of what needs doing feel a bit radical. And mistakes will be made. As an ER physician friend once told me, part of her job is to minimize scarring, but you can't let that stop you from doing the main job, saving the patient.

5.

On the other hand, be nonbinary.

Most people who call themselves progressive properly insist that we move beyond rigid binary categories concerning gender and sexuality. The progressive consensus in psychology and psychiatry also now considers the mind and consciousness itself to be fundamentally nonbinary, and individual people to be *neither* absolutely rational *nor* delusional but on continuums somewhere in between the poles, most of us clustered on the sane side. But why limit that sensible acceptance of fluidity and nuance to sexuality and mental states? It's unfortunate that so many on the left tend to be as ferociously binary as people on the right when it comes to politics and policy.

Being ideologically nonbinary can sometimes make *political* sense (bigger tent, more allies), but that's not mainly why I'm for it. It isn't my groovy synonym for *centrist* or *bipartisan*. The policy position on any given subject that appears to be at the "center," equally distant from the positions of the organized right and left, is sometimes quite wrong. What's more, old-fashioned default bipartisanship is impossible when one of the two parties is cuckoo or operating in bad faith or both. Rather, being nonbinary on economics means sticking to goals that can seem radical—lots more power for workers and average citizens, optimizing the economy for all Americans rather than maximizing it for rich ones and corporations—but then being nondoctrinaire about how we achieve the goals. It's like "hybrid vigor" in genetics, where stronger offspring are produced by outbreeding rather than by inbreeding. It's the virtue of every kind of diversity in organizations and on teams, in addition to justice and kumbaya, because seriously divergent points of view can increase the odds of finding and pursuing the best ideas, tactics, and strategies.

In a famous Supreme Court opinion during the Depression, Justice Louis Brandeis wrote that "one of the happy incidents" of America's federal system is that Washington can treat smaller governments and jurisdictions as policy proving grounds, because "a single courageous state may serve as a laboratory and try novel social and economic experiments without risk to the rest of the country." Surely we can expand our laboratories-of-democracy purview beyond U.S. states to include the virtual World's Fair of successful social and economic policies on display from which we can pick and choose.

Running a society well and fairly requires optimizing more than maximizing, going for the greatest happiness of the greatest number and the smallest possible number being screwed. Single-minded maximization of any one thing turns into crazed binary thinking—maximum profits are *everything,* regulations are *all* bad or *all* good (as it also tends to do for individuals: never apologize, constantly apologize, practice celibacy, practice promiscuity, eat as much as possible, starve yourself, and so on). Before the 1970s and '80s, back when corporate CEOs were still supposed to worry about their employees and communities and the public good as well as the price of their stock, that was optimization.

But then by focusing exclusively on one or two numbers, corporate executives become willfully simpleminded, like primitive calculators, artificially unintelligent.* The business school authors of "Theory of the Firm," that 1976 paper that became the scripture for ignoring such "stakeholders," actually argued in a subsequent paper that optimization for a whole society or diverse community or complicated individual simply *Does. Not. Compute*: "Since it is logically impossible to maximize in more than one dimension, purposeful behavior requires a single valued objective function."

Among the great examples of nonbinary thinking are the efforts of both presidents Roosevelt: they got the federal government to intervene in the free-market system in the early 1900s as it never had before in order to save the free-market system, to keep out-of-control capitalists from wrecking capitalism. The year upper-class FDR said of the forces of "business and financial monopoly" and "organized money" that he "welcome[d] their hatred" was the same year F. Scott Fitzgerald wrote that "the test of a first-rate intelligence is the ability to hold two opposed ideas in the mind at the same time."

The new Washington think tank that I mentioned a few pages ago is the Niskanen Center, and the thinkers there would remodel our economy along the lines of the Nordic social democracies. So . . . socialist? Not exactly—it was created by apostate defectors from Charles Koch's libertarian Cato Institute. "Markets are not just the natural and spontaneous consequence of government inaction," its 2018 manifesto explained. Remember: the economic right's great confidence trick in the 1980s was to redesign and reengineer the economy to privilege the rich and business—and *then* to insist that a market economy is like a precious unchangeable piece of nature, neither designed nor engineered.

> Markets are products of design—for good or ill. . . . For instance, when we design markets that do not price the costs that a firm imposes on others—for example through pollution, or in finance . . .—then we get far more of things that we don't want (like global warming and financial catastrophes). Environmental or financial regulation of this sort is not "anti-market"; on the con-

*"Because of the way the machines are changing the world," a character in Vonnegut's *Player Piano* says, "more and more of [people's] old values don't apply any more. People have no choice but to become second-rate machines themselves."

trary, it is essential to a properly constituted market where firms can't make excess profits by pushing off costs onto others.

"Countries like Canada, Denmark and Sweden," says Will Wilkinson, Niskanen's head of policy, "have become more robustly capitalist over the past several decades. They needed to be better capitalists to afford their socialism." What he calls "free-market 'socialism'"—note that he puts *socialism* in quotation marks—may seem like an oxymoron, but in fact it's acknowledgment of the range of vigorous real-world nonbinary hybrids.

The headlines on a few recent U.S. opinion surveys were basically These Crazy Kids Love Socialism, but my takeaway from the data is that younger people tend to be more ideologically nonbinary. A survey of people under thirty by Harvard's Kennedy School of Government found that majorities said they "don't support" capitalism *or* socialism, with small fractions who "identify as" either socialist (16 percent) or capitalist (19 percent). In a 2019 Survey Monkey/Harris poll of adults of all ages, six out of ten of those under twenty-five "have a positive reaction to the word *socialism*"—but six out of ten of them *also* have a positive reaction to the word *capitalism,* more or less the same as among people over twenty-five. Basically, the younger you are, the closer you come to thinking that—given no particulars spelled out—capitalism and socialism are equally okay.

But how does nonbinary thinking shape particular policies?

Our healthcare system is a grotesque jerry-built Rube Goldberg machine that's expensive, wasteful, ineffective, unfair, anxiety-provoking, and confusing. It welds together private and public components in some of the worst possible ways—such as the federal law prohibiting Medicare from negotiating prices with pharmaceutical companies, which may cost us an unnecessary $50 billion a year, 7 percent of the entire Medicare budget.* The system should get a complete overhaul. That is a binary starting point, but deciding what that means really isn't binary at all, because the range of vastly superior versions from relatively less (Switzerland) to more (Canada) to totally (the U.K.) government-run is wide. The irreducible and correct ideological binary in the politics of healthcare is

*The single senator getting the most campaign contributions from the pharmaceutical industry, by the way, has been Majority Leader Mitch McConnell, who helpfully calls proposals to regulate prescription drug costs "socialist price controls."

fair and effective versus unfair and ineffective. But a nonbinary approach is also enthusiastic about the genuinely virtuous free-market effects of government-guaranteed healthcare—everyone unshackled to switch jobs or occupations at will, to freelance or have multiple part-time jobs, to raise children, to become an artist, or to start a business.

Not all regulation is good, and not all deregulation is bad. I described earlier how the sensible deregulation of some industries, such as the overregulated airlines in 1978, was undertaken in good faith by people on the left—to increase competition to make prices lower and service better, antitrust by other means. But then conservatives turned suspicion of regulation into a true phobia and insistence on deregulation *of every kind* into dogma. That's because regulation that benefits Americans in general by making life safer or fairer or healthier also often prevents businesses from absolutely maximizing profits, which is taboo.

Or was: concerning antitrust regulation of the giant tech companies, the regulation-*bad* binary has started to crack even on the right. All sorts of antitrust experts and enforcers—federal and state, right and left—have been suddenly looking hard at Google and Facebook (and Amazon and Apple), as if it's the twentieth century again.

It is nonbinary to support the careful deregulation of urban real estate development as one necessary way to create more apartments and houses in prosperous cities that would be affordable for more people. Excessive regulations and approval processes really can drive rents and real estate prices unnecessarily higher, and the policy choice shouldn't be binary—laissez-faire Houston versus restrictive San Francisco. As with antitrust suddenly being taken seriously again, there are hopeful new models for smart, democratic *re*-regulation intended to make urban housing cheaper and cities more dense and environmentally sound—such as the fairly radical and fairly uncontroversial zoning code Minneapolis just adopted.

6.

Or else we could head straight for communism.

That's a joke. But when Andrew Yang was an infant—decades before the idea of a universal basic income began its national emergence in *Phineas Finn* fashion, from *chimerical* past *dangerous* to merely *difficult* on its way—possibly, eventually—to *absolutely needed*—a modest version went into effect in America. In fact, this shockingly successful socialist experiment began at the very moment when the rest of the country made its historic right turn in the 1970s and early '80s—and in *Alaska,* the self-consciously ultra-libertarian state that only one Republican presidential nominee has ever lost. It's a fantastic nonbinary American laboratory-of-democracy tale.

In my telling, the central character is Arlon Tussing. He grew up in Oregon's rural Rogue Valley and Berkeley, California, in the 1930s and '40s, attended the University of Chicago when Milton Friedman had just started teaching there, and graduated from college at seventeen. He went on to get an economics Ph.D.—and during the 1950s and early '60s, he become a leader of and writer for the Socialist Party of America. In 1965 he moved up to Fairbanks to teach at the University of Alaska, and while a professor there, he also served as the U.S. Senate Energy Committee's chief economist.

Shortly after Tussing became an Alaskan, North America's largest deposit of oil was discovered on the North Slope, and oil companies paid the state of Alaska the equivalent of $6.5 billion up front to start drilling, with royalties to follow. The good-looking young Alaska professor, when asked by a reporter how the oil money should be used, said, "The only way to guarantee that the money does any good to most of us is to hand it out to the people." The new Republican governor agreed, and after personally getting Milton Friedman's okay, he made it his main political project to amend the state constitution to put a quarter of the state's oil revenues into a dedicated fund, the Alaska Permanent Fund, then send a dividend check every year to every resident of Alaska, including children. Free money for everyone, no strings attached! Just as the new plan was being finalized, the governor visited China and met with Premier Zhou Enlai, who was just beginning the struggle to move his country's economic system away from dead-end Communism. "You Alaskans," Zhou told him, "are more socialistic than *we* are!"

The annual Alaska dividend varies each year, depending on how the fund's $66 billion worth of investments perform—it was $1,600 per person in 2019 and 2018, or $6,400 each year for a family of four, but it has occasionally reached the equivalent of nearly $3,000 per person and rarely dipped below $1,000. In 2007 another Republican governor got the legislature to pass an even higher tax on the oil companies' profits, an astoundingly progressive tax with rates that increased as the market price of oil increased. As a result, a year later each Alaskan got the equivalent of nearly $4,000, including the governor and her husband and five children, whose $28,000 universal basic income checks probably arrived just days before she failed to be elected the Republican vice president of the United States.* Professor Tussing died a few years ago in an old town in another archetypal western place, Silicon Valley. His two final Facebook posts are fabulous. One concerned a news story floating the possibility that Texas governor and future energy secretary Rick Perry might become president ("hell. No!") and the other was about himself: "I. Am happy on public demand to explain why and how I have long been Libertarian AND a Socialist."

It has worked out fine for Alaskans. According to the academic research, their modest universal no-strings cash entitlement hasn't made them work less, although it has made more people who hadn't worked take part-time jobs, especially women, apparently because the dividend helps them afford childcare. It also seems to make for better nutrition, with fewer underweight newborns and fewer obese toddlers, especially among the poor, and it has lifted a third of Alaska's officially poor rural Native citizens above the poverty line. The effect on overall inequality is unclear, but in the early 1980s Alaska had the highest income inequality of any state in America, and now it has about the lowest.

North to the Future is Alaska's official motto. The U.S. future will almost certainly need something like a Permanent Fund and a popular understanding, acceptance, and extension of its underlying idea of social wealth. Social wealth is really not an extreme or unfamiliar notion. Alaska's phenomenal oil strike was a one-off, but the new part was the direct sharing, giving some of the government's take from the windfall to everybody individually and equally. All Americans collectively own, through the government, 28 percent of the land in the United States, as well as the coastal seabed. A small bit of that is leased—to drilling and mining companies, solar and wind and geothermal firms, ranchers—for

*Oh, Alaska! It denies its criminals their annual dividend checks only if they're sentenced for a felony or incarcerated for any crime during that particular year, but as soon as they're out of jail or prison, they're good again. So for instance, former governor Sarah Palin's eldest child, Track, who in 2019 finished serving time for one of his assaults, should have his dividend resumed starting in 2021 if he's not sentenced or incarcerated again in the meantime.

$12 billion a year.* The money is ours, it just doesn't go to any of us individually unless we're among the Natives whose land the feds administer and lease out for them.

Before the oil age, starting in the 1860s, a large piece of America's collective wealth, one-tenth of all federally owned land, was given by the government to millions of individual Americans, to live on and farm and own as homesteaders. At that same time, the government granted another 100 million of our collectively owned acres to individual states—to sell and then use those proceeds to create the hundred public colleges and universities that became the foundation of the U.S. higher education system.

What else do all Americans own in common that could generate income and directly improve everybody's lives, like the oil under the North Slope did only for Alaskans? The air over the whole United States. Instead of just *giving away* the right to dump 5 billion tons of carbon dioxide into our air every year, we should start charging a fee for it, by means of taxes on oil and other fossilized carbon we burn. Those tax revenues could cover an annual dividend paid to every citizen, even oil-enriched Alaskans. A group of sane conservative éminences grises, including three former Republican treasury secretaries, recently proposed exactly that.

The same scheme was proposed a few years earlier by the left activist Peter Barnes in his book *With Liberty and Dividends for All: How to Save Our Middle Class When Jobs Don't Pay Enough*. As Hillary Clinton was about to launch her 2016 presidential campaign, she read it. What happened next is a sad and perfect epitome of the last few decades of Democratic political economics. "I was fascinated by this idea," she wrote in her memoir,

> as was my husband, and we spent weeks working with our policy team to see if it could be viable enough to include in my campaign. We would call it "Alaska for America." Unfortunately, we

*"In free governments the people own the land and the resources," the superlibertarian activist Ammon Bundy said recently. Social wealth! Except he's got it backward, as if individuals were entitled to use for free anything the society owns collectively. He and his father, Cliven Bundy, who grazes cattle on public land in Nevada but refuses to pay the rest of us for the privilege, organized the famous armed standoff with federal agents in 2014 to get their way.

> couldn't make the numbers work. . . . We decided it was exciting but not realistic, and left it on the shelf. That was the responsible decision. I wonder now whether we should have thrown caution to the wind and embraced "Alaska for America" as a long-term goal and figured out the details later.

I wonder if she thought about putting scare quotes around "responsible."

Another rich territory of social wealth isn't a natural resource, but it is ubiquitous and collectively created. It's the Internet. U.S. government funding was directly responsible for developing the semiconductor industry (and other fundamental pieces of computers) and for inventing the Internet, and after that for Google, Siri, and GPS, among other platforms and technologies.

If we behaved like the seed investors and venture capitalists we were and are, we'd now be collecting many billions a year from companies using our publicly funded Internet. But so far, we are not. It's as if we built the interstate highway system but then, because *free markets,* let some dudes set up tollbooths along its 49,000 miles and keep all the money they collected for themselves. But it's even more ridiculous than that. Now without all our ongoing billions of individual hours of daily keystrokes and clicks and pictures and videos, all the data and "content" that we donate to Google and Facebook and the rest of them, they'd have nothing to sell to advertisers—and selling ads is their business. So on the glorious new public digital superhighway we built, we're also now all working as volunteer staff for the insanely profitable tollbooth-and-billboard businesses that the private companies installed.

In fact, Mark Twain invented this business model in 1876 as a joke—Tom Sawyer's fence-painting grift, persuading a crowd of fun-loving young people with time on their hands that the tedious work he needed doing was *fun,* then even charging the eager fools to do it for him. Since 2013, when the digital pioneer and Microsoft philosopher-prince Jaron Lanier wrote a book about the basic unfairness of the Internet economy and proposed requiring the tech companies to somehow pay for our data, that notion has also moved from *chimerical* toward *possible*.

Ditto with universal basic income. Andrew Yang's presidential candidacy was quixotic but also successful—it gave the first extended, respectful national spotlight to the two important truths underlying his campaign: the inexorable automation of jobs, and our need to radically readjust the political economy to cope.

Who knows how or when or if a universal basic income could be rolled out, or what its precise funding mechanisms and rules would be? But it's feasible.* The Yang campaign version was $1,000 a month from age eighteen on, funded by a value-added tax and a carbon tax. In a Pew Research survey about automation and economics in 2017, pre-Yang, 61 percent of people were in favor of the government giving "all Americans a guaranteed income that would meet their basic needs" as a way of dealing with "robots and computers [that] are capable of doing many human jobs." Two surveys in 2019 asked about UBIs in a badly inaccurate way—about hypothetical government incomes paid *only* to people "whose jobs are threatened by automation" or "who lose their jobs because of advances in artificial intelligence"—that is, not a no-strings, no-stigma payment that everyone would get. But even asked that way, half or nearly half of respondents were still in favor, including as many as three-quarters of younger people.

Replacing our patchwork of existing social welfare programs with a unified, universal system of cash payments is a basic idea that conservatives from Hayek to Friedman have supported. Charles Murray proposed a full-on UBI fifteen years ago in a book published by the American Enterprise Institute, and now that "we are going to be carving out millions of white-collar jobs, because artificial intelligence, after years of being over-hyped, has finally come of age," he recently started pushing it hard once again. "Yes," he wrote in *The Wall Street Journal* in 2016, "some people will idle away their lives under my UBI plan. The question isn't whether a UBI will discourage work, but whether it will make the existing problem significantly worse." The approval of people on the right, and of tech billionaires like Mark Zuckerberg and Elon Musk, does not make universal basic income a better idea, just a somewhat more politically plausible one.

*In addition to the Alaskan success, in small-scale trials around the world, UBIs haven't made people work less. In the United States there would obviously need to be a serious discussion about optimal payment levels, because some people will take such a road paved with good intentions to hell. But affluent people who say they oppose UBI on principle—because it might encourage laziness or irresponsibility—should also support a 100 percent estate tax, in order to prevent lazy, irresponsible heirs.

29

The Plague Year and Beyond

When the original band of intellectuals and CEOs and politicians and the very rich began pursuing their dream of hijacking the U.S. political economy and dragging it back in time to the days before the New Deal, surely none of them imagined they'd wind up *here*. By which I mean either the scale and durability of their victory, or with such a front man—so deranged and unpleasant and idiotic, so brazenly racist and xenophobic and misogynistic, a businessman yet so completely incompetent as an executive. Today's evil geniuses find him embarrassing and tiresome. All they and their predecessors ever really wanted was a system permanently guaranteeing them inordinate fortunes and power, with a clubbable Bush or Romney at the helm. Over the decades, however, as they decided again and again that their ends (money, supremacy) always justified any and all means (stoking racism and other hatreds, spreading falsehoods, rousing their rabble while also rigging the system against them), it was bound to end somewhere in this horrid vicinity. In 2016, as the current generation of Fausts made their darkest bargain yet, surely some of them smelled a whiff of sulfur or heard a demonic cackle as they signed away whatever remained of their souls. And in 2020 there could be no denying it.

The obeisance of the rich right and their consiglieri to Trump and Trumpism for the last five years has exposed more nakedly than ever their compact—everything about money, anything for money—and the events of 2020 pushed that along to an even more shameless, grotesque crescendo. In early spring, when COVID-19 had killed only dozens of Americans, Stuart Stevens, a strategist for four of the five previous GOP presidential nominees but now a fierce apostate, wrote that "those of us in the Republican Party built this moment," because "the failures of the government's response to the coronavirus crisis can be traced directly to some of the toxic fantasies now dear to the Republican Party. . . . *Government is bad. Establishment experts are overrated or just plain wrong. Science is suspect.*"

He could have also listed *Believe in our perfect mythical yesteryear, All hail big business, Short-term profits are everything, Inequality's not so bad, Universal healthcare is tyranny, Liberty equals selfishness, Co-opt liberals,* and *Entitled to our own facts* as operating principles of the Republican Party and the right. During 2020 and since, all those maxims drove the responses (and the nonresponsiveness) of the Trump administration and its extended family of propagandists and allies and flying monkeys.

Stevens referred to the government's "failures," and objectively it did fail—to respond promptly and aggressively, to develop or execute an effective or even coherent strategy, to minimize the wholesale loss of American lives. But apart from this administration's special incompetence and Orwellian denial of facts, while its handling of the pandemic wound up as a *political* failure in 2020, almost every piece of the crises' exacerbation by them was inevitable because each one came directly out of the right's playbook of the last several decades.

- *Government is bad.* A Republican administration uniquely unsuited and unready and really unwilling to deal with such a national crisis? Decades before our latest show-business president defamed his entire executive branch as a subversive Deep State, the cocreator of late Republicanism announced in 1981, a few minutes after becoming our first show-business president, that "in this present crisis, government is not the *solution* to our problem, government *is* the problem," then made a shtick out of warning Americans to consider any offers of help from the government "terrifying."*

*The antisocialist Ronald Reagan most famously made his nine-most-terrifying-words crack (*I'm from the government and I'm here to help*) in 1986 in Illinois. It was in a speech

- *Believe in our perfect mythical yesteryear.* The right twisted and exploited nostalgia in the 1970s and '80s to get its way, selling people on a restoration of old-time America with storybook depictions that omitted all the terrible parts of the past—including the epidemics we had before we built a public health system and before governments required citizens to get government-funded vaccines; the economic panics and collapses we had before government intervened to help unemployed workers; the phony miracle cures that charlatan showmen marketed to us before government put a stop to them.
- *Establishment experts are wrong, science is suspect.* Since the 1980s, the oil and gas and coal industries have conspired with the right to encourage Americans to disbelieve the scientific consensus on global warming, because that science created pressure to mitigate a global crisis with government interventions that could reduce those businesses' profits. From the start in 2020, the reckless right, with the president in the lead, encouraged Americans to disbelieve virologists, epidemiologists, and other scientific experts, because trusting them would be bad for business and stock prices.
- *Entitled to our own facts.* That systematic spread of coronavirus misinformation by Trump and the right couldn't have happened without the creation in the late 1980s (Rush Limbaugh) and '90s (Fox News) of big-time right-wing mass media. Their continuous erasure of distinctions between fact and opinion has always served the propaganda purposes of the political party most devoted to serving the interests of big business and investors, and during the COVID-19 crises—*Reopen now, don't worry about disease*—they attempted to serve those interests directly.
- *Short-term profits are everything.* For years, reckless financial operators dragged healthy enterprises into leveraged buyouts and piled on excessive debt, making billions personally but the companies weak and barely able to survive in normal times. Then when things got *bad* in 2020, the LBO'd companies (such as J. Crew and Neiman Marcus) started dying off even faster than others: excessive debt turned out to

---

just before bragging that he'd given more federal billions to farmers "this year alone than any previous administration spent during its entire tenure." His antisocialist successor Donald Trump revived the tradition, repeatedly bragging since 2019 about the tens of billions his administration has given to farmers.

be a main underlying condition comorbid with the economic effects of the pandemic.

- *Liberty equals selfishness.* The right spent decades turning *brat* into a synonym for *ultra-conservative,* forging a tantrum-based politics focused on hating sensible rules that reduce unnecessary deaths and sickness—*no gun control! no mandatory vaccinations! no universal health insurance!* So in 2020, *of course* mobs of childish adults were excited to throw self-righteous tantrums on TV about being *grounded* and forced to behave sensibly by the mean grown-ups. While also playing soldier and carrying weapons at public protests all year, up to and including the murderous cosplay riot at the Capitol.
- *Inequality's not so bad.* The glaring new light of the pandemic vividly showed the results of the system we've built. The health risks and the economic burdens are borne disproportionately by people near the financial edge, black and brown people, people with low-paying jobs that can't be done from home. And on the other hand, we see more clearly than ever how the lucky top tenth, the people who own more than 80 percent of all the stocks and other financial wealth, inhabit an alternate economic universe.
- *Universal healthcare is tyranny.* A healthcare system already fractured, unfair, inefficient, confusing, and anxiety-provoking as a result of its capture by a for-profit medical-industrial complex? *Check.* And a system unique in the world for making its exceptionally expensive care a fringe benefit of (some) particular jobs—at a moment when tens of millions of jobs suddenly disappeared? *Check.*

Speaking of places with better social contracts, where governments are more trusted and permitted to be effective: as the pandemic spread, most of the countries I singled out for praise in Chapter 24, "American Exceptionalism," quickly put strict national protocols in place, and had COVID-19 death rates running half, a third, a quarter of America's. Then there's South Korea, among the most populous developed countries: in late March, 100 people had died there and 100 in the United States—but two months later, only 267 South Koreans had died, making their death rate, adjusted for population, *one-sixtieth* of ours. Other developed countries also more straightforwardly and immediately addressed the massive economic consequences, without political rancor, because providing good social safety nets to try to protect everyone from economic disaster is simply what governments *do*.

A Six-Week Case Study: Evil Geniuses, Minions, Enablers

U.S. presidents (and governors and mayors) have no more important job than preventing their citizens from dying. In 2020 ours failed to save tens of thousands. But as I've also argued in this book, running a country (or a company or one's own life) is a matter of making difficult trade-offs and balances, optimizing among different needs rather than pursuing one to the exclusion of everything else. How much is one life or death worth? How much are a hundred thousand or a million lives and deaths worth? Exactly how and how quickly do you reopen commerce and life? The instant politicization of the pandemic by the right was a case study of the folly of binary thinking. It was a character-testing episode for people and institutions. Priorities were starkly revealed.

In late February 2020, because stock prices began dropping, the president began paying attention to the epidemic—and insisting publicly that there was *no cause for alarm*. A big reason the market went down, he said on February 25, was that a Democratic presidential debate the night before had spooked investors, but no worries, because "after I win the election," "the stock market is going to boom like it's never boomed before."

The same day the Speaker of the House said of Trump's statements about the virus, "You don't know what you're talking about." *Entitled to our own facts.* That evening at his first virus-task-force press briefing, asked about a Centers for Disease Control official's latest expert judgment that "it's not a question of if but rather . . . when and how many people in this country will have severe illness," Trump said, "*I* don't think it's inevitable." Asked if he agreed with Limbaugh and others on the right that experts were "exaggerating the threat of coronavirus to hurt you politically," he said, "Yeah, I agree with that, I do, I think they are." A mere "fifteen people" in America had been infected, an untrue figure he repeated a dozen times during the briefing, and "within a couple of days," he promised, it's "going to be down to close to zero, that's a pretty good job we've done." The following day he made his magical thinking more explicit—"It's going to disappear, one day it's like a miracle, it will disappear"—and twenty-four hours after that, he held one of his big rallies, in South Carolina, where he said warnings of a viral epidemic spreading to America amounted to the Democrats' "new hoax" to make him look bad.

Co-opt liberals. On that same day, alas, a college classmate of mine, the superrational Harvard law professor and former Obama official Cass Sunstein, made himself a useful idiot for the president and the right. "One thing is clear," Sunstein wrote in his *Bloomberg News* column just as Americans had definitely started dying from COVID-19, "people are more scared than they have any reason to be," because "most people in North America and Europe do not need to worry much about the risk of contracting the disease." And the real problem was that all that needless fear was going to result in "plummeting stock prices."

Ten days later, in early March, a House subcommittee held a regular hearing on the CDC's annual budget, which the administration was trying to cut, as it had tried to do every year—large cuts that the Koch organization Americans for Prosperity had recommended because, as it complained in 2018, "CDC funding has already grown significantly over the last fifteen years." Trump's CDC director, Robert Redfield, a conservative, testified. A right-wing Republican congressman, who like Redfield is a physician, used his question time to explain why dealing with "these kind of new viruses" requires the government to continue guaranteeing high profits to the pharmaceutical industry. "On the vaccine front," he said, prospective laws like the bill the House had just passed to let the government negotiate Medicare drug prices downward "will destroy American innovation" in medicine. He instructed Redfield to agree with him that only "the private sector" can properly deal with COVID-19 and "these kinds of public health threats."

But then Redfield shared with the congressman his surprise and disappointment that the two big U.S. medical testing companies had not, on their own, "geared up sooner," starting in mid-January, to handle mass testing for the coronavirus. "I anticipated that the private sector would have engaged and helped develop it" and "be fully engaged eight weeks ago" to deal properly with this new disease, said the national director of disease control. "Here were two men wondering aloud," the journalist Alex Pareene wrote at the time, "why reality had failed to conform to their ideology. How odd that these companies, whose only responsibility is to their shareholders, had failed to make up for the incompetence of this administration."

Confirmed COVID-19 cases and deaths in the United States had just begun increasing exponentially, cases quintupling and deaths tripling in a week. However, as a rule, getting America's full attention requires show business and/or financial spectacle: starting the day after that House hearing, in one twenty-four-hour period, the NBA suspended its season, Tom Hanks announced he was sick, the president read a speech on TV, and stock prices fell 10 percent, at that time the fourth largest one-day U.S. market decline in history.

All hail big business. The next day Trump held a coronavirus press conference in the Rose Garden to promise he absolutely had everything under control. The main event was a weird parade of ten retail and health industry CEOs he emceed, "celebrities in their own right," naming each one—"great job . . . incredible work . . . tremendous help . . . tremendously talented . . . a great company"—like finalists in a Miss USA pageant. Mr. Walmart promised to "make portions of our parking lot available in select locations . . . so that people can experience the drive-thru [COVID-19 testing] experience." The Dow Jones stock average ended the day, a Friday, 1,985 points higher, 9 percent up.

The following Monday the president finally, grudgingly announced a plan, recommending that COVID-positive and sick and particularly vulnerable Americans stay home—but just for a little while, a couple of weeks, until the end of March, calling it "15 Days to Slow the Spread." By then governors and mayors began instituting the measures actually necessary to control the epidemic, mandatory closings and stay-at-home orders that drastically reduced commerce. With stock prices having fallen for three weeks, the investor class was already unhappy and anxious, but now they and the economic right *freaked.* Corporate revenues would take giant hits; keeping people solvent would require stupendous government spending; some big businesses could be temporarily nationalized; and stock prices would decline more—which they immediately proceeded to do, dropping that day alone by 13 percent on their way to a 20 percent decline in a week and a half.

Those next eleven days in March were a remarkable time to watch America's evil genius squadrons scramble the jets.

On that same Monday, March 16, when the shutdown really started, the conservative Hoover Institution published a piece called "Coronavirus Perspective" recommending against *any* restrictions on the economy because the pandemic just wasn't going to be a major public health problem. "In the United States, the current 67 deaths should reach about 500" in all, the Stanford think tank article projected, and in a quick follow-up article called "Coronavirus Overreaction," the same writer completely showed his ideological cards. "Progressives think they can run everyone's lives through central planning," he warned, so don't let them do it to fight the spread of this no-big-deal disease. The writer was neither a medical professional nor an economist, but a lawyer named Richard Epstein, a blue-chip economic right-winger from the 1970s and '80s—influential University of Chicago law professor, early Federalist Society VIP, Cato Institute scholar, editor of the Law and Economics movement's main journal. Right away, "conservatives close to Trump and numerous administration officials [were] circulating" Epstein's inexpert pronouncements, *The Washington Post* reported.*

Right around then, according to "a Trump confidant who speaks to the president frequently" and spoke to a *Financial Times* reporter about those conversations, Jared Kushner was telling his father-in-law "that testing too many people, or ordering too many ventilators, would spook the markets and so we just shouldn't do it. . . . That advice worked far more powerfully on him than what the scientists were saying."

On Friday, March 20, Americans for Prosperity issued a hysterical press release over "the recent moves by some states to shut down all non-essential businesses," because—ignoring the *non-essential* caveat that permitted grocery stores and pharmacies everywhere to stay open—"if businesses are shut down, where will people who are most in need get the things they need to care for themselves and others?" But then they got right to their other big fear: federal spending to help individual Americans with "wasteful . . . provisions that had no place in an emergency relief package."

That same night at an online "AFP activist town hall," the group's

*Five months earlier Hoover had published an Epstein article concluding that "there is today no compelling evidence of an impending climate emergency." In an interview in late March with *The New Yorker* after he published his COVID-19 articles, Epstein said his prediction of 500 total COVID-19 deaths had been an error, that he'd actually meant to say *5,000* Americans in all would die. After the reporter challenged other factual assertions, Epstein finally replied, "You're going to say that I'm a crackpot. . . . That's what you're saying, isn't it? That's what you're saying? . . . Admit to it. You're saying I'm a crackpot." Three weeks later, nearly 5,000 Americans officially died of COVID-19 in a single day, and six weeks after that, 100,000 Americans had died, 200 times Epstein's original estimate of the total deaths, 20 times his adjusted estimate. A year later, in early 2021, the total U.S. deaths were 1,000 and 100 times larger, respectively, than his estimates.

president warned that the imminent federal recovery legislation to deal with the economic consequences is "gonna have lasting ramifications for our country." When one of the AFP activists asked "how we can show others the negative effects of government-controlled socialized medicine in light of the current situation," the second main presenter, a Mississippi lawyer and vice president of Koch's umbrella political organization, simply said that "America really does have a really good healthcare system because historically we've believed in free enterprise," so everybody should just be "reminding people of how we got to where we are with a free enterprise system." *Plus*, the AFP president practically gasped—"I cannot imagine how we would be responding" to the pandemic "if the entire nation, every citizen in this nation, was trapped in a single-payer all-in government-run system." The men agreed that the federal public health bureaucracies hadn't done a good job on COVID-19, *of course,* but that the president was now cracking the whip. As for financial assistance to citizens, the lesser Koch minion said that if the federal government had "exercised fiscal discipline before now, we'd be in a position to help people more" in ways that "might include spending some money."

The economic libertarians' de facto pandemic czar for a while was Stephen Moore, the right-wing Zelig and early Trumpist so second-rate that in 2019 even the Republican Senate wouldn't consent to put him on the Federal Reserve Board. On the pandemic, his inside-outside role was, like the president's, Republicanism ad absurdum: he was responsible simultaneously for creating government policy *and* for helping to discredit and obstruct government policies. For the former, he directly advised Trump, as a member of the Economic Recovery Task Force along with his pals Larry Kudlow and Arthur Laffer. Trump held regular conference calls with those three, known in the White House as "Laffer's guys"—according to *The Washington Post,* "Trump takes them seriously because he sees the GOP tax law they pushed," the 2017 giveaway to big business and the rich, "as one of his signature agenda items."

For the outside antigovernment work, Moore collaborated with, among others, the Koch-created entity FreedomWorks; a cofounder of the Tea Party Patriots; and the head of ALEC, the influential big-business-funded organization of right-wing state legislators on whose "private enterprise advisory council" he sits with a principal Koch Companies lobbyist.

For instance, Moore appeared on the YouTube talk show of the Independence Institute, a libertarian think tank founded in the 1980s. Aggressive government responses to the pandemic were, he suggested, *intended* to damage the economy in order to damage Trump politically, and keeping nonessential workers at home was "so unnecessary," because "the only 'nonessential workers' are people who work for the government." This is all "gonna go down in history . . . as one of the great abuses of governmental power," because "*here's* what's *scary*—our government spending this year" will be so large. When a viewer asked if reopening commerce too quickly might lead to a new wave of disease, he said, "Let's pray . . . that we don't have a recurrence," although who knew, "it's not my area of expertise."

The first Sunday the shutdown was national, March 22, is particularly interesting to look at closely.

That day Moore met with a dozen CEOs and economists to plot their push to end restrictions on commerce right away, and his former employer, *The Wall Street Journal*, reported that "the group suggested Easter Sunday as a date for an 'economic resurrection,'" just three weeks away.

That same day another intelligent writer with whom I'm friendly also made himself, I'm afraid, a neoliberal useful idiot for the right by arguing blithely and prematurely for ending a public health war that had barely begun. Tom Friedman's *New York Times* column was based mainly on an interview with a celebrity physician who specializes in nutrition, not infectious disease or epidemiology, and it was all about economics—"making sure that . . . we don't destroy our economy, and as a result of that, even more lives." Only 340 Americans had died, and we had no clue how many were infected, or the nature of COVID-19 immunities. But the doctor and Friedman agreed that everybody should "basically stay home for two weeks," until early April, and then anyone who wasn't symptomatic or elderly or otherwise obviously vulnerable, the untested lot of us, "should be allowed to return to work or school." Presto, we should "'reboot' our society in two or perhaps more weeks," Friedman wrote. "The rejuvenating effect on spirits, and the economy," he quoted the physician predicting, "would be hard to overstate."

At that evening's White House task force TV briefing, the president's economic lieutenant Peter Navarro explained why they weren't going to use the Defense Production Act to make companies manufacture scarce medical gear. "We're seeing the greatest mobilization in the industrial base since World War II," he claimed, but "on a purely voluntary basis—based on the leadership of this administration—we're getting what we need without—without putting the heavy hand of government down." *All hail big business*.

That same Sunday, a couple of hours later, the next character to pop up consequentially was Steve Hilton, a Fox News anchor. He'd been a young evil genius of the U.K. right, an Oxford-educated branding expert who worked closely with prime minister David Cameron before moving to the United States in 2012 to teach for a year at the Hoover Institution.* Like Trump, he's a wealthy, cunning, well-connected showman and opportunist who presents himself as a populist fighting for "massive revolutionary change." "I'm rich, but I understand the frustration" of the "victims of elitist agenda," he says, and claims that he "probably would have supported" Sanders versus Trump in 2016. Instead, he's totally MAGA.

That night on his weekly show, *The Next Revolution,* before he brought on Kudlow, the director of the National Economic Council ("Larry, I've always loved your energy and optimism"), Hilton raved on about the urgency of America getting back to business as usual immediately but with his own fake-angry, incoherent, disingenuous Trumpy spin. The multitrillion-dollar economic recovery programs wouldn't actually help the common man, he said, but would amount to a "total government takeover of the economy." Hilton said he loved business, and he bragged about businesses he'd started, but he also said it's "our ruling class and their TV mouthpieces whipping up fear over this virus, [because] they can afford an indefinite shutdown." And finally came the demagogic Fox News version of the message Tom Friedman delivered that morning to *Times* readers: "You know that famous phrase, 'The cure is worse than the

*His wife, Rachel Whetstone, is another perfect minor character: the upper-class English daughter and granddaughter of rich professional libertarians—her grandfather a protégé of Friedrich A. Hayek and cofounder of the Manhattan Institute—Whetstone has for the last decade been the chief PR executive for, consecutively, Google, Uber, Facebook's WhatsApp, and Netflix.

disease'? You think it is just the coronavirus that kills people? This total economic shutdown will kill people."

Forty-eight minutes later Goldman Sachs's senior chairman and former CEO Lloyd Blankfein, having last tweeted more than a week earlier (about letting private industry "fix the govt's mismanaged virus testing program"), sounded exactly the same alarm—that "crushing the economy, jobs and morale is also a health issue-and beyond. Within a very few weeks let those with a lower risk to the disease return to work."

And then, just before midnight, came a tweet from devoted Fox News viewer Donald Trump: "WE CANNOT LET THE CURE BE WORSE THAN THE PROBLEM ITSELF," he declared. The country was barely seven days into his government's "15 Days to Slow the Spread" plan, but the president had already lost patience.

The next morning he retweeted himself, including his stage wink to Wall Street that he'd be ending this shutdown nonsense soon—"AT THE END OF THE 15 DAY PERIOD, WE WILL MAKE A DECISION AS TO WHICH WAY WE WANT TO GO!"—and said out loud to reporters, "We can't have the cure be worse than the problem." But the stock market nevertheless ended that day another 3 percent down.

The following morning, March 24, Trump issued an even more desperate version of his Hiltonian tweet—"THE CURE CANNOT BE WORSE (by far) THAN THE PROBLEM!"—and held a conference call with a group of big financial players, "alternative asset" multibillionaire investors who operate hedge funds and private equity firms. Among them were Stephen Schwarzman, the cofounder and CEO of the Blackstone Group, the world's largest alternative asset firm. (He's the Koch associate who'd complained that a proposal for financiers to pay income taxes at the rate paid by other affluent people was equivalent to Hitler's invasion of Poland.) In the weeks just before that conference call about the pandemic with Trump, Schwarzman had given $10 million to the super PAC devoted to ensuring that Republicans maintained control of the Senate, and $2.5 million to the GOP House super PAC. Also on the call was the head of the company that owns the New York Stock Exchange—who, with his wife, Republican U.S. senator Kelly Loeffler, had just sold millions of dollars' worth of stocks in two dozen sales starting the day she attended a private Senate briefing on the pandemic a month before the market started crashing.* (A few weeks later he donated $1 million to the main Trump reelection super PAC.) This finance industry plenum on the conference call, according to *The Wall Street Journal*, stressed "the need to . . . focus on a date" for opening up and generating more business revenue ASAP. The rest of Wall Street had apparently gotten the memo and, reassured, bid up the market 5 percent when it opened that morning.

At noon the president began his special televised live "town hall"—that is, talking to a Fox News interviewer on the White House lawn. Trump stuck to the plan hatched in the previous forty-eight hours, focusing on a date for the business resurrection. "I would love to have the country opened up and just raring to go" in nineteen days, he announced, "by Easter."

The stock market kept rising the rest of that week, but the zealots of the right, the Scrooges and Mr. Potters as well as the celebrity know-nothings, weren't about to stop using the pandemic to pick fights. As the number of newly unemployed Americans reached 10 million on its way toward 30 million, a group of prominent Republican senators threatened to keep the first big economic recovery bill from passing quickly because making those millions of citizens financially whole for a few months might give the lazy "doctors [and] nurses" among them a "strong incentive . . . to [try to] be laid off instead of going to work." By then, with almost 100,000 Americans COVID-19-positive and nearly 2,000 dead, Trump and his Fox News claque were no longer totally denying the reality of the health threat.† But Rush Limbaugh in late March was still telling his 15 million

*Loeffler, appointed to fill an empty seat in Georgia, had been a senator for only eighteen days of her total fifty-four weeks in office when she attended that early pandemic briefing. She'd worked for years for her husband's company, before and after marrying him, mainly as his head of PR but recently running its new cryptocurrencies division for $3.5 million a year.

†Right-wing fantasies and misinformation about COVID-19 on Fox News apparently caused unnecessary deaths. "[Sean] Hannity originally dismissed the risks associated with the virus before gradually adjusting his position starting late February," according to the research by economists in their paper "Misinformation During a Pandemic," but "[Tucker] Carlson warned viewers about the threat posed by the coronavirus from early February. . . . Greater viewership of Hannity relative to *Tucker Carlson Tonight* is strongly associated with a greater number of COVID-19 cases and deaths in the early stages of the pandemic." One final magnificent irony: that study was conducted and published under the auspices of the University of Chicago's institute named after Milton Friedman and his libertarian protégé Gary Becker.

listeners to doubt the Deep State doctors and scientists advising Trump. "We didn't elect a president to defer to a bunch of health experts that we don't know," the Presidential Medal of Freedom winner said. "And how do we know they're even health experts? Well, they wear white lab coats and they've been on the job for a while and they're at the CDC and they're at the NIH. . . . But these are all kinds of things that I've been questioning."

During the previous big economic crisis in 2009, the Kochs used their organizations FreedomWorks in Washington, and Americans for Prosperity just across the Potomac, to harness and amplify grassroots anxiety and confusion in the provinces. From those headquarters they'd executive-produced the politically useful shows of performative anger by Tea Party protesters against the Democratic-led federal government. In 2020 the pandemic provided a reboot opportunity—this time for protests against state and local governments, especially those run by Democrats, that weren't following the maximalist line on instantly reopening business. They mobilized their militias—old Tea Partiers, gun nuts, anti-vaxxers, random Trumpists—for demonstrations around the country that began on Easter Monday.

"There's a massive movement on the right now," Stephen Moore claimed, "growing exponentially. People are at the boiling point. They are protesting against injustice and a loss of liberties." He insisted, *The Washington Post* reported, that "the protests have been spontaneous and organized at the local level," although he admitted that "his group has been offering them advice and legal support." "I'm working with a group in Wisconsin," he told his libertarian audience on YouTube, "to shut down the capitol" with traffic, and "we have one big donor in Wisconsin, he said 'Steve, I promise I will pay the bail and legal fees of anyone who gets arrested.' The more civil disobedience the better, however you want to do it." So why, according to polls, were two-thirds of Americans in favor of the national quasi-quarantine? Because, this presidential adviser and would-be Fed governor said, "the American people are sheep."

The two Koch-created enterprises and Moore were joined by a newer organization also devoted to promoting right-wing economics, the Convention of States, funded by Robert Mercer—hedge fund billionaire, early *Breitbart News* investor, Trump's biggest 2016 donor—and overseen by a cofounder of the Tea Party Patriots and (*such* a long game) a strategist for

David Koch's 1980 Libertarian vice-presidential campaign. In Michigan, the protests were organized and promoted by existing Republican groups, one connected to the right-wing billionaire DeVos family, and in Idaho by a group funded by a new Coors, the *son* of the counter-Establishment founder Joseph.*

The mission of those demonstrations, as *The Washington Post* reported, was "making opposition to stay-at-home orders—which had been in place in most states for only a couple of weeks or less—appear more widespread than is suggested by polling." The shorthand *Astroturf* for these kinds of protests is a misnomer. Rather, they're more like *sod:* real grass but more expensive, centrally produced and harvested, then rolled out by professionals on command to look instantly picturesque. It seemed clear, from the social media posts of nominally local groups all over the country, that talking points and specific language were being issued from headquarters. FreedomWorks' protest brand Reopen America became the name for local protests all over the country—Reopen Wisconsin, Reopen Oregon, Reopen Nevada, Reopen Delaware, and many more. Their online national protest calendar stipulated that "these are not FreedomWorks events, but . . . if you're interested in planning your own event, click here for our planning guide." The professional right-wingers on K Street provided photo-op protest tradecraft instructions to the provincials—make sure to "include . . . nurses, healthcare workers, etc. as much as possible," and to "keep [signs] homemade." Americans for Prosperity held an online training session for would-be agitators on how to spread memes that they actually called "Best at Going Viral."

Because the president had been unable to hold any of his MAGA rallies for weeks, then *months,* the demonstrations also served as ad hoc reelection events, keeping the superenthusiasts excited and acting out their love for the president on TV, where he could see it. At the end of the first week of protests in April, the country was still in the middle of his government's "30 Days to Slow the Spread," as the second phase was called, but the president said *fuck that*—in four minutes one morning, he posted tweets to rev up the cultists in three swingy states: "LIBERATE

*A prominent figure in the 2020 protests in Idaho was Ammon Bundy, the forty-four-year-old member of the celebrity libertarian militant family who appeared in a footnote in the previous chapter as well. "I want the virus now," he said.

MINNESOTA!" and "LIBERATE MICHIGAN!" and "LIBERATE VIRGINIA, and save your great 2nd Amendment. It is under siege!"

In addition to that work low and outside organizing protests to make its case appear more popular and democratic, and the various operations high and inside shaping the conversation to give corporations and investors an immediate break, the economic right also started using the crisis in service of its long game. At that AFP online meeting for activists in March, the lesser Koch subordinate warned that "history shows us that what Congress does is they exploit the situation" during crises, even as his senior colleague repeatedly explained how they, the Koch network, intended to exploit this crisis themselves—for instance, by getting federal and state governments to *permanently* lift various regulatory "barriers" that had been waived temporarily for the medical industry. The Heritage Foundation, acting as if it *were* the government, created a "National Coronavirus Recovery Commission" whose "commissioners" immediately issued recommendations. Ten days after Trump took office, the evil geniuses had had him sign an executive order that cleverly sabotages federal oversight of business—it requires that two existing regulations be repealed for every proposed new one. However, the independent agencies that oversee Wall Street and energy have been exempt from the new rule, permitted to keep adding regulations as necessary; according to the National Commission, recovery from the pandemic absolutely depends on the finance and oil and gas industries also being freed from that regulatory yoke. In addition, Heritage says, the emergency requires a new "mechanism that allows for the unilateral . . . suspension" by the president of *any* "costly regulations" he chooses. People at the White House were also apparently keen on a proposal by two right-wing economists—one at AEI, the other at Hoover—for the government to give needy citizens more money right away, but only if they agreed to take less in Social Security benefits when they retire.

I've talked earlier about how *Government is bad* becomes self-fulfilling, that an unimpressive and underdelivering federal government has served the long-term political interests of the right. Trump's incompetence on the pandemic will be a test of that dynamic. In May, at the end of "30 Days to Slow the Spread," the president was still thinking magically, a de facto nostalgist for the days before modern medicine. *Believe in our perfect mythical yesteryear.* "Testing [people] is somewhat overrated," he said, and "this is going to go away without a vaccine." In other words, a reporter asked the president, Americans just had to *accept* that reopening without enough testing and contact-tracing would cause lots more deaths?

Yes. "I call these people warriors, and I'm actually calling now . . . the *nation,* warriors. You have to be warriors," by which he meant, of course, be willing to be killed by COVID-19, fallen soldiers for American capitalism.

But apart from that, everything would soon be *fantastic.* "I think you're going to have a tremendous transition. . . . I think next year is going to be an incredible year economically. . . . You see it with the stock market, where the stock market's at 24,000. . . . We're going to have a great economy very soon, much sooner than people think, much sooner." By June, he and a senior economic adviser were focused on an exciting new pandemic recovery measure—"a capital gains holiday" to cut rich people's taxes on stock profits to zero.

Before these fresh hells, as I've spent the book arguing, our political economy and society were already at a historic crossroads, Americans stuck uncomfortably on the cusp between searching for lost times and imagining a better future. We arrived at a scarier place, the inflection point even more obvious. But it's not exactly unprecedented. We've been here before.

We were in a place like this when my grandparents were young in the 1910s.

There was the global influenza epidemic, of course, which killed one in 150 people in the United States, the equivalent of 2 million Americans now. But in many other ways as well, the early 1900s looked remarkably like the early 2000s.

At the end of the nineteenth century, corporate mergers and consolidation had accelerated, and political corruption by the rich and powerful had become extreme. A Wall Street crash occurred in 1907. Americans experienced extraordinary technological change—electrification, telephones, movies, airplanes and cars, all at once. The foreign-born population of the United States had tripled. The influx of non-Protestant foreigners and the mass migration into U.S. cities of black people, accompanied by skillful racist fictions in a riveting new medium (*The Birth of a Nation*), prompted a revival of the Ku Klux Klan. Political engagement was high: the turnout in the midterm elections of 1914 wasn't exceeded for a century . . . until 2018.

The 1914 Walter Lippmann book I quoted earlier, *Drift and Mastery: An Attempt to Diagnose the Current Unrest,* is a staggering exhibit of the rhymes between then and now. Lippmann considered the consequences of feminism, a word not even twenty years old, and the imminent electoral power of enfranchised women; the homogenizing of U.S. cities; and the "overwhelming demand upon the press for . . . personal details open to the vast public. Gossip is organized; and we do by telegraph what was done in the village store."

Should the size and power of corporations be limited? What happened to old-fashioned loyalty between employers and employees? Is socialism practical? A progressive movement flourished. In the previous dozen years, Lippmann wrote, "people had begun to see much greater possibilities in the government" and "looked to it as a protector from economic tyranny." As a result, "big businessmen who are at all intelligent . . . are talking more and more about their 'responsibilities,' their 'stewardship'"—exactly as the Business Roundtable nervously did at the end of 2019. "Today if you go about the world," he wrote in 1914, "you find that countries like . . . Denmark are the ones that have come nearest the high level of social prosperity."

In America, anarchism was bubbling up on the right as well as the left, along with a general "sense of conspiracy and secret scheming" that supposedly served "labyrinthine evil." He noted the rise of nostalgic anti-modern anger and its political embodiment by the populist William Jennings Bryan, who'd just lost the presidency for the third time. "He is the true Don Quixote of our politics, for he moves in a world that has ceased to exist," but like his enemies—the "propertied bigot," the well-situated "defenders of what America has become"—he lacked "any vision of what America is to be."

Twenty years after that, in the 1930s, when my parents were young, we were also in a place like we are today. The Great Depression revealed the precariousness and excessive unfairness of our economy, then prompted a great philosophical shift and the creation by the left of fundamental changes that restored American capitalism by making it new and improved.

And we were in a place *kind of* like this when I was young in the 1970s. Following hard on the whiffs of revolution around 1970, crazy inflation and various disconcerting large events—the oil price crisis, Watergate, the Vietnam surrender, the collapse of iconic U.S. manufacturers—combined to create high anxiety and fear, of which the economic right took brilliant political advantage.*

Only a crisis—actual or perceived—produces real change, because *only then does the politically impossible become the politically inevitable,* you'll recall Milton Friedman, the new president's economic hero, explaining in 1982. *You never want a serious crisis to go to waste,* to miss *the opportunity to do things that you could not do before,* you'll recall the incoming president's White House chief of staff, Rahm Emanuel, saying in late 2008 as the financial system was melting down.

Today's evil geniuses (and obedient dimwits) of the economic right were instantly determined to exploit the pandemic crises to maintain and increase their political and economic power and thus the share of American wealth that flows to big business and the rich. So must the left use and its allies use all available crises to increase their political power and thereby begin to restore the democratic sharing of economic power and wealth we once had and even improve on it.

That's why the third-ranking member of the House Democrats, James Clyburn of South Carolina, told some fellow members, on a private conference call in the spring, that the pandemic crises were "a tremendous opportunity to restructure things to our vision." Hilariously, the right professed to be *appalled* by that, then was further "outraged," according to *The New York Times*, when the majority's proposed multitrillion-dollar recovery bill "included an array of progressive policies well beyond the scope of emergency aid." The liberals were daring to "use the crisis to advance a liberal agenda."

The leaders of the economic right in 2020 weren't as terrified by the prospects of mass death or the huge new tranche of federal debt as they were by the stunning, irresistible power of such a crisis to change political rules and ideological conventions overnight.

In the last chapter, I described the polls since the 1990s showing that

*Even my ancestors in Europe experienced a prelude to this in the late 1300s, when the Black Death changed everything economically. With the supply of workers suddenly cut by a third or half, the economic power and incomes of the surviving masses shot up, landlords lost fortunes, peasants rebelled, capitalism started replacing feudalism, and the Dark Ages gave way to the Renaissance.

more and more Americans were in favor of the federal government solving big problems. In a survey in the spring of 2020 by Suffolk University for *USA Today* about how the federal government had dealt with the health and economic consequences of the pandemic, fully half of Americans said it had done too little and only 10 or 11 percent thought it had done too much.

Imagine the elite right's shock when it saw the *Financial Times* one Friday in April 2020. The *FT* is a moderately conservative million-circulation daily published in London ("Since 1888, this newspaper has argued for free markets"), at least as influential globally as *The Wall Street Journal*. Two or three months earlier the headline on that day's main editorial could have been a gag on a prop newspaper in a fantasy film:

> VIRUS LAYS BARE THE FRAILTY OF THE SOCIAL CONTRACT
>
> RADICAL REFORMS ARE REQUIRED TO FORGE A SOCIETY THAT WILL WORK FOR ALL

These ultimate Establishment conservatives had had a conversion experience.

> As western leaders learnt in the Great Depression, and after the second world war, to demand collective sacrifice you must offer a social contract that benefits everyone. Today's crisis is laying bare how far many rich societies fall short of this ideal. . . . We are not really all in this together. . . . Better paid knowledge workers often face only the nuisance of working from home. . . . Radical reforms—reversing the prevailing policy direction of the last four decades—will need to be put on the table. . . . Redistribution will again be on the agenda. . . . Policies until recently considered eccentric, such as basic income and wealth taxes, will have to be in the mix.

If I've lost the Financial Times, some strategist on the rich side in the class war must have thought, *I've lost elite opinion*. Today suddenly everyone deemed it essential for Congress to shovel out trillions to average

American citizens by means of new debt and for the Federal Reserve to conjure trillions more by esoteric monetary magic! Tomorrow it could be wealth taxes on the superrich or true universal healthcare or carbon taxes on (cheap) oil or God knows what socialist madness!

As the *Times* columnist Jamelle Bouie wrote, "If something like a social democratic state is feasible under these conditions," then people might become convinced that it was "absolutely possible when growth is high and unemployment is low," particularly after Bernie Sanders's and Elizabeth Warren's campaigns "pushed progressive ideas into the mainstream of American politics." Before he was elected president, Joe Biden echoed this wish. "I think people are realizing," he said, "'My Lord, *look* at what is *possible*,' looking at the institutional changes we can make, without us becoming a 'socialist country' or any of that malarkey."

My case that Americans need to rediscover the defining but atrophied national knack for taking up the challenges of the *new* in new ways is suddenly undeniable and urgent. As the Columbia University economic historian Adam Tooze said early in 2020, we've entered "a period of radical uncertainty, an order of magnitude greater than anything we're used to."

We've already seen how the pandemic changed the economy and the culture and daily life temporarily—and we will continue adapting and adjusting. But what *permanent* changes will happen? For one thing, I'm betting that the automated jobless future I laid out in the last few chapters will arrive even sooner. Many of us have become habituated already to working only from home and communicating only with little talking pictures of human colleagues and clients. That's why, ten weeks after the pandemic started driving stock prices down, 495 of the 500 biggest corporations had dropped 13 percent, but the share prices of the other five companies, the five largest—Facebook, Amazon, Apple, Microsoft, and Google—were 10 percent *up*. And why, a year after the early-pandemic crash, all of those companies' shares were still up more than the rest of the stock market: the Dow Jones average had increased by 71 percent, but Google was up by 95 percent, Amazon 115 percent, Apple 121 percent.

But we really don't know where the experience of the pandemic and the protests of 2020 will lead us—the overnight upendings, the long traumas, judging how individuals and institutions and ideologies and systems worked or failed. People in 1918 and 1929 and 1970 (and 1347) had no clue what was coming next, either. Will my hypothetical grandchildren grow up as ignorant of these events as I was of the global viral pandemic that my grandparents survived and of the 1919 "race riots" that included the lynching of a black man in my hometown? For Americans now, will surviving a year (or more) of radical uncertainty help persuade a majority to make radical changes in our political economy to reduce their chronic economic uncertainty and insecurity? Will we summon the necessary will to achieve racial fairness? Like Europe six hundred years ago after the plague, will we see a flowering of radically new creative works and the emergence of a radically new economic system? Or will Americans remain hunkered forever, as confused and anxious and paralyzed as we were before 2020, descend into digital feudalism, forgo a renaissance, and retreat into cocoons of comfortable cultural stasis providing the illusion that nothing much is changing or ever can change?

The United States used to be called the New World. It's a new world again, maybe the way it was struggling to become new in the 1910s. Lippmann was pragmatic, in many ways conservative, in no way a utopian, but back at that chaotic, pivotal moment, he quoted Oscar Wilde's line that "a map of the world that does not include Utopia is not worth even glancing at," because social progress comes only by navigating toward hopeful visions of perfection. "Our business is not to lay aside the dream," Lippmann explained, "but to make it plausible. Drag dreams out into the light of day, show their sources, compare them with fact, transform them to possibilities . . . a dream . . . with a sense of the *possible*." He also wrote that the urgent national inflection point a century ago came down to choosing "between those who are willing to enter upon an effort for which there is no precedent, and those who aren't. In a real sense it is an adventure."

So let's *go* already.

ACKNOWLEDGMENTS

My old friends Bruce Birenboim and Bill Cohan and Bonnie Siegler were invaluable readers and advisers. And my new acquaintances Gabriel Chodorow-Reich and Simon Reynolds were also generous with their deep knowledge.

I'm indebted as well to David Andersen, Kristi Andersen, Kate Andersen, Lucy Andersen, Eve Bromberg, Stephen Chao, Stephen Dubner, Nick Goldberg, Ben Goldberger, Jocelyn Gonzales, Joe Hagan, Jim Kelly, Jay Kriegel, Robin Margolis, John Massengale, Lawrence O'Donnell, Liz Phair, Paul Rudnick, and Jacob Weisberg for their help.

Of the great magazine editors I've worked with over the years, among the best have been Graydon Carter at *Spy,* Jared Hohlt at *New York,* Ariel Kaminer at *The New York Times Magazine,* and Cullen Murphy at *Vanity Fair,* all of whom improved essays that became inspirations and underpinnings for this book.

Suzanne Gluck is the perfect literary agent, and Andrea Blatt the perfect agent's deputy.

It's thanks to Gina Centrello that I wrote *Fantasyland,* and it's thanks to *Fantasyland* that I wrote this book. In fact, it's thanks in large part to her and to Andy Ward, the editor of *Fantasyland* and indispensable über-editor of *Evil Geniuses*—because of their unfailing kindness, intelligence, respect, and enthusiasm—that after twenty-four years, Random House remains my home sweet publishing home.

And now thanks also to the kind, intelligent, respectful, and enthusiastic Mark Warren. His work editing this book was heroic. He was an exceptionally knowledgeable collaborator who provided hundreds of essential ideas and challenges and nudges that helped make almost every page clearer and better.

I'm grateful as well to the whole impeccably professional Random House team, in particular Janet Biehl, Benjamin Dreyer, Ayelet Gruenspecht, Greg Kubie, Matthew Martin, Steve Messina, Tom Perry, Robbin Schiff, Erin Richards, Chayenne Skeete, Susan Turner, and Dan Zitt. And Pete Garceau designed a splendid cover.

The Civitella Ranieri Foundation provided me several productive weeks of coddling in their Umbrian utopia.

And to Anne Kreamer—mind-melded daily collaborator, beloved enabler of it all—thank you once more and more than ever.

BIBLIOGRAPHY

All sources and citations are online at https://www.kurtandersen.com/Evil-Geniuses-Notes.

Abramowitz, Alan, and Ruy Teixeira. "The Decline of the White Working Class and the Rise of a Mass Upper-Middle Class." *Political Science Quarterly* 124, no. 3 (2009): 391–422.

Acemoglu, Daron, et al. "Import Competition and the Great U.S. Employment Sag of the 2000s." *Journal of Labor Economics* 34, no. S1 (2016): 141–198.

Acemoglu, Daron, and Pascual Restrepo. "Robots and Jobs: Evidence from US Labor Markets." MIT Department of Economics Working Paper no. 17-04, March 2017.

Acemoglu, Daron, and James A. Robinson. *Why Nations Fail: The Origins of Power, Prosperity, and Poverty.* New York: Currency, 2012.

Allen, Robert C. "Engels' Pause: Technical Change, Capital Accumulation, and Inequality in the British Industrial Revolution." *Explorations in Economic History* 46, no. 4 (2009): 418–35.

Alvaredo, Facundo, et al. "Global Inequality Dynamics." *American Economic Review* 107, no. 5 (2017): 404–9.

Autor, David. "The Polarization of Job Opportunities in the U.S. Labor Market." *Community Investments* 23, no. 2 (2011): 11–16.

———. "Wayward Sons: The Emerging Gender Gap in Labor Markets and Education." *Third Way Next Initiative,* March 2013.

———. "Why Are There Still So Many Jobs? The History and Future of Workplace Automation." *Journal of Economic Perspectives* 29, no. 3 (2015): 3–30.

———. "Work of the Past, Work of the Future." *AEA Papers and Proceedings* 109 (May 2019): 1–32.

Autor, David, David Dorn, and Gordon Hanson. "The China Syndrome: Local Labor Market Effects of Import Competition in the United States." *American Economic Review* 103, no. 6 (2013): 2121–68.

Bailey, James M. "'Keeping People from Being Killed': Arizona Governor Bruce Babbitt, Public Safety, and the Phelps Dodge Copper Strike, 1983–1984." *Mining History Journal* 3 (1996): 3–14.

Baird, Douglas G. "The Future of Law and Economics: Looking Forward." *University of Chicago Law Review* 64, no. 4 (1997): 1129–65.

Barnes, Peter. *With Liberty and Dividends for All: How to Save Our Middle Class When Jobs Don't Pay Enough.* San Francisco: Berrett-Koehler, 2014.

Bartels, Larry M. "Question Order and Declining Faith in Elections." *Public Opinion Quarterly* 66, no. 1 (2002): 67–79.

———. *Unequal Democracy: The Political Economy of the New Gilded Age.* Princeton: Princeton University Press, 2008.

Basu, Kaushik, and Joseph E. Stiglitz. *Inequality and Growth: Patterns and Policy.* 2 vols. New York: Palgrave Macmillan, 2016.

Baum, Sandy. "The Evolution of Student Debt in the United States." In *Student Loans and the Dynamics of Debt,* edited by Brad Hershbein and Kevin M. Hollenbeck. Kalamazoo, Mich.: Upjohn Institute, 2015.

Bell, Daniel. *The Coming of Post-Industrial Society: A Venture in Social Forecasting.* New York: Basic Books, 1976.

———. "The Cultural Contradictions of Capitalism." *Journal of Aesthetic Education* 6, nos. 1–2 (1972): 11–38.

———. *Work and Its Discontents: The Cult of Efficiency in America.* Boston: Beacon Press, 1956.

Berman, Marshall. *All That Is Solid Melts into Air: The Experience of Modernity.* New York: Verso, 1983.

Berman, Matthew, and Random Reamey. "Permanent Fund Dividends and Poverty in Alaska." University of Alaska Anchorage, Institute of Social and Economic Research, 2016.

Bernstein, Irving. *The Lean Years: A History of the American Worker 1920–1933.* Boston: Houghton Mifflin, 1969.

Biskupic, Joan. *American Original: The Life and Constitution of Supreme Court Justice Antonin Scalia.* New York: Farrar, Straus & Giroux, 2009.

Blumenthal, Sidney. *The Rise of the Counter-Establishment: The Conservative Ascent to Political Power.* New York: Union Square Press, 2008.

Bork, Robert H. *The Antitrust Paradox: A Policy at War with Itself.* New York: Basic Books, 1978.

———. "Neutral Principles and Some First Amendment Problems." *Indiana Law Journal* 47, no. 1 (1971): 1–35.

Boudreaux, Donald J., and Robert B. Ekelund, Jr. "Cable Reregulation." *Cato Journal* 14, no. 1 (1994): 87–101.

Boushey, Heather, J. Bradford DeLong, and Marshall Steinbaum, eds. *After Piketty: The Agenda for Economics and Inequality.* Cambridge, Mass.: Harvard University Press, 2017.

Bowie, Nikolas. "Corporate Democracy: How Corporations Justified Their Right to Speak in 1970s Boston." *Law and History Review* 36, no. 4 (2018): 943–92.

Bregman, Rutger. *Utopia for Realists: How We Can Build the Ideal World.* Translated by Elizabeth Manton. Boston: Little, Brown, 2017.

Brera, Guido Maria, and Edoardo Nesi. *Everything Is Broken Up and Dances: The Crushing of the Middle Class.* Translated by Antony Shugaar. New York: Other Press, 2017.

Bridle, James. *New Dark Age: Technology and the End of the Future.* London: Verso, 2018.

Broadberry, Stephen N., and Douglas A. Irwin. "Labor Productivity in the United States and the United Kingdom During the Nineteenth Century." *Explorations in Economic History* 43, no. 2 (2006): 257–79.

Broda, Christian, and John Romalis. "Inequality and Prices: Does China Benefit the Poor in America?" *European Trade Study Group,* 2008.

———. "The Welfare Implications of Rising Price Dispersion." University of Chicago, unpublished paper, 2009.

Brulle, Robert J. "Institutionalizing Delay: Foundation Funding and the Creation of U.S. Climate Change Counter-Movement Organizations." *Climatic Change* 122, no. 4 (2014): 681–94.

Brynjolfsson, Erik, and Andrew McAfee. *The Second Machine Age: Work, Progress, and Prosperity in a Time of Brilliant Technologies.* New York: W. W. Norton, 2016.

Bursztyn, Leonardo, et al. "Misinformation During a Pandemic." University of Chicago, Becker Friedman Institute for Economics Working Paper no. 2020-44, April 2020.

Campbell, Richard J. "Increasing the Efficiency of Existing Coal-Fired Power Plants." Congressional Research Service, December 2013.

Cass, Oren. *The Once and Future Worker: A Vision for the Renewal of Work in America.* New York: Encounter Books, 2018.

Cette, Gilbert, Lorraine Koehl, and Thomas Philippon. "Labor Shares in Some Advanced Economies." NBER Working Paper no. 26136, August 2019.

Chemerinsky, Erwin. "The Constitution Is Not 'Hard Law': The Bork Rejection and the Future of Constitutional Jurisprudence." *Constitutional Commentary* 6, no. 1 (1989): 29–38.

Chetty, Raj, et al. "The Fading American Dream: Trends in Absolute Income Mobility Since 1940." NBER Working Paper no. 22910, 2017.

Cobb, J. Adam. "Risky Business: The Decline of Defined Benefit Pensions and Firms' Shifting of Risk." *Organization Science* 26, no. 5 (2015): 1263–551.

Cowen, Tyler. *The Complacent Class: The Self-Defeating Quest for the American Dream.* New York: St. Martin's Press, 2017.

———. *The Great Stagnation: How America Ate All the Low-Hanging Fruit of Modern History, Got Sick, and Will (Eventually) Feel Better.* New York: Dutton, 2011.

Crane, Daniel A. "The Tempting of Antitrust: Robert Bork and the Goals of Antitrust Policy." *Antitrust Law Journal* 79, no. 3 (2014): 835–53.

Cullen, Jim. *The American Dream: A Short History of an Idea That Shaped a Nation.* New York: Oxford University Press, 2003.

Daugherty, Paul R., and H. James Wilson. *Human + Machine: Reimagining Work in the Age of AI.* Boston: Harvard Business Review Press, 2018.

Davis, Morris A., et al. "The Price of Residential Land for Counties, ZIP Codes, and Census Tracts in the United States." FHFA Staff Working Paper no. 19-01, January 2019.

Deneen, Patrick J. *Why Liberalism Failed.* New Haven, Conn.: Yale University Press, 2018.

Denning, Stephen. *The Age of Agile: How Smart Companies Are Transforming the Way Work Gets Done.* New York: AMACOM, 2018.

Diamond, Peter, and Emmanuel Saez. "The Case for a Progressive Tax." *Journal of Economic Perspectives* 25, no. 4 (2011): 165–90.

Dietz, Miranda, Peter Hall, and Ken Jacobs. "Course Correction: Reversing Wage Erosion to Restore Good Jobs at American Airports." UC Berkeley Labor Center, January 2013.

Donohue, Julie. "A History of Drug Advertising: The Evolving Roles of Consumers and Consumer Protection." *Milbank Quarterly* 84, no. 4 (2006): 659–99.

Donovan, Sarah A., Marc Labonte, and Joseph Dalaker. "The U.S. Income Distribution: Trends and Issues." Congressional Research Service, 2016.

Downes, Giles R., Ehud Houminer, and R. Glenn Hubbard. *Institutional Investors and Corporate Behavior.* Washington, D.C.: AEI Press, 1999.

Drexler, K. Eric. *Radical Abundance: How a Revolution in Nanotechnology Will Change Civilization.* New York: PublicAffairs, 2013.

Dunbar, Nicholas. *The Devil's Derivatives: The Untold Story of the Slick Traders and Hapless Regulators Who Almost Blew Up Wall Street.* Boston: Harvard Business Review Press, 2011.

Durkin, Thomas A. "Credit Cards: Use and Consumer Attitudes, 1970–2000." *Federal Reserve Bulletin* 86 (2000): 623–24.

Dynan, Karen, Douglas Elmendorf, and Daniel Sichel. "The Evolution of Household Income Volatility." *B.E. Journal of Economic Analysis and Policy* 12, no. 2 (2012).

Elliott, Michael. *The Day Before Yesterday: Reconsidering America's Past, Rediscovering the Present.* New York: Simon & Schuster, 1996.

Elmer, Peter J., and Steven A. Seelig. "The Rising Long-Term Trend of Single-Family Mortgage Foreclosure Rates." Federal Deposit Insurance Corporation Working Paper no. 98-2, October 1998.

Engels, Frederick. *The Condition of the Working-Class in England in 1844.* 1845; London: Allen & Unwin, 1926.

Enthoven, Alain C., and Victor R. Fuchs. "Employment-Based Health Insurance: Past, Present, and Future." *Health Affairs* 25, no. 6 (2006): 1538–47.

Epstein, Edwin M. "The Business PAC Phenomenon: An Irony of Electoral Reform." *Regulation* 3 (May–June 1979): 35–43.

Fabozzi, Frank J., and Franco Modigliani. *Mortgage and Mortgage-Backed Securities Markets.* Boston: Harvard Business School Press, 1992.

Fabricand, Burton P. *American History Through the Eyes of Modern Chaos Theory.* N.p., 2009.

Fenn, George W., Nellie Liang, and Stephen Prowse. *The Economics of the Private Equity Market.* Washington, D.C.: Board of Governors of the Federal Reserve System, 1995.

Ferrie, Joseph P. "Historical Statistics of the U.S., Millennial Edition: Internal Migration." Northwestern University, unpublished paper, 2002.

Finn, Ed, and Kathryn Cramer, eds. *Hieroglyph: Stories and Visions for a Better Future.* New York: Morrow, 2014.

Florida, Richard. *The Great Reset: How New Ways of Living and Working Drive Post-Crash Prosperity.* New York: HarperCollins, 2010.

Ford, Martin. *Rise of the Robots: Technology and the Threat of a Jobless Future.* New York: Basic Books, 2015.

Fourcade, Marion, and Rakesh Khurana. "The Social Trajectory of a Finance Professor and the Common Sense of Capital." *History of Political Economy* 49, no. 2 (2017): 347–81.

Frank, Malcolm, Paul Roehrig, and Ben Pring. *What to Do When Machines Do Everything: How to Get Ahead in a World of AI, Algorithms, Bots, and Big Data.* Hoboken, N.J.: Wiley, 2017.

Frank, Thomas. *Listen, Liberal: What Ever Happened to the Party of the People?* New York: Metropolitan, 2016.

Fraser, Steve. *The Limousine Liberal: How an Incendiary Image United the Right and Fractured America*. New York: Basic Books, 2016.

Frey, Carl Benedikt, and Michael A. Osborne. "The Future of Employment: How Susceptible Are Jobs to Computerisation?" *Technological Forecasting and Social Change* 114 (2017): 254–80.

Friedan, Betty. *The Feminine Mystique*. New York: W. W. Norton, 2013.

Friedman, Milton, and Rose D. Friedman. *Capitalism and Freedom*. Chicago: University of Chicago Press, 1962.

Frydman, Carola, and Raven E. Saks. "Executive Compensation: A New View from a Long-Term Perspective, 1936–2005." *Review of Financial Studies* 23, no. 5 (2010): 2099–138.

Fukuyama, Francis. "The End of History?" *National Interest* 16 (1989): 3–18.

———. *The End of History and the Last Man*. New York: Free Press, 1992.

Galbraith, John Kenneth. *American Capitalism: The Concept of Countervailing Power*. Boston: Houghton Mifflin, 1952.

Gallardo, German Gutierrez, and Sophie Piton. "Revisiting the Global Decline of the (Non-Housing) Labor Share." NYU Stern School of Business, June 2019.

Gans, Joshua, et al. "Inequality and Market Concentration, When Shareholding Is More Skewed than Consumption." NBER Working Paper no. 25395, December 2018.

Gayle, George-Levi, Chen Li, and Robert A. Miller. "How Well Does Agency Theory Explain Executive Compensation?" *Economic Research* 100, no. 3 (2018).

Giannone, Elisa. "Skill-Biased Technical Change and Regional Convergence." *2017 Meeting Papers, Society for Economic Dynamics* 190 (2017).

Gibson, William. *Distrust That Particular Flavor*. New York: G.P. Putnam's Sons, 2012.

Goldin, Claudia, and Lawrence Katz. "The Race Between Education and Technology: The Evolution of U.S. Educational Wage Differentials, 1890 to 2005." NBER Working Paper no. 12984, March 2007.

Gompers, Paul, and Andrew Metrick. "Institutional Investors and Equity Prices." *Quarterly Journal of Economics* 116, no. 1 (2001): 229–59.

Good, Irving John. "Speculations Concerning the First Ultraintelligent Machine." In *Advances in Computers,* edited by F. Alt and M. Ruminoff. Cambridge, Mass.: Academic Press, 1966.

Gordon, Robert J. "Is U.S. Economic Growth Over? Faltering Innovation Confronts the Six Headwinds." NBER Working Paper no. 18315, August 2012.

———. *The Rise and Fall of American Growth: The U.S. Standard of Living Since the Civil War*. Princeton: Princeton University Press, 2016.

Graham, John R., Campbell R. Harvey, and Shivaram Rajgopal. "Value Destruction and Financial Reporting Decisions." *Financial Analysts Journal* 62, no. 6 (2006): 27–39.

Greenwood, Robin, and David Scharfstein. "The Growth of Finance." *Journal of Economic Perspectives* 27, no. 2 (2013): 3–28.

Grove, Andrew S. *Only the Paranoid Survive: How to Identify and Exploit the Crisis Points that Challenge Every Business.* New York: Doubleday, 1999.

Grullon, Gustavo, Yelena Larkin, and Roni Michaely. "Are US Industries Becoming More Concentrated?" *Review of Finance* 23, no. 4 (2019): 697–743.

Gyourko, Joseph, Albert Saiz, and Anita Summers. "A New Measure of the Local Regulatory Environment for Housing Markets: The Wharton Residential Land Use Regulatory Index." *Urban Studies* 45, no. 3 (2008): 693–729.

Hacker, Jacob S. *The Great Risk Shift: The New Economic Insecurity and the Decline of the American Dream.* New York: Oxford University Press, 2006.

Hacker, Jacob S., and Paul Pierson. *Winner-Take-All Politics: How Washington Made the Rich Richer—and Turned Its Back on the Middle Class.* New York: Simon & Schuster, 2010.

Hayek, Friedrich A. *Law, Legislation and Liberty,* vol. 3: *The Political Order of a Free People.* Chicago: University of Chicago Press, 1986.

Hill, Seth, Daniel J. Hopkins, and Gregory Huber. "Demographic Change, Threat, and Presidential Voting: Evidence from U.S. Electoral Precincts, 2012 to 2016." *SSRN Electronic Journal,* 2019.

Himmelberg, Robert F. *Regulatory Issues Since 1964: The Rise of the Deregulation Movement.* New York: Garland, 1994.

Hofstadter, Richard. "The Paranoid Style in American Politics." *Harper's Magazine,* November 1964.

Horowitz, Michael. "The Public Interest Law Movement: An Analysis with Special Reference to the Role and Practices of Conservative Public Interest Law Firms," unpublished ms. prepared for the Scaife Foundation, 1980.

Hsieh, Chang-Tai, and Enrico Moretti. "Housing Constraints and Spatial Misallocation." *American Economic Journal: Macroeconomics* 11, no. 2 (2019): 1–39.

Hunter, Louis C. *A History of Industrial Power in the United States, 1780–1930.* 3 vols. Charlottesville: University Press of Virginia, 1979, 1985, 1991.

Husain, Amir. *The Sentient Machine: The Coming Age of Artificial Intelligence.* New York: Scribner, 2017.

Jacobs, David. Inventory of the Jude Wanniski Papers. Hoover Institution Archives, 2010.

Jacobson, Louis S., Robert John LaLonde, and Daniel Gerard Sullivan. "Earnings Losses of Displaced Workers." *American Economic Review* 83, no. 4 (1993): 685–709.

Jensen, Michael C. "Value Maximization, Stakeholder Theory, and the Corporate Objective Function." *Journal of Applied Corporate Finance* 14, no. 3 (2001): 8–21.

Jensen, Michael C., and William H. Meckling. "Reflections on the Corporation as a Social Invention." *Midland Corporate Finance Journal* 1, no. 3 (1983).

———. "Theory of the Firm: Managerial Behavior, Agency Costs and Ownership Structure." *Journal of Financial Economics* 3, no. 4, (1976): 305–60.

Jones, Damon, and Ioana Elena Marinescu. "The Labor Market Impacts of Universal and Permanent Cash Transfers: Evidence from the Alaska Permanent Fund." NBER Working Paper no. 24312, February 2018.

Jordan, John M. *Robots.* Cambridge, Mass.: MIT Press, 2016.

Katz, Arnold. "Imputing Rents to Owner-Occupied Housing by Directly Modelling Their Distribution." Bureau of Economic Analysis, 2017.

Kerouac, Jack. *On the Road.* New York: Viking, 1957.

Klein, Jennifer. *For All These Rights: Business, Labor, and the Shaping of America's Public-Private Welfare State.* Princeton: Princeton University Press, 2003.

Kristol, Irving. *Two Cheers for Capitalism.* New York: New American Library, 1978.

Krueger, Alan B., and Orley Ashenfelter. "Theory and Evidence on Employer Collusion in the Franchise Sector." NBER Working Paper no. 24831, July 2018.

Krugman, Paul R. *The Age of Diminished Expectations: U.S. Economic Policy in the 1990s.* Cambridge, Mass.: MIT Press, 1999.

Kruse, Kevin M., and Julian E. Zelizer. *Fault Lines: A History of the United States Since 1974.* New York: W. W. Norton, 2019.

Kuttner, Robert. *Can Democracy Survive Global Capitalism?* New York: W. W. Norton, 2018.

———. *Revolt of the Haves: Tax Rebellions and Hard Times.* New York: Simon & Schuster, 1980.

Lanchester, John. *I.O.U.: Why Everyone Owes Everyone and No One Can Pay.* New York: Simon & Schuster, 2010.

Lande, Robert H. "Wealth Transfers as the Original and Primary Concern of Antitrust: The Efficiency Interpretation Challenged." *Hastings Law Journal* 34, no. 1 (1982): 65–151.

Lazonick, William. "The Financialization of the U.S. Corporation: What Has Been Lost, and How It Can Be Regained." *Seattle University Law Review* 36, no. 2 (2013).

Leonard, Christopher. *Kochland: The Secret History of Koch Industries and Corporate Power in America.* New York: Simon & Schuster, 2019.

Levit, Katharine R., Gary L. Olin, and Suzanne W. Letsch. "Americans' Health Insurance Coverage, 1980–91." *Health Care Financing Review* 14, no. 1 (1992): 31–57.

Lindsey, Brink, et al. "The Center Can Hold: Public Policy for an Age of Extremes." Niskanen Center, December 2018.

Lippmann, Walter. *Drift and Mastery: An Attempt to Diagnose the Current Unrest.* New York: Mitchell Kennerley, 1914.

Litjens, Geert J. S., et al. "Clinical Evaluation of a Computer-Aided Diagnosis System for Determining Cancer Aggressiveness in Prostate MRI." *European Radiology* 25, no. 11 (2015): 3187–99.

Loecker, Jan De, and Jan Eeckhout. "The Rise of Market Power and the Macroeconomic Implications." NBER Working Paper no. 23687, August 2017.

Lowery, Annie. *Give People Money: How a Universal Basic Income Would End Poverty, Revolutionize Work, and Remake the World.* New York: Crown, 2018.

Marcuse, Herbert. *Eros and Civilization: A Philosophical Inquiry into Freud.* Boston: Beacon Press, 1955.

Marx, Karl. *Capital: A Critique of Political Economy.* Translated by Ben Fowkes. 1867; London: Penguin Classics, 1990.

———. *Grundrisse.* Translated by David C. MacLellan. 1939; London: Macmillan, 1972.

Mason, Paul. *PostCapitalism: A Guide to Our Future.* New York: Farrar, Straus & Giroux, 2015.

Mayer, Gerald. "Union Membership Trends in the United States." Congressional Research Service, August 2004.

Mayer, Jane. *Dark Money: The Hidden History of the Billionaires Behind the Rise of the Radical Right.* New York: Doubleday, 2016.

Mazzucato, Mariana. *The Value of Everything.* New York: PublicAffairs, 2018.

McAlevey, Jane F. *No Shortcuts: Organizing for Power in the New Gilded Age.* New York: Oxford University Press, 2018.

McGann, James G. "2018 Global Go To Think Tank Index Report." *TTCSP Global Go To Think Tank Index Reports* 16 (2019).

McLean, Bethany, and Joseph Nocera. *All the Devils Are Here: The Hidden History of the Financial Crisis.* New York: Portfolio/Penguin, 2011.

McQuaid, Kim. *Big Business and Presidential Power: From FDR to Reagan.* New York: Morrow, 1982.

———. "Big Business and Public Policy in Contemporary United States." *Quarterly Review of Business and Economics* 20 (1980): 59–60.

Meyer, Bruce, and Nikolas Mittag. "Using Linked Survey and Administrative Data to Better Measure Income: Implications for Poverty, Program Effectiveness and Holes in the Safety Net." NBER Working Paper no. 21676, October 2015.

Mishel, Lawrence, and Jessica Schieder. "CEO Pay Remains High Relative to the Pay of Typical Workers and High-Wage Earners." Economic Policy Institute, July 2017.

Mizruchi, Mark S. *The Fracturing of the American Corporate Elite*. Cambridge, Mass.: Harvard University Press, 2013.

Moretti, Enrico. *The New Geography of Jobs*. Boston: Houghton Mifflin Harcourt, 2012.

Morris, Ian. *Why the West Rules—for Now: The Patterns of History, and What They Reveal About the Future*. New York: Farrar, Straus & Giroux, 2010.

Morrisey, Michael A. *Health Insurance*. Chicago: Health Administration Press, 2008.

Murphy, Cullen. *Are We Rome? The Fall of an Empire and the Fate of America*. Boston: Houghton Mifflin Harcourt, 2007.

Murray, Charles A. *In Our Hands: A Plan to Replace the Welfare State*. Washington, D.C.: AEI Press, 2006.

———. *Losing Ground: American Social Policy, 1950–1980*. New York: Basic Books, 1984.

Nace, Ted. *Gangs of America: The Rise of Corporate Power and the Disabling of Democracy*. San Francisco: Berrett-Koehler, 2003.

National Center for Education Statistics. *120 Years of American Education: A Statistical Portrait*. Washington, D.C.: U.S. Department of Education, Office of Educational Research and Improvement, 1993.

National Research Council. *The Long-Term Impact of Technology on Employment and Unemployment*. Washington, D.C.: National Academies Press, 1983.

Nonnenmacher, Tomas. "History of the U.S. Telegraph Industry." *EH.Net Encyclopedia*, edited by Robert Whaples, August 14, 2001.

North, Michael. *Novelty: A History of the New*. Chicago: University of Chicago Press, 2013.

Norton, Michael I., and Dan Ariely. "Building a Better America—One Wealth Quintile at a Time." *Perspectives on Psychological Science* 6, no. 1 (2011): 9–12.

O'Reilly, Tim. *WTF? What's the Future and Why It's Up to Us*. New York: HarperCollins, 2017.

Oreskes, Naomi, and Erik M. Conway. *Merchants of Doubt: How a Handful of Scientists Obscured the Truth on Issues from Tobacco Smoke to Global Warming*. New York: Bloomsbury, 2010.

Ostry, Jonathan D., Andrew Berg, and Charalambos G. Tsangarides. *Redistribution, Inequality, and Growth*. International Monetary Fund, 2014.

Page, Benjamin I., and Lawrence R. Jacobs. *Class War? What Americans Really Think About Income Inequality*. Chicago: University of Chicago Press, 2009.

Perlstein, Rick. *Before the Storm: Barry Goldwater and the Unmaking of the American Consensus*. New York: Nation Books, 2009.

———. *The Invisible Bridge: The Fall of Nixon and the Rise of Reagan*. New York: Simon & Schuster, 2014.

Philippon, Thomas. *The Great Reversal: How America Gave Up on Free Markets.* Cambridge, Mass.: Harvard University Press, 2019.

Philippon, Thomas, and Ariell Reshef. "Wages and Human Capital in the U.S. Finance Industry: 1909–2006." *Quarterly Journal of Economics* 127, no. 4 (2012): 1551–609.

Phillips-Fein, Kim. *Invisible Hands: The Businessmen's Crusade Against the New Deal.* New York: W. W. Norton, 2009.

Pierson, Paul, and Theda Skocpol. *The Transformation of American Politics: Activist Government and the Rise of Conservatism.* Princeton: Princeton University Press, 2007.

Piketty, Thomas. *Capital in the Twenty-first Century.* Translated by Arthur Goldhammer. Cambridge, Mass.: Harvard University Press, 2017.

Piketty, Thomas, Emmanuel Saez, and Gabriel Zucman. "Distributional National Accounts: Methods and Estimates for the United States." *Quarterly Journal of Economics* 133, no. 2 (2018): 553–609.

Plunkert, Lois M. "The 1980's: A Decade of Job Growth and Industry Shifts." *Monthly Labor Review,* September 1990, 3–16.

Posner, Eric A., and E. Glen Weyl. *Radical Markets: Uprooting Capitalism and Democracy for a Just Society.* Princeton: Princeton University Press, 2018.

Posner, Eric A., Glen Weyl, and Suresh Naidu. "Antitrust Remedies for Labor Market Power." *Harvard Law Review* 132 (December 2018): 536–601.

Post, Robert, and Reva Siegel. "Originalism as a Political Practice: The Right's Living Constitution." *Fordham Law Review* 75 (November 2006).

Powell, Lewis F., Jr. "Attack on American Free Enterprise System." Memo for the U.S. Chamber of Commerce, August 23, 1971.

———. "The Attack on American Institutions." Address to the Southern Industrial Relations Conference, July 15, 1970.

Rajan, Raghuram. *The Third Pillar: How Markets and the State Leave the Community Behind.* New York: Penguin Press, 2019.

Ransom, Roger. "Economics of the Civil War." *EH.Net Encyclopedia,* August 24, 2001.

Reardon, Sean F., and Kendra Bischoff. "Income Inequality and Income Segregation." *American Journal of Sociology* 116, no. 4 (2011): 426–35.

Reich, Charles A. *The Greening of America.* New York: Random House, 1970.

Reynolds, Simon. *Retromania: Pop Culture's Addiction to Its Own Past.* New York: Farrar, Straus & Giroux, 2010.

Rich, Nathaniel. *Losing Earth: A Recent History.* New York: MCD, 2019.

Rodgers, Daniel T. *Age of Fracture.* Cambridge, Mass.: Harvard University Press, 2011.

Roine, Jesper, and Daniel Waldenström. "Long-Run Trends in the Distribution of Income and Wealth." In *Handbook of Income Distribution,* edited by Anthony B. Atkinson and François Bourguignon, 2:469–592. ScienceDirect.com, 2015.

Rosenberg, Samuel. *American Economic Development Since 1945: Growth, Decline, and Rejuvenation.* New York: Palgrave Macmillan, 2003.

Roszak, Theodore. *The Making of a Counter Culture: Reflections on the Technocratic Society and Its Youthful Opposition.* New York: Anchor Books, 1969.

Routledge, Clay, et al. "Nostalgia as a Resource for Psychological Health and Well-Being." *Social and Personality Psychology Compass* 7, no. 11 (2013): 808–18.

Rudnick, Paul, and Kurt Andersen. "The Irony Epidemic." *Spy Magazine,* March 1989.

Runciman, David. *How Democracy Ends.* New York: Basic Books, 2018.

Saez, Emmanuel. "Income and Wealth Inequality: Evidence and Policy Implications." *Contemporary Economic Policy* 35, no. 1 (2016): 7–25.

Sarnak, Dana O., et al. "Paying for Prescription Drugs Around the World: Why Is the U.S. an Outlier?" Commonwealth Fund Issue Brief, 2017.

Sawyers, June Skinner. *Racing in the Street: The Bruce Springsteen Reader.* New York: Penguin Books, 2004.

Schivelbusch, Wolfgang. *Three New Deals: Reflections on Roosevelt's America, Mussolini's Italy, and Hitler's Germany, 1933–1939.* New York: Henry Holt, 2006.

Schlesinger, Arthur M. *The Cycles of American History.* Boston: Houghton Mifflin, 1999.

———. *The Disuniting of America: Reflections on a Multicultural Society.* New York: W. W. Norton, 1992.

Schnieder, Elizabeth. "The Devil Is in the Details: Nebraska's Rescission of the Equal Rights Amendment, 1972–1973." M.A. thesis, Bowling Green State University, 2010.

Schubert, Walt, and Les Barenbaum. "Equity-Based Executive Compensation," *Journal of Leadership, Accountability and Ethics,* Fall 2008.

Schumpeter, Joseph A. *Capitalism, Socialism, and Democracy.* 3rd ed. New York: HarperPerennial, 1950.

Sedikides, Constantine, et al. "Nostalgia Counteracts Self-Discontinuity and Restores Self-Continuity." *European Journal of Social Psychology* 45, no. 1 (2015): 52–61.

Shambaugh, Jay, et al. "The State of Competition and Dynamism: Facts About Concentration, Start-Ups, and Related Policies." Brookings, June 2018.

Shambaugh, Jay, et al. "Thirteen Facts About Wage Growth." Hamilton Project/Brookings, September 2017.

Shapiro, Fred R., and Michelle Pearse. "The Most-Cited Law Review Articles of All Time." *Michigan Law Review* 110, no. 8 (2012): 1483.

Sherman, Mila Getmansky. "The Life Cycle of Hedge Funds: Fund Flows, Size and Performance." *SSRN Electronic Journal,* 2005.

Sides, John, Michael Tesler, and Lynn Vavreck. *Identity Crisis: The 2016 Presidential Campaign and the Battle for the Meaning of America.* Princeton: Princeton University Press, 2018.

Singleton, Christopher J. "Auto Industry Jobs in the 1980's: A Decade of Transition." *Monthly Labor Review,* February 1992, 18–27.

Smith, Adam. *The Wealth of Nations.* Edited by Andrew S. Skinner. 1776; London: Penguin, 1999.

Smith, Hedrick. *Who Stole the American Dream?* New York: Random House, 2013.

Snyder, Timothy. *The Road to Unfreedom.* New York: Tim Duggan Books/ Crown, 2018.

Sommeiller, Estelle, Mark Price, and Ellis Wazeter. "Income Inequality in the U.S. by State, Metropolitan Area, and County." Economic Policy Institute, 2016.

Song, Jae, et al. "Firming Up Inequality." *Quarterly Journal of Economics* 134, no. 1 (2019): 1–50.

Southworth, Ann. *Lawyers of the Right: Professionalizing the Conservative Coalition.* Chicago: University of Chicago Press, 2008.

Sprague, Shawn. "Below Trend: The U.S. Productivity Slowdown Since the Great Recession." *Beyond the Numbers* 6, no. 2 (2017): 1–11.

Srnicek, Nick, and Alex Williams. *Inventing the Future: Postcapitalism and a World Without Work.* New York: Verso, 2016.

Steckel, Richard H. "A History of the Standard of Living in the United States." *EH.Net Encyclopedia,* July 21, 2002.

Stelzner, Mark, and Daniel Taekmin Nam. "The Big Cost of Big Medicine: Calculating the Rent in Private Health Care." Hopbrook Institute Working Paper no. 1, January 2019.

Stern, Andy, and Lee Kravitz. *Raising the Floor: How a Universal Basic Income Can Renew Our Economy and Rebuild the American Dream.* New York: PublicAffairs, 2016.

Stiglitz, Joseph E. *People, Power, and Profits: Progressive Capitalism for an Age of Discontent.* New York: W. W. Norton, 2019.

Stockman, David Alan. *The Great Deformation: The Corruption of Capitalism in America.* New York: PublicAffairs, 2013.

Stout, Lynn. *The Shareholder Value Myth: How Putting Shareholders First Harms Investors, Corporations, and the Public.* San Francisco: Berrett-Koehler, 2012.

Sullivan, Teresa A., Elizabeth Warren, and Jay Lawrence Westbrook. *As We Forgive Our Debtors: Bankruptcy and Consumer Credit in America.* New York: Oxford University Press, 1989.

Tegmark, Max. *Life 3.0: Being Human in the Age of Artificial Intelligence.* New York: Knopf, 2017.

Teles, Steven Michael. *The Rise of the Conservative Legal Movement: The Battle for Control of the Law.* Princeton: Princeton University Press, 2010.

Tepper, Jonathan, and Denise Hearn. *The Myth of Capitalism: Monopolies and the Death of Competition.* Hoboken, N.J.: Wiley, 2019.

Theobald, Robert. *Free Men and Free Markets.* Garden City, N.Y.: Anchor Books, 1965.

Tobin, James. "On the Efficiency of the Financial System." *Lloyds Bank Review* 153 (1984).

Tocqueville, Alexis de. *Democracy in America.* Translated by Arthur Goldhammer. 1835–40; New York: Library of America, 2012.

Toffler, Alvin. *Future Shock.* New York: Random House, 1970.

Turney, Shad, et al. "Waiting for Trump: The Move to the Right of White Working-Class Men, 1968–2016." *California Journal of Politics and Policy,* 2017.

Vonnegut, Kurt. *Player Piano.* New York: Charles Scribner's Sons, 1952.

Waterhouse, Benjamin C. *Lobbying America: The Politics of Business from Nixon to NAFTA.* Princeton: Princeton University Press, 2013.

Watkins, Elizabeth Siegel. "How the Pill Became a Lifestyle Drug: The Pharmaceutical Industry and Birth Control in the United States Since 1960." *American Journal of Public Health* 102, no. 8 (2012): 1462–72.

Weisberg, Jacob. *Ronald Reagan.* New York: Times Books/Henry Holt, 2016.

Welch, Jack, and John A. Byrne. *Jack: Straight from the Gut.* New York: Warner Books, 2001.

West, Darrell M. *The Future of Work: Robots, AI, and Automation.* Washington, D.C.: Brookings Institution Press, 2018.

Westbrook, Wayne W. *Wall Street in the American Novel.* New York: New York University Press, 1980.

Wiener, Norbert. *The Human Use of Human Beings.* Boston: Houghton Mifflin, 1950.

Wilkinson, Will. "The Density Divide: Urbanization, Polarization, and Populist Backlash." Niskanen Center, June 2019.

Winkler, Adam. *We the Corporations: How American Businesses Won Their Civil Rights.* New York: Liveright, 2018.

Winston, Clifford. "Economic Deregulation: Days of Reckoning for Microeconomists." *Journal of Economic Literature* 31, no. 3 (1993): 1263–89.

Wolff, Edward N. "Changes in Household Wealth in the 1980s and 1990s in the United States." In *International Perspectives on Household Wealth,* edited by Edward N. Wolff. Northampton, Mass.: Elgar, 2006.

———. "Household Wealth Trends in the United States, 1962–2013: What Happened over the Great Recession?" *RSF: The Russell Sage Foundation Journal of the Social Sciences* 2, no. 6 (2014).

———. "Household Wealth Trends in the United States, 1962 to 2016: Has Middle Class Wealth Recovered?" NBER Working Paper no. 24085, November 2017.

———. "Recent Trends in Household Wealth in the United States: Rising Debt and the Middle-Class Squeeze." Levy Economics Institute Working Paper no. 502, June 2007.

Yang, Dennis Tao, Vivian Weijia Chen, and Ryan Monarch. "Rising Wages: Has China Lost Its Global Labor Advantage?" *Pacific Economic Review* 15, no. 4 (2010): 482–504.

Zaretsky, Adam M. "I Want My MTV . . . and My CNN . . . The Cable TV Industry and Regulation." *Federal Reserve Bank of St. Louis,* July 1995.

INDEX

PHOTO: © MARCO LAU

KURT ANDERSEN is the *New York Times* bestselling author of the novels *Turn of the Century, Heyday, True Believers,* and (with Alec Baldwin) *You Can't Spell America Without Me,* as well as the nonfiction titles *The Real Thing, Reset,* and *Fantasyland.* He has also written for film, television, and the stage and contributes regularly to *The New York Times.* He lives in Brooklyn.

kurtandersen.com
Twitter: @KBAndersen

ABOUT THE TYPE

This book was set in Fairfield, the first typeface from the hand of the distinguished American artist and engraver Rudolph Ruzicka (1883–1978). Ruzicka was born in Bohemia (in the present-day Czech Republic) and came to America in 1894. He set up his own shop, devoted to wood engraving and printing, in New York in 1913 after a varied career working as a wood engraver, in photoengraving and banknote printing plants, and as an art director and freelance artist. He designed and illustrated many books, and was the creator of a considerable list of individual prints—wood engravings, line engravings on copper, and aquatints.